The Psychology

of Childhood

A Survey of Development and Socialization

KARL C. GARRISON
Old Dominion College

ALBERT J. KINGSTON
University of Georgia

IN ASSOCIATION WITH
HAROLD W. BERNARD
Division of Continuing Education
Oregon State System of Higher Education

The Psychology of Childhood

A Survey of Development and Socialization

Charles Scribner's Sons

NEW YORK

The authors wish to make grateful acknowledgement for permission to quote
and to use other material from the following works indicated below. Authors are
listed in alphabetical order, and are also identified in the references for each
chapter.

Roger G. Barker, *Child Behavior and Development.* Copyright 1943 by Mc-
Graw-Hill, Inc. Used by permission of McGraw-Hill Book Company.

Collier's Encyclopedia, Vols. 5, 7, 8, 10, 11, 13, 15 and 17. Copyright 1950,
1951, 1955, 1956, 1957 by P. F. Collier and Son Corporation; Copyright 1952,
1953, 1954, 1963 by the Crowell, Collier Publishing Company. Copyright under
International Copyright Union. All rights reserved under the Inter-American
Copyright Union, and under Pan-American copyright conventions.

Jean Marquis Deutsche, *The Development of Children's Concepts of Causal
Relations.* Copyright 1937 by the University of Minnesota.

Edgar A. Doll, *Vineland Social Maturity Scale,* Minneapolis Education Test
Bureau, 1947, revised 1965. Copyright by the American Guidance Service.

James Gallagher, a figure on page 227 of *The Elementary School Journal,*
Vol. 58, Copyright 1958. Used by permission of the University of Chicago Press,
Inc.

Sidonie Matsner Gruenberg, Editor, *Our Children Today.* Copyright 1952 by
the Viking Press, Inc. Reprinted by permission of the Viking Press, Inc.

Elizabeth Hurlock, *Child Development.* Copyright 1956 by McGraw-Hill,
Inc. Used by permission of McGraw-Hill Book Company.

Earl C. Kelley, *In Defense of Youth.* Copyright © 1962 by Prentice-Hall, Inc.

Howard Kingsley and Ralph Garry, *The Nature and Conditions of Learning,*
2nd Edition. Copyright © 1957 by Prentice-Hall, Inc.

Melvin Kohn, a table on page 344–45 of *The American Journal of Sociology,*
Vol. 64, Copyright 1959. Used by permission of the University of Chicago Press,
Inc.

Dorothea McCarthy, "Language Development in Children," in *Manual of
Child Psychology,* 2nd Edition (L. Carmichael, Editor). Copyright 1954 by John
Wiley and Sons, Inc. Reprinted by permission.

Calvin H. Reed, a table on page 396 of *The Elementary School Journal,* Vol.

58, Copyright 1958. Used by permission of the University of Chicago Press, Inc.

Harold C. Stuart and Howard V. Meredith, three tables from "Use of Body Measurements in the School Health Program," *The American Journal of Public Health*, Vol. 36, Copyright 1946 by the American Public Health Association, Inc.

Mildred C. Templin, *Certain Language Skills in Children: Their Development and Interrelationships*. Copyright 1957 by the University of Minnesota.

United Press International, "Children in Slum Respond to Arts." Copyright 1963 by the New York Times Company (September 2, 1963).

PICTURE ACKNOWLEDGMENTS

Aero Service Division of Litton Industries: pp. 40–41
Paul Barbuto: p. 420
Chicago Housing Authority: p. 37
Reprinted from *Family Circle,* by permission: p. 186
Ford Foundation: p. 367 (by William R. Simmons)
Fulton County Public Schools: p. 360
Mrs. Thelma Grube: p. 279
Reprinted by permission of The Hall Syndicate, all rights reserved: p. 320
Harvard University News Office: p. 13
Los Angeles City Schools: p. 80
Monkmeyer Press Photo Service: pp. 5 (by Sybil Shelton); 129 (by Feily); 194 (by Lucien Aigner); 311 (by Jerome Wexler)
National Education Association: pp. 18, 164, 299, 353 (by Joseph Nettis); 361
The *New York Times:* pp. 94, 137, and also David Pascal for p. 329.
Susan Perl: p. 250
Reproduced from original woodcut by Leona Pierce, courtesy of Weyhe Gallery, New York City: p. 364
Portland Public Schools (Oregon): p. 412
Regional Primate Research Center, University of Wisconsin: p. 68
Nancy Rudolph: p. 184
Schoolcraft, Inc.: p. 281
From *Teacher* by Sylvia Ashton-Warner. Simon and Schuster, 1963: p. 136
United Nations: p. 298

Preface

There is a continuous production of research data and theories concerning children of all ages in all situations, and psychologists can hope to incorporate into one textbook only a small portion of the material available about child behavior and development. Drawing upon their experiences as parents and teachers, the authors of this volume have carefully selected and organized such theories and data as they consider necessary in order to fill the student's need for a better understanding of the biocultural nature and unique personality of a child growing according to fundamental principles of development. They also seek to furnish the student with knowledge for the evaluation and control of a child's environment. Special attention is given to the social forces that operate from birth in molding the child into a human being who lives in harmony with his culture. Recognition is given to the fact that these forces always operate within the framework of heredity.

The text has been organized into three major sections. The first introduces the student to historical methods and reasons for studying children, to the more recent scientific methods of child study, and to an overview of the child and his world—his heredity and his environment. The "Course of Development" is emphasized in the second part of the text, where attention is given to the principles of development as they apply to growth in certain skills, abilities, and forms of behavior. The third part deals with the socialization process as it affects individual attitudes and personality and examines the roles played by the home and school. Attention is also given to the children who experience difficulties in social adjustments and to the forces that combine and coalesce to create the well-integrated personality. By and large, the text concentrates on the years prior to adolescence, for it is during this time that the most solid foundations for adulthood are laid.

The authors wish to express their appreciation to all the sources from which material was gathered, even though many of them are specifically credited in each chapter. Especially do the authors wish to express their gratitude to Sister Mary Amatora, who carefully read the entire manuscript and offered many valuable criticisms and suggestions.

K. C. Garrison
A. J. Kingston

Contents

PART ONE Introduction

PART TWO The Course of Development

PART THREE The Socialization Process

APPENDICES

Tables

Figures

Illustrations

PART ONE
Introduction

O N E

The Study of Children

INTRODUCTION

Concerning Purposes

In the twentieth century, hardly an area of living exists that has not been and is not still being rapidly altered by science and technology. Keeping pace with the accelerated advances is an impossibility for the bulk of mankind. Moreover, those alterations which do not carry with them an inherent set of problems create problems as they become universally accepted. Certain responsible citizens, then, are faced with the tasks of educating others to accept the change, helping them to sublimate their outmoded prejudices and opinions, meeting the problems involved in change, applying new ideas and modes of behavior to harmonize with the change, and all the time planning a future that incorporates the new and the old while leaving room for the as yet unknown. There are groups of individuals—philosophers, for an example—who attempt to carry out all of these assignments within their own special field. Some groups—educators, for example—are forced to make such an attempt. Others prefer to perform their service from within the one area in which they can be authorities and yet feel that by their concentration they are serving the broader purpose of bridging a knowledge gap separating one field from another, one individual from another. A scientist is an example of such an authority. By the very nature of his profession, he expects and is expected to conduct his research with an orientation toward depth

3

rather than breadth, toward description rather than prescription. Like a miner, in other words, the scientist concerns himself with opening and tapping an obscured vein of wealth and leaves the distribution and application of the product to others.

The distinction is made between purposes here because psychologists are frequently asked questions regarding their reasons for conducting certain researches. The answer generally is analogous to the one given by the man who was asked, "Why do you want to climb that mountain?" "Because it is there," he said. Furthermore, psychologists working with children and teachers of child psychology in particular are often asked such questions as "Why do girls develop linguistic skills sooner than boys do?" or "Is aggression in a child good or bad?" The psychologist can only answer that the whys and the value judgments are not his major concern. The why is to a marked degree the concern of philosophers; making value judgments is the province of each individual's society, which determines the codes of behavior—both total and specific—by which that individual must live if he is to be a successful, well-integrated personality *in that society*.

As for the purpose of the psychologist's investigation, society also determines that. In the American culture, the psychologist is asked to bridge the gaps of knowledge regarding children, for instance, for the purpose of setting better educational standards and improving the goals and methods of education. Those improvements are considered necessary, *by our society,* because the complexities of the modern world demand more from children earlier. Society is becoming aware not only of the problems faced by adults responsible for rearing children and the problems facing the child—which some children (as well as some adults) are incapable of solving—but also of the fact that more problems than previously supposed have always existed and have never been adequately resolved. Specifically, a tremendous amount of literature is being made available which deals with such special areas as the difficulties encountered by and methods of handling the mentally deficient, the retarded, the handicapped, the slow learner (in one or more skills), the so-called average, the above-average, the gifted, and the disadvantaged.

Within this range, of course, there are as many variations in capacities and between the capacities of any one person as there are individuals who possess them. To organize a system of education that will enable each child in each category to attain optimum development is impossible; to *attempt* to organize an educational system that gives consideration to large groups of children within the broader categories is a gigantic task. As teachers and fathers in the American society, the authors of this text work toward that end. As psychologists, they can only present the results of investigations

The children of today are the hopes of tomorrow.

carried on over many decades by many people working in many different scientific fields—investigations dealing with the characteristics of children in all societies. Hopefully, the presentation will foster the understanding so necessary to the task society has assigned the adults responsible for rearing, educating, and guiding its children. To foster that understanding is the purpose of this book.

Problems and Principles

The question can now be raised, Can adults ever really understand children, even though all adults have experienced a period of childhood? Several factors stand in their way. First, adults have moved out of the child's world. They interpret happenings and conditions through the eyes and ears of accumulated experiences rather than in terms of the more immature experiences of children. Second, adults project their own feelings and egocentric natures into the behavior act of the child. Lawton (1940), who noted this fact, states: "Most of us are adultcentrics; we cannot even for a moment step outside the sphere of adult interests and concerns or set aside the grown-up way of thinking" (p. 341). Third, the scientific observations and studies of child behavior are made by adult investigators and are interpreted by adult analysts. Their feelings, prejudices, and frustrations are barriers to objective interpretations and are frequently the bases for un-conscious distortions of evidence. Fourth, there is no simple rule or formula which can be followed by adults attempting to better understand children. A child is not a mechanism to be measured and evaluated against a simple formula or standard. Those people who would ascribe all aspects of growth to one or a special combination of the forces and conditions and who think that by reducing all characteristics to a formula the prediction and under-standing of development and behavior could become relatively simple—those people are guilty of either overgeneralization or oversimplification and are easily led into forming erroneous conclusions.

The problem is to understand the multiplicity of factors that affect a particular child and make him the complex individual he is. One must first *recognize his dynamic nature*. He is not an artificial plant to be washed oc-casionally and set aside for decorative purposes; he is more like the young rose bush (not without thorns) that needs warmth, care, nutrition, contain-ment, pruning (discipline), and possibly protection from pests in order for it to attain its optimum growth. Studies have shown that one of the major differences between parents of problem children and parents of nonproblem children is the failure of the former to recognize the dynamic nature of their children.

Closely akin to the recognition of the child as dynamic rather than passive is the need to *regard each child as a unique individual*. He is unique because his hereditary characteristics are unique, unless he has an identical twin. He is unique because his immediate societal environment—family, neighborhood, school, community—is unique. No other environment exists *exactly* as his does, not even that of his siblings or his identical twin. And because his potential and experience are different his perceptions also differ. Absorbing this principle of an individual's individuality requires a study of differences in growth, abilities, and special characteristics which result in the development of highly complex, hence unique, personalities.

A third essential is an attempt to *understand the principles of growth and development*, including a knowledge of the relative roles played by heredity, maturation, and learning. This principle is particularly significant to parents, teachers, and other adults who are entrusted with the guidance and training of children. In fact, whereas a philosopher might deem it un-wise, a psychologist would deem it impracticable, for any adult to work amongst children without having a rudimentary understanding of these principles.

History of Child Study

Adult beliefs concerning the nature of the child are reflected in educa-tional methods, as well as in the customs, mores, and laws regarding the place of children in society. The current concepts of child nature and development have evolved over long periods of time and are constantly changing, although some concepts give way to new ideas more slowly than others. Certainly, interest in children's characteristics and the "proper" goals of education is not a new trend. Plato observed differences in individual capacities, and in his conception of the ideal state (*The Republic*) advocated an educational system that would help each child fully realize his potentials and develop his special capabilities. In 1690 John Locke emphasized self-denial as a means toward learning self-control. Jean Rousseau, in the eighteenth century, insisted upon the inherent goodness of nature and children and suggested bringing the two into close harmony, allowing the child to learn by questioning the experiences he encountered in his natural environment. In the same century, Wordsworth described the child as "father of the Man," a concept used by many modern psychologists as a guiding principle for their studies of childhood development. In *Little Dorrit* (1832) and *Barnaby Rudge* (1841), Charles Dickens presented his society with descriptions of mental deficiency which are often considered better than modern clinical analyses.

Biographers and autobiographers have always placed a great deal of emphasis on the childhood and education of their subjects. One of the more amazing accounts frequently cited is the *Autobiography of John Stuart Mill* (1873), the life story of an economist and philosopher who was educated at home by his father. But biographies of children, written for the specific purpose of understanding the nature of a child, were comparatively slow in appearing. Nearly a century elapsed between the "first" publications and the real beginnings of the child-study movement. Johann Heinrich Pestalozzi, regarded by many as the father of the modern elementary school, published in 1774 the notes from his observations of his son; and in 1787 Tiedemann published a tracing of the development of various abilities in a single infant. Although other "baby biographies" appeared sporadically throughout the following century, the bulk of them arrived late in the 1800's, along with published theories concerning the education of small children: Charles Darwin, *A Biographical Sketch of an Infant* (1877), W. Preyer, *The Mind of the Child* (1882), Bronson Alcott, *Observations of the Vital Phenomena of My Second Child,* and writings by educators such as Friedrich Fröbel, Maria Montessori, John Dewey, Horace Mann, and William James, among many others.

The philosophers, novelists, poets, and biographers imparted information (albeit, the observations were usually selected by a biased party), theories, and interesting speculations about the nature of children and childhood, but of greater importance is the influence they exerted in spreading a universal interest in the *scientific* study of the child. On the one hand, these writers brought into focus basic problems whose solutions lay hidden under centuries of accumulated superstitions, prejudices, and "common sense" musings. On the other, the theories were often in opposition to each other and to observable, but misinterpreted, facts. While one school of thought would believe in rigid control of a supposed inborn perversity, an inherited sinfulness of the infant, another believed in allowing extreme freedom to his (presumed) hereditary goodness. Many writers believed that, good or bad, a child's behavior was as entirely instinctive as an animal's. All of them accepted the popular and still widespread conception of the child as an immature adult, a prejudice that sublimates the child's needs and motives to those of the older generations and subjects his behavioral characteristics to interpretations arising from quite different adult perceptions.

Such contrasting viewpoints began waging their war toward the end of the nineteenth century, but unfortunately for them their only weapons were created by science; and, in a sense, science won all the battles.

THEORY AND SCIENTIFIC METHOD

... A scientific theory consists of (a) a set of clearly defined terms that refer to empirical phenomena; (b) a set of basic principles (axioms) that relate many of the concepts to each other; and (c) a further set of empirical laws that may be deduced, according to the rules of mathematics and/or formal logic, from the basic principles. For the scientist, explanation consists in the deduction of the phenomenon to be explained from the set of basic principles.

McCandless and Spiker, 1956, p. 75

For the scientist, a theory is a research tool. It is a means for furthering his understanding of a problem, and he uses it for securing additional facts not available from the results of experimental studies. It furnishes postulates from which the scientist devises theorems for testing, and it is especially useful in integrating the interrelatedness of phenomena.

Theory, then, may be regarded as the total framework that binds together the threads of knowledge acquired through the use of scientific methods in studying problems. In the case of child study, it functions to bring together the learned facts about child behavior and development into a unitary whole.

People have differing ways of arriving at what seems to be a sound theory. Some rely upon authorities, using them as sources for their quotations and empirical data; others turn to logic. The authors of this text have used both methods extensively and naturally feel that each has its place in arriving at answers to problems. However, some authorities who appear to carry a great deal of weight in many areas of knowledge deserve to be questioned, just as one would question the psychologist as an authority on weather conditions; and logic should never be substituted for evidence that might be available from scientific studies. Furthermore, logic which is out of harmony with available data should be given additional study. Even logic in harmony with "common sense" may be open to question, since "common sense" is a vague and arbitrary term.

In the scientific method there is no place for prejudices, hazy thinking, and superficial questioning. Ideally, the research scholar searches for truth without regard to the moral acceptability of his findings. Or, as Nietzsche wrote to his sister in 1865:

> ... Is it decisive after all that we arrive at *that* view ... which makes us feel most comfortable? Rather, is not the result of his inquiries something wholly indifferent to the true inquirer? Do we after all seek rest, peace, and pleasure in our inquiries? No, only truth—even if it be the most abhorrent and ugly.

Although Nietzsche can hardly be described as an objective writer, he well realized the value of science's most precious tool: an objective viewpoint from which to conduct a disinterested inquiry. That is the ideal.

The scientific investigator works within a theoretical framework, and within this framework, the problems for special study are selected. Mussen and Conger (1956) list six steps in the research: (1) a clear and accurate statement of the problem, designed to eliminate the floundering that occurs when the problem selected is too broad and to assure an adequate understanding of the purpose of the study; (2) a review of the pertinent literature; (3) preliminary observations for the purpose of (4) constructing a theory or hypothesis; (5) verification of the hypothesis; (6) application of the verified theory.

What is the best method to use for securing data? There is no *one* best method. Frequently, several are necessary, and whichever ones are selected will depend upon a number of factors, including the nature of the problem being studied, the instruments and time available for collecting and studying the data, the training of the investigator and his assistants, and the uses to be made of the data once it is collected.

Closely related to the question of appropriate method is the problem of the sample of subjects to be studied. For a sampling to be true and accurate, its size should, in general, be large, and all levels within a particular, significant area should be represented—that is, population, social class, economic status, occupation, intelligence, age, and so forth.

The quest for objectivity has brought about the widespread use of statistics, which have been invaluable to the investigator, enabling him to make relatively accurate estimates and predictions. However, statistics are not a substitute for accuracy in collecting data or for a logical analysis of the data after it is collected. There is no statistical device that will rectify the inaccuracy of a faulty instrument or a careless investigator.

To summarize briefly, no method in itself will provide useful and accurate information. The scientific worker must first of all be a "truth seeker." He will make use of any instruments available, often adapting tools from related sciences or even constructing new ones in accordance with the demands of the problem, and he will apply statistical procedures appropriate to the solution of the problem. He will, in each case, follow what Harlow (1957) calls "a trend to adapt method to problems, rather than to adapt problems to method" (pp. 489–490). And last, the scientist, in arriving at conclusions and in making generalizations, will be guided, within a theoretical framework, by the data thus gathered and by the applications of logic.

THE SCIENTIFIC METHOD OF CHILD STUDY

History of Child Psychology

The seeds of psychology as a science were germinated in philosophy and brought to its present productivity by physiology through the contributions of Ernst Weber, Gustav Fechner, and Hermann von Helmholtz, among others. Experimental psychology blossomed in the laboratory of Wilhelm Wundt, who established an institute in Leipzig in 1879, the first of its kind anywhere. From this institute James Cattell brought to America the first information concerning experimental psychology, and as the first professor of psychology in America, he began teaching at the University of Pennsylvania in 1888. William James and Hugo Münsterberg, both at Harvard, extended their investigations into the applied sciences, and for a time, Harvard became the center of psychology. In the meantime, Charles Darwin had published *Expression of the Emotions in Man and Animals* (1872) and forced the scientific community to recognize the importance of studying the early stages of human development. Galton had already illustrated the value of studying large groups of individuals, and Edward Thorndike, who was contributing heavily to the field of animal psychology, subjected Darwin's conclusions to exact measurement. Influenced by the work of such men, G. Stanley Hall, president of Clark University and founder of the *Pedagogical Seminary* (now absorbed by *The Journal of Genetic Psychology*), began his systematic study of children in the United States. He and his students published a long series of studies on a wide variety of topics, the most famous one a classic treatise on "The Contents of Children's Minds on Entering School" (1891).

The first two decades of the twentieth century saw genetic psychology almost completely submerged in the increased concentration and interest in the work of Alfred Binet: educational measurements and the testing of functional intelligence. Perhaps the greatest upsurge of interest in child psychology was created by John Watson, founder of the behavioristic movement. His studies of infant behavior, begun in 1920, gave an impetus to child psychology that was tremendous. As Jones (1956, p. 239) says:

> ... In 1918 there were only 3 psychologists who indicated a primary interest in children. By 1937 this number had increased to about 81. At the present time nearly a thousand members and fellows of the APA indicate the child, or work with children, as their first interest.

Furthermore, during the 1920's, research organizations for the study of child behavior sprang up all over the United States, many of them outgrowths of college and university course offerings in child psychology. Hundreds of research findings have come from such well-known child research centers as those at Teachers College of Columbia University, Yale, Antioch, and the universities of Iowa, Chicago, California, and Minnesota. In 1929, the Society for Research in Child Development was founded as an affiliate of the American Association for the Advancement of Science. Concerning the Society, Goodenough (1957, p. 129) says:

> ... Its purpose is to broaden the approach to the study of child behavior through bringing together the research findings from all the major scientific disciplines concerned with human welfare and conduct. Its membership includes anthropologists, physiologists, sociologists, educators, physicians, anatomists, dentists, and physiological chemists as well as psychologists.

With the flood of learned and popular literature emanating from these centers and other sources, and under the brilliant leadership of Arnold Gesell at the Yale School of Medicine's Child Development Clinic, the study of children became a highly specialized field.

Aims of Child Study

The science of child study has three major aims, consisting of studies which attempt (1) to chart the course of development for the purpose of calculating deviations (normative investigations); (2) to determine the interrelationships among specific functions and, in turn, their relations to developmental stages (correlational or predictive investigations); and (3) to study the effects of external conditions on behavior and development (experimental or comparative studies). Because of these aims, there have evolved an ever-growing number of intensive investigations of individual differences in talents, defects, intellectual capacities, mental growth rates, and characteristics both social and emotional in nature. Also, there has been a growing recognition of the influence of home and family on the child, resulting in an increasing number of studies of conditions which affect the child prenatally and of infant-mother, parent-child, child-child relationships.

During the past two or more decades, a change has appeared in the goals of child-psychology research. Formerly, anthropological and psychological studies were primarily concerned with descriptions of conditions and happenings. Such studies dealt mainly with questions relating to what children in different cultures are like and how they behave. Present-day goals, though still using much descriptive material, seem to go beyond description into the *why* of behavior (Anderson, 1954). The methods that were developed for the purpose of studying children during the latter part of the nineteenth and early twentieth centuries have been refined, and new techniques also have been created. Moreover, there has been a change in emphasis. Many students of child behavior and development have extensively used the term "whole child," or the "holistic approach," a recognition that the organism in its unity is more than and different from the sum of its parts. Where this viewpoint has been accepted, research methods have been organized in such a way as to facilitate the study of the whole child in all his complexities. The conceptual framework recognizes existing functional interrelations. This idea was stated by Sigel (1956, p. 242) when he wrote, ". . . I would prefer to think of the 'whole' child as an organization of a number of systems, which function at varying degrees of autonomy and interrelatedness."

Specific Research Methods

The complexity of the human organism and the myriad factors which influence its growth and development have prevented any one method of child study from becoming accepted as the major, or most important, technique of research. Present-day studies have moved away from the generalized observations of the nineteenth century, however, and more emphasis is being placed upon the systematic recording of specific patterns, with certain other factors controlled. The development of statistical tools for analyzing and interpreting data has resulted in more precise and specific evaluations. The following pages describe the methods most commonly employed for studying children at the present time. A more complete listing has been devised by Mussen (1960).

The natural history approach. Anthropologists as well as psychologists have used the natural history approach for studying primitive children in ordinary life situations. Careful observations are made of infants being cared for by their mother or mother-figure, children at play or work, puberty ceremonies, religious observances, etc. "In such an approach the investigator is minimally present, effaces himself or his camera as much as possible, and records the surrounding context of behavior as well as the actual behavior" (Mead, 1954).

Various techniques have been used to refine this method as well as to adapt it to a study of child behavior and development. The one-way vision screen used by Gesell (1928) gave the observer visual access to the child's behavior without the observer becoming a part of the child's social environment. At a later date, Gesell (1934) made use of a photographic dome for observing and recording the behavior of infants. This dome provided the observer with acoustic as well as visual isolation. Sometimes used are several observers who concentrate on different aspects of the situation and later combine their results in order to obtain a more complete behavioral record.

Cinematograph records, such as those obtained by Behrens (1946–48) on the growth patterns of individual children, furnish the most complete behavioral data. Through the use of two Cinematic cameras along with two miniature cameras, experimenters have been able to record behavioral sequences without any break. Although these records vary in refinement— some consisting of sort-sequences interspersed with verbal records, others being considerably more complete—the one great advantage of this technique is that the films or other records can be studied at a later date by other investigators.

Experimental classroom with one-way mirror in Larsen Hall, Graduate School of Education, Harvard University. This arrangement is similar to earlier clinics for child study.

The genetic or longitudinal method. The genetic or longitudinal method of studying children is concerned with the development of a particular characteristic or attribute throughout a given period of time. The method seeks to ascertain the day to day, week to week, or month to month relationship of some specific attributes to the individual's pattern and rate of growth (Shirley, 1931). It can be utilized whether the research worker studies a single individual or a group and has been used to investigate such factors as the development of muscular control in children, the relationship of height and weight at different chronological ages, and the relationship of the length of such appendages as legs and arms to torso size at various stages of development.

Dealing with the development of posture and locomotion, Gesell's work with infants and young children, in which motion-picture photography was used, is an excellent example of refinements made in the use of observations in longitudinal studies (1942). One of the most famous examples of the genetic method is Lewis Terman's long-term investigation of a group of very bright California school children (1959). In a series of studies extending over a thirty-five-year period, Terman followed a group of elementary-school youngsters from childhood to maturity. As a result of this monumental work, many popularly held beliefs about the "intellectual genius" or gifted child were found to be erroneous and were consequently revised.

Many research workers in the past have found themselves financially unable to devote the long periods of time necessary for the painstaking and continuous observations required by the longitudinal approach. However, in terms of the amount and quality of information gained from this method, its virtues have been impressed upon various foundations and agencies responsible for grants, and its difficulties (another one lies in the attempts to secure repeated and systematic observations within an increasingly mobile population) are gradually being decreased by the sporadic growth of longitudinal centers and by other forms of economic aid.

The normative-survey method. If the genetic method may be thought of as representing a longitudinal approach, the normative-survey method may be regarded as a cross-sectional approach to investigations. Essentially, the normative-survey method attempts to study one or more characteristics in a group which is thought to be a representative sample of the total population. If a researcher desired to know how the height and weight of ten-year-old girls differed from the height and weight of ten-year-old boys, he might determine these differences by obtaining a representative sample of ten-year-olds and then weigh and measure each of the selected children. Through the use of standard statistical techniques he could then determine the averages and variances of each of the two groups. Both similarities and differences could thus be found.

Another scholar might seek to compare the mathematical achievements of fifth-grade boys and girls. A third research worker might seek to discover whether the typical six-year-old is able to perform certain hand-eye coordinated tasks which are related to the mastery of handwriting skills. Normative-survey methods are employed in many child studies, and some of the most common ways of accumulating the data are by questionnaires, interviews, scales, and tests.

In most of the child studies where the normative-survey method is used, a lack of knowledge concerning the characteristics of the total population (whether of a hamlet or the world) prevents the investigator from properly testing the sample to determine if the obtained data are representative of the total group being studied. The sample rarely satisfies all of the criteria for randomness and representativeness. As a result of this grave limitation, the surveys are often criticized and the validity of the generalizations made from the studies are somewhat suspect.

The case study. The clinical method, or case study, has developed largely as a result of efforts on the part of specialists to understand and to assist individuals with special problems. It is widely used by psychologists, psychiatrists, remedial specialists, speech correctionists, counselors, and social workers. Ideally, complete case studies require a team approach, involving a number of specialists; however, even school teachers are finding the method increasingly helpful for gathering more accurate and pertinent information about their pupils.

The procedure may be viewed as analogous to the genetic method in reverse; i.e., it starts from the present and delves into the past developmental history of the particular individual being studied. Essentially, the case study seeks to focus upon a wide range of factors which have had some bearing on the subject's development. Usually, the investigator hopes to reveal something about the etiology of the difficulty as well as to find clues for proper treatment. The typical case study generally includes the following information:

1. *Family history.* Information regarding the physical and mental health of the various members of a subject's family is frequently helpful in determining the origin of the difficulty, whether it is organic or psychological, whether it is due to genetic or environmental factors. The investigator, for instance, makes special notations of instances of mental retardation, tendencies toward heart disease, cases of mental illness, alcoholism, and so forth.

2. *Prenatal and birth history.* Human development begins with conception, and the conditions present in the mother prior to a child's birth have a marked effect upon his later development. Infections, injuries, toxemias, poor nutrition, or other complications during the mother's pregnancy affect the child's prenatal (and hence, postnatal) development. Similarly, unusual

birth conditions such as prolonged labor, difficult delivery, or prematurity may have resulted in damage to the brain, eyes, nervous or respiratory systems.

3. *Developmental history.* A knowledge of the subject's past developmental patterns, including physical growth and the acquisition of motor and language abilities, together with a history of his illnesses, injuries, food habits, and toilet training often provides an understanding of his present problem or condition.

4. *Personal and social history.* Information in this category includes facts concerning the individual's social adjustments, his habits of eating, sleeping, and playing, the skills he has mastered, his abilities, activities, interests, likes, and dislikes. All of these items together present the clinician with a background against which the subject's present needs and behavior are illuminated.

5. *Educational history.* Particularly in cases where the subject is a child, the progress he has made in his school work and the difficulties he has encountered as he advanced through kindergarten and the successive grades provide valuable information for diagnosing his problems. General achievement, results of standardized tests, grades attained, attendance record, special abilities or disabilities are important factors for consideration.

Although physical, neurological, psychological, and pyschiatric examinations are frequently necessary to supplement the data collected for a case history, the method is obviously an exhaustive one. Its limitations lie in the fact that it is time-consuming and necessarily focused on the single individual, and, as previously mentioned, it requires the services of a team of specialists. Teachers, who are finding this method most helpful, cannot hope to function as specialists, with competencies in all the areas dealing with child behavior and development. On the other hand, the value of the case-study method has been so impressed upon educators that an increasing number of school systems are installing special services, designed to aid the teachers in their work with the children who have special difficulties.

Experimental methods. Two general types of experimental methods are used in studying children: the single-group and the parallel group. The single-group method studies either a single individual or a single group, while the parallel-group method makes use of two or more groups in examining a specific problem. Watson and Rayner (1920) studied a single infant by the single-group method in order to ascertain the conditionability of emotional responses during infancy. Gordon (1959) employed the same method in studying children's concept of the self. Teams were assigned to judge individual children in the elementary school without the observers being seen by the subjects. The parallel-group method was used by Lippitt (1940), who, with the aid of one-way-vision screens, observed the effects of democratic and autocratic social atmospheres on the behavior of children.

The experimental method seeks to test a specific hypothesis by carefully controlling all variables except the one under observation. In fact, one of the method's distinguishing features is the active role played by the experimenter as he attempts to control those variables. As an example of a problem that could well be studied by the parallel-group method, suppose a research worker hypothesized that children enrolled in the primary grades who had the benefits of a daily program of physical education would develop better muscular coordination than those who did not have the added benefits. The experimenter probably would select two groups of children, both equated; that is, they would be approximately equal in as many variables as feasible or deemed necessary. The most likely variables in this case would be sex, age, socioeconomic status, present health condition, and muscular coordination. After the experimenter felt that he had two groups of nearly the same caliber, he would hope that both groups encountered the same general treatment and experienced the same general conditions except for one thing: one group (the experimental) would receive the planned program of physical education, the other group (control) would not. At the end of the planned period of study, the experimenter would examine the muscular coordination of both groups and compare the results. If the differences between the two groups are not significant, the hypothesis is probably wrong, but there is also the possibility that the criteria of evaluation were not clearly differentiated or that important intervening variables were not sufficiently controlled.

Other purposes for which the experimental method might be used are: to ascertain the value of more frequent tests on learning, to determine the effectiveness of a particular method of instruction, to discover whether students who are taught by courses that include homework learn more than those who are taught by courses without homework. There are, of course, many hypotheses that can be tested by means of this method; however, Harlow (1957, p. 490) points out:

> For many classes of problems, simple observation methods may be more productive than rigid laboratory experiments using complex apparatus, especially during the exploratory phases of programmatic research. Actually, it should be emphasized that there is no sharp dichotomy between observational and experimental methods or between clinical and experimental methods.

The psychoanalytic method.   Sigmund Freud, the father of psychoanalysis, and other psychologists inspired by his work have been important influences upon modern child psychology through their development of the psychoanalytic interview. Originally designed as a method for studying adults suffering from emotional conflicts, the interview constructs the individual's past through the detailed examination of his behavior and experiences. Anna Freud (1928) in particular emphasized the principle that neurotic symptoms appearing in adults are the result of childhood experiences.

The analyst notes irregularities, evasions, and deceptions in the behavior of the subject. In the study of children, he analyzes and interprets valuable data collected from the observation of play activities. Through such data, the investigator hopes to find the conscious and unconscious motivations for the subject's behavior, thus arriving at a better understanding of the dynamic forces in his life. However, data obtained by the psychoanalytic method are extremely hard to evaluate and should be supplemented by data from other sources. For one reason, the method is dependent upon subjective interpretations of observed behavior; for another, it is equally dependent upon verbalizations. In order to overcome the difficulties inherent to these weaknesses, a variety of projective techniques and other unstructured devices have been developed for the purpose of studying personality. Although stemming directly from the psychoanalytic method, these techniques have been generally accepted as research instruments in their own right, and have, by themselves, become useful in studying the psychological problems of both children and adults.

Children need opportunities for the expression of many feelings.

Figure I–1. The inkblots used in the Rorschach Test are bilaterally symmetrical.

Projective techniques. The principle behind the development of projective techniques is that individuals, when given ample opportunity for free expression in any one of a number of media, will "project" facets of their personalities into the expressed product. A child, for instance, will draw or paint pictures of what he *feels* rather than what he sees. Likewise, with his inhibitions set free by the various unstructured situations devised for testing, the child (or adult) will inadvertently "act out" his feelings of aggression, and emotional difficulties and indicate his attitudes, interests, likes and dislikes—in short, his entire personality. Doll play is a popular expressive medium used by many investigators, along with finger-painting, clay modeling, dramatic skits, and other creative activities.

The two best known and most frequently used tests for eliciting expressive responses are probably the Rorschach Test (see Beck, 1937) and the Thematic Apperception Test (see Morgan and Murray, 1935). The former uses inkblots similar to the one in Figure I–1, the clinician asking such questions as, "What do you see in this?" or "What do you think this is?" The investigator scores the subject according to the number of responses he makes to any one card, the quality of such responses, the types of things seen, and whether the blot is perceived in a series of parts or as a whole. On this latter point, for instance, Barron (1958, p. 155), in speaking of the creative personality, says:

> . . . When confronted . . . with the Rorschach inkblot test, original individuals insist to a most uncommon degree upon giving an interpretation of the blot which takes account of all details in one comprehensive, synthesizing image.

Barron goes on to theorize that such a tendency illustrates the creative individual's response to disorder, "which is to find an elegant new order more satisfying then any that could be evoked by a simpler configuration."

Other aspects of personality, besides creative capacity, which investigators claim to find revealed by the Rorschach test are independence, amount of self-will, range of interests, and degree of certain mental abilities and experiences.

The Thematic Apperception Test, developed by Murray and his associates (1943) consists of pictures of people in various settings. There are
thirty pictures in all; some are specifically for boys and some for girls. For a
particular age group there are 20 pictures that are supposed to be used. The
subject is instructed to tell a story about what is going on in each picture.
Pictures of rabbits, for instance, apparently elicit longer stories from children between the ages of five and ten (Bills, 1950).

Thus, drawings, form perceptions, story telling, reactions to stories and
pictures, sentence, story, and figure completions, and figure preferences have
all been used with varying degrees of effectiveness (not, of course, without
difficulties and criticisms) for the analysis of personality characteristics and
for obtaining clues to problems and to the reasons behind abnormal behavior
patterns. However, a summary of the literature on the structure and content
of projective tests led Murstein (1959, p. 4) to conclude: "If we are to build
a theory of projective techniques, much more data are needed with regard to
the roles played by the stimulus, background, and personality variables."

SUMMARY

Numerous writers have speculated about the nature of children since
the dawn of history, some out of mere curiosity, some from the realization
that they were responsible for teaching children the skills, attitudes, morals,
and knowledge necessary for the assumption of active adult roles, and others
out of a broader desire to understand and guide the potential cornerstones
of a higher, future civilization. The early notions of child nature, based on
armchair thinking, uncontrolled observations, or faulty interpretations, have
given way to a more accurate understanding, arrived at through the accumulation of scientific studies conducted primarily in the twentieth century. Although Tiedemann, Hall, Galton, Thorndike, and Binet are some of the
names most frequently cited as having made notable contributions, the
science of child psychology is founded on the products of investigations in
all sciences dealing with animal behavior.

Several methods for studying children have been discussed. The genetic
or longitudinal method studies the development of a characteristic or attribute over a period of time. The normative-survey method studies one or
more characteristics of a sample group which is thought to be representative
of a total population. The case study investigates the entire developmental
history of a particular individual for the purpose of understanding factors
that lead to the condition, needs, or difficulties of the subject. The experimental method usually employs either a single group or two equated groups
in order to test a specific hypothesis by controlling all variables except the
one being tested.

The psychoanalytic method, developed primarily for studying adults suffering from emotional conflicts, has been found useful in studying children. Various kinds of projective testing instruments have been developed to implement this technique, including inkblots, incomplete sentences and figures, pictures that elicit stories or reactions, and children's drawings. In the hands of trained clinicians, these instruments offer much promise of furnishing investigators with clues to the behavior and needs of children with special emotional and social problems.

QUESTIONS AND PROBLEMS

1. List several generalizations you have made concerning the nature of the school-age child. How many of these viewpoints are based upon scientific evidence?
2. List several generalizations about individual differences among school-age children.
3. Compare the normative-survey and genetic approach to studying school children.
4. List some problems you feel would best be studied by each method and explain your reasons for choosing this method.
5. What are the advantages and disadvantages of each method of studying children?
6. Make a short case history of some child whom you know, using the broad topics discussed in this chapter.
7. Explain why elementary teachers should have a good understanding of the growth characteristics of school children.

SELECTED READINGS

ALMY, MILLIE, *Child Development*. Henry Holt, 1955. Ch. 4.

ALMY, MILLIE, *Ways of Studying Children*. Bureau of Publications, Teachers College, 1959.

ANDERSON, JOHN E., Methods of child psychology, in *Manual of Child Psychology* (L. Carmichael, ed.), 2nd ed. John Wiley & Sons, 1954. Ch. 1.

BERNARD, HAROLD W., *Human Development in Western Culture.*, 2nd ed. Boston: Allyn and Bacon, 1966. Ch. 1.

DINKMEYER, DON C., *Child Development: The Emerging Self*. Englewood Cliffs, N.J.: Prentice-Hall, 1965. Chs. 2 and 3.

GARRISON, KARL C., *Growth and Development*, 2nd ed. Longmans, Green (now McKay), 1959. Ch. 1.

GESELL, ARNOLD, CATHERINE S. AMATRUDA, BURTON M. CASTNER, and HELEN THOMPSON, *Biographies of Child Development. A Ten-Year Study from the Clinic of Child Development at Yale University*. Hoeber, 1939.

MCCARTHY, DOROTHEA, Trends in the psychological appraisal of children, *Child Development*, 1955, 26, 213–222.

MUSSEN, PAUL H., ed., *Handbook of Research Methods in Child Development*. John Wiley & Sons, 1960.

OLSON, WILLARD C., *Child Development*, 2nd ed. Boston: D. C. Heath, 1959. Ch. 1.

THOMPSON, GEORGE G., *Child Psychology*, 2nd ed. Boston: Houghton Mifflin, 1962. Chs. 1 and 2.

THORPE, LOUIS P., and WENDELL W. CRUZE, *Developmental Psychology*, 3rd ed. Ronald Press, 1962. Ch. 1.

REFERENCES

If a reference in the text gives a specific page number as: Jones (1956, p. 239), the page number will not be repeated identically in the references at the end of the chapter. There the reference will then show the span of the article, so that it now appears: Jones, Harold E., The replacement problem in child development, *Child Development*, 1956, 27, 237–240.

When no place of publication is given, it signifies that the place is New York. Convenient brief forms of book publisher's names are used, but the identity is always clear.

If a publisher has merged, so that the identity is not easily determined, we provide the current name also.

ALCOTT, BRONSON, Observations of the vital phenomena of my second child, cited in *Bronson Alcott, Teacher* by D. McCuskey. Macmillan, 1940.

ANDERSON, JOHN E., Methods of child psychology, in *Manual of Child Psychology* (L. Carmichael, ed.), 2nd ed. John Wiley & Sons, 1954.

BARRON, FRANK, The psychology of imagination, *Scientific American* (September 1958), *199*, No. 3, 150–166.

BECK, S. J., *Introduction to the Rorschach Method: A Manual of Personality Study.* Research Monograph of the American Orthopsychiatric Association, No. 1. Menasha, Wisc.: American Orthopsychiatric Association, 1937.

BEHRENS, H. D., *A Study in Human Development*, Parts I, II, III, IV (films). Psychological Cinema Register, Pennsylvania State University, 1946–48.

BILLS, ROBERT E., Animal pictures for obtaining children's projections, *Journal of Clinical Psychology*, 1950, *6*, 291–293.

FREUD, ANNA, Introduction to the technique of child analysis, *Monograph No. 48*, Nervous and Mental Disease Publishing Co. (Washington, D. C.), 1928.

GALTON, FRANCIS, *Hereditary Genius: An Inquiry into Its Laws and Consequences*, rev. ed., D. Appleton, 1887.

GESELL, ARNOLD, *Infancy and Human Growth.* Macmillan, 1928.

GESELL, ARNOLD, *An Atlas of Infant Behavior.* New Haven, Conn.: Yale University Press, 1934.

GESELL, ARNOLD, and HENRY M. HALVERSON, The daily maturation of infant behavior: a cinema study of postures, movements, and laterality, *The Journal of Genetic Psychology*, 1942, *61*, 3–32.

GOODENOUGH, FLORENCE L., Child psychology, in *Collier's Encyclopedia*, 1957, *5*, 128–131.

GORDON, IRA J., Inferring children's concepts of self: interobserver reliability. Paper presented at the Southeastern Psychological Association, St. Augustine, Florida, April 24, 1959.

HALL, G. STANLEY, The contents of children's minds on entering school, *Pedagogical Seminary*, 1891, *1*, 139–173.

HARLOW, HARRY F., Experimental analysis of behavior, *The American Psychologist*, 1957, *12*, 485–490.

JONES, HAROLD E., The replacement problem in child development, *Child Development*, 1956, 27, 237–240.

LAWTON, GEORGE, Can adults ever really understand children? *Childhood Education*, 1940, *16*, 341–346.

LIPPITT, R., An experimental study of the effect of democratic and authoritarian group atmospheres, *University of Iowa Studies in Child Welfare*, 1940, *16*, No. 3, 43–195.

LOCKE, JOHN, *Some Thoughts Concerning Education: 1690, Sections 38 and 40.* London: Cambridge University Press, 1913.

MCCANDLESS, BOYD R., and CHARLES C. SPIKER, Experimental research in child psychology, *Child Development*, 1956, 27, 75–80.

MEAD, MARGARET, Research on primitive children, in *Manual of Child Psychology* (L. Carmichael, ed.), 2nd ed. John Wiley & Sons, 1954, p. 746.

MORGAN, CHRISTIANA D., and H. A. MURRAY, A method for investigating fantasies: The Thematic Apperception Test, *Archives of Neurological Psychiatry, Chicago*, 1935, *34*, 289–306.

MURRAY, H. A., *Thematic Apperception Test.* Cambridge, Mass.: Harvard University Press, 1943.

MURSTEIN, BERNARD I., A conceptual model of projective techniques applied to stimulus variations with thematic techniques, *Journal of Consulting Psychology*, 1959, *23*, 3–14.

MUSSEN, PAUL H., ed., *Handbook of Research Methods in Child Development.* John Wiley & Sons, 1960.

MUSSEN, PAUL H., and JOHN J. CONGER, *Child Development and Personality.* Harper & Brothers, 1956.

NIETZSCHE, FRIEDRICH, Letter to his sister, in *The Portable Nietzsche* (Walter Kaufmann, ed. and trans.). Viking Press, 1954, pp. 29–30.

PESTALOZZI, JOHANN HEINRICH, A father's diary, 1774, cited in *Pestalozzi, His Life and Work* by R. DeGuimps. D. Appleton, 1906.

ROUSSEAU, JEAN JACQUES. The "return to Nature" theme referred to in this chapter is the basis for two of Rousseau's novels, *The New Héloïse* (1761) and *Émile* (1762).

SHIRLEY, MARY, The sequential method for the study of maturing behavior patterns, *The Psychological Review*, 1931, *38*, 507–528.

SIGEL, IRVING E., The need for conceptualization in research on child development, *Child Development*, 1956, 27, 241–252.

TERMAN, LEWIS M., and M. H. ODEN, *The Gifted Group at Mid-Life: Thirty-five Years' Follow-up of the Superior Child.* Genetic studies of Genius, Vol. V. Stanford, Calif.: Stanford University Press, 1959.

TIEDEMANN, D., *Beobachtungen über die Entwickelung der Seelenfähigkeiten bei Kindern.* Altenburg: Bonde, 1787.

WATSON, JOHN B., and ROSALIE RAYNER, Conditioned emotional reactions, *Journal of Experimental Psychology*, 1920, *3*, 1–14.

WORDSWORTH, WILLIAM, "My Heart Leaps Up" (1802), line 7.

T W O

The Child and His World

HEREDITY ←——→ ENVIRONMENT
The Basis of Heredity

The child is a product of a germ cell from a female (an egg) which has been fertilized by a germ cell from a male (a sperm). The fertilized cell (zygote) contains twenty-three pairs of chromosomes, and of these forty-six, twenty-three are received from the mother and twenty-three from the father. Each chromosome contains a string of molecular units called *genes*. Estimations (Thomas, 1954) have placed the number of genes received at 72,000 from each parent. These genes are the carriers of heredity, and the ways in which they interact under normal conditions have been referred to as the laws of heredity.*

The particular combination of genes received by a child is a matter of chance. Each gene from the mother's chromosomes is paired with a gene from the father's. If the genes in a pair are similar in their performance of a particular function, the traits influenced by them will appear—provided they are not interfered with by some other pair of genes or some environmental factors. Of the latter, for example, X rays, radium rays, ultraviolet light, and certain chemical substances have been found to greatly increase

---

* A complete discussion of techniques used in analyzing hereditary characteristics in man is presented by J. V. Neel and W. J. Schull in *Human Heredity*, Chicago: University of Chicago Press, 1954.

the rate of mutation, which occurs through the disturbance of the chemical arrangements within the gene molecule (Muller, 1947).

If the genes in a pair are dissimilar, the two genes may blend to produce an intermediate characteristic, or one gene may prevail and thus conceal the effect of the other. For example, a gene for tallness may combine with a gene for shortness and produce an individual of medium, or average, height; or, the combination may produce a tall individual. In the latter case, the prevailing gene, which produces a trait (tallness) in the presence of the other gene (shortness), is referred to as *dominant;* the concealed gene is *recessive.* The recessive gene, although concealed, remains intact and may be passed on to a child in a succeeding generation. If, in the next generation, this recessive gene is matched with a like recessive gene, the characteristic influenced by them will appear.

Determining the nature and methods of gene operation is one of the most interesting research projects being conducted today, and, as a review of the recent "genetic code" literature will show, the operations are exceedingly complex. What little we know about heredity and its effects has been derived from studies of plants, animals, viruses, and, infrequently, human embryos. The scientific study of human heredity is obviously difficult because of the inability of humans to reproduce offspring in large numbers and in short spaces of time. When one considers that many characteristics are carried in the recessive genes through several generations before some chance combination produces those characteristics in any one descendant of a family, the magnitude of the geneticist's task becomes evident.

An individual's traits and characteristics are a result of (1) the particular genes which appear and are combined at the time of fertilization; (2) the interaction between the genes; and (3) the influence of environment during the prenatal, natal, and postnatal periods. Within this statement lies the foundation of the heredity-environment controversy that has waxed and waned over the past century. The problem began when an attempt was made to separate and define accurately the two concepts. Gradually, the realization came that such a separation was impossible: For one reason, not enough is yet known about heredity and its effects; for another, the beginnings (and hence the extent) of environmental influences are as yet impossible to determine, and may remain obscured even after the precise nature of gene operations is described. As Snyder (1965, p. 70) has said:

> ... As the zygote divides and forms a ball of cells, some cells are on the outside, some on the inside. Already different conditions exist for different cells. Slightly different chemical reactions are set up by the same genes under these differing conditions, and these lead in turn to still differing reactions; or, in some cases, certain genes act strongly under certain conditions of the surrounding cytoplasm, less strongly under other conditions.

"Heredity probably does determine limits, both upper and lower, within which development can occur," says J. P. Guilford (1962, p. 164). But so far as science is concerned, all that we are sure of is that, genetically, a child brings into the world a physical and psychological *potential* for development. Menninger (1961) asserts that what we actually inherit "is probably confined to physical structure, including brain patterns" (p. 23)—for example, the general shape of the face and head, the pigmentation of the skin, color of the eye, body build. That is, our entire hereditary endowment, received at the moment of conception, determines the special nature these characteristics may have if unacted upon by environmental factors. However, both before and after birth, structural characteristics can be greatly altered by adverse environmental conditions (Shuttleworth, 1949). A disease such as rickets changes normal bone structure, a syphilitic mother can bear a congenitally blind child, a mother who contracts German measles early in her pregnancy runs a high risk of bearing an infant with a heart or vision defect. Difficult births which necessitate the use of instruments are responsible for a great many cases of cerebral palsy, and it is not uncommon for infants born by Caesarian operation to live a life of chronic respiratory ailments. Each of these is a case of structural change resulting *from* environmental influences and resulting *in* functional change.

Some Tempered Theories

Concerning such conditions as those described, there is general agreement about the roles of heredity and environment. But, once we go beyond a discussion of *structure* to determine the effects of heredity, we meet with overwhelming difficulties, and controversy. One of the most common "proofs" that a particular characteristic is inherited is summed up in the words, "It runs in the family." The phrase has been applied to such traits and conditions as genius, feeblemindedness, ingenuity, nervousness, indigestion, alcoholism, instability, various mental diseases, asthma, epilepsy, and rheumatic fever, among others. The pure and simple fact is, we don't know positively whether these things are inherited or acquired. Menninger (1961, p. 25) maintains that all functional propensities—that is, all behavior patterns in general are usually acquired. He says:

> . . . a great many people believe and will go on believing that not only personality traits but personality defects and personality diseases are inherited. . . . The truth is that at the present time we have no convincing scientific evidence that "insanity" or any generally prevalent form of mental disease likely to result in insanity is definitely transmitted by heredity. There are a few exceptions to be noted—one or two degenerative conditions of the nerve tissue which seem to run in families but which are very rare. Epilepsy is often described as hereditary but the trend of scientific opinion is against this. . . . Even feeblemindedness, which we once felt to be quite definitely and regularly hereditary in certain forms, is in the vast majority of cases, not transmitted.

Many attempts have been made to link heredity and intelligence, and the controversy reached its height when intelligence tests came into common usage. However, the tests, besides becoming outmoded, or at best inadequate, with each succeeding generation, measure only the *functioning* of inherent neural structures, not the structures themselves. Some correlations have been found between mental measurements and genetic relationship (see Chapter VII), but in most of the investigations environmental factors could not be discounted as contributors. Parental attitudes, to name one, are too subtly transmitted to be easily observed or analyzed.

Perhaps, then, for those people who would offer their proof by saying "It runs in the family," the most tempering answer is, "So do the most influential aspects of environment."

A Few Truths

The theory that the child inherits a potential for development is borne out by Illingworth (1949), who grouped boys and girls according to their birth measurements and recorded their weights and heights at half-yearly intervals up to the age of thirteen. He found that the measurements generally followed the direction of differences recorded at birth. And the hypothesis that physical characteristics are inherited is supported by a number of correlative studies. One study by Newman, Freeman, and Holzinger (1937) shows height (and intelligence) correlation coefficients of .94 for identical twins, .58 for fraternal twins, and .50 for siblings. Correlations in the .60's and .70's were obtained between parents and their children.

Menninger does admit the possibility that we also inherit "peculiar neural arrangements which facilitate certain types of reaction" (p. 27). This theory gains support from the findings of Jost and Sontag (1944) who became interested in the pronounced individual differences in the excitability and intensity of emotional reactions observable among children even during the first year of life. Using pairs of identical twins, siblings, and unrelated children ranging in age from six to twelve years, the investigators obtained measurements of skin resistance, pulse, salivation, respiration, vasomotor persistence, autonomic balance, "heart period," and volar conductance. The results furnished evidence for a pattern of relationship between the different physiological measurements and heredity, as indicated by the following correlations:

Identical twins	.43 to .49
Brothers and sisters	.26 to .40
Unrelated pairs	.02 to .16

Thus, the conclusion drawn from this study is that the child does inherit a structure that predisposes him to react emotionally according to a pattern set forth by environmental circumstances and conditions. Through indoctrination, imitation, and cultural demands, he develops certain emotional responses within limits set forth by his heredity. More recent studies, cited by Levin (1965), lend full support to the investigators' conclusions. (See pp. 213–14.)

Sex. Of all the physical characteristics inherited by the individual, probably none is more important to him than the sex he receives—and probably no other endowment is such a matter of chance. The female germ cell contains a pair of chromosomes designated as XX, and the male germ cell contains a pair of chromosomes designated as XY, the only unmatched pair in either sex. When these chromosomes split and unite at fertilization, one female X choromosome is paired with *either* one male X chromosome (forming an XX, or female, cell) *or* one male Y chromosome (forming an XY, or male, cell). At the moment of union, the sex of the unborn infant is unalterably determined once and for all. There is no way of forcing a union of X with X or X with Y, there is no way of changing the union once it has been made, and there is no one-hundred per cent reliable way of predicting what the infant's sex will be before birth.

Obviously a child's sex will make a difference to him in direct proportion to the difference it makes to his parents. A parent who wanted a boy but received a girl will most likely develop specific attitudes of rejection or overcompensation for feelings of rejection, depending upon how strong the original desires for a particular sex were. (Dinitz and his associates (1954) found that prospective parents express a preference for boys more often than for girls.) Conversely, the parents of several girls are apt to pamper and have higher expectations for the boy-child born to them. The nature and effects of such parent-child relationships are taken up in Chapter XI.

Sex characteristics have an even more direct influence on the child's development than occurs through parental attitudes. Boys appear to be at a slight overall disadvantage, although there are more of them born and their birth weights and lengths are usually greater than girls'. The mortality rate for infant boys is greater, they come in for a larger share of sex-linked characteristics (color blindness, baldness, hemophilia), and they acquire more speech defects among them, which adversely affect the acquisition of language. Girls carry four per cent more genetic material, which may account for their advantage in longevity (*Time*, 1963), and besides being more advanced in all phases of language development, they are superior in color vision, they mature sexually earlier, and their skeletal growth is more accelerated. As a result of these and other factors, girls (in the American culture) become more highly socialized and make better social adjustments (Bonney, 1942, 1944).

All societies are divided into a masculine and a feminine culture, and even before the child is born every adult begins to channel him into one or the other prescribed mode of behavior. The culture into which a child is born dictates, according to his sex, what games he plays, and the toys he plays with, the clothes he wears, the language he uses, and his behavior in general. These cultural dictates, and possibly others, are responsible for the stories he prefers to read and the television programs he prefers to watch. On this subject, Hurlock (1956) says:

> Every social group has an approved pattern of behavior for members of the two sexes. From earliest childhood, the girl learns to conform to this pattern by identification with her mother, just as the boy learns to be "masculine" by identifying himself with his father or with older boys. Through differential training in the home and social pressures from their peers, teachers, and other adults, children learn their approved sex roles. Boys are allowed greater freedom, their emancipation is speeded up, and they are held to less exacting codes of behavior than are girls. Once a stereotype of appropriate "masculine" or "feminine" behavior is learned, the child can be assured of social acceptance. Lack of conformity to the socially approved sex role, on the other hand, leads to criticism and social ostracism. . . .

Thus, the assimilation of an appropriate sex role becomes one of the most important developmental tasks of childhood (see Chapter III). The well-integrated male or female who has mastered this task is a supreme example of the complex interactions between heredity and environment.

Race.   Because a child inherits his physical structures, he also inherits a race. This term, although much maligned and misused, is nothing more or less than a useful concept in human biology. Shapiro (1965, p. 593) defines it as follows:

> . . . Races . . . are distinct groups of mankind differing from each other by recognizable physical or anatomical features which are inherited and are not materially altered by environment. But above all, in their combination of distinctive traits they are unique and represent some degree of independent development or evolution.

Despite a widespread tendency to refer to "the Italian race" or "the Scandinavian races" or "the Jewish race," the fact remains that there are only three primary races—Negroid, Caucasoid, and Mongoloid—with various subraces and composite races within the three categories, none of which carry the names of the ethnic or religious groups so commonly called races.

Many investigators have attempted to prove or disprove a supposed superiority of one race over another. For the most part, they have failed to establish any correlations between race and inferiority-superiority except insofar as membership in a particular race affects the caste or the socioeconomic status of an individual. Concerning race differences in intellectual capacity, Cobb (1960, p. 939) concludes: "Given an equal chance for education the young of any race can equal in intellectual capacity that of any other." Frequently, comparisons are made merely between Negroes and whites, not between Negroes and whites from the same general environment. That is, the Negro's home environment is often one of slum-like conditions, which have a demonstrably deleterious effect on child development (see pages 42–3).

Likewise, the findings regarding racial influence upon the rate of development are inconclusive. Early studies failed to take into consideration the socioeconomic status of the subjects; later studies concluded that, in general, where living conditions are similar, differences in rate of development as measured by the age of pubescence disappear (Garrison, 1965).

Statistics, then, present no evidence for racial advantages or disadvantages that cannot be explained by environmental conditions or familial differences within a racial group. Therefore, generalizations about physical growth or inherent capacities based solely upon race are unsafe, unsound, and certainly unscientific.

About Interactions

Regardless of how little we know about heredity and its effects, we can recognize its importance. The infant's inherited gene structure determines the kind of biological potential with which he starts life and probably determines the extent to which much of his abilities and characteristics emerge at later stages as a result of his interaction with his environment (Boyd, 1953). And a continuous interaction does take place. About that there is universal agreement. "The nature and extent of the influence exerted by each type of factor depend upon the contribution of the other" (Anastasi and Foley, 1948, p. 241).

Environment, according to a noted geneticist, is all that is not genetically determined. "It means," he says, "the intrauterine surroundings of the embryo and fetus, the food and climate which impinges on the child and adult, and the psychological and cultural influences of the home, school and society in their complex reactions upon the personality" (Stern, 1956, p. 48).* The implication is obvious: A child's environment will have a profound and lasting effect upon his physical, psychological, mental, and emotional development and upon his total behavior patterns. And, although controllable to an extent, the effects of environment are inescapable. However, the influence of any environmental factor will depend upon the nature of the hereditary materials upon which it operates, and, conversely, any single

---

* One term that deserves consideration here is *congenital*, which means "being born with." To some people, congenital factors may therefore appear to be inherited. The fact is that congenital conditions are those in which the hereditary potential is influenced in some way by intrauterine or birth processes (prolonged or instrument births) prior to the infant's emergence into the external environment. Congenital factors are more amenable to human control than are hereditary factors but they are, at present, less readily controlled than the external environmental factors.

hereditary factor may operate differently between individuals as a result of environmental conditions (Kallmann, 1956–57). The danger of accepting any viewpoint other than that of a continuous, reciprocal interaction between hereditary and environmental factors is implied by Menninger in his statement that, in essence, World War II was a "conflict between theories of hereditary superiority and theories of environmental determination" (p. vii).

At no time, and in no instance, can the effects of heredity and environment act independently of each other. This statement must be repeated over and over again, especially in view of the fact that, seemingly, whole books on child development and child psychology deal exclusively with environmental factors, and this text is not substantially different in that respect. The reason for the emphasis being so placed is a logical one. The role of the genes, carriers of heredity, has been played out long before the infant ever arrives on the scene, their force unchanging and uncontrollable. That is, the potential for growth exists at the moment of cell fertilization; and, while environment can fulfill or fail to fulfill that potential, it cannot change the potential itself. Until more information concerning the operation of heredity is available, students would be wiser to concentrate on the environmental influences, which are more readily analyzable (and controllable), even though such an emphasis places an added burden of responsibility upon society. It means, of course, a reorientation that forces society to regard the individual not as a finished work of art to be praised or criticized, but as a fresh canvas to be filled in. Only thus can society become a dynamic, positive force in shaping the future of mankind.

SOCIETIES AND CULTURES

Within the child's most comprehensive environment, the world, there are many broad groupings of peoples—communities, states, nations, regions, continents—having common traditions, institutions, and collective activities or interests. Each grouping has its own culture—the complex of knowledge, religion, art, values, beliefs, and customs that affect the ways of life in a given society (Linton, 1945). These ways of life are a product of accumulated heritage handed down through customs, habits, and various media of communicative interaction and are directly responsible for the manner in which each society handles the problems revolving around such areas of living as health, survival, marriage and mating, rearing of children, education, socialization, recreation, religion, care of the aged, and death and burial (Alpenfels, 1957; Benedict, 1934). Because a child is born into a culture (and many subcultures) as well as a physical and social world, the practices and attitudes involved in dealing with these problems have a direct and intimate bearing on his ultimate development.

In order to be viewed as "successful," a child must behave in accordance with the ways of life peculiar to the society into which he is born. The child in America, for example, cannot dress the same as the Australian aborigine; his sexual habits are not the same as those of the Samoan child; his diet is quite different from that of the Eskimo. Similarly, an adult cannot behave as a young child does, and the elderly gentleman plays a different role than does the man "in his prime." Furthermore, these roles differ in various societies. Thus, behavior at all stages and ages is influenced by what is expected and demanded by the cultures of continents and nations, regions within a nation, local communities, parents and peers. Each society has its social "norms" which become immediate, individual pressures.

Biocultural Behavior

Whenever a mother makes a dress or prepares a meal, or a father drives a nail, or a small child shovels sand on the beach, some genetically inherited body parts are used in ways and for the purposes determined by the culture of the society in which each individual exists. Such actions have been termed by Titiev (1959) and other anthropologists as *biocultural behavior*. Titiev described four possible combinations of stimuli and response: (a) Both the stimulus and the response fall within the field of inherited biological factors, e.g., the dryness in the throat alleviated by glandular secretion. (b) The stimulus to action may originate in culture but induces a biological response, e.g., when a child is not allowed to "bang" on furniture, he becomes angry, thus increasing his pulse rate. (c) Stimuli which arise within the body are responded to in a culturally determined manner. For example, muscular contractions within the body may produce the feeling of being hungry, but the individual awaits mealtime for the satisfaction of his hunger, a culturally prescribed mode of behavior. (d) Both the initiating impulse and the response are determined by culture. American males, for instance, usually arise when a lady enters the room in which they are seated.

In each of these four types of activity, some aspect of the biological self is brought into play and is, except in the first type, interrelated with a cultural environment. The child is guided, beginning at an early age, toward making these interrelationships. Throughout childhood, he is required to modify his behavior in accordance with the cultural demands for different age levels. Through some form of disapproval, such as punishment, for failure and some form of reward for success, the child acquires the desire to do what is expected of him. When this stage of development is reached, he may be said to have *internalized* the values of his society.

Enculturation

The internalization of cultural values, which is closely related to the development of conscience, is brought about in the child through maturation and learning. The process whereby he is taught the social behavior required for adequate adjustment to his environment is called *enculturation.** Through this process the child adjusts his innate characteristics to the prevailing culture practices of his society. He is born with the potentials to do so, potentials for maturing and for grasping, at different age levels, his inherited society's language, ways of behaving, attitudes, and values.

A large number of individuals contribute to the child's cultural education, most of them connected with his home and his community institutions —the school, the church, and the mass media.

> Since the major source for what we learn, including what we react to emotionally, is the human environment into which we are born, the core responsibility for the younger generation's progress towards humanity, individuality, and inner integration rests squarely on the shoulders of the older generations, who represent and reflect the society into which the new generation is born. Whether we are aware of it or not, we teach our version of human-ness and our social values and practices to younger persons through our relations with them, *not through lip-service, word-magic, admonitions*—whether these relations involve direct personal interaction, or are indirect, as in the case of adult-controlled mass media.
>
> Milner, 1959

Acculturation

We have stated that the child is born with the potentials for adjusting his inherited characteristics to his inherited culture. He is also born with potentials for later reorganizing and remodeling his culture in harmony with the changed conditions and needs which frequently manifest themselves as one culture comes into close contact with a more advanced one. This process of modification is called *acculturation.* One might say that acculturation is accomplished, to an extent, when a child (a primitive culture) internalizes the values and behavior patterns of his parents (an advanced culture). In this instance, the process can never be a total one, because the child throughout his life has contacts and interrelationships with more than one significant adult (Lazarus, 1961). Moreover, as a child enters public school and turns more often to his peers for approval, he finds himself faced with the problem of adjusting to many different ethnic, racial, religious, and social-class cultures. Such situations occur with consistent frequency in overcrowded, concentrated areas, such as large cities or climatically popular regions, where literally hundreds of different cultures are represented in any one educational or recreational area. Many small internal or borderline areas in Europe have experienced varying forms of acculturation for centuries, particularly Alsace-Lorraine in France, which has been used as a political

---

* The anthropological meaning and use of *enculturation* is presented here. See Melville Herskovits, *Man and His Work*, Knopf, 1948, pp. 40–41.

football passing back and forth between the jurisdictions of France and Germany, and Switzerland, which is culturally and geographically divided into four parts, each using a different language—Romansch, French, Italian, and German.

Under these and like circumstances, the children often accomplish a subtle form of acculturation, which results, according to Redfield, Linton, and Herskovits (1936, p. 149), " 'when groups of individuals having different cultures come into continuous first-hand contact, with subsequent changes in the original cultural patterns of either or both groups.' "

Cultural Diversity

Of the many cultures and subcultures throughout the world, two divisions have been mentioned in connection with heredity—the two-way division based on the sexes and the three-way division based on race. Race is also included in a more comprehensive division, ethnic culture, which includes peoples grouped according to religious faith, geographical locations or nationality, system of government, caste system, and so forth. The United States is made up of a great variety of ethnic cultures: English, Scots, Irish, German, French, Italian, Scandinavian, Greek, Chinese, Japanese, Negro, Puerto Rican, Cuban, Mexican, Indian, Polynesian, Filipino, Jewish, Mormon, Mennonite, to name but a few. Each group, as might be expected, has its individual culture patterns, manifested in child-rearing practices, food habits, recreational preferences, language expressions, religions, or attitudes toward different governmental, economic, and social problems.

In the American "melting pot," each of the ethnic cultures is represented within one of the country's major regions, which in turn have cultures peculiar to them. New England, the Deep South, the Middle West, the Mountain States, the Southwest, the West Coast, and the Alaskan and Hawaiian communities all have different historical backgrounds, traditions, climates, resources, language patterns, and major religious and occupational groups.

Within the regions are, of course, the community and the family cultures, and all the cultures are further combined and shuffled under another classification—socioeconomic status, or social class. These latter cultures, however, have such an immediate bearing upon the child's education and personality that they will be taken up separately in this chapter.

The greater mobility of our society and the advanced forms of communication are contributing to more frequent first-hand contact between many of the cultures and are fostering a better understanding between the groups, but any fusion is accomplished only gradually, if at all. The cultural lessons a child learns are deeply ingrained into ways of looking at himself and his world. Furthermore, all members of a cultural group share and are influenced by the cultural heritage of that group to such an extent that certain behavior patterns are sometimes regarded as inborn. For instance, we speak of "Yankee ingenuity," "Southern hospitality," "Midwestern industriousness," and the "Western mode of casual living." A further study of the nature of the apparent "inbornness" shows that the cultural pattern has been internalized to so great a degree that it is completely integrated into the lives and personalities of the group members and hence is passed on generation after generation through attitudes and symbolic behavior. These deeply internalized behaviors are not easily uprooted, supplanted, or fused.

Dangers of Cultural Demands

Specific practices within any of the broader cultures will, no doubt, always be open to some form of criticism because no one culture is able consistently to take into consideration the uniqueness of the individual. Not only is his immediate environment the only one of its kind, but also his neuromuscular characteristics, constitution, emotional patterns, and the biochemical ingredients contained in his body are peculiar to him. Few, if any, societies consider the possibility that a child or an adult might not be equipped to handle the role he is expected to assume, that he might be better equipped for another. In America, for instance, the major responsibility for the care of the infant is assigned to the mother without giving cognizance to the fact that while she is anatomically suited for bearing children she might not be psychologically or constitutionally suited for rearing them. The mother in the Alorese society returns to the fields to work when her baby is three weeks old, leaving the care of the infant to older members of the tribe and thereby "robbing" the child of what our society considers an important affectional relationship. Mentowie children are adopted by their mother's father, and their mother's brothers assume the task of feeding them —a custom of patriarchal custody which raises the same doubts and questions as have been raised by critics of our own matriarchal society.

Some cultures do not take nutrition or food availability into consideration when they pass on their food habits and preferences. A poor family of Caucasoids in the United States would reject a free meal of plump gophers, while the Navaho Indians would regard them as delicacies. Until recent years, cow's milk, generally haled in the United States as one of the most nutritious foods, was unacceptable to many Orientals.

Methods of punishment have always created controversies. Some tribes frown upon striking children, and the efficacy of such a method is a matter for frequent discussion among American adults. Among Hopi Indians, children are not punished by striking them, but once each year Kachinas (masked adult male relatives dressed in terrifying costumes) are called in to frighten the child into behaving (Dennis, 1940).

As we mentioned in Chapter I, Jean-Jacques Rousseau believed firmly in an educational method by which a child would roam the fields, observing nature and asking questions; yet, our society decrees by law that every child, regardless of his constitution, physical makeup, or aptitudes, must attend a formal school upon reaching the age of six. If one were to build an educational system based upon evaluations of individual children, both methods, and probably newly devised ones, would have to be given recognition.

In these and other ways, the demands of a culture force upon its members a conformity to modes of living that are not always in the best interests of the individual or even of the society itself. Sometimes whole cultures are eliminated or drastically modified because of their own unrealistic demands, as we witnessed in America when the static, inflexible Indian cultures attempted to withstand the dynamic sweep of the pioneer society.

CULTURE AND THE CHANGING COMMUNITY

Within almost every community one can find a wide diversity of occupations, religions, and organizations, developed to fill the needs of a complex way of life and molded largely by the culture of the people making up the community. The ways in which the social structure affects the developing child depends upon his family's position in relation to the total community, whether it retains a majority or minority position. The child whose father is an unskilled or semiskilled worker will quite likely find himself living in a large industrial community where his peers will be from the same sociocultural level as himself, the families large, the playground and park facilities public, the youth organizations oriented toward some civic or religious groups. The child of a professional man, on the other hand, might find himself living in a college town where his peers are from the middle class, the families of average size, the playgrounds and parks few, small, and central to the community, the cultural emphasis on musical concerts, libraries, lectures, and art museums, and the religious affiliations casual. The adjustments of such children are far easier than those expected from, for instance, the child of a lower-class restauranteur who moves to a resort area culturally oriented toward the upper-class transient, where the child's activities are limited to sports in a natural setting and the pursuit of transitory pleasures—where, in short, there are wide discrepancies between his family culture and his community culture.

Furthermore, the child's adjustment to a particular culture is made more difficult by the fact that each type of community is constantly changing. Continuing advances in technology have assured us that few, if any, social units of American society will remain static or become stable.

Urbanization

For two centuries, America was predominantly rural, with scattered

Slum housing on South Dearborn Street, at 35th Street on Chicago's South Side. The site was rebuilt, with apartments and recreational areas.

Stateway Gardens, a low-rent public housing development on Chicago's Near South Side. Site was once part of what was characterized as "the largest contiguous slum" in the nation. Buildings are owned and operated by the Chicago Housing Authority.

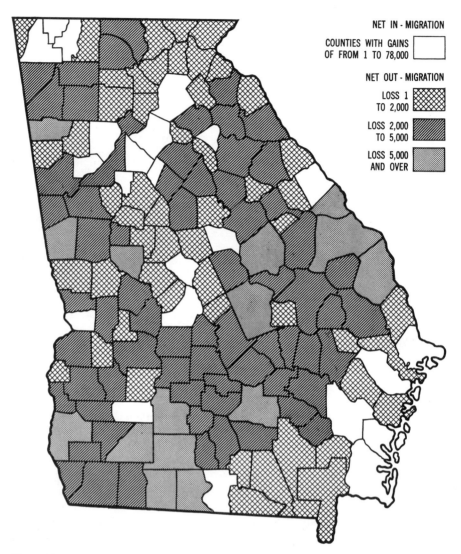

NET IN - MIGRATION

COUNTIES WITH GAINS
OF FROM 1 TO 78,000

NET OUT - MIGRATION

LOSS 1
TO 2,000

LOSS 2,000
TO 5,000

LOSS 5,000
AND OVER

Figure II–1. Between 1950 and 1960 the population of Georgia has shifted, causing heavy losses in the farm-oriented counties (*Atlanta Journal and Constitution*, 1963, Section C).

towns serving as trading centers. As late as 1890, seventy-two per cent of the population was classified by the U. S. Bureau of Census as rural; whereas only 30 per cent was listed as rural in the 1960 census. In 1900 farmers and farm workers made up 36 per cent of the working population; whereas in 1960 farmers and farm workers totalled only 6 per cent (Hauser, 1962).

The changing population in the Southeast may be observed in the in-migration and out-migration of the 159 counties of Georgia, as shown in Figure II-1. Only twenty of the 159 counties gained population in a state where there has been a substantial gain in the total. These twenty counties included urban areas or counties adjacent to urban areas. The rapid growth of these sections, accompanied by a rapid decline in the population of rural areas, not only has changed the complexion of a large percentage of communities in the United States, but also has been partially responsible for the increased instability of the people and institutions making up the various communities. Finally instability, conflicts in values, emotional insecurity, and economic dependency have resulted from the continuing urbanization of our society.

The Vanishing "Hick"

Formerly, the child reared in a small, rural area experienced, almost exclusively, social contacts of an inbred nature—within his church, school, and grange groups, rarely outside his particular community. His peer group was small and stable, and he had far more interactions with adults than with children. The concept of the "hick" who was comically awkward in social relations and sadly deficient in knowledge of the world became a favorite stereotype thirty years ago. Today, the "hick" has all but disappeared. Although there are still many children in rural communities in the United States, the widespread use of automobiles, the development of local and interstate highways, the establishment of local and regional hospitals and libraries, the consolidation of schools, the construction of community centers, and the universal presence of radios and television in the home have greatly reduced the differences in educational and recreational opportunities between children in rural and urban homes. Moreover, the development of parks, campsites, and other recreational centers, along with the ever-widening circle of suburban areas,* have placed the children from all the various districts in closer proximity, enhancing the cultural exchanges.

Suburbia

Modern suburbia is a relatively recent development, made possible by improved standards of living. Its culture is primarily one of segregation, because the housing developments that are an integral part of suburbia have

* Prior to 1950, Suffolk County, New York, was totally given over to farming, which is still the big industry in the eastern part of the county. The western part, however, which is approximately forty to fifty miles from New York City, has been subjected to a fantastically rapid suburbanization. In 1954, for example, the district of Commack had one school with 250 pupils. Ten years later, the fields had given rise to new split-level homes instead of potatoes and strawberries, the one school had multiplied eighteen times, and the 250 pupils found themselves with 12,000 school-mates (McCarthy, 1964).

Before Levitt and Sons arrived the region shown in this aerial photograph was Pennsylvania farmland. Land use had changed little in two centuries. The only distinctly modern feature is the oval track of the Langhorne raceway, one mile in circumference.

After Levitt arrived in 1952 the land was put to new use. Between 1952 and 1958 more than 17,000 homes, most of them priced below $15,000 were built in the new community called Levittown, Pa. Only about two-thirds of the eight-square-mile development appears in this photograph. If Levittown were a political entity, which it is not, its present population of more than 65,000 would make it the 11th largest city in the state.

been designed for certain income levels. Schools have been built to serve one or two housing developments, or one housing development could well fill several schools. Thus, the children experience a segregation according to social class, in the home, the school, the church, and in their recreation.

Within suburbia, which is predominantly middle class, there are strong pressures for conformity. Parents are preoccupied with "keeping up with the Joneses," and they expect their children to behave in the ways that will enhance their own reputation and self-esteem. In a sense, the adults in suburbia are building a whole new set of values centered on leisurely living. Their goals are indistinct, obscured by the newness of their way of life, and the traditions under which they were reared have, in most cases, been left behind with the extended families—with the parents and grandparents, aunts and uncles, who remained in the older portions of the country.

To a marked degree, suburbanites are as young as their communities. A large portion of the population is made up of young parents, children, and teenagers. The grandparents and older relatives seldom live in close proximity and rarely, because of the moderate size of the homes, do they reside under the same roof. Thus, the children are isolated from the past family culture. They grow up in an environment that is protective and permissive rather than one that is characterized by "old-fashioned" restraint and discipline. In many ways, they consider themselves privileged individuals set loose in an amusement park. By the time they have reached adolescence, the children have adopted the attitudes and patterns of behavior of the adults of their community—they are as insecure, their roots are as lightly planted in fresh topsoil, and their goals are as nebulous.

Slum Districts

As an increasing number of middle- and lower-middle-class families leave the cities for the suburban areas, a proportionate amount of the city is turned over or left to the lower-class families who cannot afford to go elsewhere. The culture of these families is of a primitive nature; therefore, the areas in which they are forced to live become primitive in cultural facilities. Conant (1961), although speaking of schools in particular, could well have been referring to any educational or recreational center when he said that what it *"should do and can do is determined by the status and ambitions of the families being served."* Obviously, then, any area made up predominantly of poor and unstable families, parents of low moral character with no aspirations, and unsupervised, underfed, deprived children will provide nothing better than streets for the children to play in. (See Whyte, 1955.)

The slums are a challenge to education in particular and are discussed in that respect in Chapter XII. But education is not the only challenge. Here we find civilization at its worst. Medical care and disease, diet and vigor (or lack of it), apathy and ignorance are problems of awesome size and complexity. And, although juvenile crime and delinquency can be found in places other than slums, the incidence there is considerably higher. Thus, it is not surprising to find that those conditions which are frequent concomitants of delinquency turn out to be the same ones which frequently describe life in the slum areas (Kvaraceus and others, 1959).

Community Institutions

Every community, no matter how small, is served by at least one organization which helps to teach the ways of life of that community. The school, of course, carries the greatest influence, if only because of the amount of time a child is required to spend within its environs. The size and quality of its plant, the number and effectiveness of its personnel—these are reflections of community concerns, beliefs, and goals. (See Chapter XII.) The mass media, too, carry a persistent weight, although the three major vehicles—newspapers, radio, and television—usually serve many cultures and many communities.

Frequently, the only organization for out-of-school activities that is available to children from small communities is the church. It is perhaps the greatest, sometimes the only, socializing force in the rural child's life. And even in the larger communities, the church is often responsible for sponsoring, housing, or organizing the major clubs in which the children participate: Boy Scouts, Girl Scouts, YMCA, YWCA, CYO, and so forth.

Although some churches or denominations cross-cut the community's social structure, with memberships fairly representative of all socioeconomic levels, in most cities there are characteristic social-class distributions for different denominations (Havighurst and Neugarten, 1957, p. 131). Within a large city, for instance, there is likely to be a social graduation of Catholic parishes, with those in the more favorable residential areas being at the top of the status hierarchy and those in the slum areas at the bottom (Havighurst and Neugarten, 1962, p. 177). The same is usually true of the well-established Protestant denominations. The type of fellowship services, then, will vary even within the different denominations in harmony with the needs and aspirations of the groups being served. Therefore, the child who regularly attends church, either as a member of the worshipping body or as a participant in the church-housed social activities, learns not only the religious beliefs and practices of the church, but also a social class pattern of behavior.

Table II–1 lists many of the major youth groups to be found in communities throughout the country and gives a representative percentage of group membership among boys and girls of a certain age level. Other or-

Table II–1   Group Membership of Boys and Girls Aged 11 to 13 (From Havighurst and Neugarten, 1962, p. 175)

Organization	Per cent of Boys and Girls Holding Membership	
	Boys	Girls
Church Groups	18	33
School Clubs—Latin Club, Math Club, Band, Glee Club, Chess Club, etc.	18	27
Religion Oriented—YMCA, YWCA, YMHA, Hi-Y, Tri-Hi-Y, CYO	4	5
Social and Informal Clubs	2	7
Other National Youth Organizations:		
Boy or Girl Scouts	25	18
Rural—4-H, Future Farmers of America, Future Homemakers	10	16
Junior Achievement, Camp Fire Girls, etc.	5	6
No Club Membership	41	32

Note: Data taken from national samples obtained in 1953, 1956, and 1959 of 2,480 boys and 1,925 girls in public and private schools. Percentages total more than 100 because some belonged to more than one organization.

ganizations, such as dancing schools, day camps, nursery schools, art classes, and similar specialized groups, generally are private institutions and are designed to teach certain desirable skills and attitudes. Many of these schools and groups attain a prestige status—even in middle-class suburbia, where they are most prevalent.

Oftentimes, through membership in one or more of these institutions, and especially through interorganizational competition, the children become culturally mobile, particularly in the larger urban areas where class lines are less rigidly observed; however, in most cases, the organizations serve to perpetuate the cultural values of one segment of the population, and the child experiences a strong reinforcement for the values and behavior patterns he has absorbed at home.

THE FAMILY—BEARERS OF CULTURE

The smallest environmental and cultural unit to affect the development of a single child is his family. Through his parents and grandparents, the child inherits the basic structures that make it possible for him to acquire and modify his cultural heritage, a heritage directly transmitted by his parents and colored by their interactions with each other and with the larger society to which they belong. They function as mediators of the world to which the child is exposed, explaining the life he experiences in their own inimitable fashion, and, in so doing, they impose their attitudes and behavioral patterns upon him, make certain demands of him, and expect certain actions from him—all in keeping with the culture they have internalized. A child's family and his home life establish the standards by which he lives, his perceptions of right and wrong, his values and attitudes toward himself and others. In short, the home and its emotional-social setting has the earliest and greatest influence upon the child's social development.

An outstanding characteristic of American families is diversity. They are small or large or broken, father-dominated, mother-dominated, or even child-dominated, healthy or handicapped, urban, suburban or rural. They are classified according to social class, ethnic background, race, religious denomination or lack of church affiliation, geographical location, amount of education, or occupation—and usually according to more than one of these categories. Ackerman (1958) has developed an interesting and valuable system for discussing various types of family groups based upon their forms of adaptation.

1. The externally isolated family group, characterized by excessive isolation from the community, few or no friends, and some or no contact with members of the extended families. The essential pattern is one of failure of emotional integration into the community.
2. The externally integrated family group, characterized by active participation in the community, friends, and contact with extended families. In many instances, this external integration is compensatory for a basic failure of unity in the internal life of the family. The family has an incomplete or fragmented internal life.
3. The internally unintegrated family group, characterized by failure in internal unity with mutual alienation of the two parents or conflict of both. In some instances the effort to compensate takes the form of a mutually protective alignment of the members of one family pair, sometimes parent and child or parent and own sibling, which sets itself against another family pair.
4. The unintended family group, characterized by a primacy of the parents' motivations and needs and the subordination or exclusion of the needs of the child. Sometimes there is a mutually protective alliance of the parents with emphasis on sexual and social satisfaction but no intent to build a family or to have offspring and no goals for the family as a group. The goals of egocentric fulfillment of each parent's individual needs is paramount.
5. The immature family group, characterized by immaturity of the parents, each one parentifying the other. The immature, dependent needs of each parent are fixated to the grandparents and the responsibility for fulfilling family roles is not accepted. Therefore, the family unit is not independent and tends to lean on the extended family.
6. The deviant family group, characterized by rebellion against community mores, nonconformity in standards and organization, deviant goals and values for family and child rearing and a revolt against standards of ex-

tending families. The deviant family group can be divided into two types: (a) internally integrated but consistently in rebellion against community standards; (b) failure of internal integration, with rebellion occurring both inside and outside the family.

7. The disintegrated or regressed family group, characterized by trends that have the potential of breaking up the group, lack of integration, immaturity, excessive conflict, lack of compatibility, mutual attack, mutual isolation and inappropriate and unclear goals.

Ackerman could well have included another classification at the beginning of his list, a family group which may be thought of as both internally and externally integrated. Such a family is characterized by unity and cohesiveness of the different members of the family, and by active participation in varied community activities. This may be observed in their attendance at church, participation in school-related activities, and close ties with relatives of the family.

As cultural patterns change, the family unit changes and as large groups of families change their patterns of behavior and their values, the cultural patterns of a society change. With the rise in standards of living throughout the world and increased opportunities for acquiring knowledge of other societies, the family unit is constantly adjusting itself to new ideas and new modes of living. And, as we have indicated previously, the population shift has caused thousands of families to face the problem of adjusting to new locations, making new friends, and joining different institutions. The large trend toward suburban living has created situations in which many fathers leave home early in the day, commute to work, and return late at night. They see little of their children, and often fail to become identified with the communities in which they live.

The attitudes of parents and their ability to provide a favorable environment for a child's growth depends upon many factors, the most important of which is the parents' own family background—how their parents felt about them and dealt with them, what their parents considered of fundamental or superficial importance, and the values their parents held and passed on. Many of the young parents of today who are experiencing difficult adjustments to the rapidly changing patterns of family living are those very "latch-key" children of the war and postwar years who experienced little if any positive family interaction because of fathers being away most or all of the time and mothers being employed in factories or defense jobs. The children, left to care for themselves if they were old enough or in the care of maids, nursery-school personnel and grandparents if they were not, found their environment insecure, ever shifting. It is not surprising, then, that the parent of today finds his role slightly changed in the same way that he is changed. As Carrier (1959) maintains, parents no longer manage the lives of their children. Education and discipline are delegated to the schools, recreation and skills to youth groups, and ethical and spiritual guidance to the church. Naturally, the child frequently finds himself forced to look outside the family for judgments regarding his behavior and to find greater satisfaction than ever before in the approval of his peers.

Concerning the family crisis, Vaughan (1961, p. 355) states:

> The many agencies and institutions in our cities are not strong enough to make up the lacks in such things as security, love experience, direction, discipline and control and identification models. Children, who comprise our future adult society, live in the midst of a paradoxical situation—a life with material comforts and prerequisites never before known to man, but a life with a dearth of meanings, of direction, of clear and definite purpose.

Hopefully, the student of child psychology will examine the new experiences of modern families, attempt to relate them to older ones, absorb the knowledge gathered from research concerning family relationships (see Chapter XI), and synthesize a more progressive and well-balanced attitude toward the importance of a close, personal family unit to a healthy society.

THE CULTURE OF THE CLASSES

At various times throughout this chapter we have had occasion to use the terms "social class" or "middle class" or "socioeconomic status," until the reader must now be aware that the social status of a child's family has a direct, profound, and encompassing effect upon the child's entire personality. It has, as we shall briefly discuss, an influence on his motivations, perceptions, emotional behavior, success in school, and acceptance by his peers, as well as upon the external presentation of his self—dress, language, conduct. Such influences are brought about as a direct result of the child-rearing practices and parental expectations peculiar to the social class of which his family is a member.

Social class is defined as "two or more orders of people who are believed to be, and are accordingly ranked by the members of the community, in socially superior and inferior positions" (Warner and Lunt, 1941). The class idea is not a welcome one in America, steeped as we are in the democratic tradition of liberty, fraternity, justice, and equality; the existence of a society divided into classes seems inconsistent with that tradition. However, pertinent to this apparent inconsistency is a statement by Loeb (1953, p. 173):

> The essence of the democratic way does not consist in the obliteration or denial of social class differences. Rather it involves providing each person with the opportunity of learning those behaviors and values which can lead to "success" with a minimum amount of frustration and hostility toward self, family, or the original culture.

Unlike caste, social class is a sociological phenomenon. It is neither legally determined nor inherited and rigid. One may, by acquiring appropriate values and behaviors and status symbols, change his class (be mobile) either upwardly or downwardly. Moreover, differences between classes are continuous so that lines of separation are not clearly demarcated. One may possess some characteristics of one class, a few from another, and still others from a third.

Characteristics of Social Class

Warner has devised an Index of Status Characteristics which has been widely used, with modifications in some cases, to make case studies of communities. For its criteria, the ISC employs (1) occupations, ranging from professional to unskilled workers, (2) source of income, ranging from inherited wealth through salaries and wages to public relief, (3) house types, from large houses in good condition to houses in very poor condition and dwellings not originally intended for homes, and (4) areas lived in, from exclusive "Gold Coast" sections to slums (Warner and Warner, 1953).

Other criteria most frequently used to identify one's social class are amount of education, and behavior. The latter, which includes dress, language usage, and attitudes, is perhaps the most obvious characteristic of social status. The words a man uses, his interests, his regard for and relationships with both his immediate and remote associates, his hopes and aspirations, and his regard for and use of social amenities are all reflections of the class in which he was reared (Warner, 1944).

In some communities there may be only two or three social classes, while in others there may be six that are distinguishable. Older and larger cities of the east coast—those in which a shifting process has taken place over the years, and those which have changed more slowly—may have six classes. Newer and more rapidly growing and changing communities may have fewer classes and the demarcations may be less evident.

Using a five-class categorization, Havighurst and Neugarten (1962) have described the class characteristics, which we have adapted here. The reader must remember, though, that differences between classes are continuous and that the following divisions are but rough approximations.

The upper class consists of individuals who possess family wealth, have income from rents and royalties, belong to exclusive clubs, are often the power behind the throne in politics. They behave "properly" but not compulsively, since there is no problem of "keeping up with the Joneses": they *are* the Joneses. Education is important to them but the quest for advanced degrees is not assiduous. Offspring may go into law, medicine, politics, or architecture, but rarely do they become teachers or social workers. Marriages occur at ages later than the national average, the marriages are stable, and typically there are only one or two children. Foreign travel is common. Their homes (and they often have more than one) are spacious, with well-kept yards and buildings, and are located in exclusive areas. The women are not employed outside the home, and, as a rule, are aided inside the home by domestic servants.

The upper-middle class individuals are engaged in business administration and professional work. They are people with a wide range of economic resources (many are earning more than the average of the upper class) which they have gained through education and diligent and effective work. They are active in community and political affairs, live in new and expensive homes adjacent to the *most* exclusive areas.* Marriages are stable. Their two or three children, who have good books, travel opportunities, and robust health protected by thorough medical service, are a source of much gratification to teachers. Children are given special developmental opportunities such as dancing and music lessons; membership in clubs provides the setting for play at individual sports and with artistic media. Parents and their children are said to have an education compulsion.

The lower-middle class is the part of the population which best fits the stereotype of the typical American (Hollingshead, 1949, p. 97). The majority own their own homes, and families are a bit larger than in the classes above them. Marriages are characterized by instability. Kahl (1957) states that an extreme form of upper-middle class behavior is snobbery but of the lower-middle class it is respectability and prudery. In general, the latter class exercises moderation—in homes, work, education, and leisure-time pursuits. Some of the mothers work as teachers, secretaries, and book-keepers to supplement the incomes of their husbands, who work in white-collar jobs, as foremen in stable industries, as building contractors, or in their own small businesses. They make long and frequent trips by automobile, but foreign travel is unusual. Children are verbally encouraged to go to school and are obedient and hard-working pupils in the elementary grades and high school; however, parental example is such that only about one-third of them go to college.

The upper-lower class consists of the industrious bluecollar workers and their families. They live in small but well-kept houses near or on the "wrong side of the tracks." The women, when not confined at home by their four or more children, may work in factories, restaurants, or retail stores. Frequently, parents or the grandparents are recent immigrants. A third of the homes are broken by divorce, separation, desertion, or death. They are consciously or unconsciously striving for upward mobility. Leisure-time activities for the men consist of gathering in pool halls, watching baseball

* See Robert J. Havighurst, *et al.*, *Growing Up in River City*, John Wiley & Sons, 1962, p. 8 for a map of residential areas by social class.

games, and talking. Men, women, and children tend to be avid watchers of television. Husband and wife carry on independent recreation, and, at an early age, children are expected to take care of themselves. There is little reading of books and magazines by parents or children.

The lower-lower class is made up of sporadic laborers, cropfollowers, and reliefers. All the rest of society looks down on this class. They are regarded as trash, and they do contribute disproportionately to delinquency, crime, and sexual promiscuity. Focal concerns in this culture include: getting into and staying out of trouble; appearing "tough" to family, friends, and authorities; being smart enough to impose on others; being one's own boss rather than accepting external authority; and being controlled by, rather than controlling, fate (Kvaraceus and others, 1959). Parents in this group are likely to be "passive and fatalistic about their status" (Havighurst and Neugarten, 1962, p. 29). They work sporadically, move frequently, and live in the poorest dwellings. Mothers often supplement the meager income of their husbands and children by working as waitresses, dishwashers, or domestic help. Although there is an average of over five children per mother, more than half of the homes are broken by separation, desertion (divorces are too expensive), or death. The instability of marital status has led to the terminology *tandem marriage* or *serial monogamy,* meaning repeated, successive marriages of the "common law" or "trial" type. Many siblings carry different last names, and in Elmtown (Hollingshead, 1949, p. 116) twenty to twenty-five per cent of the births in the lower-lower class are illegitimate.

Many of the characteristics of the lower classes can be explained in terms of their most consistent personality trait: the placement of a high value upon the immediate gratification of needs and desires rather than upon a delay of satisfaction for a possible greater good (Leshan, 1952; Straus, 1962). America's prevailing middle-class culture regards as a mark of immaturity the inability to postpone the gratification of impulses; yet it is virtually impossible for the lower classes to react otherwise.

> . . . Lower-class people look upon life as a recurrent series of depressions and peaks with regard to the gratification of their basic needs. In their lives it is all or nothing, or next to nothing. When they have fire, their homes are stifling hot, and everyone sits as close to the fire as possible. For they remember anxiously what it was to be cold—to be too cold to sit in the house, so cold that the whole family must go to bed to keep warm. Just as their deep anxiety about hunger leads them even in good times to glut themselves, as middle-class people view their eating, so the acquired fear of deprivation drives them to get all they can of the other physical gratifications "while the getting is good."   W. Allison Davis, 1952

Such a value so placed results in many of the behavior patterns and characteristics we have described. Early, unstable marriages, so prevalent in the lowest class, indicate a disinclination to hold sex impulses in abeyance; quitting school to go to work is clearly evidence of the inability to plan long-term satisfactions. As we have said, they frequently change jobs, residences, and spouses; in addition, they have a tendency to spend all their money as soon as they acquire it.

In contrast, both adults and children of the upper-middle and upper classes typically will forego immediate wants with the hope that the ultimate outcome will be magnified.

The Impact of Social Class on Children

The assertion that class means deprivation and hardship for some and privilege and opportunity for others becomes most convincing when we consider the impact that class status has on children.* For the lower-class infant, his chances of handicap before birth are greater due to lack of prenatal medical care and advice for the mother. Furthermore, she is often overtired from working outside the home and caring for a large family; she is usually under emotional strain resulting from health and financial worries and the turmoil which accompanies the leaving of one spouse and the adjustment to another. Lack of education to deal with life's problems is a common characteristic of the lower-class mother, and stress is to a marked extent the chronic pattern of life for her (and for the youngsters). These conditions affect the health and emotional stability of the child, for the mother whose major concern is mere survival has little time or energy to satisfy any but the most basic needs of food, clothing, and shelter for herself and her children.

Obviously, a family's economic condition will have an impact upon the child even during his early infancy (Harrower, 1934). It will affect his amount of play space, his opportunities for broadening his experiences by way of travel, his time and recreations with his parents, the style, variety, and cleanliness of his clothing, and his nutrition—therefore, his physical growth. Meredith (1951) found that boys whose fathers were in professional or managerial occupations were, at seven and ten years of age, one inch taller and three pounds heavier than those whose fathers were semi-skilled. This relationship is even more pronounced in areas of the world where social and economic classes are more clearly stratified (Berry and Cowin, 1954).

---

* For the most part, we shall use the popular three-class categorization—upper, middle, and lower. Although in any system of social stratification there is bound to be a great deal of overlapping, the three categories are generally composed of the characteristics distributed throughout five or six subdivisions; i.e., *upper class* refers to a composite of upper-upper class and lower-upper class characteristics, *middle class* to upper- and lower-middle class, and *lower class* to upper- and lower-lower class.

Relationship of class to motivation and perception. Socioeconomic status has an apparent effect upon a child's motivations, according to Terrell and his associates (1959). Children ranging in age from six to eleven were given the task of discriminating the size of three-dimensional geometric figures. Social class was indicated by using Warner's ISC scale. Middle-class children learned more quickly when they were given non-material rewards—told they had reached a norm or praised—although these children also responded to the promise of a monetary reward. The motivation of lower-class children dropped significantly when there was no promise of material reward. These differences in attitude toward the test are explained in one way by questionnaires on which the middle-class youngsters reported that they would prefer to do something for the fun of it rather than to be given something for doing it.

The reader will notice that the motivations of the lower-class child are most often need-oriented. He is more preoccupied with the material things in life than with the symbolic. This tendency also shows up in a test administered by various investigators in which children of differing socioeconomic statuses were required to estimate the size of coins, either with the coins present or from memory or by comparisons with spots of light. Children from the slum areas in particular overestimated the size of coins, distorting the value of the larger ones especially (Bruner and Goodman, 1947; Tajfel, 1957).

Socioeconomic status and social acceptance. As a result of the differences in the conditions just mentioned, children will vary greatly in their development of attitudes toward themselves and other people. For example, awareness of appropriate sex roles (an important concomitant to social adjustment) develops earlier in the lower-class children. Differences are especially great between girls of the lower and middle classes (Rabban, 1950).

Other contrasts in peer culture prestige values among twelve-year-olds are described by Pope (1953). Ability to take a joke was more often a criterion for acceptability by both boys and girls in the high socioeconomic groups than by those in the low groups; restlessness was unacceptable behavior to the highs, but not to the lows; the "good student" was not accepted by the highs as a leader but he was not rejected by them as he was by the lower-class group; and tomboyishness was definitely unpopular with the high girls, who identified the trait with other attention-getting devices. The lower girls regarded the tomboy with a certain amount of admiration because of her advanced sexual interests and her ability to go out with boys. Concerning the major differences between the two groups, Pope states (pp. 216–217):

> The high groups of both sexes expect their members to show an appropriate tendency to conform to adult standards within the classroom.

They also show a positive evaluation of certain conventional rules of decorum, when attending parties and dances with the opposite sex. These qualities are not at all stressed by the low socio-economic groups. It is perhaps in these two respects that we find the most significant differences.

In order to win peer approval within his own social class, the lower-class boy must learn to be a good fighter—he must learn to stand up for his rights, generally by way of physical action. Lesser (1959) found that such aggression, providing it was provoked, was acceptable among lower-class preadolescent boys. However, differences between the high and low groups disappeared with certain types of undesirable behavior, such as unprovoked physical aggression against others or their possessions; indirect aggression, consisting of ignoring, rejecting, or using critical remarks and gestures as a means of showing displeasure toward others; and methods of getting attention.

Class status and emotional behavior. The number of fears and worries of children is related to their home and community background, as may be clearly seen in Table II-2, which indicates the close relationship between experiences, learning, and emotional behavior. As children become more aware of conditions which their experiences have shown to be potentially dangerous, they develop emotional reactions to the conditions. (Such objects or situations do not necessarily have to be physically dangerous; they can threaten a child's self-esteem or his relations with other people.) As might be expected, then, children from underprivileged homes with a paucity of experiences have fewer anxieties than those from the upper socioeconomic groups. On the other hand, lower-class children are more aware of the personal and social disorganizations wrought by poverty, and they

Table II-2   Summary of Means for the Total Number of Fears and Worries Indicated by Both Boys and Girls from Two Differing Socio-Economic Levels in Each of Ten Categories (Angelino, *et al.,* 1956, p. 265)

	Boys		Girls	
Category	Upper S-E (N = 179)	Lower S-E (N = 383)	Upper S-E (N = 178)	Lower S-E (N = 390)
I. Safety	1.07	1.05	.87	1.30
II. School	1.32	1.06	1.39	1.14
III. Personal Appearance	.04	.02	.06	.17
IV. Natural Phenomena	.28	.13	.25	.35
V. Economical & Political	.49	.44	.40	.27
VI. Health	.26	.16	.34	.20
VII. Animals	.20	.51	.22	.64
VIII. Social Relations	.43	.37	.63	.58
IX. Personal Conduct	.28	.22	.27	.28
X. Supernatural	.04	.04	.09	.04

visualize the problem as being near at hand. Undoubtedly, poverty is a condition with which these children are all too familiar (Estvan, 1952).

Angelino and his associates (1956) summed up their findings (Table II-2) thus: "Socio-economic background may be considered as an important variable in the self-expressed fears of different social groups, especially so when the qualitative nature of these fears is examined" (p. 276).

Child-rearing practices. Certainly it seems safe to make the observation that the class characteristics manifested by children are products of the practices by which their parents deal with them, and many investigators have been able to show significant contrasts in the attitudes and practices of parents within different classes. Within the lower classes, for example, more relaxed and permissive practices prevail in feeding and toilet training; yet, there is a hierarchical and rigid parental relationship with the children (Maas, 1951). The children expect punishment and authoritarian control in relation to their behavior, and, indeed, will generally prescribe punishment for wrongdoing to a greater extent than do other children. Further-

Table II–3 Comparison of Child-Rearing Practices of Middle- and Lower-Class Families in the United States

Lower class	*Middle class*
Children frequently breast-fed; pacifiers often used	Children usually given bottled milk to supplement breast feeding; infants held during bottle feeding
Casual attention and consideration given to weaning and to development of ability to use spoon and fork for self-feeding	Early weaning; guidance in the development of the ability to use spoon and fork in self-feeding
Toilet training usually starts late; little concern for soiled diapers	Toilet training starts early; attention given to cleaniness of diapers
Children's play unsupervised; girls allowed freedom and permitted to engage in rough-and-tumble games	Consistent supervision of play and playmates of children, particularly girls
Children are allowed to spend freely whatever money they obtain	Children are given an allowance and are encouraged to save money for future use
Children are taught fear of police and other law enforcement agencies	Children are taught to respect the law and its enforcement agents
Homes are authoritarian; parents mete out physical punishment	Democratic type of homes; children are reasoned with and punished by denying privileges

more, certain types of behavior are considered by them to be inherently wrong rather than harmful because of consequences or unfairness.

Children in the middle-class groups, on the other hand, enjoy a more democratic family life, a more equalitarian atmosphere, although the parents in general do wean and toilet train their children earlier, are more likely to schedule feedings rigidly, and exercise more control over choice of playmates, play activities, and movie-going. Despite the closer supervision, communication between the middle-class child and his parents is more free and open and the general permissiveness is greater amongst these mothers, who believe that love and understanding guidance should prevail. The parents discipline less severely, they are usually pleased about the birth of a child, and they are more warmly demonstrative.

A comparison of some child-rearing practices is presented in Table II-3. (Incidentally, investigators believe that these differences are not simply a function of education, because when educational level was held constant, the differences between the classes were still sizable. For corroboration and more detailed discussion of these practices, see Orlansky, 1949; Klatskin, 1952; Maccoby and Gibbs, 1954; Kohn, 1959; Bayley and Schaefer, 1960.)

Parental expectations. As for certain attitudes which have an effect upon the child-rearing practices, Kohn (1959) made an interesting study of the characteristics chosen by mothers as most desirable in their children. The results of two such studies are combined in Table II-4. The first classification is according to the occupation of the mother, the second according to social class. Apparently, the lower-class mother regards her children as being good only when they are obedient and respectful. The higher the socioeconomic status, the greater the probability a mother will choose consideration, curiosity, self-control, and happiness as desirable traits.

If generalized value judgments were to be made regarding such parental expectations, they would probably take the form of maintaining that lower-class expectations are too low and middle class too high. As stated previously, middle-class parents have an education compulsion. Their children are guided and gently pressured into attending nursery schools, kindergarten, a full four years of high school, and at least two years of college or business school. During that time, they are encouraged to obtain good grades. These expectations, no matter how subtly transmitted, are often unrealisticaly high, and, in truth, a high percentage of the anxiety neuroses observable among children occur in those from the middle class. Conversely, school attendance and high grades are not so important to the parents and children of the lower classes. Learning to fight for their rights, gaining early independence, and assuming responsibility at an early age are of greater concern. However, because parental expectations are fatalistically low, the children do not usually develop high aspirations.

Table II–4 Characteristics Chosen by Mothers as "Most Desirable" in a Ten- or Eleven-Year-Old Child (Combined from Kohn, 1959, pp. 344, 345)

Tabulated According to Working-class Mothers' Own Occupation and Mothers' Socio-economic Status

Characteristics	Proportion Who Select Each Characteristic			Class *				
	White-collar Job	No Job	Manual Job	I	II	III	IV	V
Obedience	.26	.35	.53	.14	.19	.25	.35	.27
Neatness, Cleanliness	.16	.18	.42	.06	.07	.16	.18	.27
Consideration	.39	.21	.05	.41	.37	.39	.25	.32
Curiosity	.10	.04	.00	.37	.12	.09	.07	.03
Self-Control	.13	.14	.11	.24	.30	.18	.13	.14
Happiness	.33	.40	.26	.61	.40	.40	.38	.30
Honesty	—	—	—	.37	.49	.46	.50	.65

* Class ratings are based on Hollingshead's Index. Class I is the highest class; class V is the lowest class.

Social class and education.   Nowhere is the idea of privilege for some
and deprivation for others quite so evident as in the fields of education,
whose major problems—dropouts, underachievement, motivation—are basically functions of social class. The child who is not encouraged to stay in
school or to achieve a good academic standing, whose intellectual abilities
are inhibited by lack of educational experiences, and who is further handicapped by unacceptable manners, speech, and dress is assuredly at a distinct
disadvantage in an atmosphere filled predominantly with middle-class attitudes and behavior patterns. And, in a cultural sense, the school milieu
is—as is all of America—predominantly middle class. The largest percentage of teachers come from middle-class origins—they perceive in terms
of their socioeconomic status and aspirations and are therefore more comfortable in the presence of middle-class behaviors, manners of dress, language usage, and attitudes (NEA, 1957). Unconsciously, without intent or
malice, they are biased in favor of the clean, well-dressed, well-behaved
pupil who speaks "properly." Yet, the lower class makes up approximately
half the population of the country (Havighurst and Neugarten, 1962, p. 21).
Obviously, this constitutes a problem from the very outset for children of
the lower class who must cope with one set of standards at home and in his
neighborhood, another set from his teachers, and as few as three sets at
one time from his classmates. It is small wonder, then, that even at the
nursery-school level children from economically and educationally underprivileged backgrounds enter into more conflicts than those from a higher
socioeconomic level (Appel, 1942; Body, 1955). Competition, likewise, appears earlier and is more intense among the lower-level children, and aggression is more common (McKee and Leader, 1955).

By tabulating according to a six-class categorization the proportion of
the youth population attending (or not attending) school beyond the elementary grades, Table II-5 shows how social status influences the dropout

Table II-5   Quota Fulfillment Indices * (Davie, 1953, p. 178)

Class	Non-Attendant	Trade School	High School	Private School	Liberal Arts College	Higher Vocational School
I	6	70	79	348	494	155
II	39	24	110	168	303	132
III	60	79	106	162	164	119
IV	92	76	110	96	61	90
V	105	100	106	66	55	100
VI	151	159	82	62	18	77

* A "Quota Fulfillment Index" of 100 indicates that the same proportion of the total
population from a given social level is in the indicated school category as is found in
the total population.

Table II–6   Social Class and Intelligence in Relation to Dropouts (Adapted from Havighurst and Neugarten, 1957, p. 226)

Did not finish high school IQ 115 and above—(12 pupils)		Did not finish high school IQ 101–114—(35 pupils)	
Upper and upper-middle	0	Upper and upper-middle	0
Lower-middle	3	Lower-middle	2
Upper-lower and lower-lower	9	Upper-lower and lower-lower	33

phenomenon. The "non-attendant" column is of major interest to the student of child development, but the other columns are significant in terms of showing the persistence of social class influences in education subsequent to the childhood years. Table II-6 adds the factor of intelligence to the relationship between dropouts and social class, although the sample is too small to permit unqualified generalizations.

Tables II-7 and II-8 present data which suggest that grades also are a function of the social-class status of pupils. However, Havighurst and his associates (1962) have tempered that generalization by concluding that social class, intelligence, personal-social adjustment, and achievement motivation must be considered in accounting for success in school and staying in or leaving school.

Social class and organized activities.   Significant differences have been observed in the nature of the out-of-school activities engaged in by children and adolescents from different cultural backgrounds. Upper-class children, for instance, attend summer camps, where the tuition would exclude the major portion of the youth population. They travel to resort areas and stay at hotels patronized by a select group. A great many of their activities are centered around country clubs and yacht clubs, where they participate in small-group sports such as tennis, golf or sailing.

While the activities of upper-class children are by nature relatively exclusive, those of the middle class may best be described as selective. Because of financial considerations, middle-class children are required to use public facilities. They are usually found in the public schools, parks, theaters, skating rinks, bowling alleys, and so forth. However, a selective process is continuously operating among middle-class children and their parents. The parents try to choose the parks, the playground areas, and the forms of entertainment on the basis of middle-class values. That is, these parents, especially in modern suburbia, where success is usually defined in terms of upward mobility, are more discriminating and put greater pressure upon their children to achieve and to move ahead socially. Even in their games, the youngsters manifest an emphasis on individual achievement rather than on team effort, although they run in larger "packs" than do the upper-class boys and girls.

Table II–7   Per Cent of Social Class with Mean Grade of

Class	85–100	70–84	50–69
I & II	51.4	48.6	00.0
III	35.5	63.2	1.3
IV	18.4	69.2	12.4
V	8.3	66.7	25.0

Table II–8   Intelligence Test Scores by Class IQ (Number)

Class	120–139	111–119	91–110	70–90
I & II	8	15	12	0
III	19	72	59	2
IV	11	82	128	8
V	0	11	70	10

Both tables are slightly adapted from A. B. Hollingshead, *Elmtown's Youth*, New York: John Wiley & Sons, 1949, pp. 172, 175.

The activities of lower-class youths have been described as residual in nature: They pursue those activities available to them, whether they be on a nearby playground or in clubs for "underprivileged children," sponsored by some civic group. Welfare services are usually welcomed, and where community centers are opened, the children, in general, flock to take advantage of the various recreations and games. Although these lower-class children are encouraged to fight for their rights and consequently place a great deal of emphasis on individual competition in athletics, physical strength, and stamina, the community centers attempt to organize large-group games and sports where team effort and team spirit become focal concerns. Many such centers institute classes in social dancing, youth choirs, and dramatics; they encourage participation in orchestral groups, even if it means using toy instruments.

Equipment and space is also made available for sports such as basketball, softball, volley ball, wall tennis, dodge ball, wrestling, and tumbling.

Thus, even in the recreations he finds and the type of games he plays, socioeconomic status, filtering through the child's immediate community origins and experience, enters deeply into the fabric of his daily living and developing personality.

SUMMARY

Through the linkage of male and female chromosomes, each of which contains hundreds of molecules called genes, the individual inherits, through his ancestors, the ability to develop particular anatomical and psysi-ological structures in a specific form. At the moment of chromosomatic union, the entire hereditary endowment is awarded. Also at that moment, various forms of environmental influences begin their operations; and be-cause human embryos and genetic histories are so difficult to obtain for studying, scholars have been unable to determine the exact nature of the separate influences of either heredity or environment. They overlap, they are indefinable except in terms of the operations they perform, they interact in such a manner as to further cloud the issues under investigation.

So far as is known, no behavior patterns are inherited, nor any mental diseases except those rare ones resulting from degenerative nerve tissue; and opinion is swaying away from theories concerning other diseases sup-posedly transmitted through the genes.

The most important characteristic inherited by the normal child is his sex—yet he receives it purely as a matter of chance. The male parent car-ries the only unmatched pair of chromosomes in any germ cell, and when this pair divides and unites with the divided female chromosome, the new pair is either matched or unmatched. More unmatched chromosomes are united than matched, although the mortality rate in the resultant male in-fants is higher. In most areas of development, girls have an advantage over boys, but in many societies, which have their accepted patterns of masculine and feminine behavior, the boy is given more freedom than the girl and his independence is established earlier.

The biologic concept of race is based upon inherited physical character-istics, primarily anatomical ones. Despite much popular opinion to the con-trary, scientific research has been unable to prove any race superior to any other in rates of development or in capacities. Racial differences other than physical appearance can be attributed to such environmental factors as nu-trition, higher standards of living, and climate.

In a sense, the infant also inherits a culture and many subcultures, in-cluding a community, a family, and a social class. Each cultural unit has an impact upon the growing child, but perhaps none has such a demonstrable effect upon so many facets of his personality as does the socioeconomic status of his family. It affects what he gives of himself and what he receives, what he sees of himself and his environment and how others see him, what he feels he is capable of attaining and how much he accomplishes with that capability. It reaches deeply into his inner life and extends into the outer periphery of his actions.

QUESTIONS AND PROBLEMS

1. Describe the operation of genes in connection with some hereditary charac-teristic or trait. Differentiate between dominant and recessive traits.

2. What are some characteristics or traits commonly supposed to be inherited? Explain how environmental conditions might account for them.
3. What did Karl Menninger mean when he said that World War II was a "conflict between theories of hereditary superiority and theories of environmental determination"?
4. What are some of the major categories that make up different culture modes?
5. What are some of the subcultures that operate in your life? Show how these differ from those of some other people in the United States.
6. Show how culture may either expand or limit a child's life activities.
7. Define and illustrate by example biocultural behavior.
8. Show how internalizing the values of a culture is closely related to the development of conscience. How is this brought about?
9. Name three or four marked cultural changes of the past one hundred years which you consider to be most important in terms of human life. How do these influence child development?
10. Show ways in which cultural diversity may be observed even among children from the same city.
11. What is meant by *ethnic* culture? What ethnic cultures are you familiar with? What are some problems posed for the six-year-old child brought up in an ethnic culture?
12. Compare the child-rearing practices of the middle- and lower-class families as presented in Table II–4. How do these compare with your observations and experiences?
13. Present arguments for and against the proposition that how a child is fed (or toilet trained) influences his subsequent perceptions.
14. Some people contend that no attempt should be made to raise the socio-economic level or aspirations of lower-class children because when and if they fail (and the prospects for failure are strong) they will be more unhappy and ineffective than they were previously. What position do you take on this proposition?
15. How do you account for the fact that many slum children ultimately rise above their community origins? Can you cite an example of this from your own observations or readings?

SELECTED READINGS

BENEDICT, RUTH, *Patterns of Culture*. Boston: Houghton Mifflin, 1934; New York: Penguin Books, 1946.

BERNARD, HAROLD W., *Human Development in Western Culture*, 2nd ed. Boston: Allyn and Bacon, 1966, pp. 86–118.

BRODY, S., *Patterns of Mothering*. International Universities Press, 1956.

COLE, LAWRENCE E., and WILLIAM F. BRUCE, *Educational Psychology*. rev. ed. Harcourt, Brace & World, 1958. Ch. 1.

CONANT, JAMES B., *Slums and Suburbs*. McGraw-Hill, 1961.

FRANK, LAWRENCE K., *Personality and Culture*. Danville, Ill.: Interstate Printers and Publishers, 1948, pamphlet.

HAVIGHURST, ROBERT J., and BERNICE L. NEUGARTEN, *Society and Education*, 2nd ed. Boston: Allyn and Bacon, 1962.

HUTT, MAX L., and ROBERT G. GIBBY, *The Child: Development and Adjustment*. Boston: Allyn and Bacon, 1959. Ch. 3.

LEWIN, K., The effects of social climate, in *Readings in Child Psychology*, 2nd ed. (Wayne Dennis, ed.). Englewood Cliffs, N.J.: Prentice-Hall, 1963.

MEAD, MARGARET, *Childhood in Contemporary Cultures*. Chicago: University of Chicago Press, 1955.

PRESSEY, SIDNEY L., FRANCIS P. ROBINSON, and JOHN E. HORROCKS, *Psychology in Education*. Harper, 1959. Ch. 6.

RIESMAN, DAVID, The suburban dislocation, *The Annals of the American Academy of Political and Social Science*, 1957, *314*, 123–146.

SEARS, ROBERT R., ELEANOR E. MACCOBY, and HARRY LEVIN, *Patterns of Child Rearing*. Evanston, Ill.: Row, Peterson (now Harper's), 1957.

WHYTE, WILLIAM F., *Street Corner Society: The Social Structure of an Italian Slum*, 2nd ed. Chicago: University of Chicago Press, 1955.

REFERENCES

ACKERMAN, NATHAN W., *The Psychodynamics of Family Life*. Basic Books, 1958, pp. 329–330.

ALPENFELS, ETHEL, Culture shapes self, *Childhood Education*, 1957, *33*, No. 7, 294–296.

ANASTASI, ANNE, and JOHN P. FOLEY, JR., A proposed reorientation in the heredity-environment controversy, *The Psychological Review*, 1948, *55*, 239–249.

ANGELINO, HENRY, JOSEPH DOLLINS, and EDMUND V. MECH, Trends in the "fears and worries" of school children as related to socio-economic status and age, *The Journal of Genetic Psychology*, 1956, *89*, 263–276.

APPEL, M. H., Aggressive behavior of nursery school children and adult procedures in dealing with such behaviors, *Journal of Experimental Education*, 1942, *11*, 185–199.

BAYLEY, N., and E. SCHAEFER, Relationships between socioeconomic variables and the behavior of mothers toward young children, *Journal of Genetic Psychology*, 1960, *96*, 61–77.

BENEDICT, RUTH, *Patterns of Culture*. Boston: Houghton Mifflin, 1934. (Also, New York: Penguin Books, 1946.)

BERRY, W. T. C., and P. J. COWIN, Conditions associated with the growth of boys, 1950–1, *British Medical Journal*, 1954, *1*, Pt. 2, 847–851.

BODY, M. K., Patterns of aggression in the nursery school, *Child Development*, 1955, *26*, 3–11.

BONNEY, MERL E., A study of social status on the second grade level, *The Journal of Genetic Psychology*, 1942, *60*, 271–305.

BONNEY, MERL E., Sex differences in social success and personality traits, *Child Development*, 1944, *15*, 63–79.

BOYD, W. C., *Genetics and the Races of Man*. Boston: Little, Brown, 1953.

BRUNER, JEROME S., and CECILE C. GOODMAN, Value and need as organizing factors in perception, *The Journal of Abnormal and Social Psychology*, 1947, *42*, 33–44.

CARRIER, BLANCHE, *Integrity for Tomorrow's Adults*. Crowell, 1959, p. 5.

COBB, STANLEY, Brain and personality, *American Journal of Psychiatry*, 1960, *116*, 938–939.

CONANT, JAMES B., *Slums and Suburbs*. McGraw-Hill, 1961, p. 1.

DAVIE, JAMES S., Social class factors and school attendance, *Harvard Educational Review*, 1953, *23*, 175–185.

DAVIS, W. ALLISON, Social and economic factors in learning, in *Our Children Today* (Sidonie M. Gruenberg, ed.). Viking Press, 1952, pp. 270–271.

DENNIS, WAYNE, *The Hopi Child*. Appleton-Century, 1940.

DINITZ, SIMON, RUSSELL R. DYNES, and ALFRED C. CLARKE, Preferences for male or female children: traditional or affectional? *Marriage and Family Living* (May 1954), *16*, 128–130.

ESTVAN, F. J., The relationship of social status, intelligence, and sex of ten- and eleven-year-old children to an awareness of poverty, *Genetic Psychology Monographs*, 1952, *46*, 3–60.

GARRISON, KARL C., *Psychology of Adolescence*, 6th ed. Englewood Cliffs, New Jersey: Prentice-Hall, 1965, pp. 40–41.

GUILFORD, J. P., Creativity: Its measurement and development, in *A Source Book for Creative Thinking* (Sidney Parnes and Harold F. Harding, eds.). Charles Scribner's Sons, 1962, p. 164.

HARROWER, M. R., Social status and the moral development of the child, *British Journal of Educational Psychology*, 1934, *1*, 75–95.

HAUSER, P. M., More from the census of 1960, *Scientific American*, 1962, Vol. 207, pp. 35–37.

HAVIGHURST, ROBERT J., PAUL H. BOWMAN, GORDON P. LIDDLE, CHARLES V. MATTHEWS, and JAMES V. PIERCE, *Growing Up in River City*. John Wiley & Sons, 1962, p. 43.

HAVIGHURST, ROBERT J., and BERNICE L. NEUGARTEN, *Society and Education*. Boston: Allyn and Bacon, 1957; 2nd ed., 1962. Both editions cited.

HOLLINGSHEAD, AUGUST B., *Elmtown's Youth*. John Wiley & Sons, 1949.

HURLOCK, ELIZABETH B., *Child Development*, 3rd ed. McGraw-Hill, 1956, p. 296.

ILLINGWORTH, R. S., *et al.*, Relation of birth weight to physical development in childhood, *The Lancet*, 1949, 257 Pt. 2, 598–602.

JOST, HUDSON, and LESTER W. SONTAG, The genetic factor in autonomic nervous system function, *Psychosomatic Medicine*, 1944, *6*, 308–310.

KAHL, JOSEPH A., *The American Class Structure*. Rinehart (now Holt, Rinehart and Winston), 1957, pp. 204–205.

KALLMANN, FRANZ J., The genetics of human behavior, *American Journal of Psychiatry*, 1956–57, *113*, 496–501.

KLATSKIN, E. H., Shifts in child care practices in three social classes under an infant care program of flexible methodology, *American Journal of Orthopsychiatry*, 1952, 22, 52–61.

KOHN, MELVIN L., Social class and parental values, *The American Journal of Sociology*, 1959, *64*, 337–351.

KVARACEUS, WILLIAM C., and others, *Delinquent Behavior: Culture and the Individual*. Washington, D.C.: National Education Association, 1959.

LAZARUS, RICHARD S., *Adjustment and Personality*. McGraw-Hill, 1961, pp. 291–292.

LESHAN, LAWRENCE L., Time orientation and social class, *The Journal of Abnormal and Social Psychology*, 1952, 47, 589–592.

LESSER, GERALD S., The relationships between various forms of aggression and popularity among lower-class children, *The Journal of Educational Psychology*, 1959, 50, 20–25.

LEVIN, PHYLLIS LEE, "There Are Babies and Babies," *The New York Times Magazine* (September 12, 1965), pp. 132, 134.

LINTON, RALPH, *The Cultural Background of Personality*. Appleton-Century, 1945.

LOEB, MARTIN B., Implications of status differentiation for personal and social development, *Harvard Educational Review*, 1953, 23, 168–174.

MCCARTHY, JOE, "Long Island Is Becoming Long City," *The New York Times Magazine* (August 30, 1964), pp. 17, 66–67.

MACCOBY, ELEANOR E., and PATRICIA K. GIBBS, *et al.*, Methods of child-rearing in two social classes, in *Readings in Child Development* (William E. Martin and Celia B. Stendler, eds.). Harcourt, Brace, 1954, pp. 380–396.

MCKEE, JOHN P., and FLORENCE LEADER, The relationship of socio-economic status and aggression to the competitive behavior of preschool children, *Child Development*, 1955, 26, 135–142.

MENNINGER, KARL A., *The Human Mind*, 3rd ed. Alfred A. Knopf, 1961.

MEREDITH, HOWARD V., Relation between socioeconomic status and body size of boys seven to ten years of age, *American Journal of Diseases of Children*, 1951, 82, 702–709.

MILNER, ESTHER, *The Failure of Success*. Exposition Press, 1959, p. 152.

MULLER, HERMANN JOSEPH, C. C. LITTLE, and LAURENCE H. SNYDER, *Genetics, Medicine and Man*. Ithaca, N.Y.: Cornell University Press, 1947.

National Education Association, The status of the American public-school teacher, *National Education Association Research Bulletin*, 1957, 35, No. 1.

NEWMAN, H. H., F. N. FREEMAN, and K. J. HOLZINGER, *Twins: A Study of Heredity and Environment*. Chicago: University of Chicago Press, 1937.

ORLANSKY, H., Infant care and personality, *Psychological Bulletin*, 1949, 46, 1–48.

POPE, BENJAMIN, Socio-economic contrasts in children's peer culture prestige values, *Genetic Psychology Monographs*, 1953, 48, 157–220.

RABBAN, M., Sex-role identification in young children in two diverse social groups, *Genetic Psychology Monographs*, 1950, 42, 81–158.

REDFIELD, ROBERT, RALPH LINTON, and MELVILLE J. HERSKOVITS, Memorandum for the study of acculturation, *American Anthropologist*, 1936, 38, 149–152.

SHAPIRO, HARRY L., Race, in *Collier's Encyclopedia*, 1965, 19, 593.

SHUTTLEWORTH, FRANK K., The adolescent period: a graphic atlas, *Monographs of the Society for Research in Child Development*, 1949, 14, No. 1.

SNYDER, LAURENCE H., Heredity, in *Collier's Encyclopedia*, 1965, 12, 70.

STERN, C., Hereditary factors affecting adoption, in *A Study of Adoption Practices* (M. Schapiro, ed.). Child Welfare League of America, 1956, II, 47–58.

STRAUS, MURRAY A., Deferred gratification, social class, and the achievement syndrome, *American Sociological Review*, 1962, 27 Pt. 1, 326–335.

TAJFEL, H., Value and the perceptual judgment of magnitude, *The Psychological Review*, 1957, 64, 192–204.

TERRELL, GLENN, JR., KATHERINE DURKIN, and MELVIN WIESLEY, Social class and the nature of the incentive in discrimination learning, *The Journal of Abnormal and Social Psychology*, 1959, 59, 270–272.

THOMAS, H., New wonders of conception, *Woman's Home Companion* (November 1954), 7–8, 100–103.

TITIEV, MISCHA, *Introduction to Cultural Anthropology*. Holt, Rinehart & Winston, 1959.

VAUGHAN, WARREN T., JR., Children in crisis, *Mental Hygiene*, 1961, 45, 354–359.

WARNER, WILLIAM LLOYD, *Who Shall Be Educated? The Challenge of Unequal Opportunities*. Harper & Bros., 1944, p. 33.

WARNER, WILLIAM LLOYD, and PAUL S. LUNT, *The Social Life of a Modern Community*. New Haven, Conn.: Yale University Press, 1941, p. 82.

WARNER, WILLIAM LLOYD, and MILDRED H. WARNER, *What You Should Know About Social Class*. Chicago: Science Research Associates, 1953, pp. 22–25.

WHYTE, WILLIAM F., *Street Corner Society: The Social Structure of an Italian Slum*, 2nd ed. Chicago: University of Chicago Press, 1955.

T H R E E

The Needs and

Motives of Children

According to the current theory of the origin of life, the first living organisms were required to mutate in order to sustain themselves through a period of famine. The organisms followed two lines of evolution, resulting in plants having a complex enzyme system for converting their environment into food, and animals having a neuromuscular system for obtaining the food they need (Moment, 1963). Needs, therefore, have always been basic to activity, which is synonymous with "living," and were basic to the development of spontaneous action, or motility, in animals. In the evolution of the human individual, the embryo could be likened to the plant which depends upon and converts its surroundings for sustenance, an automatic process; at birth, the infant becomes a motile, or motivated, animal, retaining some automatic processes—breathing, sleeping, eliminating—but experiencing states of disequilibrium—hunger, thirst, pain, thermal variation—which are not automatically resolved. These states lead to activity aimed at bringing the organism (infant) back into a state of equilibrium, or internal balance, or homeostasis.

Activity, then, is intrinsic to all living cells. It begins with need satisfaction. However, once we speak of human (or animal) activity we must include two intermediary conditions—disequilibrium and drive, an addition that changes the word "activity" to "behavior." Thus, we say that all behavior is motivated. The active organism strives, seeks, is motivated, to satisfy a particular need.

THE CONCEPT OF NEEDS

Basic and Acquired Needs

Many writers have devised lists of basic and acquired needs only to be caught up in the overlapping which occurs from one to the other. For instance, all living tissues need food, but the infant receives food *from someone,* usually his mother. The intake of food eliminates discomfort and simultaneously instills warmth via bodily contact, and the infant learns to need the contact when he does not need the food. Furthermore, as Frank (1948) says:

> When a child is fed whenever he is hungry, he gets more than food—he gets a feeling of confidence that his needs are going to be met; he feels that he can trust his world. As all successive difficult lessons of social adjustment come along, he has this basic security and confidence to build upon. If, on the other hand, he is left hungry and thwarted by an inflexible feeding schedule, he may begin to doubt and fear the world, and is likely to approach his subsequent experiences with doubt, fear, and insecurity.

The processes of learning in such cases are nearly inseparable from the need fulfillment, and the dividing line between them is difficult to establish. Even when we say that humans require certain basic things to stay alive and other things to stay *healthily* alive, individual differences in human beings must be taken into consideration. Some infants have actually died for lack of maternal love, others have led a mentally unhealthy existence, a few have survived the deprivation to live out normal lives. As a result, some psychologists maintain that love is a basic need, a primary drive, while others insist that it is a secondary need, a learned drive. Evidently, those in the former group believe that the truly basic need—oxygen, food, water, rest, thermal stability, defecation, and urination—are automatically or easily met, and thus turn their attention to needs of a higher order, ones which require *behavior* in less elementary forms.

The lists formulated by some of the authorities who consider also as basic the "secondary" or ego needs include the following motivations:

Thomas (1923): security, new experiences, response, recognition

Symonds (1934): Be with others, gain attention, approval, be a cause, mastery, maintain self, security, affection, curiosity

Prescott (1938): Physiological well-being, social security (or status), integrative behavior (adjust to the physical and social world)

Trow (1950): Bodily activity, knowledge, sensory enjoyment, security, mastery, service

Carroll (1955): Physical security, emotional security, mastery, status
Schneiders (1955): Affection and belonging, security and status, attention,
    independence, achievement, experience

The Hierarchy of Needs Theory

A helpful list of needs, derived from experimental studies, observation,
and clinical experience is that proposed by Maslow (1954). He presents the
theory that, in general, needs have a sequence of priority from low to high
order. When needs of a low order have approached gratification, those at the
next higher level become prepotent. The concept of purpose, which makes
human needs different from animal needs, is pervasive throughout the
hierarchy.

Physiological needs.   These are the needs of the organism for food,
water, oxygen, sleep, activity, and sensory satisfaction. Such requirements
are easily satisfied in America where most people are well fed and adequately
housed. Satisfaction of these needs may best be indicated in the statistics
on infant and child mortality, which since the turn of the century have been
so low that many years have been added to the average person's life expect-
ancy. Actually, in American society, physiological needs are emergency
needs, that is, are satisfied almost immediately, and the behavior of but
very few individuals can be explained by their denial. Motivational needs
of a higher level are dominant in most babies and children of our culture.

A crying, fretful, restless baby may be indicating that he is hungry,
thirsty, or in need of rest. But when feeding, sleeping, bathing, and activities
are carefully scheduled by mothers, physiological motives rarely, if ever,
become very dominant. Often, the crying, restless baby will be as readily
comforted by being picked up, cuddled, kissed, and talked to as he will be
by being presented the breast or bottle. His restlessness then may be indicating needs other than the physiological. He wants attention. This observation illustrates an important principle of behavior: Motives are never single
and simple; they are multiple and complex. No claim is made here that physiological needs are unimportant—they are simply so readily satisfied that
they quickly become fused with higher-order needs.

Safety needs.   Once an individual's physiological welfare is assured
he experiences varying degrees of anxiety concerning threats to his body
and his sense of security. Emotionally neglected children appear to be dominated by safety-seeking behavior. Usually, the sensory organs, muscular
activity, and the intellect warn the individual of danger and carry him away
from it. However, every generation, apparently, has seen considerable anxiety reflected in its parents and has felt the need for aid and comfort in times
of stress. Succorance, or security, is the heading under which fall the needs
most commonly expressed by preschool children (Shirley, 1938).

There are some things that can be done to promote that security. Children need an orderly world; routines are appreciated—regular meals, a schedule for sleep, play, and cleanliness. In school, regular, dependable routines help make the necessary introduction of new subjects, experiences, teachers, and playmates a desirable venture instead of an upsetting irregularity.

Permissive parents and teachers have been puzzled at their apparent failure and view with wonder the admirable success of firm, directive adults. As often happens, misunderstanding of the merits and liabilities of permissiveness lead to its over-use, especially with preschool and primary youngsters, and a resultant disruption of family and school life (Henry, 1961). The explanation is the simple one of expecting too much of children. Their immaturity leads to frustration with freedom they are not prepared to handle. Children *need* discipline—not punishment, autocracy, and complete obedience, but firm direction, letting them know what is expected, and the establishment of firm limits. That is the kind of discipline which satisfies the child's safety needs and pushes him toward the exploration of higher level satisfactions.

The need for security may be noted among monkeys as well as among children. Frightening objects such as a mechanical teddy bear causes almost all infant monkeys to flee blindly to the cloth mother. Once reassured by pressing and rubbing against her, they would then look at the strange object.

Belongingness and love needs.   According to W. C. Menninger (1950), many adults spend a lifetime seeking to satisfy the need to give and receive love, never quite able to develop a normal affectional pattern and consequently never able to rise beyond this need level. (See also Karl Menninger, 1963). At least two experimenters attribute this failure in part to hereditary emotional characteristics but primarily to the quality of mother-child relationships before and just after the time of weaning. Harlow (1959) discovered that to deprive monkeys of physical contacts with mothers or cloth surrogates during their first eight months "evidently left them incapable of forming a lasting affectional tie" (p. 74). Denenberg (1963) concluded from an exhaustive study of social relations among rats that "the mother in her interaction with the young between birth and weaning brings about a relatively permanent change in the emotional behavior of the offspring" (p. 139). Children who are given love show less evidence of dependency (they need not seek what they have); they show less overt aggressive behavior, but initiative is higher (Antonovsky, 1959).

These conclusions should help to resolve the conflicts concerning specific methods and timing of infant feeding and toilet training by showing that the emotional atmosphere in which the child is fed and trained is far more important. And, we can continue to say, the atmosphere in which the child learns in school is more important than the particular methods employed. Children, indeed all people, need to feel that they are wanted, that they belong to someone and belong in some place, that they are a part of the groups (family, peers, school classes) around them. Accepting a child who does not feel that he is loved or that he belongs is a difficult task for adults. His defenses against deprivation lead him to be aggressive or sullen. His justified lack of trust in others leads him to test those who proffer love. Yet, when the child is most unlovely he is most in need of love. Adults who understand that such behavior—or misbehavior—is caused by the lack of need fulfillment can go the "second mile" in accepting the child while he seeks to overcome his lack of trust. In this connection, Sams (1957) describes how a substitute mother was able to keep overlooking waywardness and disobedience as she helped two girls become contributing citizens.

Status or esteem needs.   At the receiving-love level, the child is content to be loved merely because he exists, but as he moves to the status level, he seeks to merit that acceptance and respect by his performance, unusualness, or superiority. Status needs are being sought when the child shifts from a "Here I am" orientation to a "See, I can do this" phase. If, for instance, he receives praise or reward for accomplishments of good conduct at home, satisfactory grades in school, or good citizenship in peer groups, the youngster has reason to congratulate himself for earning esteem and to establish the habits that earned it rather than revert to a more primitive method of gaining attention, such as temper tantrums or other aggressive behavior.

Maslow (p. 90) lists two levels of esteem needs: (1) the strength, adequacy, accomplishment, and competence needs (so that one can be independent and free) and (2) the desire for reputation and prestige. Both of these are dependent upon self-esteem (see Chapter X) which itself is a reflection of the view taken of the individual by others. Unless the child perceives that he is well liked, he cannot acquire the self-esteem that permits him to venture forth courageously and seek skills, knowledges, and prowess that will earn his status. Obviously, this is a cyclical process having neither beginning nor end. The child attempts a task, succeeds, and gains self-confidence to try a similar task. His chances of succeeding the second time are far greater than those of the child who meets with failure and has his self-confidence and motivation diminished. The child who has met with continuous failure develops a sense of unworthiness and generally compensates for that feeling with conduct that is unacceptable to both peers and adults. Such a student presents a real challenge to his teachers, who must search for tasks at which he can be successful and thus help him to construct a better self-picture.

Self-actualization needs. Man has a tendency *"to become his potentialities,"* according to Carl Rogers (1962, p. 66).

> . . . By this I mean the directional trend which is evident in all organic and human life—the urge to expand, extend, develop, mature—the tendency to express and activate all the capacities of the organism, to the extent that such activation enhances the organism or the self. This tendency may become deeply buried under layer after layer of encrusted psychological defenses; it may be hidden under elaborate façades which deny its existence; it is my belief however, based on my experience, that it exists in every individual, and awaits only the proper conditions to be released and expressed.

Throughout infancy and childhood, the child develops a compulsion to use and exercise each physiological characteristic as it matures. If the individual is compelled to develop one skill, such as walking, when a more complex ability presents itself for practice (language, for example), the higher-order task must wait. So it is in the hierarchy of needs. Only when persons have had their physiological, safety, love, and status needs fairly well satisfied are they in the fortunate position to realize their potentials, separately and in their totality. Life becomes an adventure, and the individual crosses the frontier of his own physical existence into the interesting unknown.

The last half of infancy is particularly devoted to this great adventure. Once the infant learns to crawl his behavior becomes almost frenetically exploratory and manipulative. No portion of his environment is free from minute examination by way of taste, touch, and smell.

> . . . The behavior that leads to the building up of effective grasping, handling, and letting go of objects . . . is not random behavior produced by

a general overflow of energy. It is directed, selective, and persistent, and it is continued not because it serves primary drives, which indeed it cannot serve until it is almost perfected, but because it satisfies an intrinsic need to deal with the environment.

White, 1959, p. 318

In order to help the child actualize himself, to help him achieve fulfillment of this highest order of needs and thus good mental health, the adult is required to establish the proper climate. Descriptions of that climate permeate the literature on fostering creative talent in the home and schools, particularly in the works of Viktor Lowenfeld (1954, 1957), E. Paul Torrance (1962), and James I. Gallagher (1964). Rogers (1962), however, sums it up by listing two prerequisite conditions: psychological safety and psychological freedom. Three processes are involved in the first condition. (a) The parent or teacher must show unconditional faith in the worth of the child, regardless of his present pattern of behavior. Such faith, provided it is genuine, gradually assures the individual that he need not pretend to be anything or anyone other than himself. (b) The child needs to develop and retain his own "locus of evaluation." To aid this, the adults in his environment must repress their evaluations of any product of the child's imagination. That is, the adult may *react:* he may say he does not like it; but he may not say it is good or bad. The point is a subtle one, but it means the difference between the child expressing *himself* and being overly concerned with what others will think of him. (c) The child must receive empathic understanding. The significant adults in his life, the key personalities, must be able to see things from the child's point of view. If, from that vantage point, the adults still accept him, the child has reached the ultimate in psychological safety.

The second necessary condition, psychological freedom, means that the child has permission to express himself *symbolically.* Certain overt behaviors are prohibited or controlled by society, and for the child to give vent to them openly is to foster feelings of guilt and a rigidity which narrows his imaginative vision. Freedom of symbolic expression allows the individual to free, and thus control, his innermost thoughts and emotions. "It is permission to be *free,* which also means that one is responsible. The individual is as free to be afraid of a new venture as to be eager for it; free to bear the consequences of his mistakes as well as of his achievements" (p. 71).

Incidentally, the perceptive reader will have realized that neither Maslow nor Rogers imposed any age limit on their theories. The prescriptions they offer are as applicable to adult social relationships as they are to the establishment of an optimum environment (external and internal) for children.

Value of the Needs Theory

The big advantage of the needs concept is that we can examine the lists to see how the developmental environment of the child might be improved. If he is a happy, growing, well-behaved individual, we know that his currently insistent needs are approaching satisfaction. If he is developing slowly, failing in school, acting contrary to expectations, "storing up trouble for himself," we should know that some needs are being rather consistently denied. Because one kind of behavior in different children may spring from various deprivations, only careful study of the individual child will reveal which needs are being denied (Allen, 1953).

Another value of the needs concept is that it provides a basis for understanding the perceptions and motives of children. The reader will remember that Bruner and Goodman (1947), after noting how poor children overestimated the size of coins, concluded that needs have an important bearing on a child's perception of things in his world.

A third, and probably the most important, advantage of the theory of needs is that the student of child psychology should be better able to see that the overall environment, not the specifics of child training, is the important consideration. One of the recent brilliant insights about child growth is that the temporary, occasional denial of a need will not result in maldevelopment. One mistake by a parent or teacher is not fatal—it is the consistent, pervasive, chronic atmosphere that bears so heavily on need gratification (Sewell, 1955, p. 339).

DEVELOPMENTAL TASKS

The human infant cannot attain need satisfaction in a vacuum: He must in some form come into daily contact with some other human being. Assuming that he is physically normal, the infant notices and responds to those contacts—he experiences. Through experiencing, learning takes place; yet, no form of learning can come about until the essential neuromuscular mechanisms have reached a particular stage of development. When they are ready, the individual is able to notice and to respond, and, in keeping with his need to be active, is compelled to do so. Furthermore, as the mechanisms develop and reach maturation, the child's society decrees that he *must* use them and that he must use them in prescribed ways for prescribed purposes.

Thus we arrive at the concept of developmental tasks, which effects a coalescence of empirical and experimental knowledge about child development and motivation because it embraces physical development, psychological development, and cultural requirements. Zachry in 1940 made references to life-adjustment tasks, and Havighurst in 1945 and 1953 gave impetus to the terminology, until today the concept permeates much of the literature on child and adolescent development as well as the growing body of knowledge concerning problems of middle and old age.

The Meaning of Developmental Tasks

A developmental task is a problem which arises at or about a given time of life and has its roots in (1) the physical and physiological growth and capacities of the individual, (2) the phase of his intellectual and emotional growth, and (3) the expectations and demands of the total culture and socio-economic class in which he lives. Successful achievement of a developmental task prepares one for his next tasks and is conducive to happiness because it leads to approval, status, and actualization. Failure, of course, has opposite effects (Havighurst, 1953).

Developmental tasks, then, are (1) necessary learnings if one is to attain a normal, wholesome, and satisfactory adjustment to himself and society (See Figure III–1). They must (2) be learned within a rather restricted period of time, though some tasks may persist in varying degrees of intensity through several phases of chronological development. (For example, developing a wholesome concept of self is closely related to adjusting to one's age mates.) Obviously (3) progress often takes place in several places at the same time, and success in one task conditions success in the other concurrent and subsequent tasks. Each task (4) involves varied types of learning —attitudes, skills, knowledges—both in and out of school. Perhaps most important from the standpoint of salutary development (5) the tasks define the concerns of childhood (Corey and Herrick, 1955). Adults who are engaged in promoting optimum development are thus afforded a view of children's immediate concerns, however dimly the children themselves may perceive them, and can better appreciate what the motivations really are.

The reader should bear in mind, while perusing the following pages, that several tasks overlap the phases of development which we can call infancy, babyhood, and early, middle, and late childhood. Moreover, because there are multitudes of things one must learn, the tasks mentioned are representative and indicative rather than inclusive.

Developmental Tasks of Infancy and Early Childhood

1. Learning to walk depends upon the biological development of bones and muscles and upon the maturation of a sense of equilibrium. Those parents who "push" their children into walking at an early age create as much physical and psychological damage to the child as they would if they themselves were to decide suddenly and without preparation to walk or sleep on a bed of nails Hindu-fashion. ("Physical damage" does not refer to bowed legs,

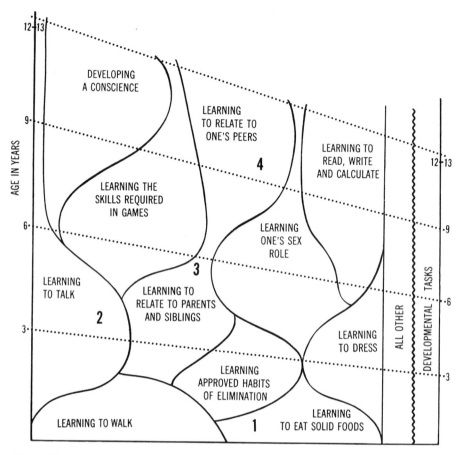

Figure III–1. Schematic Representation of Developmental Tasks. Only a few tasks at any age are represented—as indicated by the broken space to the right. Some tasks are learned and completed (1 above), others continue (2 above), and still others merge into new tasks (3 and 4 above). The different levels on which one chronological age is represented indicate that children are involved in a given task at somewhat different ages. (Figure adapted from Bernard, 1966, p. 27)

which are common in early walkers and which are straightened by the muscles after walking begins.) Prior developmental tasks—creeping, crawling, and standing with the aid of furniture—prepare the child for walking and he should be allowed to exercise freely. Encouragement can be provided by seeing that the floors are not too cold, cluttered or slippery, and that the child's clothes, shoes and socks are not too tight or cumbersome.

2. Learning to eat solid foods and developing control over the time and place for elimination are developmental tasks that have been examined carefully and extensively by parents, pediatricians, psychologists, and anthropologists. There are wide differences in the timing of weaning and toilet training in different parts of the world, and, possibly, differing personality

orientations in various cultures are partially due to the specific nature of the indigenous practices. The fact that there are such differences in timing and methods seems to support the current opinion that the exact nature of the practices is not important: The really significant factor is the personality of the mother—her attitude toward both the child and the task itself. A fearful, resentful, irritable, impatient mother who considers the tasks time-consuming, messy, and "not quite nice" will probably encounter feeding and toilet training problems no matter what the culture dictates as to timing.

But that is not to imply that any practice will do! The schedules and methods must be geared to the homeostatic processes and developmental stages of the baby (Hunt, 1960). He must be able to manipulate his tongue in order to get the food in the proper position for swallowing, he must learn how to masticate, and later he must learn how to chew with his molars; his awareness of bodily processes must be sufficiently developed to facilitate recognition of the signs preceding elimination, and his intellect has to be mature enough to relate those signs to a desired pattern of behavior. Once that stage has been reached, the child is expected to actuate or to control his sphincter and bladder muscles—tasks analogous to ear wiggling and not blinking before a bright light. They require maturation, concentration, and practice.

3. Learning to talk, like other tasks and behaviors, cannot be separated from the total pattern of the child's life. The importance of mental and emotional maturity, the provisions of stimulation through being talked to, and the importance of reinforcement are dealt with in Chapter VI. Here it is necessary to mention only that talking is so important to success in other tasks and as a means for the child to control his overwhelming environment that in the American culture a tremendous amount of attention is paid to the specifics of learning to talk.

4. Learning to recognize sex differences and to accept the appropriate sex role begins at an early age. Generally, mild curiosity attends the initial observation of physical differences, and unless that curiosity is thwarted or the child is made to feel shame and embarrassment because of it, he accepts the fact without any sense of shock or abnormal interest.

Almost immediately, if not beforehand, both sexes become aware of differences in dress, length of hair, and patterns of behavior. During this time of early awareness of sex differences, girls become identified with their mothers and boys with their fathers, and through imitative behavior they begin to assimilate appropriate sex roles. Boys will show a decided (and approved) preference for guns, cars, spacecraft, fishing equipment, construction toys; girls prefer dolls, tea sets, sewing, cooking and cleaning utensils, personal clothing. Boys realize that they receive smiles for aggressive, "manly" acts and frowns for "sissiness." Girls, although met with tolerant amusement for "tomboyishness," know that they are expected to be gentle, docile, and "a little lady." All of which helps the children establish identity as an individual and aids them in forming a healthy self-concept. (See also Chapter X.)

Contrary to popular opinion, the fact that questions concerning where babies come from arise at this time is more coincidental than it is evidence of an interest in sex, and the answers to those questions do not constitute sex instruction. The "sex" connotation is a product of adult thought-expression. Simple, truthful answers to the questions young children ask about babies are the beginnings of instruction in biology, not sexual behavior, and therefore should be answered. With as much detachment as one would have for such questions as Where do flowers come from?, How do you make coal?, or What is thunder? It is the emotional tone with which these questions are asked *and answered* that establishes the mood and nature of the specific sex instruction received by the adolescent.

The following is a list of some typical questions asked at this time, with some perhaps not-so-typical answers:

> Where do babies come from? (Where did I come from?)
>> They grow in their mother's belly.
> How do they get there?
>> From an egg that gets bigger and bigger.
> Who grew me? . . . . Who grew you?
>> I did. . . . . Grandma.
> I'm going to grow a baby. Can I?
>> When you get big like me you can.
> Why can't I grow one now?
>> Because you're not old enough to make an egg.
> I'm not going to get married, but I'm going to have seven babies. Can I do that?
>> Yes, but who would buy the baby's food? Babies need a daddy to work and make money so they can eat.
> Will you grow me four babies for Christmas?
>> It takes a long time to grow a baby, and most mothers grow only one at a time. Let's wait until you grow your own.
> But then they wouldn't be my brothers. I want four brothers all at once.

Questions such as these cropped up over a period of two years. That is, the simple question plus the simple answer often keeps the child satisfied for many months. When it is asked and answered a second time, the parent usually finds that a second question has been added. In the meantime, the child is relating each item to other observations in the world of biology—a pregnant woman, a mother's breasts, an animal giving birth, suckling kittens or puppies. These things are an inevitable part of his environment, about which he is intensely curious. If his questions are not answered as objectively as Nature herself would answer them, his curiosity becomes intensified.

5. Learning to give and receive affection and to relate to others are overlapping tasks which begin in babyhood and continue in some dimension throughout life. The foundations of social personality are laid in early life and what happens then will, in large measure, determine whether that personality will be friendly or indifferent, outgoing or seclusive, confident or timid. Several specifics in the total child-rearing climate are worthy of mention: (1) The child must learn to think well of himself by being cuddled and talked to, by receiving admiration, and by being praised for worthy behavior and effort. (2) Children need to be given TIME as well as love. Parents may love their child, but if there are many priorities to giving him some time he will not be sure he has love. Moreover, giving time may lead to parental development of love—as is demonstrated by mothers of illegitimate children who have decided, after feeding and cuddling the infant, that they do not want to give him up for adoption. (3) The child should be talked to, even though he seems not to understand. Again, time is involved. (4) Each child needs to feel that he is an important and necessary member of the household. When an infant sibling is introduced into the family, the older child, regardless of his age, should be allowed to share and enjoy the new member—bringing a dry diaper, holding the bottle, presenting the can of talcum after a bath. Helping daddy load autumn leaves into a basket or placing soiled clothing in the washing machine are other examples of ways the very young person can share in family life.

6. Learning to accept and internalize rules (developing a conscience) is dependent upon the child's being able to trust his parents. Very early in life (as he begins to take solid foods, for example), the youngster becomes concerned about displeasing the adults close to him. As he grows and matures mentally and physically, more is expected of him and he evidences a comprehension of what is right and what is wrong. Toddlers are frequently observed reaching tentatively toward some "forbidden" object and pulling back with the verbal equivalent of "No, No." He is, at this level, accepting and internalizing at least some of the rules.

As successive lessons in "Yes" and "No" are given the child and as his world (life space) expands, he finds it necessary, for continued safety, to learn not to be dependent upon the actual presence of authority. Here again we can see the importance of the patient acceptance by parents of childish deviations and inconsistencies. If the child behaves correctly because of fear—as he is likely to do in a strict, authoritative atmosphere—he becomes inclined to "take a chance" and misbehave in the absence of authority. If, on the other hand, rapport and respect for parents is such that he would not displease them, present or absent, he has internalized the social privileges and prohibitions. He is developing a conscience that can be a positive factor for subsequent development, a conscience that prepares him for the pursuit of higher level needs. (See also Chapter IX.)

Developmental Tasks of Later Childhood

During the years from six to about twelve, some of the developmental tasks begun earlier are continued; e.g., learning of sex roles and development of conscience. Others shift somewhat in nature: self-care shifts from eating and the control of body wastes to complete independence in dressing and then determination of one's activities; social tasks shift from adapting to parents to adapting to an expanded social world—peer groups. Still other tasks, despite their dependence on earlier ones, are essentially new.

1. Learning the skills necessary for games requires physical growth of bones and muscles and the maturation that leads to large-muscle coordination. The psychological basis of the tasks is inherent in the rewards achieved through peer approval. Our culture is somewhat more demanding of boys than of girls in achieving these skills. Girls who are not adept at games may still be accepted by peers, though those who are adept are not frowned upon if they become "tomboys." Boys are less likely to be approved if they do not play well; and if their ineptitude leads them to seek other, more sedentary, activities, they may be regarded as sissies by their peers—and parents.

Typically, all the help that need be given in learning games skills is freedom to participate. Clubs, community centers, and school-affiliated activities are invaluable aids; however, regardless of the amount of play space available, children of all classes usually find some way to practice the required skills of throwing, catching, kicking, jumping, running, and scuffling.

2. Learning the give and take of getting along with age mates is a continuation of the earlier task of getting along with siblings and parents, although the lessons may be a little more traumatic because peers feel less compulsion to tolerate blunders. This task is an exceedingly important one because so much of the culture of wider society is learned in the context of peer groups. Here the children encounter the adult values that are reflected in a vast community of young people.* Not only do they receive instruction in sportsmanship, cooperation, honesty, and responsibility, but they learn more about sex roles, etiquette, self-government; and they thus take strides toward ultimate maturity (Havighurst and Neugarten, 1962).

* The organized gang is a special kind of peer group which has not responded to adult values. Although such gangs have received much publicity in connection with juvenile delinquency, they include such a small portion of all those in the middle childhood age group that they should be separated in our thinking from informal and casual peer groups.

Parents and teachers can best give assistance in this task, not by direct intervention, but by providing the basis for building a sound ego concept. This self-picture, as was emphasized earlier, is a product of the overall atmosphere in home and school; but some specifics are: acceptance of individual differences, tolerance of shortcomings, praise for accomplishment, and the presentation of tasks that are challenging but which, with stretching if necessary, can be accomplished.

3. Learning to read, write, and use arithmetic are tasks which depend, of course, on the intellectual maturation of the child, but also to be considered is the experiential background of the learner. Those who come from homes where there are few books and periodicals lack not only contact with printed words and pictures but also the motivation (example) for getting acquainted with reading. Experiences related to what is being read are also a part of the readiness of the child for reading and written communication (Gates, 1953).

Arithmetic is a special kind of communication tool, and factors similar to those involved in reading must be considered: mental maturity, experiences, meaningfulness to the child. Because arithmetic, like reading, involves a series of steps, there are also various stages of readiness. Recent research indicates that precise stages are difficult to define because current methods of teaching and the new concepts in mathematics are proving to be increasingly more successful, especially in what once might have been considered difficult cases. In other words, children apparently can learn better than formerly because of teachers' increased knowledge of the processes and the appropriateness of various methods (Freeman, 1954).

While the teacher's attitudes and methods are important in the successful achievement of communication tasks, so too is the view the child has of himself and his world. If he thinks well of his abilities and is confident of the likelihood of success—both being reflections of parental attitudes toward him—he can better marshall his intellectual resources and experience background for task accomplishment.

4. Broadening one's intellectual concepts of time, space, distance, quantity, number, money, weight, and causal relationships is one of the continuous tasks of maturing. The particular nature of these concepts is indigenous to one's culture, and the subtleties are such that we are often unconscious of what has been learned. For example, events in our culture are rigidly scheduled by clock time, but such time to the Pueblos does not exist. Their events take place "when things are ready" (Hall, 1959). Distance is measured in kilometers or miles; money in pennies or shillings or francs; weight in avoirdupois or troy or "stone"; height in inches or hands, and so forth.

To aid in the formation of these concepts, of which there are hundreds, teachers broaden the experiences of pupils outside of the school by field trips, travel to governmental institutions, visits to museums, stores, industrial plants, dairy farms, national and state parks, and the like. Although these events have always been a part of the elementary-school programs, the Higher Horizons Program in New York City, coordinated by Daniel Schreiber (1960) supplements such trips for high-school students by visits to theatres, ballets, concerts, operas, colleges, and points of historical interest.

Contact with adults who are interested in children is one of the most effective aids to learning the concepts necessary for everyday living. Parents and teachers who travel with youngsters, explain what is being seen, and relate experiences to printed material, movies, television, and radio are giving appropriate aid in achieving this task.

5. Developing a scale of values and internalizing rules is a task which continues from early childhood. Whereas the earlier part of the task was accomplished through identification with parents, the latter part is dependent upon school and peer contacts. From experience in groups, one learns the necessity of rules.

Increasing maturity in moral judgments is represented by a shift (1) from literal rules to a concept of what is right and wrong, (2) from arbitrary edicts to a perception of reasons for rules, (3) from external demands to

Young nature students are excited about learning.

internalized standards, and (4) from judging others' actions by rigid standards to judgment in terms of intentions (Piaget, 1932). This development is not necessarily a sequential process—children vary in the ages at which they reach these stages and they vary in the final results (Durkin, 1959). The problem has been well stated by Caudill (1952, p. 13) for a child with a cultural background somewhat different from that in which he must learn to live.

> ... The problem of the child, as a new member of a society, is to learn how to gratify his biological and acquired social needs in ways which are expected and rewarded by his society. To help him, the society places the growing child in a number of social contexts wherein the child may learn to organize his behavior in forms acceptable to the social group and satisfactory to himself.

Much can be learned from the case in which a child fails to learn the scale of moral values approved by his culture. Such a case shows the need for a strong ego concept, for an adult model, and for salutary peer contacts.

> Mary was a bright twelve-year-old who was referred to the counselor because of low grades and behavior problems. Specifically, she "sneaked" away from home and school affairs to associate with a girl of questionable moral virtue and several boys. Study of the case revealed: Early repudiation of the girl for thumb sucking and maloccluded teeth (treatment for which emphasized her unworthiness), comparison of her grades with her brighter older sister's record, supplementary reading sessions with her mother that typically ended in a "storm," and lack of communication with a taciturn father whose most frequent contact with Mary concerned her scholastic ineptitude. Mary's lack of supportive communication (it seems) contributed to her developing habits of seclusion which made it difficult to establish contacts with other girls her age. This may have been either the cause or the result of her failing to develop social, game, and play skills that would form the basis for normal peer contacts. The outcome was a reaching for love and affection outside the realm of ordinary gratification.

6. Gaining personal independence from adults is a task that varies greatly in terms of age and speed in our culture. In the lower social classes, where families are large or where mothers work, it may be accomplished at an early age—most often before the child is able to handle it. In middle- and upper-middle-class homes the speed varies with the attitude of the parents. Some mothers prepare a child to face the experience of attending kindergarten or first grade by sending him on errands and allowing him to move and play freely in the neighborhood. Other mothers hover over their children and physically bring them to kindergarten or the early grades, manifesting extreme reluctance to leave. At a most important stage, when the child needs time to grow by himself quietly, this same type of parent will organize a youngster's time with dancing, music lessons, swimming, junior theatre, and club activities. As a result, the child not only feels constantly pressured

to attain but does not learn to act independently of supervision—or, if he does, he internalizes and intensifies the pressures (Strong, 1964).

Here again is an area where the "golden mean" is difficult to determine. Complete lack of adult direction is shattering to the child, but so too is such close supervision that he has no chance to learn independence. Obviously, this is as much a task for parents as it is for children (Havighurst, 1957). In fact, the ultimate success of men and women as parents is revealed in the degree of autonomy achieved by their offspring. But the lesson must be begun early and continued (Goodenough and Tyler, 1959). Childish rebellion against parental authority can then be regarded as healthy evidence that parents are achieving their goal—the child has enough initiative and "backbone" to want to try his own powers in adjusting to the world.

7. Developing healthy attitudes toward social groups and institutions is basically a task of learning to live democratically. It requires an atmosphere of peace, liberty and dignity, affection and understanding, and it requires the right of the child to live without discriminating or being discriminated against. These requirements are the responsibility of the child's entire environment. If, during middle childhood, the individual has salutary experiences in his home, school, and community, he will develop positive attitudes which will not be easily changed in his adult years as he makes a constructive contribution to social groups and institutions.

In the home, implementation of this task resides in allowing the child to express his views, listening politely to what he has to say; allowing him, appropriate to his maturity, degrees of freedom to determine his own activities; explaining the rules, even though explanations result in "But why?"

At school, the methods are similar: progressively giving greater attention to his voice in the determination of activities, allowing him to vote in the establishment of regulations, student councils, advisory committees, and in other ways regarding the child as a growing individual.

SUMMARY

Behavior does not just happen; it is caused. Causes spring from physical, mental, and emotional growth and development as well as from the surrounding environment, especially the social (cultural) milieu. These causes are called needs—both organic and learned—motives, goals, and incentives.

There have been many statements of needs, and the attempt to make the statements embrace more of the possible varied conditions is continuing. Maslow has proposed a helpful theory of needs in terms of a hierarchical order, with higher order needs becoming functional as lower needs are satisfied. The categories include physiological, safety, love, esteem, and self-actualization needs.

Like the needs theory, the concept of developmental tasks is also used to categorize the causes of behavior. The concept is helpful because it takes account of physical growth, psychological development, and cultural demands. Developmental tasks begin in infancy and persist throughout one's life span. Success in early tasks results in self-satisfaction, in approval by society, and in preparation for one's next tasks. The milieu most helpful to children's task development is composed largely of adults who accept children for the developmental stage they are in at any given time, and of adults who can let individuals be autonomous and unique.

QUESTIONS AND PROBLEMS

1. If the human desires a state of homeostasis, how do you account for the fact that a child will do things he knows will irritate his teachers—or that he will keep practicing after he makes the ball team?
2. Give reasons why you accept or reject the notion that specific child-rearing practices are less important than the overall emotional atmospheres of the home.
3. Do you agree that in the American culture, physiological needs function as emergency, rather than basic, needs? Give reasons for your answers.
4. What are some ways in which safety needs can be approached in the school?
5. Evaluate the statement "It is more important to give the child time than it is to love him."
6. What are some ways in which the teacher might satisfy the status needs of ALL of his pupils?
7. What are some of the broad developmental tasks that you are now facing? How are they related to the tasks of later childhood?
8. How does the child learn about sex differences?
9. What are some of the specific situations which you think contributed to the development of your conscience? At what chronological stage did most of them occur?
10. Looking at our culture, what typical experiences of childhood may have contributed to the indifference which many citizens manifest toward participation in government?

SELECTED READINGS

BERNARD, HAROLD W., *Human Development in Western Culture*, 2nd ed. Boston: Allyn and Bacon, 1966. Chs. 6, 7, 8.

BROWN, JUDSON S., *The Motivation of Behavior*. McGraw-Hill, 1961. Ch. 5.

DEMBER, W. N., and R. W. EARLY, Analysis of exploratory, manipulative, and curiosity behaviors, *The Psychological Review*, 1957, 64, 91–96.

D'EVELYN, KATHERINE E., *Meeting Children's Emotional Needs*. Englewood Cliffs, N.J.: Prentice-Hall, 1957. Chs. 2, 3.

FRANK, LAWRENCE K., *The Fundamental Needs of the Child*. The National Association for Mental Health, 1952, p. 28.

HAVIGHURST, ROBERT J., and BERNICE L. NEUGARTEN, *Society and Education*, 2nd ed. Boston: Allyn and Bacon, 1962. Ch. 4.

HYMES, JAMES L., JR., *Behavior and Misbehavior*. Englewood Cliffs, N.J.: Prentice-Hall, 1955. Chs. 1, 2.

MASLOW, ABRAHAM H., *Motivation and Personality*. Harper & Row, 1954. Chs. 5, 8.

PEARSON, GERALD H. J., *Emotional Disorders of Children*. Norton, 1949.

PRESCOTT, DANIEL A., *The Child in the Educative Process*. McGraw-Hill, 1957. Chs. 1, 4.

ROE, KATHERINE H., Your child's self-picture, *Childhood Education*, 1962, *38*, 333–336.

THORPE, LOUIS P., *Child Psychology and Development*, 3rd ed. Ronald Press, 1962. Ch. 3.

REFERENCES

ALLEN, F. H., Special problems of infancy and childhood, *Annals of the American Academy of Political and Social Science*, 1953, *286*, 65–73.

ANTONOVSKY, HELEN F., A contribution to research in the area of the mother-child relationship, *Child Development*, 1959, *30*, 37–51.

BERNARD, HAROLD W., *Human Development in Western Culture*. Boston: Allyn and Bacon, 1966, p. 27.

BRUNER, JEROME S., and CECILE C. GOODMAN, Value and need as organizing factors in perception, *The Journal of Abnormal and Social Psychology*, 1947, *42*, 33–34.

CARROLL, HERBERT A., Motivation and learning: their significance in a mental health program for education, in *Mental Health in Modern Education, Fifty-fourth Yearbook of the National Society for the Study of Education*, Part II. Chicago: University of Chicago Press, 1955, pp. 61–70.

CAUDILL, WILLIAM, Japanese American personality and acculturation, *Genetic Psychology Monographs*, 1952, *45*, 1–18.

COREY, STEPHEN M., and VERGIL M. HERRICK, The developmental tasks of children and young people, in *Readings in Educational Psychology* (Jerome M. Seidman, ed.). Boston: Houghton Mifflin, 1955, pp. 37–43.

DENENBERG, VICTOR H., Early experience and emotional development, *Scientific American* (June 1963), *208*, 138–146.

DURKIN, DOLORES, Children's concepts of justice: a comparison with the Piaget data, *Child Development*, 1959, *30*, 59–67.

FRANK, LAWRENCE K., *Personality and Culture*. Danville, Ill.: The Interstate Printers and Publishers, 1948, pamphlet, pp. 7–8.

FREEMAN, FRANK N., What research says to the teacher, *Teaching Arithmetic*, Pamphlet No. 2. Washington, D.C.: National Education Association, 1954, pp. 6–8.

GALLAGHER, JAMES J., *Teaching the Gifted Child*. Boston: Allyn and Bacon, 1964.

GATES, ARTHUR I., What research says to the teacher, *Teaching Reading*, Pamphlet No. 1. Washington, D.C.: National Education Association, 1953, pp. 7–13.

GOODENOUGH, FLORENCE L., and LEONA E. TYLER, *Developmental Psychology*, 3rd ed. Appleton-Century-Crofts, 1959, p. 337.

HALL, EDWARD T., *The Silent Language*. Garden City, N.Y.: Doubleday, 1959, pp. 31–32.

HARLOW, HARRY F., Love in infant monkeys, *Scientific American* (June 1959), *200*, 68–74.

HAVIGHURST, ROBERT J., *Human Development and Education*. Longmans (now McKay), 1953, p. 2.

HAVIGHURST, ROBERT J., Middle age—the new prime of life, in *Aging in the Modern World* (Clark Tibbitts and Wilma Donahue, eds.). Ann Arbor, Mich.: University of Michigan Press, 1957, p. 36.

HAVIGHURST, ROBERT J., and BERNICE L. NEUGARTEN, *Society and Education*, 2nd ed. Boston: Allyn and Bacon, 1962, pp. 129–131.

HENRY, JULES, Permissiveness and morality, *Mental Hygiene*, 1961, 45, 282–287.

HUNT, J. MCV., Experience and the development of motivation: some reinterpretations, *Child Development*, 1960, 31, 489–504.

LOWENFELD, VIKTOR, *Your Child and His Art: A Guide for Parents*. New York: Macmillan, 1954.

LOWENFELD, VIKTOR, *Creative and Mental Growth*, 2nd ed. New York: Macmillan, 1952; 3rd ed., 1957.

MASLOW, A. H., *Motivation and Personality*. New York: Harper & Row, 1954, pp. 80–122.

MENNINGER, KARL, *The Vital Balance: The Life Process in Mental Health and Illness*. New York: The Viking Press, 1963, p. 295.

MENNINGER, W. C., Mental health in our schools, *Educational Leadership*, 1950, 7, 510–523.

MOMENT, GAIRDNER B., Animal-plant differences, in *The Harper Encyclopedia of Science*, 1963, 1, 68–69.

PIAGET, JEAN, *The Moral Judgment of the Child*. Harcourt, Brace, 1932.

PRESCOTT, DANIEL A., *Emotion and the Educative Process*. Washington, D.C.: American Council on Education, 1938.

ROGERS, CARL R., Toward a theory of creativity, in *A Source Book for Creative Thinking* (Sidney Parnes and Harold F. Harding, eds.). Charles Scribner's Sons, 1962, pp. 63–72.

SAMS, JESSIE B., *White Mother*. McGraw-Hill, 1957.

SCHNEIDERS, ALEXANDER A., *Personal Adjustment and Mental Health*. Holt, Rinehart and Winston, 1955, pp. 186–190.

SCHREIBER, DANIEL A., *The higher horizons program, 1959–1960*. Board of Education of the City of New York, 1960, pp. 42–43.

SEWELL, W. H., Infant training and the personality of the child, in *Mental Health and Mental Disorders* (A. M. Rose, ed.). Norton, 1955; also, *The American Journal of Sociology*, 1952, 58, 150–159.

SHIRLEY, MARY, Common content in the speech of preschool children, *Child Development*, 1938, 9, 333–346.

STRONG, LYDIA, "The Case for 'Intelligent Neglect,' " *The New York Times Magazine* (June 7, 1964), pp. 97–98.

SYMONDS, PERCIVAL M., Human drives, *The Journal of Educational Psychology*, 1934, 25, 681–694.

THOMAS, W. I., *The Unadjusted Girl*. Boston: Little, Brown, 1923.

TORRANCE, E. PAUL, *Guiding Creative Talent*. Englewood Cliffs, N.J.: Prentice-Hall, 1962.

TROW, W. C., *Educational Psychology*, 2nd ed. Boston: Houghton Mifflin, 1950, pp. 134–142.

WHITE, ROBERT W., Motivation reconsidered: the concept of competence, *The Psychological Review*, 1959, 66, 297–333.

ZACHRY, CAROLINE B., *Emotion and Conduct in Adolescence*. Appleton, 1940.

PART TWO

The Course

of Development

F O U R

Development:

Concept and Process

As pointed out previously, the human organism is intrinsically active and activity takes place in order for the organism to satisfy its needs. In the smallest unit of living matter, the satisfaction of needs produces changes in terms of both quantity and quality. Assuming that the changes are progressive, rather than regressive or degenerative, development takes place. In human beings, active cells produce physiological growth, which modifies each structure and enables it to modify its function and to relate itself to other structures and other functions, thereby producing a more complex, ineractive function for each of them. (This portion of development is *maturation.*) These functional changes create the possibility of varied patterns of behavior and simultaneously provide the organism with the need to fulfill those possibilities. As the individual is driven to action by this need, he gains experiences, and, as a result, changes occur in his pattern of behavior and, to an extent, in other physical structures. The spiral of development has taken a full turn. (This portion is *learning.*) In other words, in the realm of human behavior, the course of development is such that the individual acts and reacts; thus, he experiences. He experiences and responds; thus, he learns. He learns and he modifies his actions and reactions. Change has taken place. Development has occurred.*

* Frequently, the word *growth* is used synonymously with *development,* as when we speak of growth in language ability or mental growth. However, in this text we have attempted to use the word *growth* in its true sense: "a progressive increase in volume, weight, number, or other measurable attribute" (Rudnick, 1963). The word

Development, then, is the complex product resulting from the cyclical actions that occur between physiological growth and learning. And because all development, whether it applies to one structure, one skill, a series of behaviors, or an entire personality, follows certain natural laws and consists of universal characteristics, it can best be defined as *a rhythmic flow of quantitative and qualitative changes proceeding in specific directions in a predictable sequence.*

Beginning with maturation, let us examine the components of development in order.

MATURATION

Maturation has been variously defined as "readiness," "the process of becoming," "the unfolding of potential," and "the net sum of the gene effects operating in a self-limited life cycle" (Gesell, 1952). Hall-Quest (1957, p. 612) calls it "a process toward an integrated self" and continues by saying:

> ... At any moment of organic maturation new traits and powers appear which are not only the sum of separate gains of development but wholly new manifestations of realized organic potentiality. Thus, ability to conceptualize is more than a sum of particular sense perceptions; it is a new, integrated, emergent power of the maturer organism. This emergent characteristic is well illustrated in the individual's power to reproduce or procreate. Not until certain anatomical and glandular maturation has been attained is parenthood possible. Similar emergence of powers is true of the individual's mental life.

In maturation, the emphasis is on intrinsic rather than extrinsic factors—a movement toward the full realization of self. That "self" could be a bone, a gland, the nervous system, the ability to jump rope, the capacity to perform complicated mathematical computations, or the well-integrated individual living a full life in his own way by his own standards.

As with physiological growth, maturation begins at the moment of conception and continues throughout the organism's life. Most physical structures reach maturity by the time the individual is twenty years old, although some (nose and ears) continue to grow until death; however, there is no

---

measurable is the clue to the difference in the two processes. Growth is, in fact, used to measure development. We speak of growth in size and proportion, and qualitative and quantitative changes in muscles, bones, skin, hair, and glands. Development, on the other hand, includes traits and characteristics (e.g., prejudice, snobbishness, integrity, dignity, some forms of intelligence) which can be observed and evaluated, but not measured by absolute standards. Thus, development, besides being an integrating process, is an all-inclusive, unifying concept, bringing together all the patterns of change that involve the organism as a whole. Growth is a necessary part of both the process and the concept, and in many cases is the only means *for observing* or analyzing development.

reason to believe that all mental, emotional, or social behaviors ever attain full maturity in every individual.

But, maturation is more than physiological growth changes: it also incorporates functional changes. As the individual's life equipment reaches its ultimate growth, it is used for more complex actions. That is, units which were at one time independent, or self-contained, subordinate themselves in the service of higher-level functions; they become "part-functions of larger activities" (Stone and Church, 1957). The young child who has learned to walk and then to run combines and subordinates these activities in order to ride a tricycle. Likewise, at a later age, many separate motor skills are combined in the playing of games.

To repeat an important point, the individual is compelled to exercise each new capacity or function as it matures. Jersild (1960) calls this compulsion *indigenous motivation*. The newly mature muscle, or the well-fed, happy infant, strives to satisfy the need of self-actualization. The impulse is strong, and by means of this innate drive the organism behaves (acts), responding to both internal and external stimuli. Maturation, then, determines and influences behavior; *and* without behavior no learning can take place.

LEARNING

In his book on the theories of learning, Hilgard (1956) has stated:

> Learning is the process by which an activity originates or is changed through reacting to an encountered situation, provided that the characteristic of the change in activity cannot be explained on the basis of native response tendencies, maturation, or temporary states of the organism (e.g. fatigue, drugs, etc.).

McGeoch (1924) considers learning an alteration of behavior because of practice; and Smith (1962) offers the simplified definition: "*Learning is the acquisition of new behavior or the strengthening or weakening of old behavior as the result of experience.*"

The word *experience* is a necessary component in any discussion of learning. Learning cannot take place without a behavioral response to environmental stimuli, which is experience. Maturation can and does occur in dormant periods through simple organismic activity and it also can and does occur at higher levels through behavior. Learning occurs *only* through the interacting influences of maturation and behavior and experience.

Many of the characteristics that we identify as human result from learning, and all facets of development are affected by it. Nevertheless, the complexity of the human organism and the integrated patterns of behavior which characterize the child at all stages in his development make it difficult, if not impossible, to evaluate the exact influence of learning on development.

Parents, for instance, speak of the child who is "learning to walk," a phrase commonly used to describe the development of motor skills involved in locomotion. Although learning plays some part in the child's early attempts to master these skills, maturation apparently plays a more important role. Once the child has reached the appropriate maturational stages in bone, muscle, and balance development, he freely exercises and practices the arts of creeping, crawling, standing, and walking without any purpose or encouragement other than the sheer thrill of doing so. The thrill is so intense that children often practice a new skill far beyond their natural endurance, making themselves temporarily lame, overtired, or overexcited.

At birth, the stage is set for learning. A number of interesting observations have come about through studies dealing with the acquisition of a "conditioned response" during infancy. In a study by Marquis (1931), eight infants were bottle fed from birth. At each feeding a buzzer was sounded. Following a period of three to six days, seven of the infants showed an increase in sucking and mouth-opening and a decrease in general activity involving restlessness and crying in response to the buzzer alone. In a later study, Kantrow (1937) experimented with sixteen slightly older infants and found that sucking in response to the buzzer alone was established in some cases after three days (sixteen bottle-buzzer presentations) and in other cases up to nine days, or fifty-three presentations. However, even though the conditioned response had been established, the infants gave the sucking response to the buzzer *only when they were hungry*. The motive of hunger had to be present. Partially sated infants failed to respond at all to a buzzer unaccompanied by food.

Another indication that learning takes place during infancy is evident in the infant's adaptation to a feeding schedule. Marquis (1941) obtained the records of general bodily activity in infants on a three-hour, four-hour, and self-demand schedule. The infants on the three-hour schedule apparently "learned" to expect food at the end of three hours, and when their schedule was changed to four hours, they displayed excessive bodily activity. The infants on the four-hour schedule "learned" to wait; whereas, those on the self-demand schedule were fed when they appeared to be hungry, which turned out to be every three hours. Obviously, infants are sufficiently pliable to adapt to a four-hour schedule, even though they prefer more frequent feedings.

All learning is influenced and, at the same time, limited by conditions and forces in the external environment. However, significant aspects of learning consist not only of the process of adapting to external environmental conditions, but also of the process of inner organization. In order to help the child realize his full potentialities, opportunities for learning must be provided in the motor, intellectual, and emotional spheres of life. To achieve this end, the child must function in an environment which provides the opportunities to acquire the needed skills and knowledge, and in a psychological climate that is sufficiently permissive and warm to furnish the security he should have to reinforce his emotional needs. There is also some evidence that physiological well-being (normal sensory equipment and bodily vigor) is a part of the learning situation. For example, the hungry baby is distracted from learning or play and therefore does not function well as a learner. One who has a headache or burning eyes or fever is not concerned about any learning situation, any more than an adult can perform efficiently under similar conditions.

MATURATION ←——→ LEARNING

Because maturation depends upon inherent potential and learning depends upon external stimuli, the two concepts are analogous to and as inseparable as heredity and environment. Each one can work to the advantage or disadvantage of the other; each is necessary to and an outgrowth of the other. Neither is an independent process; both are parts of the larger process of development.

Until the required physiological properties have attained a particular stage of maturation, the individual cannot perform acts for which those properties are necessary. To give intense vocal training to an infant whose neural tissues, larynx, and intellect are underdeveloped is futile, a waste of time. He cannot be taught to sing or mimic or speak in sentences. Forcing the child to attempt something beyond his immediate capabilities (no matter what his age) may even retard learning by creating in him feelings of failure and frustration, as well as attitudes of negativism and resistance. Moreover, delay or training often works to the advantage of the trainee, as demonstrated by Strayer (1930). He found that a maturational advantage of as little as five weeks had a positive influence on the relative effectiveness of vocabulary training during early childhood. Using identical twins as subjects, Strayer observed that the twin whose practice was delayed not only learned more easily than the one who had already undergone five weeks of training, but also had a more mature pattern of response. In other words, the individual needs to have developmental readiness before he can fully benefit from instruction. If tasks and skills are geared to his maturing needs and capacities, he is more highly motivated and has a greater chance of the success so necessary to a good self-concept.

We should point out, however, that too great a delay is likely to result in an atrophy of interest. Unless challenged or allowed to exercise their newly formed capabilities, children often become bored, intractable, and destructive. This type of behavior, incidentally, is common in low-income homes

The development of the ability to use tools requires both maturation and practice.

where there are few toys and little encouragement to create playthings from materials at hand. The case against excessive delay of practice is well illustrated by the many children who are bed-ridden because of illness while motor abilities are maturing and demanding exercise: not only do these young invalids tend to select sedentary tasks as they grow older, but they manifest an inhibiting awkwardness of movement at a time when social acceptability depends somewhat upon litheness and competency in games skills.

The implications for education should be obvious—especially when one considers that children of the same age and grade level are regularly found to differ considerably in maturation. Many children entering school at the age of six are too immature to begin reading or to undertake other educational tasks with which first-grade children are confronted. And many six-year-olds lack the physical, emotional, or social maturity necessary to operate effectively in the typical first-grade group situations. Yet, because of its convenience as an index (and because maturity scales across the many areas of development are neither fully formulated nor accepted as yet), chronological age is used as a basis for determining the child's readiness to enter school. Naturally, failures and frustrations result among both pupils and teachers. Critics of the chronological-age-scale basis for school entry are probably justified in believing that the use of individual maturity-indicator lists would result in first-grade children making better adjustments to the school program—and thus to themselves and their peers. Conceivably, the children would also benefit from a continued use of such scales throughout their period of physiological growth, since maturation does not occur simultaneously in all areas. The child who has not yet attained reading readiness may, at a later date, greatly benefit his reading lag by concentrating his current efforts on singing, for example, or any other task in which he has shown a decided ability and interest. Admittedly, the administration of maturity tests, if available, would be difficult and time-consuming for the teacher or guidance counselor, and adjusting the curriculum to fit the variations would be impracticable in many cases. But to attempt to keep well within the extremes of forced instruction and no instruction is a commendable goal (by scientific standards) for the alert parent and teacher. And those alert adults have one of the best maturity indicators ever-present before their eyes—a child's spontaneous and persistent interests. Even as it is with adults, the child remains interested in those subjects or activities which accord him some measure of success or satisfaction.

THE PATTERNS OF DEVELOPMENT

Development is a rhythmic flow of quantitative and qualitative changes proceeding in specific directions in a predictable sequence.

Quantitative and Qualitative Changes

Meredith (1965) lists six classifications of change in human anatomic growth:

Complexity—from a single cell to a multicellular embryo to a fetus with partially developed appendages, to the neonate with appendages but lacking visible teeth and various bones, to an adolescent with teeth and a full complement of bones but undeveloped sex organs, to an anatomically mature adult.

Size—height, weight, length, and volume of organs, glands, and bones.

Shape—the heart, for instance, passes through its stages as a tube, a helix, and finally a pyramid. The face is short, then long, then short again. The characteristic "voice break" of the adolescent male is a result of the elongation of the larynx as it assumes its permanently elliptical shape.

Position—body organs and segments pass through periods of migration (nerves extend outward, kidneys move upward, testes downward), tilting (heart from right to left, stomach from left to right, ovaries from vertical to transverse), and rotation (at the shoulders, feet, toes, teeth). Most of the organs change by way of all three movements.

Pigmentation—the iris, hair, skin, and some fibers (as in the heart) follow varying cycles from lightness to darkness.

Texture—as the organism grows older, there is a decrease in tissue water content, bone and kidney organic material, and skin elasticity.

These changes are measurable, in keeping with the definition of *growth* stated earlier. However, there are developmental changes involving quality which should be given more attention than is usually given. Because of the ease with which most changes are observed or analyzed, adults frequently place a great deal of emphasis on quantitative growth to the exclusion of the qualitative. Teachers, for instance, in an attempt to maintain objectivity, construct tests to measure the amount of material a student has retained, i.e., they test his memory. Gradually, they have little time to ascertain whether or not the pupil has absorbed, understood, and related the material.

Besides placing undue emphasis on only one phase of intellect (recall), attention so directed endangers a sound educational program by forcing the pupil to spread himself too thin across many fields of endeavor—an orientation toward superficiality rather than depth. In an age of increasing specialization, the student needs early guidance and practice in acquiring an *intensive* understanding of a broad range of subjects.

A Rhythmic Flow

Growth and development are continual processes, characterized by rise and regression, quickening and quiescence, peaks and plateaus. Each part of the body, each system, ability, or skill develops at its own rate, follows its own pattern, and reaches maturity at its own time. Neural and sensory development have their greatest acceleration during the prenatal period (wherein the growth emphasis shifts from cranial structures to heart to limbs to respiratory system); the lymphoid tissue, brain, and nervous system grow most rapidly from birth to early childhood and then continue to develop slowly until puberty. The sex organs, respiratory and digestive systems, the kidneys, torso, pulmonary trunk, musculature, the total skelton, and the blood volume increase sharply during adolescence (Harris, 1930).

Maturation for the total organism, then, proceeds inexorably, but with shifts in emphasis—forming, pictorially, a helical pattern. Evidence that such shifts take place can also be found among the various skills, as, for instance, when the young child concentrates all his efforts on the development of motor skills before he turns his attention to vocalizations (Arlitt, 1946). (See also Chapter VI on language development.)

Behavioral shifts are evidenced in the revision (and reversal) of habits and interests. The activities that are useful at one level of maturity are changed or abandoned at another stage. Block-playing is superseded by drawing, which in turn is subordinated to writing, followed by a phase often called the "reading craze." Habits and interests are revised, of course, in harmony with growth in motor coordination, understanding, and problem-solving ability. When they are not changed, when old patterns persist, one may infer that some of the individual's developmental needs are not being satisfied. And also that he is in for trouble (Jersild, 1960).

Further illustration of the focal change in development is presented in Table IV-1. Although the ten-year-old child has attained seventy-eight per cent of the height he will probably reach by the age of eighteen, he has developed only thirty-seven per cent of his predicted grip strength. If growth were proportionate and the shifts of concentration did not occur, one might expect that a child half as old would have half the given percentages; but such is not the case. The Boyntons (1938) discovered from a longitudinal study of children's anthropometric measurements that a typical five and a half-year-old boy did have half the grip strength of the ten-year-old, but

Table IV-1   Developmental Status of a Ten-Year-Old Child (Hollingworth, 1933)

Trait	Per Cent of 18-year Status
Strength of grip	37
Weight of the body	48
Sensitiveness to pain	65
Stature (standing)	78
Rate of tapping	82
Size of skull	96

he already had sixty-five per cent of his ultimate (predicted) height. In other words, the ten-year-old Hollingworth boy (Table IV-1) had followed a typical height growth curve, slowing down considerably after the age of six, and was biding his time until his sex hormones were released at puberty, after which he would rapidly attain his mature size. (He probably grew as much as four or five inches in a single adolescent year.)

Within the larger life cycles, there seem to be yearly cycles of growth. Hurlock (1956) noted that the period from July until the middle of December was the most favorable for increase in weight, whereas the least favorable was from May until early July. Height, on the other hand, was found to increase most between April and the middle of August, and least from August to November.

In Specific Directions

Superimposed on the helical pattern of total development are the growth curves peculiar to the individual parts of the human personality, each of which has its own rhythmic flow. That is, all growth curves for height look generally alike: there is a spurt following infancy, a period of slow,

steady growth throughout the fourth, fifth, and sixth grades, then a period
of rapid development that begins when the child starts to mature sexually
and continuing until the child is fifteen or sixteen when growth again slows
down and finally tapers off quite abruptly (Thompson, 1954). The growth
curve for a single hair is quite different. Hair grows rapidly to maturity, then
maintains a nearly equal period of quiescence, after which it falls out and a
new hair grows out of the same follicle (Trotter, 1954). Other growth curves,
typical for specific aspects of human growth, are pictured in Figure IV-1.

Top to bottom (cephalocaudal)—Just as the first prenatal growth concentrates on cranial structures, so does body control begin with the head
and move downward. The infant raises his head first, then his chest. He
next acquires the ability to roll his trunk and later gains control of his lower
abdomen in order to sit. His leg muscles are still developing at this point,
and subsequently he is able to stand. He is not ready to walk until his feet
muscles and his sense of balance (which also begins developing in the head)
are mature enough.

Inner to outer (proximodistal)—The trunk of the body is formed before
the arm buds, and the formation continues outward gradually to the fingers.
The child can control his arm movements (from the shoulders) before he can
manipulate small objects with his fingers. Almost every internal organ has
reached full maturity before the appearance of facial, armpit, and pubic hair.

General to specific (differentiation, individuation)—The total body of
the infant responds to stimuli first. When he cries, he kicks his feet, waves
his arms, agitates his head, all at the same time. Later, he uses his voice
alone. He responds to all people before he selects one from the crowd—
usually his mother—to turn his attention to. In language development, the
child calls all men "Da-da"; all four-legged creatures are "doggies." Later, one
name is applied to one man and dogs are differentiated from horses or wolves
or coyotes or cows. Reactions to early fears are identical. Only with age are
specific fears accompanied by specific patterns. The child perceives a whole
word and a whole plant for quite some time before he can tell the difference
between *three* and *tree* and between a petunia and a carnation.

Simple to complex (integration)—As with anatomical growth, every
facet of an individual's development begins from a single unit—language
from one syllable and one word, art from one line and one color, writing from
one letter and one name (his own)—and proceeds with relentlessness toward an integration of that unit with a similar one, forming not two units
but a single, more complex structure.

A Predictable Sequence

The general pattern of development for any one structure or system
is the same for every individual and is unaffected by the speed at which the

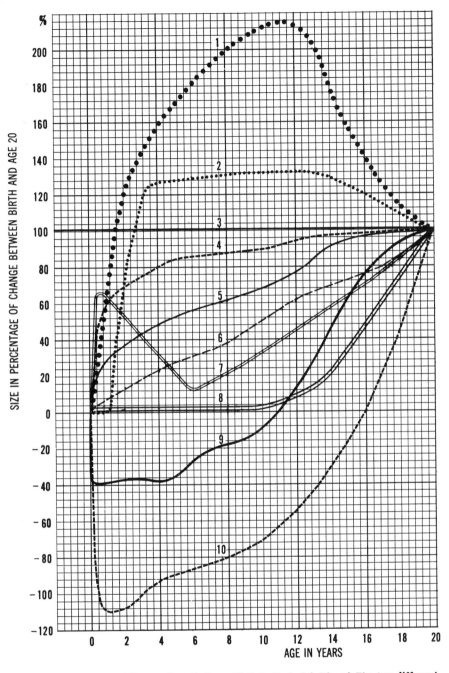

Figure IV-1. Patterns of Human Growth From Birth to Early Adulthood. The ten different patterns shown are for (1) weight of the thymus gland, (2) size of the pharyngeal tonsil, (3) size of the bones of the inner ear, (4) width of the head, (5) width of the hips, (6) weight of the pituitary gland, (7) thickness of the fatty tissue on the chest, (8) size of the testes, (9) length of the uterus, and (10) weight of the suprarenal glands (Meredith, 1965, p. 475)

various steps succeed one another. Each stage in the flow is an outgrowth of an earlier one, not a mere addition, and the steps follow one another in a reliable, predictable manner. Every normal infant acquires the ability to creep first, then crawl, then stand alone, then walk, run, and jump—in that order. In learning to speak, he cries, gurgles, coos, babbles, utters syllables, then words, and finally sentences. What occurs at one stage carries over and influences subsequent growth stages. Moreover, every child must go through every stage and at approximately the same chronological age. We can, then, make generalized statements concerning the characteristics, developmental tasks, height and weight "norms," etc. of specific age groups; and others, by referring to the lists, can determine whether or not a child is developing "normally." On the whole, this method of comparison works adequately for average children—if there are any children who are *totally* average. Even so, the lists are meant to be used only as general guides. Better ways have been devised for determining and predicting development, and those methods came about through the application of two growth principles: (1) the individual's overall rate of growth tends to remain the same throughout his lifetime, and (2) all growth is correlated, or interrelated.

Overall growth rate is relatively constant. A study by Richards and Newbery (1938) is but one of many demonstrating the relative constancy of an individual's growth rate. As shown in Table IV-2, the investigators were able to establish positive correlations between fetal activity and postnatal development (as measured by the *Gesell Developmental Schedule*).

Table IV–2   Rank Difference Coefficients Between Activity Scores and Performance on the Gesell Schedule at Six Months Postnatally (Richards and Newbery, 1938, p. 80)

Month	Number of subjects	Correlation
Seventh	6	.84
Eighth	9	.65
Ninth	11	.72
Tenth	12	.54
Ninth and Tenth	12	.71

Figures IV-2 and IV-3, aside from showing graphically the individual variations in growth patterns, demonstrate that one individual does not in any sense "catch up" to another. He begins growing at his own rate and pattern until his own maximum is attained. Except in rare instances, the "slow learner" will always remain a slow learner. However, using a foot race for analogy, we must point out that the slow runner may reach the same goal as the fast runner eventually, and may even run beyond the goal after the fast man has stopped, but he will never be able to compete successfully in a

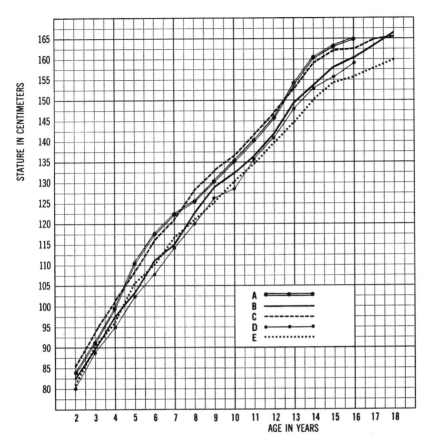

Figure IV–2. Individual Growth Curves for Five Sisters (After Ford, 1958)

Figure IV–3. Average and Individual Growth Curves (After Meredith, 1935, p. 112)

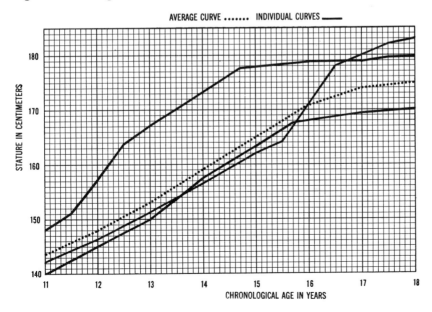

Table IV-3 Selected Percentile for Children of Northwest European Ancestry, for Weight in Pounds and Height in Inches *
(After Stuart and Meredith, 1946, pp. 1378–1380)

BOYS

Age (Years)		Percentiles				
		10	25	50	75	90
5	weight	36.6	39.6	42.8	46.5	49.7
	height	41.5	42.6	43.8	45.0	45.9
6	weight	40.9	44.4	48.3	52.1	56.4
	height	43.8	44.9	46.3	47.6	48.6
7	weight	45.8	49.7	54.1	58.7	64.4
	height	46.0	47.4	48.9	50.2	51.4
8	weight	51.2	55.5	60.1	65.5	73.0
	height	48.5	49.8	51.2	52.8	54.0
9	weight	56.3	61.1	66.0	72.3	81.0
	height	50.5	51.8	53.3	55.0	56.1
10	weight	61.1	66.3	71.9	79.6	89.9
	height	52.3	53.7	55.2	56.9	58.1
11	weight	66.3	71.6	77.6	87.2	99.3
	height	54.1	55.3	56.8	58.7	59.8
12	weight	72.0	77.5	84.4	96.0	109.6
	height	56.1	57.2	58.9	60.4	62.2
13	weight	77.1	83.7	93.0	107.9	123.2
	height	57.7	58.9	61.0	63.3	65.1
14	weight	87.2	95.5	107.6	123.1	136.9
	height	59.9	61.6	64.1	66.3	67.9
16	weight	111.0	118.7	129.7	144.4	157.3
	height	64.1	65.8	67.6	69.5	70.7
18	weight	120.0	127.1	139.0	155.7	169.0
	height	65.5	67.1	68.7	70.4	71.8

Table IV-3 (continued)

GIRLS

Age (years)		Percentiles				
		10	25	50	75	90
5	weight	36.1	38.6	41.4	44.2	48.2
	height	41.3	42.2	43.2	44.4	45.4
6	weight	39.9	42.9	46.5	50.2	54.2
	height	43.5	44.6	45.6	47.0	48.1
7	weight	44.5	48.1	52.2	56.3	61.2
	height	46.0	46.9	48.1	49.6	50.7
8	weight	48.6	53.1	58.1	63.3	69.9
	height	48.1	49.1	50.4	51.8	53.0
9	weight	52.6	57.9	63.8	70.5	79.1
	height	50.0	51.1	52.3	54.0	55.3
10	weight	57.1	62.8	70.3	79.1	89.7
	height	51.9	53.0	54.6	56.1	57.5
11	weight	62.6	69.9	78.8	89.1	100.4
	height	53.9	55.2	57.0	58.7	60.4
12	weight	69.5	78.0	87.6	98.8	111.5
	height	56.1	57.4	59.6	61.7	63.2
13	weight	79.9	89.4	99.1	111.0	124.5
	height	58.7	60.1	61.9	63.6	64.9
14	weight	91.0	99.8	108.4	119.7	133.3
	height	60.2	61.5	62.8	64.4	65.7
16	weight	100.9	108.4	117.0	127.2	141.1
	height	61.5	62.4	63.9	65.2	66.5
18	weight	103.5	111.2	119.9	130.8	144.5
	height	61.5	62.6	64.0	65.4	66.7

race that demands only fast runners. Referring again to Figure IV-2, for instance, we notice that sisters B and C attained the same height as sister A, but it took them two years longer to do so. Sisters A and D grew equally rapidly to maturity but with a two-inch discrepancy in their maximums. Which is to say that fast growth or slow growth is neither "good" nor "bad" in the absolute sense. It is merely individual.

In attempting to determine the developmental progress of a child, investigators found the earlier methods of calculating averages for height and weight somewhat unfair to those children who did not have average build. Consequently, attempts were made to devise a system for determining whether or not a child maintains his *relative* position among his age group in height and weight. One technique which seems to work fairly well is the utilization of percentile ranks. In a study reported by Stuart and Meredith (1946), scales based on percentile ranks were constructed after measurements were taken of the children in attendance one or more years from 1930 to 1946 at the University of Iowa experimental elementary and high school. Each child was measured and weighed within two weeks of his birthday. Five percentile ranks (the tenth, twenty-fifth, fiftieth, seventy-fifth, and ninetieth) were indicated.* Table IV-3 gives the norms derived from this study. By using these or similar tables, one can determine if a youngster who is slight of build is growing at a rate similar to that of other children of comparable proportions.

The determination of optimum weight is a bit more difficult. Modern methods attempt to set up standards which take into account the enormous number of variations to be found in both body build and rate of growth. Massler and Suher (1951) studied 3200 measurements taken on 531 children and found that calf girth, when used in relation to height, was helpful in arriving at the appropriate weight of a child. With this information, a chart was devised, the use of which, they believed, would help to determine the "normal" weight for a boy or girl.

Such predictability enables interested adults to estimate not only the approximate maturity any one child is likely to attain, but also the amount of progress he is making along his own growth channel. The guidance counselor, for example, can attempt to direct the boy who is six inches taller than his age-mates away from a desire to train as a jockey. A pediatrician would be likely to check into the food habits, emotional status, or possible internal disorders of the preschool child who, from a birth length of twenty-one inches (above average), attained a height four inches below his age group.

---

* The percentile ranks for the measurements of children are arranged according to size. Generally, the lowest is considered to be on the first percentile and the highest on the hundredth. If a child were on the tenth percentile for height, he would be taller than nine but shorter than ninety of his group.

All growth is correlated. The various aspects of development are interrelated: Growth in one organ or system affects growth in another; one defect influences the entire personality; any factor, external or internal, that affects any part of the organism affects the entire organism. The old notion that a child compensates for weakness in one area by being strong in another is, by and large, fallacious. The popular stereotypes of the sickly bookworm who is intellectually gifted but stunted in physical and social development or the superbly skillful, physically attractive athlete who is academically backward are based on readily accepted, but erroneous, beliefs in compensatory development. Naturally, in exceptional circumstances, the superior and the inferior do exist side by side, so to speak; yet by far the greater tendency is for all areas of individual growth and development to be correlated. As a group, children who are mentally superior are also taller, heavier, more attractive and have fewer physical defects than mentally retarded children. They have a wider range of interests, are friendlier, and continue throughout life to be better adjusted (Terman and Oden, 1951). The retarded children, especially in the extreme cases of morons and idiots, are underdeveloped in many more aspects than just the mental. Usually, their development of motor abilities is arrested at a low level, and they tend to be unresponsive, suspicious, sadistic, and physically unattractive.

When studied longitudinally, height, weight, and anatomical development, then, may be more predictive of a child's school achievement than such indices as the quality of teaching, amount of drill, or the course of study pursued. The results of early studies by Courtis (1935), for instance, suggested that a growth curve based on one set of data tends to express an underlying individuality which was reflected in other growth measures. This notion was given support in the results of a study by Millard (1940). By calculating "height quotients" for forty boys, he was able to predict intelligence quotients about as accurately as when they were measured by intelligence tests. And when we consider that methods of predicting an infant's ultimate mental development are already "more reliable than those used to predict his ultimate physical development" (Hurlock, 1956, p. 19), the immense value of predictability in child development should become clear. Adoption agencies in particular are able to do a better job than nature often does in providing an optimum environment for the children left in their care. Education and counseling, also, have been able to extend themselves further into the child's future and, in a measure, exercise control over his welfare as an adult.

In this connection, Olson and Hughes (1942) have emphasized that any phase of school achievement by the child is a function of his total growth, a concept exemplified in the educational orientation toward guidance and consideration of the *whole child*. We should keep in mind that it is the total child who is growing and developing. Learning and maturation do not take place in a piecemeal fashion: Unrelated items do not appear at different periods only to become fused into a unified pattern at a later date. The whole child is involved in learning to read or to skate. His emotional nature, motor abilities, social self, and physical person, along with his intellectual self, are involved in the acquisition of skills and knowledge. Diagnostic and remedial activities that fail to take into account this total growth of the child are ineffective in producing permanently improved achievement (Tilton, 1947).

> . . . Unity and integration (oneness of action) characterize all biological development. The human organism (the child) does not *achieve* biological integration or oneness in the process of growth, it *maintains* an originally present integration at increasingly more complex levels of development. General growth thus may be thought of as being unified and interlocked.
>
> Thorpe, 1962

ASSESSING MATURITY

Aside from the methods of determining development which we have already mentioned—height and weight in particular, the onset of puberty and the state of the bones and teeth are the most commonly used indicators of physiological maturity. The stage is far more easily determined amongst girls, because their adolescent growth spurt is accompanied by the onset of the menarche, or menstrual cycle. Unfortunately, there is not such a simple or exact measure for determining the age at which boys become physiologically mature. Authorities turn to other evidence of sex-hormone action.

Growth of Bones

The child's bones differ from those of the adult in proportion, shape, composition, position, and even in number. During the growth period, children's bones contain more water and less mineral matter than adults' and they are more vascular in nature, allowing larger quantities of blood to flow through them. Although enabling a child's nutritive needs to be more adequately satisfied, the larger quantity of blood causes the child to be more susceptible to bone diseases resulting from infection.

The bones of the young child are not firmly knit together. They grow in length by becoming longer at the ends; therefore, young joints are longer and the ligaments are rather loosely attached. X-ray pictures taken at frequent intervals during the developmental period show a strip of cartilage which serves to separate the bone shaft from the other bony masses at the ends. As long as this cartilage exists, children's bones continue to grow. When the bones fuse, skeletal growth stops. Authorities believe that the fusion is brought about through the release of a sex hormone developed at puberty.

Ossification

X-ray pictures of the hand and wrist bones not only show the development at the ends of the bones, the epiphyses, but also reveal the stage of ossification, or hardening of the bones. Ossification depends upon the secretion of a hormone from the thyroid gland and upon the nutrition of the child. If there is inadequate mineralization as a result of dietary or thyroid deficiency, bone deformities are likely to occur. Bowed legs are one of the more obvious results. (The reader should keep in mind that we are speaking of a condition resulting from deficiency and occurring several years later than the common result of early walking, which is usually self-correcting as the leg muscles develop and tighten.)

Through the use of X rays of the hand and wrist, investigators are able to determine at what rate a child is progressing in his osseous development and to predict puberty as well as other aspects of development. (Harding, 1952.) By the age of thirteen, an average girl will have about seventy per cent ossification of her wrist area. (After the age of five or six, girls generally show a more advanced bone development than boys, and a more rapid growth continues in girls until maturity.) A more recently developed method of assessing skeletal maturity utilizes the pattern of ossification at the epiphyses rather than at some other specific area.

Dentition

The age at which a child's permanent teeth erupt has also been used to indicate the stage of anatomical or skeletal development. Dental age scales are now available for both boys and girls. Generally, a youngster six years of age will have one or two permanent teeth; at eight he will have ten or eleven; at ten, fourteen or sixteen; at twelve, twenty-four or twenty-six; and at thirteen, twenty-seven or twenty-eight. The "wisdom teeth" usually erupt between the seventeenth and twenty-fifth years. As in the growth of other parts of the body, there appears to be uneven spacing in the eruption of teeth. However, the acquisition of permanent teeth closely follows the growth pattern set for height and weight—with girls ahead of the boys at all stages. (See Figure IV–4.)

FACTORS INFLUENCING DEVELOPMENT

Every child is subject to the same principles of development as are the individual anatomical structures. He grows at his own rate, maintains his unique patterns, attains his particular maximums in his own time, alters his

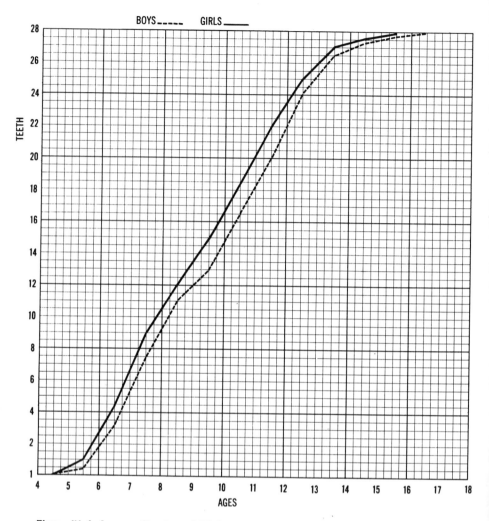

Figure IV–4. Average Number of All Permanent Teeth (Except Third Molars) Erupted at Specified Ages (After Palmer, Klein, and Kramer, 1938, p. 157)

behavior according to his specially absorbed learning, which came about through his peculiarly individual perceptions of his distinctly uncommon environment. And, in keeping with the principle of correlative development, any factor which influences one part of the child influences the entire child.

Heredity

In the face of overwhelming evidence, we must conclude that large variations do occur in individual patterns of physiological growth (see again Figures IV–2 and IV–3), and we must further deduce logically that heredity is responsible for many of the variations. Heredity influences, among other characteristics, a child's intellectual potential, the size, strength and appearance of his physical structures, his metabolism, the stability of his nervous system, and his susceptibility to disease. Because each of these characteristics affects the ways in which the child responds to his environment, they affect the kinds of things he learns and his ability to learn them, understand them, and relate them to his experiences. The child who is highly motivated to satisfy his safety needs is likely to be cautious and timid in play, dependent in the home, a quiet conformist in school, an overanxious adult. If his physical appearance is admired by his society, he will experience a form of success that will be reinforced if he also assimilates his appropriate sex role.

Heredity, as emphasized previously, is responsible for and interacts with elements in the child's environment, such as family, community, class, culture. The family, besides passing on certain physical potentials, determines the climate, both geographical and emotional, into which the infant is born, and his class and culture. Geographical climate affects the amount of fresh air and sunlight the child receives, the nature of his outdoor play, his interests, even the style of shelter he has. A steady, warm emotional climate is important to good mental health and obviates overanxiety. Social class and culture make myriad behavioral demands upon the individual and influence the manner in which others behave toward him.

In short, there is nothing in a child's development that is not "a product of an interplay between his heredity and his environment" (Jersild, 1960, p. 15). Certain facets of environment act toward the individual according to his heredity, and the individual acts upon and responds to his environment on the same basis.

Heredity plays its strongest role by determining the child's sex, which greatly influences development. Although girls are more advanced in physical development throughout the elementary-school years, boys tend to be slightly taller and heavier. An exception is found in the period between eleven and fourteen, when girls exceed boys in both measurements. When the growth rates for certain areas of the body are compared, it is found that boys are larger than girls in thoracic circumference and girth of forearm, whereas girls generally have larger thighs. These differences, along with the larger oxygen consumption for boys, especially after the age of eleven, account for some of the sex differences in the amount and characteristics of motor activity.

Prenatal and Birth Conditions

A wide range of environmental factors present during a woman's pregnancy can produce malformations in her offspring. When those factors are present, "gremlin" or destructive forces operate on the germ cell, the ovum, the embryo, or the fetus; and some operate continuously throughout the prenatal period. If the germ cell is injured before or after fertilization, the condition produced may be regarded as a result of environmental conditions. (See footnote, p. 30.) Some factors which may produce congenital defects in the intrauterine organism are listed as follows:

1. Malnutrition of the mother deprives the fetal organism of necessary food from the maternal blood stream. Experimental and clinical observations have furnished valuable information about the effects of the mother's dietary deficiencies on the development of the embryo and fetus. During the embryonic and fetal stages, the child develops as a parasite, obtaining the required nutrition from the mother, provided the maternal tissues are not exhausted. The fetus seems to draw vitamin C from the mother as long as appreciable amounts of ascorbic acid are present in the maternal plasma (Warkany, 1948). Also, the vitamin C content of the blood plasma of the fetus is higher than that of the mother. In the case of vitamin A, the fetal plasma usually has a lower content than the mother's; however, when the mother's intake is low, the intrauterine development of the individual is endangered. Malformations, including congenital blindness and other visual abnormalities, have been observed where the mother's diet is deficient in carotene and vitamin A.

2. Infection from the parent, especially syphilis in its active state, affects the fetal nervous system. (The results of such an infectious condition may not be apparent until some time after birth.)

3. A wasting disease in the mother, such as cancer or tuberculosis, may deny the fetus food.

4. Some viral diseases, German measles among them, contracted by the mother during her first twelve weeks of pregnancy, are often responsible for defects in the newborn.

5. The position of the embryo and fetus before birth may, under abnormal conditions, affect the development of the organism. A relatively common defect is a bone malformation in the legs or feet. Some doctors attribute the defect, usually correctible, to a stable fetal position in the womb which occurs when the fetus becomes too large or too long to move freely.

6. The birth process itself can endanger the normalcy of the organism, especially through injuries inflicted by the instruments a doctor must use when he encounters difficulties while assisting the mother; e.g., incorrect position of the fetus or fetal size out of proportion to the mother's pelvic structure.

7. Maternal toxemia and eclampsia may cause insufficient oxygen in the blood (anoxia) of the newborn.

8. The use of analgesics, anesthetics, and drugs during labor and at the time of birth increases the possibility of the newborn being anoxic.

The Glands

Recently, scholars in the field of endocrinology have provided valuable information concerning the importance of certain glandular secretions as they affect growth. Seemingly, even slight hyperactivity or hypoactivity of the growing child's ductless glands may bring about changes in mental and physical development during his growth period. Nor do such glands function independently. Each influences and is influenced by the activity of the other, as well as maintaining a reciprocal influence with the individual's emotional state, his blood chemistry, and his nervous system. For example, some of the symptoms of a hyperactive thyroid gland are inability to concentrate, emotional states changing abruptly from extreme depression to exhilaration, itching and sensitivity to heat, rapid heartbeat, and various hindrances to eye coordination, endurance, and finger dexterity. Needless to say, a child with a "thyroid condition"—particularly in extreme cases— would be handicapped in his intellectual, motor, and social development.

The pituitary gland, located under the brain, regulates growth in stature and sexual development. Overactivity of the anterior lobe during childhood causes giantism; underactivity produces a symmetrical dwarf with normal intelligence but with subnormal sexual development.

Two other glands, the pineal at the base of the brain and the thymus in the chest, are influential in controlling growth during infancy and childhood. They seem to regulate both the rate of growth and the appearance of the secondary sex characteristics.

Closely associated with the glands that affect growth are the gonads, the ovaries, and the testes. If the sex glands begin to function at the requisite level too early, growth is arrested and the youngsters will be abnormally short. If functioning is insufficient for too long a period of time, growth, particularly in the limbs, continues beyond normal bodily proportions.

Visual and Aural Defects

There is evidence for the conclusion that defective vision or hearing handicaps the youngster in his acquisition of knowledge and in gaining a true understanding of the world in which he lives (Schwartz, 1940). The impressions the organism receives are made possible only through the stimulation of the sense organs, and learning depends in large part upon the number and kind of those impressions. Limitations of auditory experiences narrow a child's background of information and make communication difficult within the home and classroom. At times, an unsuspected hearing impairment is responsible for an apparent lack of interest in oral language, music activities, and many kinds of social activities. It may also be the cause of what seems to be deliberate disobedience or an inability to understand and follow directions.

Once the alert teacher has discovered the possibility of such a handicap in a pupil and has made arrangements for hearing tests by means of an audiometer in the school or community, she can further aid the pupil suffering a hearing loss by adjusting the seating arrangement and altering the mode of instruction. Severe cases may need lip reading instruction or special speech therapy. However, even deaf children now obtain much of their school instruction along with youngsters who have normal hearing, in order that they may learn to get along in the community with little special attention.

As with hearing difficulties, visual defects may account for a child's lack of interest or his inability to absorb certain subject matter. The most common defects of vision are myopia (nearsightedness), hyperopia (farsightedness), astigmatism (blurred or imperfect vision due to incorrect refraction of light rays through a defective lens or an irregular cornea), and strabismus (the lack of proper adjustment of the muscles, which often produces a turning inward or outward of one or both eyes). Also, some youngsters may be color blind, a condition more prevalent among boys than among girls.

The scope of the visual defect problem may be shown by surveys which estimate that from fifteen to thirty-five per cent of school children have vision impairments serious enough to require medical attention (Dalton, 1943; 1953).

Passing consideration should also be given here to the child who has received the proper attention and is subsequently required to wear glasses. These children usually lose some peripheral vision, which frequently causes them to appear awkward or to miss events on the fringes of their visual field.

Health

For proof that a child is not merely a miniature adult, we need only turn to the field of pediatrics, whose emergence into prominence, whose very foundation in fact, is based on the fact that children are smaller than adults, are immature anatomically, physiologically, and immunologically. Not only do they contract illnesses that adults do not usually contract, but the seriousness and results of all illnesses differ from child to adult. Moreover, the child's health needs and the nature of diseases and illnesses change as the child grows and develops.

There is evidence that self-regulation in growth follows a period of illness. Meredith and Knott (1962, p. 151) report a study designed to determine the effects of illness on the physical growth of North American white children reared in surroundings favorable to health care. They conclude:

For none of the anatomic variables considered is there a dependable difference between children representing the "healthiest 20%" and "least healthy 20%" of the illness continuum. Succinctly, the results give *no support* to the view that schoolchildren who are frequently ill during middle childhood tend to be smaller, more slender, or slower growing than those who are rarely ill. Rather they allow the interpretation, *for the population studied*, that (1) there is no systematic association of body size or form during the next several years, and (2) in the period of middle childhood, differential amounts of illness have no influence on over-all absolute or relative change in body dimensions.

The illnesses of youngsters vary from acute cases of short duration to those which are chronic and require hospitalization over a long period of time. The most frequent causes of disabling illness, especially during the preschool and early school years, are the respiratory ailments (including influenza and bronchitis) and the acute communicable diseases of childhood. From the standpoint of pediatrics, congenital defects, accidents, and appendicitis provide the major portion of surgical problems. Yet, the most difficult long-term problems presented to the pediatrician are those involving cardiac patients (Stuart, 1954).

Cardiac children. Children with heart trouble, or cardiac children, fall into two groups: the congenital—those who were born with the disease or deformity, and the rheumatic—those who acquire it. According to Parsons (1954, p. 209), the former "is almost always due to arrested foetal development during the period of organogenesis in the first three months of pregnancy." The heart malformations that result may vary from those that do not interfere in any way with life activities to those which are so serious that the infant is unable to survive. However, because of the remarkable advances in surgical techniques, more and more children are falling into the former classification—those who are handicapped but little, if at all, by their condition.

The onset of rheumatic fever occurs most often between the ages of five and fifteen, and the ailment may attack several parts of the body simultaneously. The acute inflammation of the joints and the high fever so characteristic of the disease are responsible for its name. The condition is serious because healing leaves scars in the heart.

The child with heart trouble may be handicapped in his social relations. Rheumatic fever, in particular, most often affects individuals during the latency period of emotional maturation. Josselyn (1949, p. 99) points out:

... The long period of isolation from a social group and normal social activities lessens the opportunity for friendships to partially replace the parents. Furthermore, and more significant, aggressive behavior, expressed in the healthy pattern of the normal child through aggressive, active games, is again dangerous. Such expression of aggression carries with it the possible punishment of death! The danger in aggressive behavior thus becomes a real one, and the sublimation usually found by children is forbidden.

At home, the child is likely to be pampered because he cannot be allowed to perform many of the duties which exist around the house, to fight his own battles lustily, or to receive physical punishment. As a consequence, he may become overbearing, egotistic, selfish, or lazy. Newhaus (1954) noted that cardiac children aged eight through fourteen exceeded normal children of the same age in degree of neuroticism and dependency. A cardiac condition also affects the child's agility, strength, and activity. Inability to participate freely in physical activities will in turn limit the child's choice of friends.

Allergies.   Children with allergies are common in our schools. Some are hay fever victims, sensitive to dust, feathers, or pollen; some have reactions that center in the gastrointestinal tract and cause digestive disturbances; others have skin reactions such as eczema or hives; and still others suffer from a bronchial condition that we refer to as asthma. Many of the children who had eczema or hives during their early years complained of hay fever and asthma at a later age. At least half of the country's asthma victims are children. Of this group, about ten per cent have chronic, intractable asthma, a serious, sometimes fatal, ailment. It is characterized by coughing, wheezing, and gasping for breath; and drugs which generally help the other ninety per cent of all asthma sufferers do not relieve those who have this type.

"Asthma is caused by an allergy, and no one ever really gets cured of an allergy. But we do say that we can *control* asthma. We can remove the emotional overload which is preventing these children from recovering" (Tuft, 1955). In other words, there is a close relationship between the occurrence of allergy and a child's emotional life. This statement is supported by reports of behavior patterns characteristic of asthmatic youngsters. Like cardiac children, they are more maladjusted than normal children, displaying greater anxiety, insecurity, and dependency. They may have short attention spans and give evidence of other behavior difficulties. Youngsters who suffer from skin irritations are more irritable and have more tantrums than other children (Newhaus, 1954).

In order to help the child who is suffering from an allergy, parents should see that he has a careful physical examination and thereby determine, if possible, both the source of the irritation and the nature of the condition. Thus, parents and teachers can work to keep the youngster from using his condition as an excuse for gaining attention or for noncooperative behavior, and they can help him maintain a climate of security.

Epilepsy.   Epilepsy is not a disease, it is a symptom. Exactly what epilepsy is a symptom of is not always known. Sometimes it is symptomatic of a clinical, organic condition—a brain tumor, syphilis, uremic poisoning. More often the etiology of the seizures characteristic of the epileptic is undiscernible. Some authorities believe that epilepsy is caused by "cellular alterations in the brain tissue too fine for microscopic detection, changes in vascular supply, or chemical alterations" (Brussel, 1954).

How seriously epilepsy affects the youngster's behavior depends upon the severity of the condition, the effectiveness of treatment, and the attitude of his parents and other associates. The *grand mal* type of seizure is characterized by violent convulsions and loss of consciousness; the *petit mal* type, which is far less serious, can consistently attack the child while he is sleeping, leaving him with nothing more than a headache or the indistinct remains of a nightmare. Many children who suffer *petit mal* seizures are able to lead relatively normal lives without their peers knowing of the disorder. However, all children who have epileptic seizures are likely to be fearful, anxious, and frustrated. There is a definite relationship between the occurrence of the seizures and the emotional stress suffered by the patient. Although medication is an effective agent for keeping the patient in a calm state, it is important that parents and teachers give special attention to the development of good mental hygiene among epileptic children at all age levels.

Other health problems. Social stress, parental pressures, and tension are apparently responsible also for an increase in the incidence of ulcers among children, as reported by Weiss (1962), who studied 344 ulcer patients ranging in age from four to fourteen. An atmosphere of anxiety in the home, where expectations are high and where parents make an effort to see that the child excels in school work, may create tension and uneasiness in the child.

Youngsters who develop ulcers are usually tense, high strung, and nervous. They seem to crave love, approval, and an extra amount of praise. Often they overeat without seeming to satisfy their appetite. The most common symptoms are repeated stomach pain, nausea accompanied by vomiting—especially after breakfast, and irritability.

Other gastrointestinal symptoms occur frequently during adolescence, again partially attributable to increased social pressures and tension. Girls, particularly, complain more often than boys do of stomach pains and similar disturbances, and the symptoms last longer for them. Also, girls are more subject to appendicitis.

Hygiene of the nose and throat during the early development period is important, because the conditions of the respiratory passages determines to a large extent the child's susceptibility to the many infectious diseases which reach their peak during the early school years. In most cases, diphtheria, scarlet fever, measles, mumps, whooping cough, influenza, ordinary colds, infections of the middle ear, pneumonia, and tuberculosis gain entrance to the body through the nose and throat passages. Furthermore, the secretions of these areas are capable of harboring the organisms of many, if not all, of these diseases for a long period of time.

The nose and throat passages are provided with certain safeguards against the invasion of disease germs: the tonsils, the mucus secretions, the ciliated cells of the epithelium of the nose and bronchial tubes, and the hair lining of the outer portion of the nasal passages. Anything that interferes with the health of these areas renders the body more liable to infection. Consequently, adenoids, enlarged and inflamed tonsils, small follicular tonsils, nasal catarrh, and obstruction of the nasal passages by polyps or enlarged turbinates break down the natural barriers against disease germs. The removal of such conditions that are serious handicaps to a youngster's health and development should be the first consideration of those people who are concerned with the guidance and training of the school-age child. Because of the commonness of many of the ailments—upper respiratory infections, colds, tonsilitis, measles—and because the medical advances toward controlling the effects of such diseases as tuberculosis and poliomyelitis have taken tremendous strides forward, many adults have a tendency to treat childhood diseases, especially measles, lightly. During the yearly "epidemics" that occur in many areas of the country, parents are likely to treat the illnesses as unimportant, hardly worth calling the doctor about, forgetting that complications arise frequently and with possibly serious results. Furthermore, communicable diseases are not selective: they attack children already weakened by other diseases as readily as they attack healthy children, and the accompanying high fevers in particular are dangerous.

Nutrition

Cross-sectional studies of height and weight have shown the influence on youngsters of improved medical care and the increased attention to diet and nutrition so characteristic of our scientific age. The average boys and girls of today are considerably advanced in maturation rate over those born several decades ago. According to Hale (1958), the average fourteen-year-old boy is five inches taller and twenty-four pounds heavier than the average fourteen-year-old boy of 1880. In the same period of time, the average ten-year-old girl has gained four inches in height and fourteen pounds in weight over her counterpart of one or more generations ago.

However, throughout the world, malnutrition is still one of the most serious health problems. In our own country, poor nutrition may appear in environmental circumstances otherwise favorable,* although it is usually

* Surveys of the diets of children from different socioeconomic groups in Georgia show that poor dietary practices may be found in homes where the weekly expenditure for food is ample. The surveys reveal that some of the greatest deficiencies occur in the consumption of fruit and green and yellow vegetables (Unpublished data).

found along with other conditions unfavorable for maximum physical growth and health. Whether as a result of poverty, eating idiosyncracies, or lack of parental attention, children who suffer from nutritive deficiencies tend to be smaller and lighter than those who have an adequate diet (Dreizen, *et al.,* 1953).

Food habits of children. The mean daily intake of food and nutrients was estimated from seven-day dietary records of 1188 Iowa school children at successive ages from six through eighteen. Except for calcium, the boys generally had a progressively larger daily intake at each age level. The girls' mean daily intake was highest between the ages of six and twelve. After twelve, their diets tended to fall below the recommended allowances (Eppright and and Roderuck, 1955).

Any consideration of diet should give special attention to what a child eats as well as how many calories he eats. A survey of the literature on dental caries reveals that the amount of dental work necessary for children increases rapidly during childhood and reaches a maximum during adolescence (National Research Council, 1952). Many authorities relate the high incidence of caries to the excessive use of refined foods, especially sweets. They feel that if the child eats the quantities of food necessary for his nutritional requirements he will have no special need (hence, desire) for additional refined carbohydrates between meals.

Obesity. For a long time, obesity has been a problem that scientists have grappled with, and its cause has been variously attributed to glands, overeating, unbalanced diet, lack of exercise, feelings of being unloved, overprotection, and disturbances in the mechanisms regulating ingestion, digestion, absorption, utilization, or excretion, resulting in faulty nutrition. (See Boyd, 1938.) Of all these supposed causes, glandular malfunction has proved to be extremely rare as a cause of obesity and no longer serves as a valid excuse in most instances. The remaining causes are apparently valid in some cases; or overweight in a specific individual may be the result of all these conditions. For example Bruch and Touraine (1940) indicated that the obese children they studied typically lived in an environment of overprotection frequently characterized by a dominating mother and a submissive father. However, the oversolicitude of the mother did not completely hide her possessiveness and often hostile attitude toward the child. Such a home failed to provide for the child's basic needs of affection and acceptance; thus, he resorted to eating as a substitute.

Although the investigators did not mention the type of food generally eaten by the obese children, lay observers have noticed that when eating is used apparently as a substitute for acceptance the foodstuffs most often selected are sweets—as though the individual rewards himself for behavior he considers worthy of recognition. Obviously, such a pattern leads to diet imbalance, faulty nutrition, excess fat cells, and consequently a lack of exercise—because it is too tiring.

Mayer (1950) distinguishes three types of obesity: (1) metabolic, with lesions involving biochemical factors, (2) regulatory, produced by a dysfunction in the central nervous system, and (3) inactivity, characterized by a life of low energy output. Experimenting with rats, Mayer noted that high-fat diets will cause extreme obesity only in certain strains of rats and mice, and thus she implies that diet for the obese child is not so important as had been previously assumed.

Stefanik and his associates (1959) have emphasized the importance of exercise. Obese children are extraordinarily inactive; and when they are subjected to exercise requiring a considerable energy output, they will lose weight.

Recent tests on obesity lend support and credence to the various theories. Although most authorities agree that in the vast majority of cases problems of overweight center on the mechanisms by which the intake of food is regulated, modern research is primarily concerned with finding out *why* fat people eat too much. Drs. Hashim and Van Itallie at St. Luke's Hospital in New York are quoted by Osmundsen (1965) as having discovered that obese people "have an astonishing lack of hunger and lose weight rapidly when they are put into [a special] feeding situation."

Osmundsen continues:

> The St. Luke's feeding situation was designed to reduce the act of eating to its basic essentials. A bland, purified and homogenized diet was eaten in solitude. The food was dispensed from a machine through a tube that the subject held in his mouth. A mouthful of the preparation was delivered every time the subject pressed a button.
>
> In that way, all social, ritualistic trappings were stripped from the eating ceremony—even down to the elimination of traditional eating utensils. . . .
>
> The idea was to see if eating did not serve some psycho-social function to which persons who tended to overeat responded over and above their physiological hunger.
>
> The daily caloric intake of all obese persons tested so far in this way dropped precipitously to less than 250 calories, or below one-tenth of their normal daily requirement, Dr. Hashim said. The subjects did not seem to suffer from this experience.
>
> When the obese subjects were allowed to drink their meals ad libitum from a glass, say while watching television—a more social setting—the intake doubled. . . .

A control group, composed of lean subjects, was not bothered by this feeding situation and the members maintained their usual daily intake of calories.

From this preliminary study, Hashim presented the theory that "the obese person may relate to the setting in which he eats and the meaning food has come to assume for him aside from its use as a fuel." These findings, along with the ones reported by Bruch and Touraine, imply that the obese person is different from his leaner companions in ways other than weight, that there is a psychological basis for his malfunctioning mechanisms.

Emotional Climate

When economic conditions at home are favorable but the growth lag of children is greater than chance, investigators probe into family histories and other areas of the children's lives to determine the cause. Many of them have found that emotional stress at home or at school is associated with a growth lag (Fried and Mayer, 1948). A favorable emotional climate at home contributes to optimum physical and mental health, whereas adrenalin released into the blood stream in connection with emotional disturbances inhibits digestion and increases the heart rate and blood pressure. If stress is continued for a long period of time during childhood, then obviously growth will be adversely affected.

The prime responsibility for providing a climate in which a child can develop a well-integrated personality in accordance with his individual needs and capacities is, of course, usually delegated to his parents. The nature of the various climates parents create for their children is discussed in Chapter XI.

Population Density

In the twentieth century, when the phrase "population explosion" is exciting a great deal of controversy in newspapers and magazines, a brief resumé of the experiments conducted by Calhoun (1962) on wild and domesticated Norway rats might interest students of child development. The experimenter confined the rats under optimum conditions of food availability, disease control, and spacious quarters. Their social behavior was the only factor allowed to influence their productivity. At the end of twenty-seven months, the population of the wild rats had become stabilized at 150, when 5,000 was the number to be expected under the circumstances. The extreme stress from social interaction suffered by the wild female rats caused such a disruption of their maternal behavior that the infant mortality rate was very high.

The domesticated rats were held under observation for sixteen months, and the details of their modifications in behavior were noted. Under conditions of population density, the rats developed social pathologies, sexual deviations, cannibalism, withdrawal, and other behavior disturbances, whose consequences showed up most readily in the females. Some were unable to carry pregnancy for a full term, others died during or just after delivery of a litter, and a larger group neglected their maternal functions, leaving their pups to die. In some cases, the mortality rate for infants reached eighty per cent, in other cases, ninety-six per cent.

Of those infants who did survive, the eight healthiest were selected for a second series of experiments in which the eight (four males and four females) remained in an environment no longer overcrowded. This second generation produced fewer litters, and not one pup from any litter reached maturity.

The details of Calhoun's experiments give rise to some ironic analogies between the behavior of the overcrowded rodents and that of human beings in modern cities—even in suburbia, and there would seem to be support for the inclusion of population density in a list of factors influencing development. However, as Calhoun admits, before we can draw significant conclusions concerning human behavior in like situations, a refinement of the procedures and interpretations of his studies is necessary.

SUMMARY

Development is a concept that unifies all the anatomic, physiological, and behavioral aspects of an organism into a single, complex entity. It serves to make inseparable such terms as heredity and environment, mind and body, behavior and personality. Development in the human organism is the product of maturation and learning, which are also made inseparable under the concept.

Maturation is the gradual fulfillment of organismic potential and is the result of physiological growth leading to functional changes. Although it can take place without learning, maturation carries its own "built-in" drive, or motivation, to experience. Learning is a modification of the behavior with which an individual responds to his environment and his needs; it cannot take place without maturation. Thus, the two concepts become fused into one: development.

Development is also a process whereby the individual strives for self-fulfillment. It is a rhythmic flow of quantitative and qualitative changes proceeding in specific directions in a predictable sequence. Although enormous variations in rates and patterns of growth are observable among individuals, overall growth rates are relatively constant and the patterns are correlated under normal growth conditions. By applying these laws of development, adults responsible for the guidance and training of children are able to assess the various phases of a child's growth and to provide the proper care, climates, and direction for additional maturity.

There is nothing in the child's heredity or environment that does not in some measure influence his development. Some of the factors that have more immediate effects upon growth and development are the sex of the child; parental and birth conditions; the glands; defective hearing and vision; health; nutrition; emotional climate; and population density. The effects on child development of family, culture, class, and socioeconomic status have been implied, but these are discussed in other chapters of the text.

QUESTIONS AND PROBLEMS

1. Contrast by definition and illustration the meaning of the terms *maturation* and *learning*.
2. What are the educational implications of the principle, *All growth is correlated*? Show how this principle might work in the case of growth in reading ability.
3. Show how the child's growth in ability to walk tends to follow an orderly sequence. How would you account for some children learning to walk earlier than others?
4. Study the height, weight, or some other measurement available on a number of children of the same chronological age. What conclusion do you draw from the differences in their rate of growth? What cautions should be observed in predicting the level of growth or development on the basis of chronological age?
5. Show how individual growth curves may be helpful in appraising the growth of a child. How do these curves differ from average growth curves?
6. What problems sometimes emerge as a result of the differential rate of development of boys and girls?
7. Study the items listed under prenatal and birth conditions. Show how these are frequently important in relation to the development of the infant.
8. Describe the random and uncoordinated movements of the infant. Show how these movements gradually become more specific in nature. How do maturation and experiences interact to produce behavior of a more specific nature?
9. How would you account for the excessive neuroticism and dependency among children afflicted with a rheumatic heart disability? What are some things the home and school can do to lessen the intensity of these characteristics?
10. List school conditions which are sometimes hazardous to the optimum physical growth of children.

SELECTED READINGS

BAYER, LEONA M., and NANCY BAYLEY, *Growth Diagnosis*. Chicago: University of Chicago Press, 1959.

BERNARD, HAROLD W., *Human Development in Western Culture*, 2nd ed. Boston: Allyn and Bacon, 1966. Ch. 3.

BRECKENRIDGE, MARIAN E., and E. LEE VINCENT, *Child Development*, 4th ed. Philadelphia: Saunders, 1960. Chs. 1, 7.

HAWKES, GLENN R., and DAMARIS PEASE, *Behavior and Development from 5 to 12*. Harper, 1962. Ch. 6.

HURLOCK, ELIZABETH B., *Child Development*, 4th ed. McGraw-Hill, 1964. Ch. 4.

MARTIN, WILLIAM E., and CELIA B. STENDLER, *Child Behavior and Development*, rev. ed. Harcourt, Brace, 1959. Chs. 4, 14.

MILLARD, CECIL V., *Child Growth and Development in the Elementary School Years*, rev. ed. Boston: Heath, 1958. Chs. 2, 3.

OLSON, WILLARD C., *Child Development*, 2nd ed. Boston: Heath, 1959. Chs. 2, 14.

THOMPSON, GEORGE G., *Child Psychology*, 2nd ed. Boston: Houghton Mifflin, 1962. Ch. 4.

THOMPSON, HELEN, Physical growth, in *Manual of Child Psychology* (L. Carmichael, ed.), 2nd ed. John Wiley & Sons, 1954. Ch. 5.

WATSON, ROBERT I., *Psychology of the Child*. John Wiley & Sons, 1959. Ch. 3.

REFERENCES

ARLITT, ADA HART, *Psychology of Infancy and Early Childhood*. McGraw-Hill, 1946, p. 379.

BOYD, JULIAN D., The nature of American diet, *Journal of Pediatrics*, 1938, *12*, No. 2.

BOYNTON, PAUL L., and J. C. BOYNTON, *Psychology of Child Development*. Minneapolis: Educational Publishers, 1938, p. 114.

BRUCH, H., and G. TOURAINE, Obesity in childhood: V. The family frame of obese children, *Psychosomatic Medicine*, 1940, *2*, 141–206.

BRUSSEL, JAMES ARNOLD, Epilepsy, in *Collier's Encyclopedia*, 1954, 7, 385.

CALHOUN, JOHN B., Population density and social pathology, *Scientific American* (February 1962), *206*, 139–148.

COURTIS, S. A., Maturation as a factor in diagnosis, in *Educational Diagnosis. Thirty-fourth Yearbook of the National Society for the Study of Education*, 1935, pp. 169–187.

DALTON, M. M., A visual survey of 5000 school children, *Journal of Educational Research*, 1943, *37*, 81–94.

Dental, eye, and preventive medical service, *Public Health Monograph*, No. 16, U. S. Department of Health, Education and Welfare, 1953.

DREIZEN, SAMUEL, CATHERINE CURRIE, ELLIE JO GILLEY, and TOM D. SPIES, The effect of nutritive failure on the growth patterns of white children in Alabama, *Child Development*, 1953, *24*, 189–202.

EPPRIGHT, ERCEL S., and CHARLOTTE RODERUCK, Diet and nutritional status of Iowa school children, *American Journal of Public Health*, 1955, *45*, Pt. 1, 464–471.

FORD, E. H. R., Growth in height of ten siblings, *Human Biology*, 1958, *30*, 107–119.

FRIED, RALPH, and MORRIS F. MAYER, socio-emotional factors accounting for growth failure in children living in an institution, *Journal of Pediatrics*, 1948, *33*, 444–456.

GESELL, ARNOLD, Developmental pediatrics, *Nervous Child*, 1952, *9*, 225–227.

HALE, CREIGHTON J., Changing growth patterns of the American child, *Education*, 1958, *78*, 467–470.

HALL-QUEST, ALFRED LAWRENCE, Genetic psychology, in *Collier's Encyclopedia*, 1957, 8, 611–613.

HARDING, V. S. V., A method of evaluating osseous development from birth to 14 years, *Child Development*, 1952, *23*, 247–271.

HARRIS, J. A., *et al.*, *The Measurement of Man*. Minneapolis: University of Minnesota Press, 1930.

HASHIM, SAMI, and THEODORE B. VAN ITALLIE, see Osmundsen, 1965.

HILGARD, ERNEST R., *Theories of Learning*, 2nd ed. Appleton-Century-Crofts, 1956, p. 3.

HOLLINGWORTH, HARRY L., *Educational Psychology*. D. Appleton-Century, 1933, p. 111.

HURLOCK, ELIZABETH B., *Child Development*, 3rd ed. McGraw-Hill, 1956.

JERSILD, ARTHUR T., *Child Psychology*, 5th ed. Englewood Cliffs, N.J.: Prentice-Hall, 1960.

JOSSELYN, IRENE M., Emotional implications of rheumatic heart disease in children, *American Journal of Orthopsychiatry*, 1949, *19*, 87–100.

KANTROW, R. W., *An Investigation of Conditioned Feeding Responses and Concomitant Adaptive Behavior in Young Infants*. University of Iowa Studies in Child Welfare, 1937, *13*, No. 3.

MCGEOCH, J. A., *The Psychology of Human Learning*. Longmans, Green (now McKay), 1942.

MARQUIS, D. P., Can conditioned responses be established in the newborn infant? *The Journal of Genetic Psychology*, 1931, *39*, 479–492.

MARQUIS, D. P., Learning in the neonate: the modification of behavior under three feeding schedules, *Journal of Experimental Psychology*, 1941, *29*, 263–282.

MASSLER, M., and T. SUHER, Calculation of "normal" weight in children (by means of normograms based on selected anthropometric measurements), *Child Development*, 1951, *22*, 75–94.

MAYER, JEAN, Regulation of food intake and the multiple etiology of obesity, in *Weight Control; A collection of Papers Presented at the Weight Control Colloquium* (Ercel S. Eppright, Pearl Swanson, and Carroll A. Iverson, eds.). Ames, Iowa: The Iowa State College Press, 1955.

MEREDITH, HOWARD V., The rhythm of physical growth, *University of Iowa Studies in Child Welfare*, 1935, *11*, No. 3, p. 112.

MEREDITH, HOWARD V., Physical growth, in *Collier's Encyclopedia*, 1965, *11*, 475.

MEREDITH, HOWARD V., and VIRGINIA B. KNOTT, Illness history and physical growth, *American Journal of Diseases of Children*, 1962, *103*, 146–151.

MILLARD, CECIL V., Further comments on the November issue ["Intelligence in a Changing Universe"], *Educational Method*, 1940, *19*, 445–447.

National Research Council, Food and Nutrition Board, *Survey of the Literature of Dental Caries*. Washington, D.C.: National Academy of Science, 1952.

NEWHAUS, EDMUND C., *A Personality Study of Asthmatic and Cardiac Children*. Ph.D. Dissertation, New York University, 1954, p. 70.

OLSON, WILLARD C., and BYRON O. HUGHES, The concept of organismic age, *Journal of Educational Research*, 1942, *35*, 525–527.

OSMUNDSEN, JOHN A., Tests on Obesity, in *The New York Times* (January 17, 1965), p. 10E.

PALMER, CARROLL E., HENRY KLEIN, and MORTON KRAMER, Studies on dental caries. III. A method of determining post-eruptive tooth age, *Growth*, 1938, 2, 149–158.

PARSONS, CLIFFORD G., The general practitioner and the child with heart disease, *British Medical Journal*, 1954, 2 Pt. 1, 208–212.

RICHARDS, T. W., and HELEN NEWBERY, Studies in fetal behavior: III. Can performance on test items at six months postnatally be predicted on the basis of fetal activity? *Child Development*, 1938, *9*, 79–86.

RUDNICK, DOROTHEA, Growth, in *The Harper Encyclopedia of Science*, 1963, *2*, 532–533.

SCHWARTZ, F. O., Ocular factors in poor readers, *American Journal of Ophthalmology*, 1940, *23*, 535–539.

SMITH, HENRY PETER, *Psychology in Teaching,* 2nd ed. Englewood Cliffs, N.J.: Prentice-Hall, 1962, p. 260.

STEFANIK, P. A., F. P. HEALD, and J. MAYER, Caloric intake in relation to energy output of obese and non-obese adolescent boys, *American Journal of Clinical Nutrition,* 1959, 7, 55–62.

STONE, L. JOSEPH, and JOSEPH CHURCH, *Childhood and Adolescence.* New York: Random House, 1957, p. 35.

STRAYER, LOIS C., Language and growth: the relative efficacy of early and deferred vocabulary training studied by the method of co-twin control, *Genetic Psychology Monographs,* 1930, 8, 209–319.

STUART, HAROLD C., Pediatrics, in *Collier's Encyclopedia,* 1954, 15, 497–501.

STUART, HAROLD C., and HOWARD V. MEREDITH, Use of body measurements in the school health program, *American Journal of Public Health,* 1946, 36, 1365–1386.

TERMAN, LEWIS M., and M. H. ODEN, in *The Gifted Child* (P. Witty, ed.). Boston: Heath, 1951.

THOMPSON, HELEN, Physical growth, in *Manual of Child Psychology* (L. Carmichael, ed.), 2nd ed. John Wiley & Sons, 1954, pp. 292–334.

THORPE, LOUIS P., *Child Psychology and Development,* 3rd ed. The Ronald Press, 1962, p. 322.

TILTON, J. W., An experimental effort to change the achievement test profile, *Journal of Experimental Education,* 1947, 15, 318–323.

TROTTER, MILDRED, Hair, in *Collier's Encyclopedia,* 1954, 9, 473.

TUFT, HAROLD S., quoted in For the forgotten, *Newsweek* (November 28, 1955), pp. 70, 72.

Unpublished data on file, College of Education, University of Georgia, Athens, Georgia.

WARKANY, JOSEF, Dietetic factors in pre-natal development, *Proceedings of the Spring Conference on Nutrition in Relation to Child Development and Behavior of the Child Research Clinic of the Woods School,* Langhorne, Pa., 1948, pp. 26–30.

WEISS, JEROME, quoted in Keep up with medicine, *Good Housekeeping* (February 1962), p. 28.

F I V E

The Development
of Motor Abilities

A child's motor development—the development of his strength, coordination, speed, and precision in the use of his arms, legs, and all the body muscles—has been called a "handmaiden" of mental development. The child explores and experiments with his environment, gratifies much of his intellectual curiosity, and satisfies his needs by way of motor activities. With growth and learning, new skills are acquired, furnishing opportunities to develop strength in skeletal muscles and increase organic development—power and endurance in heart, lungs, organs of digestion and elimination, etc.—which is essential to good health. Motor behavior also serves as a vehicle for a large proportion of the child's social contacts and his learning to cooperate with others. It strengthens his ability to think, interpret, solve problems, and make quick decisions. And, further, motor development has an important bearing on a child's emotional behavior because his strength, speed, coordination, and skill very often determine whether he will succeed or fail, whether he will be thwarted and angry, threatened and afraid, or self-confident and eager for challenges. The quality of those motor characteristics determines the child's ability to engage in team sports, wherein the more powerful emotions of joy, fear, and anger are given expression in acceptable forms and under natural controls such as special techniques, rules, traditions, and game officials, not to mention the control exercised by the individual as he moves toward growth in good sportsmanship.

GROWTH IN GENERAL BODY CONTROL

Every motor skill that a child is required to learn is dependent upon two major developmental processes—the sequence of events leading to locomotion and the one leading to prehension, or manipulation with the fingers. Both sets of motor activities are dependent upon coordination of various parts of the body with the eyes and ears. That is, eye-hand coordination is necessary to prehension; eye-ear-cerebellum coordination (balance) is a primary component of walking; eye-hand-mouth coordination is a prerequisite to self-feeding (and exploring).

In keeping with the principles of development, growth in motor abilities begins with control of the head and neck and works downward, and proceeds from the central portions of the body outward. Aldrich and Norval (1946) observed an unselected group of 213 infants in respect to twelve aspects of neuromuscular growth and presented a graph of average ages for the ap-

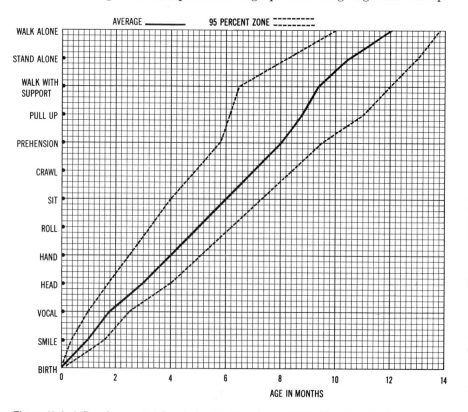

Figure V–1. A Developmental Graph for the First Year of Life Showing the Average Age for the Achievements Selected and the Zone in Which 95 Per Cent of the Infants' Developmental Graphs Fell (Aldrich and Norval, 1946, p. 306)

pearance of the developmental steps (Figure V–1). The timing of the sequence, of course, varies from child to child.

The locomotion and prehension phases of development are based primarily on a trial and error method in the early stages of learning. The neonate, whose movements are random and uncoordinated, stretches, kicks his legs, and waves his arms—in short, moves his entire body. After three months of such generalized action, the infant begins to isolate the movements that produce results for him and he learns to manage his body. Also, at this time his nerves acquire their fatty (myelin) sheath, enabling some of the elementary reflexes with which the child is born to be supplanted by responses of a higher order. Not until after myelinization, for example, is the child able to sit for very short periods, with support. Once that is accomplished, he improves rapidly in the length of time he can maintain an unsupported sitting posture.

Locomotion

Cinema-analysis records of creeping and stair climbing reveal the appearance of specific behavior patterns in a sequential order (Gesell and Halverson, 1942), and in Figure V–2 McGraw (1935) shows the early developmental phases leading to creeping and crawling. In the case of stair climbing, a single pattern was observed in eleven of the twelve cases studied and has been described by Ames (1939, p. 315) as follows:

> . . . It starts with placement of the left foot on the first stair. The left hand is then placed on the second stair, and immediately afterward, the right foot on the first stair. There is a short pause, then right hand moves to the third stair and left foot to the second. After another short pause, the left hand and right foot move up again. And so it goes.

And so goes the course of development toward locomotion, through stages of creeping, crawling, pulling to an erect position, learning how to let go, hitching on foot from one piece of furniture to another, standing without support, and then walking. None of these stages appear full blown. Not only is each an outgrowth of a former one, but also several stages are used simultaneously, or alternately, depending upon the goal and the motivation toward that goal. Many parents have observed the child who has successfully taken his first steps revert to creeping (often on hands and feet rather than on hands and knees) when he is anxious to obtain an interesting bauble that has crossed his vision. And conversely, when his practice motivation is high, he will use the slower form of locomotion, walking, through repeated falls and failures to obtain an object of only passing interest.

As soon as the child learns to walk he begins incorporating the elements of walking into larger and more complex patterns of motor behavior, and especially does he practice refinements on the basic skill. Some ex-

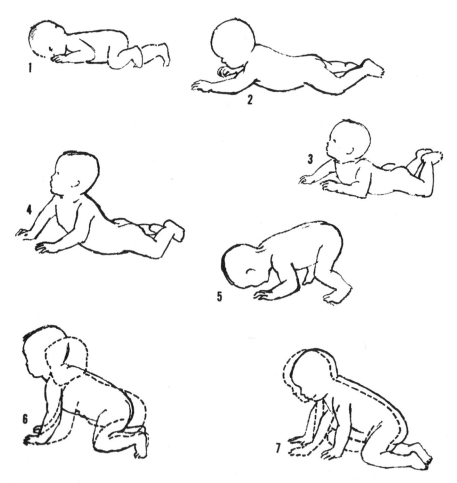

Figure V–2. Postural Phases in Development of Crawling and Creeping. 1. Newborn crawling movements. 2. Less activity in lower extremities; begins to hold head up. 3. Increased control over movements of head and shoulder girdle. 4. Marked development in upper part of body; pelvis rests on the surface. 5. Conflict in action of pelvic and shoulder regions; when pelvis is raised, head and shoulders are lowered. 6. Rocking movements; maintains abdomen above surface. 7. Associated creeping movements (McGraw, 1935, p. 70)

amples may be observed in the schedule of the *California Infant Scale of Motor Development,* based on the performance of a somewhat selected group of approximately fifty children (Bayley, 1935).*

* Such a table of averages as the one which follows should not be permitted to dull the reader's appreciation of the very wide differences in normal development. Some *normal* children will not walk at all at 16.9 months, or even at 20.3 months.

16.9 months	Walks backward
20.3 months	Walks upstairs with help
24.3 months	Walks upstairs alone
30.1 months	Walks on tiptoe
32.1 months	Jumps from chair
39.7 months	Distance jump, 36 to 60 cm.
49.3 months	Hopping on one foot 2 or 3 hops

With maturation and practice, the child develops a smoother gait of walking and better balance, which is so immature at the early stages of walking that the child cannot turn quickly in any direction. Later, he will walk up and down inclined boards, he will "dance," and he will twirl until he makes himself dizzy. Still later, he will hop, skip, and gallop, although these activities take several years to perfect. During this time—after walking has been fairly well established, the child becomes interested in other forms of locomotion, such as kiddie cars, wagons, scooters, fire engines with pedals, tricycles, and bicycles. And again, once the skill of operating them is mastered, the child elaborates on the skill and practices backing up, turning around, surmounting or circumventing obstacles, pulling other vehicles, forming "trains," and so forth.

The child develops as a unified whole. The hands and arms, head, and other parts of the body are involved in the act of walking.

Prehension

At birth, the infant is unable to use his fingers as separate units because they are under the control of cortical regions of the brain, which are as yet undeveloped. However, the hand is already an effective conductor of sensations and is "a most important avenue for the infant's first impressions of the world about him" (Halverson, 1943). Indirectly, the hand—because of its sensitivity—is probably responsible for a large part of the motivation with which the infant exercises his upper-arm muscles. After he has thoroughly examined his fingers and toes, he reaches for an object (with both arms) in order to touch, taste, and otherwise explore the unique properties of something outside his own body, and thus he begins to differentiate between himself and the external environment.

The ultimate development of prehension, then, is important to the child's growth in intellect as well as to his growth in motor abilities, and the parent who understands the sequence by which it is reached is able to provide the child with playthings appropriate to his level of achievement and for the encouragement of further development.

The subjects of an investigation by Halverson (1931) ranged in age from sixteen to fifty-two weeks, and through photographic records the investigator was able to reach the following conclusions regarding the infants' behavior in relation to a one-inch red cube:

1. At sixteen weeks no infants are likely to touch the cube. Accuracy in reaching improves gradually and steadily from sixteen to fifty-two weeks, the distinguishing differences between the older infants being the time actually required to grasp the cube, amount of cube displacement, number of adjustments necessary for a firm grasp, and the type of grasp.

2. The critical age in infant prehension is twenty-eight weeks. At this age they have the longest single regard and the greatest total duration of regard for the cube. The hand at this time begins to free itself from forearm control in reaching for objects. Instead of directing the whole hand toward the cube, the infant passes only the index and medius fingers over it. Finger manipulation is beginning to replace the pawlike behavior of the hand, and active thumb opposition is beginning to replace the palm grip.

3. Prior to the age of twenty-eight weeks, the aid of the second hand is required in grasping. The most common forms of lifting the cube from the table are (a) a purely elbow flexion, and (b) a hand-elbow action, in which the hand, after grasping the cube, rotates on the edge of the little finger before elbow flexion begins.

4. The development of reaching and grasping follows the course of maturation from the larger to the finer muscles. The early approach patterns

consist largely of crude shoulder and elbow movements, illustrating the principle of development from the general to the specific.

5. The increase in the number of higher types of grasp and in the amount and variety of finger manipulations of the cube by infants from sixteen to fifty-two weeks of age are due in part to the skeletal development of the fingers, in part to neuromuscular maturation, in part to training and practice, and in part to increase in cutaneous sensibility of the fingertips.

By the end of the first year, then, a child is able to use his finger and thumb in pincer movements, and within a few months he will manage to propel himself from place to place with amazing rapidity. At this point in his development of motor control, the toddler has a strong motivation to practice his newly acquired abilities to move and to manipulate, along with an intense curiosity about his environment. With frenetic activity, he runs from one room to another, from his yard into streets and other yards; he pokes, prods, pulls, twists whatever he encounters; and because his attention span is very short he searches persistently for new items and new areas to analyze.* Danger has little meaning for him, and he comes into repeated conflict with danger-conscious parents who frustrate his curiosity. The parents themselves find it increasingly discouraging to protect their bundle of human energy from serious harm and yet continue to provide him with opportunities to improve his motor skills and his intelligence. The wise and knowledgeable adult can make use of the child's impulse to manipulate by creating "busy work" for him, by allowing the young child to draw with crayons, string beads or buttons, construct something with blocks, cut paper with blunt scissors, or punch, pinch, poke, and prod dough, clay, or Plasticene. As the young child grows older, he is able to occupy himself at creative tasks for longer periods of time, and usually to everyone's benefit, especially his own. Ashton-Warner (1963), who has taught for more than two decades among the Maori and white children in New Zealand, believes that all children have only two sides to their nature—the constructive and the destructive; and she insists that to the extent a teacher encourages the one, she diverts energy from the other.

* Again we call the reader's attention to the fact that these are generalized statements. The attention spans of children are as subject to wide variations as any other facet of personality. Not only do some children, especially the more placid ones, remain for hours at a task—such as fitting pots and pans together; but also an extremely active, curious child may at times become so interested in a project that he, too, will spend long periods of time completely absorbed. The appeal of sand and water, used separately or together, does not favor any particular constitutional type. Universally, children of all ages find many hours of satisfaction in digging, pouring, building, trampling or wading—at a beach or in a backyard sandbox. Possibly because of the simplicity and availability of these two media, many parents fail to recognize them as valuable aids to a child's creative expression and gross motor coordination, not to mention the soothing effect they have upon his turbulent spirit and his parents' ever-watchfulness.

GROWTH IN MOTOR ABILITY

Beyond the early years, most of the differences found among children when learning complex motor skills—especially the differences in higher beginning success—result from variations in experiences and motivation (Millard, 1958). Where gross motor skills involving the large muscles are concerned, the differences in strength observed at succeeding age levels give a significant advantage to older children, who also have a greater ability to sustain attention and to follow directions and rules.

Similarly, as the body develops and changes, new motor learnings are needed. With the growth of additional wrist bones, an increase in freedom at the knees and ankles, and changes in the amount and distribution of weight, new adjustments are necessary in maintaining balance and in the manner of performing certain activities. Furthermore, society expects each age level to acquire motor abilities that are different in kind and degree.

One might theorize, then, that growth in motor ability occurs with age. The theory is substantiated by Sloan (1955), who developed and standardized the *Lincoln-Oseretsky Motor Development Scale*, consisting of thirty-six items, in order to furnish careful data about motor development of boys and girls at the different age levels.* Normative data for the scale were secured from administering the test to 380 children between the ages of six and fourteen years. The mean scores for boys and girls at different ages are shown in Table V–1.

These norms should not, of course, be looked upon as being applicable to all groups of boys and girls. Teachers and parents may expect exceptions

Table V–1 Mean Scores of Boys and Girls on the *Lincoln-Oseretsky Motor Development Scale* (After Sloan, 1955, p. 241)

	Males			Females	
Age [1]	Mean	SD		Mean	SD
6	32.53	16.12		33.33	14.55
7	56.74	15.64		49.95	15.18
8	65.39	15.71		64.85	17.67
9	81.39	15.07		67.74	16.91
10	89.05	20.69		84.66	18.47
11	106.48	17.47		98.77	19.36
12	112.83	21.30		114.10	18.69
13	122.63	11.05		127.81	17.07
14	130.81	11.35		130.83	8.67

* This scale is available from C. H. Stoelting Co., 424 N. Huron Ave., Chicago, Illinois.

[1] Age 6 means 5 years 6 months to 6 years 5 months.

to any general rule. Some children will have such highly individual growth patterns that they will, at all ages, be unable to compete with their age-mates. Clumsy, inept children should not be pushed into games or instructional activities which require the mastery of complex motor skills: they should be given training in more simple and direct motor activities.

The question may be raised, Are there any combinations of physical and motor traits that will differentiate slow and fast learners of motor skills? Smith (1956) attempted to answer that question. One hundred boys and girls ranging in age from six to nine years were given tests designed to measure motor ability, motor educability, dynamic balance, static balance, speed, flexibility, strength, and kinesthesis, after being allowed to practice a skill and to learn it without individual guidance. Statistical analysis of the results indicated that there are physical and motor measures that differentiate significantly between the fast learners and the slow. Strength of grip, for instance, was the test which best differentiates the two learning groups among girls. The balance test was the best indicator for boys.

LEARNING MOTOR SKILLS

Through the influence of maturation, the child is brought into the best position to learn, and through his motor learning experiences, properly timed with maturation, he is able to achieve the optimum degree of efficiency in motor skills. This achievement, aside from illustrating the interrelationship of maturation and learning, presents a graphic example of the developmental principles of progression from simple to complex and from general to specific. However, children who receive training in the acquisition of motor skills such as running, jumping, throwing, and catching will be superior to those who receive no training (Seils, 1951).

In many performances children will concentrate for a time on establishing a simple level of skills and then move on to a higher level. At various stages in their progress, they will combine the new skills with others that at an earlier time were practiced independently. When mastery of the new, higher skill is achieved, the different operations involved may be subordinated to the more complex task. Development proceeds from whole to part and from parts to larger wholes, as the act of running is combined with the art of catching when a child playing softball makes a "running catch."

Many motor tasks require not only complex motor coordinations but also increased attention span or concentrated mental processes—requirements which increase the learning difficulty. In other words, movement from simple to complex is not limited to motor skills alone. Writing as a motor skill also involves spelling, grammar, and other intricate mental processes in addition to the ability to manipulate the finer muscles of the arm, hand, wrist, and fingers. The game of tennis requires the motor skills of running forward and backward, leaping, stopping short, twisting the body, shoulders, arms, wrists, and hands, aiming, striking, grasping with fingers, coordination of eyes, hands, arms, and legs—all combined with a knowledge of the rules of the game, the ability to make quick decisions, and cooperation with other members of the team. Metcalf (1954, p. 33), incidentally, asserts that "the greater the variety of basic natural skills employed in a single game, the greater the resulting satisfaction and educational value of that game or sport."

Learning Motor Skills during Early Childhood

Before attending kindergarten, most youngsters have developed varying abilities in running, skipping, hopping, and climbing. Gutteridge (1939) made a study of nearly two thousand children between the ages of two and seven. He found that in the early stages of climbing stairs, low inclined planks, packing boxes, jungle gyms, and so on, going up was much easier than coming down. By the age of three, however, about fifty per cent of the youngsters were proficient in both skills. Jumping, hopping, and skipping were also learned during the preschool years, if opportunity to practice was provided. Forty-two per cent of the three-year-olds were rated efficient at jumping, whereas the percentage given a similar rating increased to seventy-two per cent for those who were four and a half and eighty-one per cent for those who were five. The ability to hop on one foot was mastered by the majority of children before the age of six. Skill in skipping developed more slowly. A few were able to skip at four. However, most of the youngsters were between six and seven years of age before they learned the technique.

Gutteridge also reported that children practiced ball throwing from the age of two but that it was not until after the age of four that any (twenty per cent) attained any measure of proficiency. By the end of the fifth year, eighty-five per cent were rated as being able to throw well. Bouncing a ball was more difficult. Of the five-year-olds, only forty-five per cent were proficient in this skill, and of the six-and-a-half-year-olds, only sixty-one per cent.

Learning Motor Skills during the Elementary-School Years

Between the ages of six and twelve, the majority of youngsters continue to enjoy and practice refinements on basic motor skills. During their play hours they run, chase, jump rope, hike, climb trees, play hopscotch, roller skate, ride bicycles, swim, dive, and so on. Nevertheless, a large portion of their daily routine is now taken up with motor skills of a more complex nature.

Many adults fail to recognize that almost every academic skill which the elementary-school child must master involves certain motor tasks. Reading requires eye-movement control, holding books, turning pages, etc. Handwriting and drawing require manipulative skills, arm movements, and hand-eye coordination. One of the major reasons why children with physical disabilities so often need special attention in their school work is a lack of adequate motor development.

Ability to manipulate pencils, scissors, and other such implements is achieved by many youngsters before they enter kindergarten. However, at this age they are still concerned primarily with large-muscle activities. Fine sewing, detailed drawings, and the reading of small print should not be encouraged until the child reaches the age of eight or ten (Hildreth, 1950). That does not mean, of course, that opportunities to write, paint, and enjoy books should be limited in the earliest grades. If large pieces of paper, heavy leaded pencils, and books with clear pictures and large print are used, boys and girls will be given the preliminary help they need to develop control of the smaller muscles.

Today the majority of schools teach manuscript writing in the primary grades. Since all letters in manuscripts are composed of straight lines, circles or parts of circles, inability to make and to read fine detail does not handicap children in their learning efforts. Through kindergarten experiences that involve eye-hand coordinations, the development of certain sensorimotor abilities is aided and interest in writing is often aroused. If nothing else, most children are interested in writing their own names, and oftentimes a "letter to Santa Claus" becomes an absorbing project. It is this gradual development of fine skills, attitudes, and interests that leads to a readiness for learning to write—and read.

From seven to nine. The child from seven to nine is challenged by activities requiring speed and accuracy. Movements have become more accurate because his sense of direction is much improved and eye-hand coordinations are developing rapidly. The sense of equilibrium, which is still poorly developed in the average four- and five-year-olds, is improving as a result of maturation and the practice gained in skipping rope, tumbling, skating, bicycling, and spontaneous dancing.

The activities of this age group are extremely diverse, although they revolve primarily around uses of the body rather than around mental exercises. The children display a great deal of creativeness in their behavior as they experiment with motor activities of a complex nature and with projects requiring the use of smaller muscles. They use hammers, nails, and saws; paints, paper, and brushes; clay, papier-mâché, and plaster of Paris; mud, wet sand, and snow, among many other media used in the fine and practical arts. Any school program which provides and encourages the use of such materials goes a long way toward enhancing the develop-

Dancing helps a child to develop graceful coordination and equilibrium.

ment of individuality, which is so often harmed at this stage by the introduction of competition between children and an insistence upon group
conformity.

From ten to twelve. Skill in the use of small muscles develops rapidly
under the stimulus of creative activities. However, ten- and eleven-year-olds
are still at a distinct disadvantage in speed writing and in the delicate and
rapid fingering necessary to play some musical instruments or to use certain
tools. At this age, steadiness and strength (particularly among boys) takes
on an added importance. With this added maturity and experience, exact
coordination between the two hands, the feet, the sense organs, and the
brain is more easily accomplished. Jumping rope, foot races, use of parallel
bars, and games with specific rules are useful for that purpose. Baseball
becomes extremely interesting to boys, as though they sensed its developmental value. Nor is there any physical reason why girls too cannot enter
into this kind of activity. In terms of better coordination and physical fitness, good results have been obtained by girls who have engaged in soft-

Soviet boys build a house.

ball. On the other hand, participation in body-contact sports such as football, wrestling, and field hockey is seriously questioned by the American Academy of Pediatrics on the basis of the young child's susceptibility to bone and joint injury. The Academy likewise cautions against sports of a highly competitive nature, which lead to excessive strain on children twelve years of age or under.

Although competition furnishes badly needed motivation to exercise and develop good coordination and physical fitness, it frequently militates against the youngster with an immature physique. Because of the wide variations in physiological maturity and strength among children in this age bracket, a boy of slight build may be pitted against and subsequently injured by a nearly mature age-mate, particularly in the nonselective "sandlot" competitions; or he may receive a severe emotional bruising by being consistently eliminated from the more selective teams made up by such adult supervisors as the high-school gym teacher or the Little League coach.

Many boys at this age feel inadequate, unpopular, and "sissified" if they are unable to join in team sports because they lack coordination, skill, or muscular maturity. And, in truth, if the majority of a youngster's friends consider proficiency in sports a criterion for social acceptance, the clumsy, inept, immature child will feel isolated from the group; and unless he has strong inner resources or the ability and opportunity to make friends with other similiarly "handicapped" children, his ego concept may suffer considerable damage. (See pp. 142–43.)

The Value of Training

Whereas the simple skills develop largely as a result of maturation and general practice, the more complex ones require a longer period for full maturation, and they benefit from early, directed training. Handwriting, for instance, is a relatively complex skill that begins to develop when the child is able to hold a crayon or pencil and proceeds slowly until physical maturity is reached. Proficiency in handwriting results in large part from learning.

When a task is simple, little, if any, differences appear as a result of directed training. Mattson (1933), who analyzed the effects of training on maze threading, found that, although the performance of the trained group was better than that of the untrained group in threading a complicated maze pattern, the more the pattern increased in complexity, the more significant became the superiority of the trained group.

From the developmental point of view, the correct starting of motor skills is very important. Investigators have found that although learning cannot transcend maturation there is a time range beyond which the child will be handicapped by not acquiring certain motor skills if he is sufficiently mature to learn them. This is perhaps more true of the skills that involve finer coordinations of developing muscles than of those dependent upon large muscular movements (Jones, 1939).

Using twin boys, Johnny and Jimmy, as subjects, McGraw (1935, 1939), studied the effects of delay over a relatively long period of time. Johnny, the experimental twin, was given an opportunity to practice certain motor activities which he was capable of learning. Jimmy, the control twin, was given no special practice but was given certain motor tests at varying intervals. This situation existed from the time the subjects were twenty-one days old until they were twenty-two months old. The results showed that Johnny made phenomenal progress in learning to roller skate when he was a little more than one year old and learned to propel a tricycle several months later—one or two years before the average child even makes the attempt! McGraw concluded that those activities which a child must acquire as part of our way of life, such as sitting, walking, and the like, are the least affected by directed practice, or training; whereas, development of skills which an individual may or may not use in our culture, such as roller skating and tricycle riding, is considerably accelerated by special attention. In other words, the exercise of a developing function is inherent in the process of growth and excessive encouragement of the natural skills is fruitless, even harmful; yet, if ample opportunity and direction is given to the practice of more complex, culturally prescribed skills *at the proper time*, specific achievements can be advanced beyond the level normally expected of children and adults. Once again we can suggest that an individual's interest is an excellent indication of proper timing. In the case of Johnny, who was taught and encouraged to practice feats of balance and propulsion unusual for his age, the investigator must have been acutely aware of the child's intense interest in all kinds of refinements on the art of locomotion.

MOTOR GROWTH AND INTERRELATIONSHIPS

Correlation studies involving many kinds of performances have been conducted in order to determine whether motor ability is general or specific in nature. The results vary. McCaskill and Wellman (1938), who used preschool children as subjects, offer evidence that a close relationship does exist between the different motor abilities and that it appears at an early age. Ninety-eight children from two to six years of age were given tests involving ascending and descending ladders and steps, hopping, skipping, jumping, balancing on a path and a circle, and throwing, catching, and bouncing balls. The scores for the different activities were combined into common categories as shown in Table V-2. Correlations obtained between

Table V–2   Correlations Between Scores on Various Motor Achievements of Preschool Children (McCaskill and Wellman, 1938, p. 143) *

Measures Correlated	Boys		Girls	
	Num-ber	Corre-lation	Num-ber	Corre-lation
Total Group				
Steps and ladders with ball activities	50	.54 ± .10	48	.72 ± .06
Steps and ladders with hopping, skipping, etc.	50	.69 ± .07	48	.79 ± .05
Ball activities with hopping, skipping, etc.	50	.69 ± .07	48	.47 ± .06
Younger Group (26 to 53 months)				
Steps and ladders with ball activities	16	.40 ± .21	29	.66 ± .10
Steps and ladders with hopping, skipping, etc.	16	.72 ± .12	29	.72 ± .09
Ball activities with hopping, skipping, etc.	16	.69 ± .13	29	.75 ± .08

* Reprinted by permission of the Society for Research in Child Development and the author.

these categories were positive and statistically significant, indicating an interrelationship of these abilities even at such an early age.

Hartman (1934) did not support the notion that motor ability is general in nature. The following motor tests were administered to fifty-six children between the ages of four and six and a half: hurdle jump, jump-and-reach, standing broad jump, baseball throw, and the thirty-five-yard dash. Correlations between scores on the five tests ranged from .36 to .56 and suggest that although the tests have something in common, different motor abilities depend upon different combinations of muscular coordination.

Carpenter (1940) supports the results reported by Hartman. Children enrolled in grades one through three were tested by means of a number of measures such as right-hand and left-hand grip, ball-throwing, hopping, jumping, and running. She obtained correlations ranging from −.10 to .77, although most of them were between .20 and .50, indicating a low but positive relationship between the different motor skills possessed by elementary-school children.

The lack of a close relationship among the motor abilities probably indicates that they are specific in nature with perhaps certain common factors appearing in some motor skills. Also, size of limbs, weight in relation to height, and similar physical characteristics influence children's achievement on a number of motor tasks. Bayley (1935) points out that there seems to be a closer relation between motor abilities in infancy and early childhood than during a later period of childhood—when individual physical differences are more exaggerated. Those differences, therefore, as well as amounts of motivation and experiences, must be taken into consideration when one attempts to study and evaluate a child's motor ability. On any performance test of motor skills, certain children should be expected to be below average and some to be above average, a good enough reason for instituting learning programs that will enable all children to develop their particular motor aptitudes.

Motor Abilities and Physical Growth

Conflicting testimony is also offered by several investigators concerned with the correlations between motor abilities and measurements of physical growth, although the bulk of the studies support the theory that positive, if low, correlations do exist. An analysis of data presented by Seils (1951) shows that the mean performance of both boys and girls becomes higher at each grade level; however, correlations between gross motor skill performances and height and weight are low. A more positive, significant correlation was to be found between gross motor performance and skeletal maturity.

Latchaw (1954) selected tests to measure the basic skills of running, jumping, throwing and catching, striking, and kicking and administered them to a group of sixty-seven boys and girls enrolled in the fourth, fifth, and sixth grades. The results tended to corroborate those of Seils, showing a relatively low relationship between height and weight and performance as measured by the tests.

A different conclusion was reached by Govatos (1959), who found significant correlations between motor skills and the various aspects of growth, tabulated in Table V-3. The lowest correlations were found in connection with weight and reading, a fact to be expected since each is affected by somewhat extraneous forces or conditions.

Motor Ability and Mental Capacity

Despite popular opinion and the developmental principle of correlative growth, there is no apparent relationship between intelligence and motor growth except on the lower end of the intelligence scales. There does appear to be a relationship, albeit a low one, between mental retardation and retarded motor development. Francis and Rarick (1959) gave a battery of eleven gross motor tests to 284 mentally retarded boys and girls, and observations were made to determine the age and sex trends for each skill tested. The extent of retardation was determined by comparing the scores

Table V-3   Correlations Between Motor Skills and Various Aspects of Growth in Elementary School Boys and Girls (Govatos, 1959, p. 336)*

Motor Skills		Aspects of Growth						
		Height	Weight	Grip	Carpal	Dental	Reading	Mental
Jump and	B	.55	.42	.63	.50	.63	.45	.66
Reach	G	.67	.53	.66	.70	.69	.54	.51
Standing	B	.60	.44	.71	.55	.70	.54	.71
Broad Jump	G	.62	.51	.63	.69	.72	.65	.65
Soccer Kick	B	.70	.68	.75	.70	.80	.61	.66
for Distance	G	.73	.64	.71	.78	.77	.63	.66
Twenty-five-	B	.53	.41	.59	.46	.57	.38	.61
yard Dash	G	.59	.41	.52	.62	.63	.50	.51
Ball Throw	B	.70	.64	.84	.66	.71	.55	.65
for Distance	G	.68	.60	.71	.77	.77	.59	.60
(Overhand)								
Ball Throw	B	.67	.63	.77	.63	.70	.55	.64
for Distance	G	.79	.68	.75	.77	.80	.57	.64
(Underhand)								
Ball Throw	B	.60	.54	.63	.47	.56	.40	.53
for Accuracy	G	.48	.35	.46	.62	.51	.45	.46
(Overhand)								
Ball Throw	B	.57	.54	.58	.60	.61	.42	.55
for Accuracy	G	.58	.52	.67	.63	.65	.53	.56
(Underhand)								

* Reprinted by permission of the Society for Research in Child Development and the author.

with those obtained by Carpenter (1940) and McCloy (1938) on normal subjects. The age trends in motor performance for each sex followed approximately the same pattern as those for normal children—but, at a lower level for each age.

This study was supported in 1951 by Sloan, who also found that mental deficients exhibited poor motor coordination.

Past generations once feared that a child who did not walk until he was nearly two years old would prove to be feebleminded. Modern scientific studies and their recognition of wide variations in individual growth patterns have shown that such a child may even be superior in intelligence. Likewise, Dennis (1943) has dispelled another myth by reporting that, as a group, gifted children do not begin to walk earlier than average or below-average youngsters.

Motor Abilities and Social Maturity

Rarick and McKee (1949), working among third-grade children, showed those superior in motor proficiency to be active, calm, popular, resourceful, and cooperative; those with inferior motor abilities were inclined to be shy, withdrawing, and tense. (In the 1951 Sloan study just mentioned, the investigator found that the mental deficients who were poor in motor coordination were also inferior in social maturity.)

Wherever cultural conditions combine to make motor proficiency a necessary characteristic for social adaptability, the cyclical interactions of ego concept, social adjustments, and emotional adjustments create a situation in which the child with inferior motor abilities is decidedly handicapped in attaining social maturity. Unless he can be guided by understanding teachers and acceptant parents into a realization of other special abilities and into successes in less physically demanding areas, his self-concept—particularly as it relates to maleness—may be negatively altered. However, we must emphasize the importance of those cultural aspects. Motor skills become important to a child only if his society—family, peers, and community—regards them as such. The American community as a whole places a rather high value on athletic ability, and the average American boy selects many of his heroes from the sporting world. Oftentimes, when an American child is driven by high parental expectations, or other forms of parental rejection, to crave acceptance from his peers, he experiences disappointments and less subtle emotional crises if the peer group expects him to be a skilled athlete.

But generally all these conditions must combine before serious maladjustment occurs. The child who is unconditionally accepted by his family, regardless of his physical makeup, has a comparatively smooth path, if only because his need for acceptance outside his family is not so acute and thus his motivation to conform to peer-group standards is not so intense (Schonfeld, 1964).

FACTORS INFLUENCING MOTOR DEVELOPMENT

Physical Fitness

Espenschade (1958), using fourth-grade pupils as subjects, found a positive correlation between scores on the *Kraus-Weber Test of Muscular Fitness,* which tests strength and flexibility, and the quality of performances of boys in running, jumping, throwing, and sit-ups. For girls, the relationship was less significant, which may be accounted for by the fact that fourth-grade girls do not exert themselves in physical activities as much as the boys do.

Ikeda (1961) designed a study to compare the physical fitness of children (ages nine to twelve) in Iowa with those in Tokyo. Over seven hundred children were tested. In anthropometric measurements, the Iowa girls and boys were taller, heavier, and had longer legs; yet, the Japanese groups exceeded the Iowa groups in all physical fitness tests but one—sit-ups. A summary of findings from a checklist of activities of the groups showed that the Tokyo children pursued various physical activities more than the Iowa children, although the physical education classes in Tokyo were larger and had less desirable facilities. Such findings, combined with other studies which compare American children unfavorably with European children, have led writers to suggest that American children spend altogether too little time in exercise and too much time sitting—at school, at home reading or watching television, in automobiles.

Sex Differences

Table V-4 presents the results of various tests administered to three hundred children enrolled in public schools and shows that, in general, boys were superior to girls except for the fifty-foot hop. The McCaskill and Wellman study previously mentioned made further differentiations and showed sex differences in favor of boys for steps, ladders, and ball activities and in favor of girls for hopping and skipping. A study by Jokl and Cluver (1941) showed that both boys and girls improved in efficiency up to the age of thirteen, after which the boys continued to improve but the girls manifested a considerable loss, not only in efficiency as reflected in their running time, but also in their physical condition as revealed by their pulse rate, respiration, and fatigue.

Table V–4   Mean Scores Obtained by Five-, Six-, and Seven-Year-Old Boys and Girls in Certain Motor Performances (Jenkins, 1930)

	Five-Year-Olds		Six-Year-Olds		Seven-Year-Olds	
	Boys	Girls	Boys	Girls	Boys	Girls
N =	50	50	50	50	50	50
Running Broad Jump (Distance in inches)	34.40	28.60	45.20	40.00	58.80	50.80
Standing Broad Jump (Distance in inches)	33.70	31.60	39.30	38.00	42.20	41.00
Jump and Reach (Vertical distance in inches)	2.52	2.22	4.02	3.48	4.98	4.28
Thirty-five-yard Dash (Time in seconds)	9.30	9.70	8.52	8.84	7.92	8.02
Fifty-foot Hop Without Error (Time in seconds)	10.82	10.33	9.20	8.89	8.81	7.59
Ball Throw (Distance in feet)	23.60	14.50	32.80	17.80	41.40	24.40
Baseball Throw at 10-foot Distant Target (Error in inches)	8.87	16.90	5.40	13.17	4.20	8.50

These apparent sex differences are explainable on the basis of culturally encouraged habits and practices. At a fairly early age, girls show an increased interest in social activities and a lack of interest in athletics and other muscle- and endurance-building activities. Even at the kindergarten level, teachers will, for instance, forbid a girl to climb on the monkey bars unless she adequately covers her underwear with slacks or shorts, and yet, in most schools, girls are customarily required to wear dresses, not play clothes. Throughout the elementary grades, girls are encouraged to enter "genteel" sports that have a minimum of rough and tumble activity and a maximum of ladylike modesty. Thus, in spite of the results of scientific studies relating to the development needs of boys and girls, many schools hold to conventional ideas about what a boy or girl should do, using policies and developing learning programs that aggravate sex differences rather than capitalize on abilities that both boys and girls have in common. It is a peculiarly inconsistent form of segregation, with the two sexes receiving academic instruction together but being guided into playing separate, non-coeducational games.

Freedom to Practice

At all age levels, motor development is influenced by opportunity to practice and by the amount and quality of the space available for that practice. Within reasonable limits, restrictions and constrictions are decidedly not beneficial to a child's development of motor skills, nor to his intellect or emotional well-being. Attention to adequate clothing is important: many parents insist upon overburdening children with clothes that are too heavy, too warm, too confining, forgetting that a healthy, well-fed child needs less clothing than an adult (Spock, 1957). The heavily bundled youngster, overheated before he begins to play, uses more energy for less exercise, becomes more heated as a result.

Motivation

Illness robs a child of interest, as well as endurance and the opportunity to practice his motor activities. So do attitudes of overprotectiveness on the part of his parents and their subservience to his wishes. Whether for lack of patience or "time" or because of a misguided sense of responsibility, the parent who anticipates the child's every action removes many of the goals or objects for which he strives. If he is anxious to obtain the ball he sees across the room and the alert parent fetches it for him, the infant will not exercise his creeping and crawling, reaching and grasping abilities. Likewise, the parent who persists in tying a child's shoelace far beyond the age when he should be gaining proficiency in the task actively encourages his dependency and retards both his motor and emotional development.

Emotional Factors

The guidance of the infant is essential for his well-being, and his explorations of the things in his environment are necessary for his development. Frequently, these turn out to be opposing conditions which haunt the conscientious parent and create a dilemma (Erikson, 1951). The "Golden Mean" for action is difficult to determine. Parental overanxiety lest a child should injure or endanger himself yields restrictions on his exploratory and manipulatory actions, as well as transmitting a like sense of anxiety to the child. Fear produces timidity, a lack of courage and daring, that places heavy modifications on a child's interest and practice. On the other hand, anxiety, along with conflict and frustration, can be fostered in a child by overenthusiastic parents who push him into accomplishing what he is not ready to attempt.

An adequate knowledge of the sequence of motor growth can help adults to make inroads in the dilemma. Coupled with an acceptance of a child's individuality, whether his attainments are achieved rapidly or slowly, that knowledge can provide parents and teachers with an understanding that will lead to the gearing of activities and play materials to the child's maturational level.

SUMMARY

The development of motor abilities is essential to good health—physical, mental, and emotional. The degree of efficiency a child attains in the various skills affects his learning of complex behavior patterns, his social relationships, and his academic success.

All motor abilities are based primarily on the development of locomotion and prehension. The stages through which a child passes toward proficiency in those skills illustrates many of the principles of development—progression from head to foot, inner body parts to outer, simple to complex, general to specific, in predictable sequences, with a constancy of rate.

The more complex a skill is, the longer it takes to develop and the better it lends itself to improvement by training, provided the training is begun at an early stage of maturation.

Concerning the interrelatedness of motor abilities and correlations between motor abilities and such factors as physical growth and intelligence, investigators have presented conflicting reports. However, positive relationships have been found between various skills and strength of grip; and low, positive correlations can be found between mental and motor retardation.

Motor development and physical fitness exercise a reciprocal influence upon each other. In spite of up-to-date facilities, American children apparently have less endurance, strength, and flexibility than either Japanese or European children, presumably because they spend more time at sedentary occupations and less time at physical activities.

At first glance, sex appears to have an influence on the quality and duration of growth in motor skills, but further examination shows that girls are more proficient in those activities which are culturally acceptable for their sex, and boys achieve higher scores on tests of those skills that society encourages them to engage in, thus adding support to the theory that skill in motor activities is a product of motivation and practice.

Other factors influencing motor development are freedom to practice and participate, and motivation.

QUESTIONS AND PROBLEMS

1. Why is the development of prehension in the infant important in relation to child training?
2. Discuss the notion presented in this chapter concerning the relation of maturation to the learning of motor skills. What are the educational implications of this idea?
3. Specifically, what help can a teacher give the child who is learning to ride a bicycle? What are the major essentials in such a learning problem?
4. Show how the motor skill involved in learning to somersault requires a single growth cycle, whereas that involved in learning to play a piano requires a longer growth cycle, perhaps two growth cycles.
5. Show how the fundamental principle that the child develops as a whole operates in connection with motor development.
6. Trace changes in body proportions from birth to adulthood. What bearings do these changes have on the development of motor skills at different ages?
7. What conditions in modern living contribute to the lack of physical fitness of children in the United States as compared to that found among European and Japanese children? What are some of the responsibilities of the school in this matter? Of the home?

SELECTED READINGS

BRECKENRIDGE, MARIAN E., and E. LEE VINCENT, *Child Development,* 4th ed. Philadelphia: Saunders, 1960. Ch. 8.

GARRISON, KARL C., *Growth and Development,* rev. ed. Longmans, Green (now McKay), 1959. Ch. 6.

HAWKES, GLENN R., and DAMARIS PEASE, *Behavior and Development from 5 to 12.* Harper, 1962, Ch. 7.

HURLOCK, ELIZABETH B., *Child Development,* 3rd ed. McGraw-Hill, 1956. Ch. 5.

JERSILD, ARTHUR T., *Child Psychology,* 5th ed. Englewood Cliffs, N.J.: Prentice-Hall, 1960. Ch. 5.

MARTIN, WILLIAM E., and CELIA B. STENDLER, *Child Development and Behavior,* rev. ed. Harcourt, Brace, 1959. Ch. 14.

MILLARD, CECIL V., *Child Growth and Development in the Elementary School Years*, rev. ed. Boston: Heath, 1958. Ch. 5.

OLSON, WILLARD C., *Child Development*, 2nd ed. Boston: Heath, 1959. Ch. 4.

THOMPSON, GEORGE G., *Child Psychology*, 2nd ed. Boston: Houghton Mifflin, 1962. Ch. 7.

THORPE, LOUIS P., *Child Psychology and Development*, 3rd ed. The Ronald Press, 1962. Ch. 5.

REFERENCES

ALDRICH, C. ANDERSON, and MILDRED A. NORVAL, Physical and motor development. *Journal of Pediatrics*, 1946, *29*, 304–308.

AMES, LOUISE B., Some relationships between stair climbing and prone progression, *The Journal of Genetic Psychology*, 1939, *54*, 313–325.

ASHTON-WARNER, SYLVIA, *Teacher*. New York: Simon and Schuster, 1963, pp. 99–100.

BAYLEY, NANCY, The development of motor abilities during the first three years, *Monographs of the Society for Research in Child Development*, 1935, *1*, No. 1, 1–26.

CARPENTER, AILEEN, Tests of motor educability for the first three grades, *Child Development*, 1940, *11*, 293–299.

DENNIS, WAYNE, On the possibility of advancing or retarding the motor development of infants, *The Psychological Review*, 1943, *50*, 203–218.

ERIKSON, ERIK H., *Childhood and Society*. Norton, 1950.

ESPENSCHADE, ANNA, Fitness of fourth grade children, *Research Quarterly*, 1958, *29*, 274–278.

FRANCIS, ROBERT J., and G. LAWRENCE RARICK, Motor characteristics of the mentally retarded, *American Journal of Mental Deficiency*, 1959, *63*, 792–811.

GESELL, ARNOLD, and HENRY M. HALVERSON, The daily maturation of infant behavior: A cinema study of postures, movements and laterality, *The Journal of Genetic Psychology*, 1942, *61*, 3–32.

GOVATOS, LOUIS A., Relationships and age differences in growth measures and motor skills, *Child Development*, 1959, *30*, 333–340.

GUTTERIDGE, M. V., A study of motor achievements of young children, *Archives of Psychology*, N.Y., 1939, No. 244.

HALVERSON, HENRY M., An experimental study of prehension in infants by means of systematic cinema records, *Genetic Psychology Monographs*, 1931, *10*, 122–129, 270–280.

HALVERSON, HENRY M., The development of prehension in infants, in *Child Behavior and Development* (Roger G. Barker, Jacob S. Kounin, and Herbert F. Wright, eds.). McGraw-Hill, 1943, p. 49.

HARTMAN, DORIS M., The hurdle jump as a measure of the motor proficiency of young children, *Child Development*, 1943, *14*, 201–211.

HILDRETH, GERTRUDE, The development and training of hand dominance: V. Training of handedness, *The Journal of Genetic Psychology*, 1950, 76, 101–144.

IKEDA, NAMIKO, *A Comparison of Physical Fitness of Children in Iowa, U.S.A. and Tokyo, Japan*. Ph.D. Dissertation, State University of Iowa, 1961.

JENKINS, LULA M., *A Comparative Study of Motor Achievements of Children at Five, Six, and Seven Years of Age*, Teachers College, Columbia University, Contributions to Education, 1930, No. 414, *passim*.

JOKL, ERNEST, and E. H. CLUVER, Physical fitness, *The Journal of the American Medical Association*, 1941, *116* Pt. 2, 2383–2389.

JONES, T. D., *The Development of Certain Motor Skills and Play Activities in Young Children*, Child Development Monographs, No. 26, 1939.

LATCHAW, MARJORIE, Measuring selected motor skills in fourth, fifth, and sixth grades, *Research Quarterly*, 1954, 25 439–449.

MCCASKILL, CARRA L., and BETH L. WELLMAN, A study of common motor achievements at the preschool ages, *Child Development*, 1938, *9*, 141–150.

MCCLOY, C. H., Appraising physical status: methods and norms, *University of Iowa Studies in Child Welfare*, 1938, *15*, No. 2.

MCGRAW, MYRTLE B., *Growth: A Study of Johnny and Jimmy*. Appleton-Century, 1935, p. 70.

MCGRAW, MYRTLE B., Later development of children specially trained during infancy: Jimmy and Johnny at school age, *Child Development*, 1939, *10*, 1–19.

MATTSON, MARION L., The relation between the complexity of the habit to be acquired and the form of the learning curve in young children, *Genetic Psychology Monographs*, 1933, *13*, 299–398.

METCALF, HARLAN G., Physical education, in *Collier's Encyclopedia*, 1954, *16*, 33–34.

MILLARD, CECIL V., *Child Growth and Development in the Elementary School Years*, rev. ed. Boston: Heath, 1958, p. 104.

RARICK, G. LAWRENCE, and ROBERT MCKEE, A study of twenty third-grade children exhibiting extreme levels of achievement on tests of motor proficiency, *Research Quarterly*, 1949, *20*, 142–152.

SCHONFELD, WILLIAM A., quoted in "Of Youth and Health" by Robert and Phyllis Goldman, *The New York Times Magazine* (September 6, 1964), p. 26.

SEILS, LEROY G., The relationship between measures of physical growth and gross motor performance of primary-grade school children, *Research Quarterly of the American Physical Education Association*, 1951, *22*, 244–260.

SLOAN, WILLIAM, Motor proficiency and intelligence, *American Journal of Mental Deficiency*, 1951, *55*, 394–406.

SLOAN, WILLIAM, The Lincoln-Oseretsky Motor Development Scale, *Genetic Psychology Monographs*, 1955, *51*, 183–252.

SMITH, JEAN A., Relation of certain physical traits and abilities to motor learning in elementary school children, *Research Quarterly*, 1956, 27, 220–228.

SPOCK, BENJAMIN, *Baby and Child Care*. Pocket Books, 1957, p. 157.

S I X

The Development

of Language

Language is the most valuable adjustment mechanism that man possesses. With it he acquires the prevailing culture of the society into which he is born; without it he remains aloof from and ignorant of his heritage. Language is the key to his participation in social life, a vehicle for self-realization, expression and communication, and an instrument for the organization of his mental processes. To a remarkable extent it is language which makes us human. It is also peculiarly revelatory of character and background, according to Young (1959), who says:

> Language is a uniquely revealing type of behavior. It identifies a person with amazing effectiveness. Language habits reflect one's past life, the geographic area where childhood years were spent, grammatical errors copied from uneducated associates, and the critical or kindly attitude of the speaker.

The scope of language includes reading, writing, art, vocalization, and the comprehension of vocalizations, facial expressions and gestures. However, the word "language" commonly carries the strong connotation of "the *spoken* word." The act of speaking involves complex muscular coordination and is thus dependent upon the maturational process, as is every phase of child development. The processes of speech development are virtually the same for children all over the world; but the rates vary according to each child's intelligence, maturity, environment, emotional well-being, and motivation. About motivation, or stimulus to speech, Sampson (1956, p. 199) wrote, after observing and analyzing the speech development of fifty children:

> ... It was, for example, frequently noted at the interviews that the child's efforts were goal-directed; he had a motive to make himself understood and improvement seemed to result because of this. ... Among the children of the sample a struggle for the right expression was sometimes witnessed. Strong feeling also provided motive and under its impact the standard of expression often improved. Thus, a girl was moved to elaborate on her one-word cry of "sweetie!" to "I want my sweetie!" when she feared that she was not understood.

PATTERNS OF PRESPEECH

An individual's language begins when someone understands and responds to his efforts to communicate his wants. The infant whose mother feeds him as soon as she observes him stroking his tongue back and forth between his lips has developed a language. He has not developed speech, however, which has its beginning in some form of vocalization. Crying is the commonest form, and the earliest. Although the infant is conditioned to use crying as a means for relieving distress, he learns rapidly (generally within three months) to use crying as a method for gaining attention. Sometime between the second and fourth month, he engages in spontaneous cooing, makes sucking, smacking and gasping sounds, and generally experiments with vowels, which are the earliest non-crying speech sounds. At two months, as many as four different vowels may be heard, with a new one being added every two or three months until the end of the second year, when most children are able to reproduce all the vowel sounds.

According to Shirley (1933), some babies are combining vowels and consonants by the age of five months, repeating them several times in succession, as "mum-mum-mum," "da-da-da," "gully-gully-gully," and so forth. By the time the child is eight or nine months of age, he is able to make a variety of such babbling sounds. Combining these babblings, the infant soon produces sounds similar to those heard in his environment. The babbling stage is considered by most authorities an extremely important one. McCarthy (1954) calls this type of vocalizing "play speech," maintaining that the child is indulging in a form of vocal gymnastics for the pleasure of hearing his own voice—exercises which, of course, serve to develop the vocal mechanism.

A baby shows evidence of being able to understand the meanings of words before he is able to reproduce them. (This phenomenon, incidentally, accompanies the individual into adulthood. Most adults have a passive vocabulary far superior to their active one.) Certainly the infant understands the tone of voice used to produce the words he hears, and because these tones are so frequently associated with such pleasurable sensations as feeding, bathing, and snuggling, the next logical step would seem to be for him to discriminate the sounds made—if only as a means to recreating the sensations. Through trial and error he succeeds in reproducing the syllables, the tones, even the rhythms he hears; and the recognition he receives from making a meaningful sound serves to reinforce his efforts. Thus, through both imitation and conditioning, the infant learns that he can "control" his environment by the use of language.

ORAL LANGUAGE

Theoretically, the development of speech involves the building of both a passive vocabulary and an active vocabulary; the formation of sentences; and pronunciation. As with the infant, the two-year-old's comprehension of words (passive vocabulary) far outstrips his ability to use them. The development of this understanding vocabulary depends first upon inner maturation, and, second, upon the amount of language the child hears. Because sounds and words are largely undifferentiated at the early stages, the child builds his understanding primarily through his reactions to tones of voice and through his understanding of gestures. The eighteen-month-old child, by using gestures and some vocalizations, is able to communicate his needs and desires to other members of the family. Long before he enters school he is able to understand commands and directions given by people other than those in his family; and he understands the stories that are told or read to him.

Early Vocabulary Development

According to principles of growth and maturation, the ability to engage in a brand new skill generates the impulse to do so, and, for the most part, children's efforts and energy are concentrated on the completion of each new task as it is presented to them. For this reason, language development suffers a series of lulls, the major one occurring when the child is learning to walk (Shirley, 1933). For instance, on page 156 the list of vocabulary sizes at certain age levels shows that, from twelve months—when the first word is generally produced—until eighteen months, the child acquires only twenty-two words; six months later—when upright locomotion is well-established—his vocabulary has increased by 250 words.

Throughout the preschool years, interest in language waxes and wanes as other new motor skills are acquired; however, the acquisition of vocabulary progresses with extreme rapidity when children do become interested, since talking, like any new skill, is practiced continually—as most parents and nursery-school teachers can testify.

Qualitative and Quantitative Differences

The language of the small child is largely a matter of naming and labeling, since the child is verbalizing his percepts and attaching labels to his activities in order to retain them. The lack of pronouns and the preponderance of nouns in the very young child's speech is quite noticeable. The preschool child learns the names of objects first, and his speech patterns contain a greater number of nouns and verbs. The former, by the way, constitute over half the speech of two-year-olds. However, pronouns, particularly *me* and *my*, appear frequently with the development of an increased awareness of self. Davis (1938) found that by the age of four children seem to have acquired the commonly used pronouns, prepositions, and conjunctions. At least a study of the further growth of their vocabulary does not reveal an increase in these categories. The number of nouns, obviously, increases as the child masters new ideas at school and in his ever-expanding environment. Percentages computed on the basis of different words used at four and one-half, five and one-half, six and one-half, and nine and one-half years of age are shown in Table VI–1. Notice that nouns and verbs make up over seventy per cent of the different words used after the age of five and one-half years.

Studies of children's speech show wide differences not only in the number of different words used at various age levels, but also in the total number of words used. In one study (McCarthy, 1930), the length of time required by children to produce fifty remarks varied from seven to fifty minutes. Jersild and Ritzman (1938) studied the relationship between lo-

Table VI–1   Mean Percentage of Each Part of Speech Used by Children According to Age and Sex, Based on Number of Different Words Used (Davis, 1938, p. 310) *

	McCarthy		Davis					
	4½ years		5½ years		6½ years		9½ years	
	Boys	Girls	Boys	Girls	Boys	Girls	Boys	Girls
Nouns	36.0	36.8	43.1	45.9	41.4	44.4	41.4	42.5
Verbs	27.8	25.5	26.9	26.0	29.9	27.7	30.3	29.8
Adjectives, adverbs	21.2	21.0	18.3	17.9	17.1	16.7	19.4	19.1
Pronouns	6.5	7.1	2.7	2.5	3.6	3.5	2.6	2.6
Conjunctions	1.2	2.4	1.3	1.3	1.7	1.7	1.3	1.4
Prepositions	3.6	3.8	2.6	2.6	3.3	3.1	2.9	2.8
Interjections	2.0	1.4	4.2	3.0	2.0	2.1	1.4	1.0
Miscellaneous	1.7	2.1	0.8	0.8	0.9	0.8	0.7	0.8

* Reprinted by permission of the Society for Research in Child Development and the author.

quacity and the number of different words used by nursery-school children. As Table VI–2 shows, the number of different words used at the various ages does not increase so fast as the quantity of speech throughout the nursery-school period. Perhaps the best explanation for these findings is that, as children grow older and use adult sentence constructions, they use more pronouns and articles.

Content of Speech

Although the numbers and kinds of word used by children may be of interest to students of child psychology, the question of why the child uses language is more significant to an understanding of the dynamics of child behavior. Piaget (1926), who was primarily interested in studying his thought processes, divided the conversation, or talk, of two children into two large groups—egocentric speech and socialized speech. In egocentric speech, according to Piaget, the child "does not bother to know to whom he is speaking nor whether he is being listened to. He talks either for himself or for the pleasure of associating anyone who happens to be there with the activity of the moment. . . . [He] does not attempt to place himself at the point of view of his hearer. Anyone who happens to be there will serve as an audience" (p. 9). (Egocentric speech also occurs during adolescence and adulthood, but to a lesser degree.) The child's speech is related to his own actions and thoughts, but the child is not actually speaking to anyone. He is merely talking in the presence of others, a pseudo-conversation, or collective monologue. This particular kind of egocentricity, incidentally, is a product of the child's intellectual limitations, and egocentric speech aids the development of his thinking.

Table VI–2   Comparison of the Median Number of Words Spoken and Median Number of Different Words Used by Boys and Girls in Relation to Chronological Age (From Jersild and Ritzman, 1938, p. 253) *

Half-yearly	Number		Words spoken per three hours		Different words used per three hours	
	Boys	Girls	Boys	Girls	Boys	Girls
24–29	3	8	299	428	75	82
30–35	11	9	753	682	149	173
36–41	10	12	978	1468	194	265
42–47	13	13	1679	1843	292	321
48–53	3	2	714	1645	164	282

* Reprinted by permission of the Society for Research in Child Development and the authors.

Socialized speech, which is an aid to a child's social adjustments, is subdivided into (1) *adapted information,* involving an exchange of thought or ideas; (2) *criticism* of the behavior or work of others, directed to an audience; (3) *commands, requests, and threats;* (4) *questions;* and (5) *answers.* During this stage of a child's speech development, says Piaget, "the child speaks from the point of view of his audience. The function of language is no longer merely to excite the speaker to action, but actually to communicate his thoughts to other people" (p. 19). In other words, whereas the pronoun "I" is especially frequent in the language of two- and three-year-old children, there is an increase during the preschool years in the use of such words as *we, you, he, she, they,* and *it* (Jersild and Ritzman, 1938).

Basing his observations on the spontaneous expressions of children, Piaget noted that socialized speech predominated between ages five and six. On the other hand, Vigotsky (1939), while agreeing that much of the three-year-old child's speech is egocentric in structure, maintained that it was social in general function. His examination of the relation of children's speech to the social situations in which they were used revealed that even at three years of age the use of speech for communication to others was quite important. By the age of seven, the child's speech was clearly social both in structure and function.

Of course, the age for crossing the bridge from egocentric speech to socialized speech varies. Among other factors, personality plays a dominant role—an egocentric self-concept, for instance, will require more time for the necessary interest in others to begin operation. Also, the number of opportunities a child has to share experiences with both children and adults will determine his degree of social maturity.

Further Vocabulary Development

There is such a close relationship between intelligence and language development that psychologists have devised tests involving vocabulary to measure intellectual ability. In using the *Stanford-Binet Scale,* for instance, psychologists frequently administer the vocabulary section first, because it helps to determine the appropriate basal mental age of the child. Thus, the importance of adequate vocabulary development is so well recognized that both psychologists and educators, among others, have sparked many studies of this area of language skills.

During the elementary-school years, the child's oral language capacity develops at a fairly even, although rapid, pace. Usually the first-grade child possesses a greater vocabulary than is required by basal reading books. This condition is illustrated in a study by Hughes and Cox (1949). They recorded the free conversations of a group of first-grade children during the first two months of the school year, analyzed their oral language, and then compared the speech patterns with the vocabulary contained in first-grade reading books. They found a large percentage of common words both in the speech of the children and in the basal readers but concluded that children talk about a greater number of things, used descriptive words in a richer manner, utilized a greater number of verbs and verb forms, and used a larger number of relational words in correct and mature ways.

A relatively steady and continuous growth in vocabulary was reported by Madorah Smith (1926) in a study of the general size of the English vocabulary at different grade levels. The following average number of words were spoken:

Fifteen months	19 words
Eighteen months	22 words
Two years	272 words
Three years	896 words
Four years	1,540 words
Five years	2,072 words
Six years	2,562 words

In a later study, Mary Smith (1941) recorded the basic vocabulary scores obtained for the different chronological age groups in grades one through twelve, shown in Figure VI–1. Considerable overlapping was noted.

Seashore (1947) used a vocabulary test consisting of eighty-nine items in which pictures were used to give the child an opportunity to display his knowledge of words. The test was given individually to 117 children ranging in ages from four to ten years. The following estimates of vocabulary size were based on the results of this test:

Age four	5,600 basic words
Age five	9,600 basic words
Age six	14,700 basic words
Age seven	21,200 basic words
Age eight	26,300 basic words
Age nine	29,300 basic words
Age ten	34,300 basic words

The reader will have noticed a great deal of variation in the findings of these studies, variations which are accounted for by the differences in sampling and methods for obtaining the data and in scoring and interpreting results. When the child is very young, observers can easily tabulate the words he can use. Later, when the vocabulary is increasing rapidly, other techniques must replace the counting method. Then, problems relating to eliciting responses (the use of word lists or pictures), acceptability of the responses (whether to accept synonyms, explanations, or illustrations), and

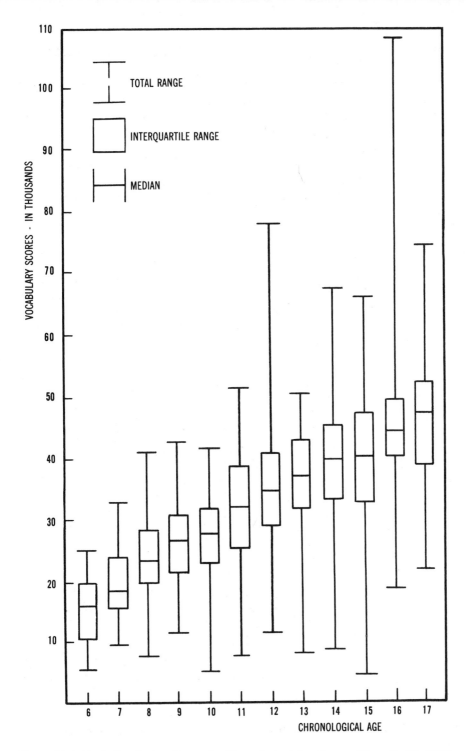

Figure VI–1. Basic Vocabulary Scores by Chronological Age Groups (From Smith, 1941, p. 332)

the extent of understanding (the child may be able to use the word and recognize it only when it is in context) make the study of vocabulary development difficult. Furthermore, many vocabulary studies have used small samples of words. There is evidence that the larger the dictionary used as a basis for sampling, the larger the estimated vocabulary will be.

However, such vocabulary counts are useful in showing the general development of the child's speech vocabulary, although care should be taken that they are not regarded as being established norms for the different age levels.

Forming Sentences.

The young child beginning to talk uses single words, each of which, with varying inflections or gestures, serves as a sentence. As shown in Figure VI–2, there is a gradual and continuous increase in the mean number of words per response. That is, sentence length increases in much the same pattern as vocabulary size. This increase, according to McCarthy, is the best single index of the linguistic ability of boys and girls.

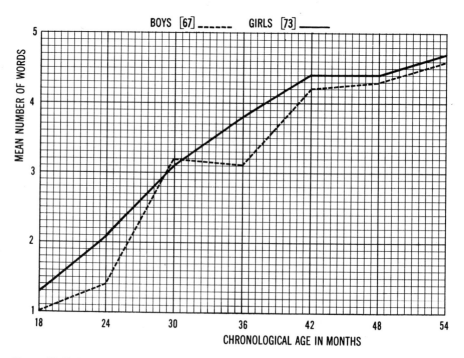

Figure VI–2. Mean Number of Words per Response by Age and Sex (From McCarthy, 1930, p. 53)

Sentence structure also improves as the child moves from the use of simple noun-verb combinations in which there is rarely any subject through the use of all parts of speech in simple, but complete, sentences, and finally to complex and compound-complex sentences which utilize more verbs and verb tenses. This final stage of speech requires an advanced mental grasp of relationships and is usually not found until a child is between four and five years old. By the time he is six, he has used, at times, almost every form of complete sentence structure. As with other phases of language development, girls, bright children, and children with high socioeconomic status manifest an observable advantage.

Pronunciation

A child's correct pronunciation of syllables and words usually lags behind his acquisition of them. The act of imitation is not a discriminating one, and bad speech or poor grammar is as easily imitated as is good speech. Furthermore, even an adult with above-average diction will slur words and certain sounds. Van Riper (1950) says:

> Many of the errors made by little children are due to their perceiving words as lumps of sounds. They often omit sounds that are of low intensity. They say "ike" for "like," "way" for "away"; they omit the final s sounds from plural words; they may even omit a whole syllable if it is unstressed in the word. . . .

Aside from the auditory perception required for correct pronunciation, an accurate, controlled adjustment of muscles in the vocal apparatus is necessary. Thus, maturation plays its usual developmental role. Strayer (1930) found that a maturational advantage of as little as five weeks had a definite influence on the relative effectiveness of vocabulary and pronunciation training during early childhood. Using identical twins as subjects, she determined that the twin whose practice was delayed not only learned more easily, but also had a more mature pattern of response.

If good models, guidance, and practice each play supporting roles, motivation perhaps plays the strongest one. As suggested earlier in the excerpt from Sampson's study, the child has a motive to be understood, even a fear of being misunderstood. Frequently, the frustration is so great that the child reverts to an earlier form of relieving tension, such as crying.

Incomprehensible speech is less appreciated by children than by adults, for children have neither the patience nor the inclination to "stand and wait." On the other hand, Anna Freud (1952, p. 91) cautions against placing the child with delayed speech development in a nursery-school situation in the hopes of providing him with incentive and a variety of good models. Even if all the other children speak correctly, she says, the "child's poor speaking ability will deteriorate rather than improve under the added strain."

Unless a child's faulty articulation has been well established by habit, or his "baby talk" has been unwisely encouraged by adults who think it's "cute," he will correct his own errors in accordance with the principle of development which calls for the revision of habits with maturity. (See p. 96.) In general, mispronunciations disappear from the child's speech shortly after he enters school.

SPEECH DISORDERS

Speech is produced by the movements of the organs of articulation, i.e., the jaws, lips, tongue, and soft palate. Any failure of these organs to make the correct movements may result in an articulatory defect. Auditory deficiency, too, is responsible for a great many speech disorders, since obviously a child must be able to hear what it is he is expected to reproduce. However, speech is also a part of the child's general behavior pattern and is closely associated with his aspirations, his attitudes, and his feelings. It can never be separated from his *self*. Anything that affects a child's well-being will also affect his speech. Thus, a child who is having a difficulty with his speech may also be struggling with other problems.

Types of Speech Disorders

Disorders of speech may result from such organic defects or conditions as cleft palate, cerebral palsy, nasal obstruction, muscle paralysis, and laryngeal malformations. Other types of speech and language disorders have been classified by Karlin (1958, p. 372) as follows:

1. Delayed speech—retardation in acquisition and use of words
2. Articulatory disorders—the distortion, omission, and substitution of consonant sounds
3. Voice disorders—the absence of voice or abnormal production of the qualities (intensity, pitch, or melody) of voice
4. Cluttering—rapid speech, associated with slurring and distortions of sounds
5. Stuttering—disorganization of the rhythmic flow of speech
6. Aphasias—disorders of linguistic symbolization

Immature Speech

Kindergarten and first-grade children frequently substitute one sound for another, as may be observed in the case of Harriett, who substituted *w* for *l* and *r*. Instead of *run* she said *wun*, and instead of *log* she said *wog*. The normal process of maturation, along with correct examples, will usually remedy these conditions. In this connection, Davis (1938) has presented the ages at which most children are able to articulate certain sounds. *S*'s and *z*'s are listed at two age levels because, although they appear consistently at four and five years of age, dentition produces a spacing between the teeth, making these sounds almost impossible for the child to produce; thus, at the age of eight, the correct articulation of *s*'s and *z*'s is equivalent to a brand new skill.

> 3.5 years: *b, p, n, w, h*
> 4.5 years: *t, d, n, g, k, ng, y*
> 5.5 years: *f, v, s, z*
> 6.5 years: *sh, zh, l, th* as in *then*
> 8.0 years: *s, z, r, wh*

Roe and Milisen (1942) noted that substitutions characterize the faulty speech of children in grades one to six; however, during the first three grades, many improvements are made in articulating individual consonants without formal speech practice.

Lisping is quite frequently found among preschool children and in the lower grades. It includes the inability to pronounce certain letter sounds or combinations of letter sounds and a tendency to omit, transpose, or slur sounds. This inability, or tendency, constitutes the most characteristic feature of baby talk and is found in a greater or lesser degree among very young children. When lisping persists beyond the age of five and six years, it may be classified as a speech difficulty. The frequency of this condition decreases rapidly in the upper grades. Garrison and Force (1965) state:

> . . . The undue persistence of lisping may be attributed to (1) lack of practice in the proper use of the articulatory organs, due to bad models in the child's language environment; (2) damage to auditory pathways from end organs to higher centers; (3) incomplete development of the speech organs; (4) anatomical abnormalities of teeth, lips, tongue, jaws, soft or hard palate, nasal or pharyngeal cavities, etc.; (5) a general deficiency of the motor centers; or (6) poor listening habits.

The child's ability to articulate consonant sounds accurately and distinctly furnishes a partial basis for determining his physical, mental, and emotional maturity. By the time he is three and a half years old he should be using the sounds *m, p, b,* and *w* correctly and consistently in words. Children in the kindergarten and lower elementary grades will derive satisfaction, as well as develop speech skills, from listening to and imitating the sounds of the things about them. A trip to the country or to the zoo will bring them into contact with the sounds made by animals: the *moo-moo* of the cow; the chirping of the bird—*peep-peep-peep;* the barking of the dog— *bow-wow, bow-wow;* and the buzzing of the bee—*b-z, b-z-z.* Certain objects in the environment produce sounds whose imitations require vocal skill. For example, the ticking of the clock—*tick-tock, tick-tock;* the buzzing sound of the airplane—*b-z-z-z, b-z-z;* the ringing of the bell—*ting-a-ling, ting-a-ling;* and many others.

Articulatory Disorders

Some investigators of speech defects among children point out that most of them are articulatory in symptom and functional in origin (Powers, 1957). Clinical evidence has increasingly stressed the emotional and personality disturbances that appear among children as symptoms of functional speech disorders referred to as "baby talk," "delayed speech," and "speech inhibition" (Allen, 1947; Russell, 1944).

A study reported by Solomon (1961) was designed to test the possible relationship between functional articulatory speech defects in children and personality and behavior patterns. Forty-nine boys and girls with functional defects of articulation were matched in pairs with a control group of normal children. Mothers of both groups were asked to describe their children's behavior over the previous two years in the following areas of child development and personality: (a) eating behavior, (b) sleeping behavior, (c) toilet training, (d) fears and anxieties, (e) comfort patterns, (f) tension, (g) aggression, (h) dependency, and (i) peer relations. Four of the nine selected areas, in addition to the overall adjustment rating, were found to show differences between the two groups which were statistically significant at the .01 level or better. The four areas were sleeping, fears and anxieties, peer relations, and tension. Solomon concludes: "The speech-defective group tended to be passive children who internalized their responses and were characterized by submissiveness, timidity, and a need for approval" (p. 734).

Stuttering

A child's speech reflects his emotional and personality characteristics, especially observable in the case of stuttering, in which there is repetition of speech sounds of a rapid and compulsive nature accompanied by muscular tension. The entire body functions in the act of stuttering, not just some discrete portion of it, such as the speech apparatus. It usually has its onset between the ages of two and four. Frequently, experiences in this period have a deep-seated effect upon the individual and keep the stuttering in force. It differs from lisping in that there is usually an increase in its incidence from grade to grade up to the fourth or fifth.

Studies bearing on the incidence and causes of stuttering have brought forth some interesting and useful results. In the first place, there is statistical evidence that stuttering often runs in families (West, *et al.,* 1939). That some children of a family where one of the parents stutter develop the tendency while others from the same family do not indicates that imitation alone is not a sufficient explanation for the onset of stuttering. The popular conclusion is that a hereditary constitutional condition present in some individuals enables them to develop the habit more readily than the average person.

However, there is apparently little likelihood that a child would develop the habit of stuttering if his general environment were completely satisfactory. Moncur (1952) concluded from his study that there is a syndrome of environmental factors that precipitate and aggravate the stuttering condition. This syndrome largely involves parental actions of domination, overprotection, oversupervision, excessive standards of performance, and adverse criticism. Such conditions tend to produce nervous tension, which is likely to set off the beginnings of stuttering. A developmental theory of stuttering presented by Wyatt (1958) involves significant feelings of stuttering children toward their mothers.

> The stuttering child has experienced a developmental crisis, a disruption of the patterns of complementary behavior between mother and child which are of vital importance for the learning of language in childhood. A disturbance of the mother-child relationship occurring at the time when the child is in the practicing stage of early grammatical speech results in inability on the part of the child to continue language learning successfully. Stuttering is the overt symptom of this disturbance.

Speech Defects and Mental Retardation

The consistent findings of studies of speech defects among the mentally retarded are verifications of the theory that a relationship exists between mental growth and language growth. According to Gens (1950), seventy to seventy-five per cent of institutionalized mentally deficient children have some sort of speech disorder. The articulation profiles of 209 mentally retarded school children from ages seven years and three months to seventeen years and five months in eighteen classes in Kern County, California, were studied by Russell (1952). The IQ range was from 40 to 79, with a mean of 65.5. A matched group of children showed a greater incidence of errors typified by indistinct sounds, a finding which may be accounted for by their larger vocabulary and the inability to pronounce certain words in it. In the case of vowel errors, Russell noted that there were approximately four times as many distorted sounds among the retarded than among the matched group. (No significant sex differences were noted. The mean number of errors on the complete test for boys was 14.7, while that for girls was 12.9.)

Although both Craig (1951) and Everhart (1953) have reported a relationship between low intelligence and the incidence of articulatory disorders, one must be careful of making broad generalizations. Certainly the school work of these children suffers; yet, even with the intelligence factor disregarded, children with defective speech are, in general, retarded in any school activities requiring the use of language (FitzSimons, 1958). In reading clinics, for example, case studies reveal that a substantial number of children with reading difficulties also have speech difficulties. Thus, superior school work— and scores on intelligence tests—must be attributed, in part at least, to superior articulatory development.

Considering these findings, and especially those of Solomon and Moncur, functional speech problems are not isolated phenomena but are a part of a total adjustment pattern, a fact which would suggest a broadening of the speech correction program to include studies of and guidance for the child's personality and behavior, and his adjustments at home and elsewhere.

FACTORS INFLUENCING LANGUAGE DEVELOPMENT

Speech is deleteriously affected by maturation in the sense that its development must await the growth of teeth, the changes in size and shape of the vocal mechanism—for instance, the tongue—and the growth of muscle coordination. Later, the acquisition of motor skills absorbs all the energy of the growing child, and speech development must again wait.

Through careful diagnosis and remedial work most children can acquire good speech habits.

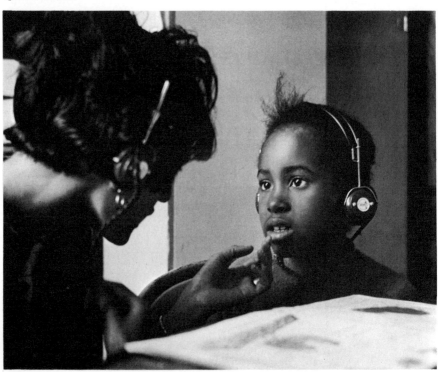

Thus, regardless of one's viewpoint as to whether there is an advantage or disadvantage, maturation is perhaps the primary influence on language development. Other factors, such as intelligence, motivation, and physical defects, have already been touched upon in this chapter. There remain a few influences worth considering: sex differences, environment, ordinal position, and bilingualism.

Sex Differences

It was earlier intimated that there is a slight sex difference in language development in favor of girls, especially in the preschool years. McCarthy (1954) summarized the results of fourteen studies, each of which compared the mean length of response (according to McCarthy, the best single index of linguistic ability) of boys and girls and disclosed that in sixty-four comparisons, forty-three favored the girls, three were identical for each sex, and eighteen favored the boys. She states:

> Whenever groups of boys and girls are well matched in intelligence and socio-economic background, and when the situation in which responses are recorded does not tend to favor the interests of one sex or the other, there appear slight differences in favor of girls. Whenever such sex differences fail to appear, or in rare instances are reversed, the result can nearly always be accounted for, when the data are available, in terms of selection on the basis of one of the aforementioned factors.

Such a difference may be related to the more advanced maturation of girls. There is a tendency for them to vocalize at an earlier age and also to progress more rapidly in total language development than boys do. By the time they enter the first grade, they enunciate more clearly, have larger vocabularies, and employ longer sentences in speaking.

The extent to which the language superiority of girls remains apparent throughout the developmental period is difficult to determine. There is evidence from McCarthy's summary that sex differences decrease with age. Out of fourteen comparisons in which the children were five and a half years of age or older, seven were in favor of the boys. Furthermore, a study which analyzed the written and tape-recorded oral language activities of pupils in the fourth, fifth, and sixth grades revealed little sex difference (Murray, 1953). Probably such slight differences as were noted at these grade levels represent a manifestation of boy-girl competition rather than actual sex differences.

Although Havighurst (1953) disclaims any knowledge of why differences should appear at all, even at the preschool level, McCarthy (1953) attempted to explain them on the basis of a closer mother-daughter than father-son relationship (due to discrepancies in the amount of time they spend together) and a less satisfactory "echo" reaction between father and

son because of the difference in the tonal qualities of the two voices. Mc-
Carthy further suggests that boys are emotionally less mature than girls,
which could account not only for the inferiority of language development,
but also for the fact that speech defects, especially stuttering, are far more
common in boys than in girls.

While it appears that these general sex differences in language development do occur, it should be pointed out that differences within the sex
are greater than those between the sexes. That is, some boys will be superior
in language development to all others in their age-sex group and will thus
be superior to most girls: and conversely, some girls will show language
abilities inferior to all other girls in their group and to most boys.

Environmental Factors

Many environmental factors appear to influence the language development of the child, most of which affect his opportunities to hear quantities
of good speech. The child who is brought up in a home where the language
he hears is limited to simple communications about rather concrete ideas
or objects does not have the opportunities for learning words or expressions of a more abstract nature. If the language his parents employ is
grammatically incorrect or loaded with slang, cursing, and colloquialisms,
the child will naturally learn these speech patterns. At an early age, he
will reflect these patterns in his language activities, as borne out by a study
of two groups of children attending the nursery school at the University
of Georgia (Young, 1941). For a period of time, the nursery school was run
as a Federal Emergency Relief Project, and only children from families on
relief were admitted, tuition free. Language records were compared for
seventy-four youngsters, half of whom attended during the time when
tuition was charged and half of whom attended later. The tuition group
surpassed the relief group in every aspect of language analyzed.

An interesting speculation arises as to whether these differences result
from fundamental differences in the language present in the children's
homes or whether they result from variations in the child-rearing attitudes
and practices of parents at each socioeconomic level. Generally, the child
from the higher socioeconomic home has greater opportunity for free oral
expression and interaction with his mother and father than does the lower-
class child. Usually, too, there are fewer cultural opportunities in the
homes of the financially and socially less fortunate: there are fewer activities, less traveling, fewer books, magazines, and pictures, all of which evoke
more elaborate speech patterns. Also, in these homes, examples of correct
speech are less apt to be available.

Interestingly enough, although the widespread use of television at all
cultural levels has demonstrably improved the child's comprehension of
oral language, there is no evidence that it has a marked effect upon his

grammar, despite the preponderance of cartoon shows which utilize slang and grammatically incorrect speech constructions. Apparently, the child's family still exerts the stronger influence. One five-year-old girl, who was an inveterate watcher of television cartoons, consistently spoke the same correct grammar that her mother used, until after each of her serviceman father's infrequent visits, when for a brief time she would use the poor grammar that he employed. At no time, even in the face of mild corrections, did she point out any similarities between her father's speech and that of the cartoon characters.

More scientific evidence of parental influence on children's speech has been presented by Noel (1953), who studied the language usage of 177 children and their parents. The conclusion was that to a very large degree the language an elementary-school child hears from his parents determines the quality of his own.

The results of a study by Dawe (1942) furnish evidence of the value of a stimulating environment upon the language development of young children. Her subjects consisted of twenty-two orphaned children divided into one experimental and one control group on the basis of school group, age, sex, mental age, IQ, scores on a spoken vocabulary test, and answers to the "home living and general science" part of an information test. The experimental group was given special training involving experiences designed to promote comprehension of words and concepts. The control group was given no special training. Following the training period, both groups were retested. The results showed that the group exposed to special training and enriched experiences made a marked improvement on the intelligence and vocabulary tests and on the home living and science information test, whereas the control group showed significantly less improvement. The results presented in Figure VI-3 show that in all areas tested the experimental group surpassed the control group. In light of this study and theoretical considerations, the enrichment of an impoverished environment will have a beneficial effect upon language development.

Closely related to Dawe's study is the one by Moore (1947) in which the language abilities of orphanage and nonorphanage children of the same chronological age were compared. The findings of this study showed that the orphanage group was inferior to the nonorphanage group in all aspects of language studied.

The conception of stimulus to speech as perceived by Sampson (1956) was somewhat distinct from such background factors as social class, educational level of the parents, and occupational status of the father; however, certain other aspects of the home background do have an important bearing on the child's language. The following conditions and situations have been found to encourage speech and language development:

(1) The emotional atmosphere of the home. A home in which there

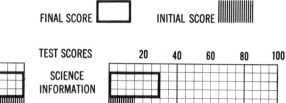

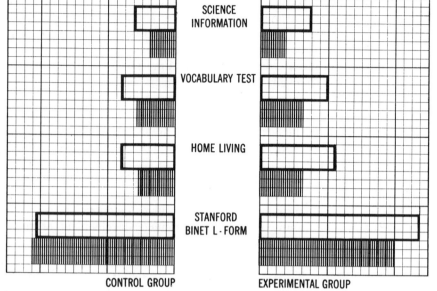

FINAL SCORE ☐   INITIAL SCORE ▓

Figure VI-3. The Effects of an Enriched Environment on Test Scores (After Dawe, 1942, p. 203)

is a warm, affectional relationship between different members of the family encourages language activity. A home where tension and discord are lacking provides a favorable climate for talking.

(2) The provision of toys, books, and other sources of stimulation.

(3) Example and encouragement in speech. The number of people and symbols (words in particular) in the child's environment determine whether his experiences will be barren ones or rich ones. The words used by others furnish him with the models that he imitates, and the attitudes of others toward him furnish the drive.

Ordinal Position

Evidence that favorable contacts with the mother are significant for language development is supported by findings that an only child, who need not share his mother's affection with other children, is usually advanced in his language development when compared with the child who has brothers and sisters. Furthermore, some studies have indicated that the language development of twins, triplets, and multiple-births is in general somewhat slower than that of singletons (Davis, 1937; Howard, 1946). In Figures VI-4 and VI-5, the findings of several studies are brought together

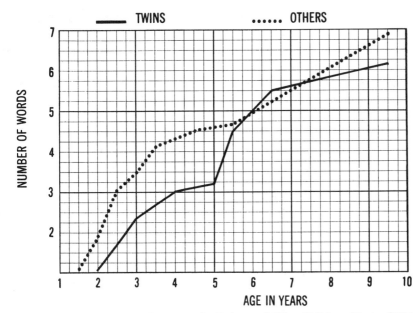

Figure VI-4. Mean Length of Response for Twins and Other Children (Davis, 1937, p. 136)

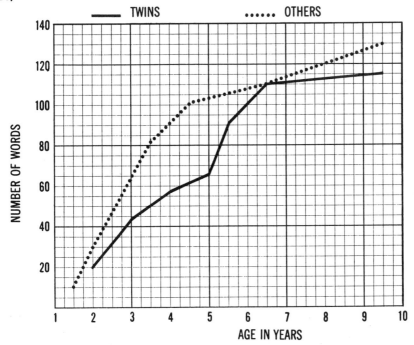

Figure VI-5. Mean Number of Different Words Used by Twins and Other Children (Davis, 1937, p. 136)

for two measures of language development—mean length of remark and mean number of different words (Davis, 1937). In this study, twins were compared with a group of singly born children, some of whom were siblings and some who were only children. The curves labeled "others" are descriptive of the scores of this combined group. The study showed twins to be inferior in their language development to the combination of other children.

Although Davis' evidence is not wholly conclusive regarding the rate of language development for only children as compared with that of children with siblings, his study indicates a superiority for only children, a reflection perhaps of the greater amount of time the mother and other adults spend with an only and a first-born child. Possibly, too, socioeconomic factors enter into the picture, for a higher percentage of only children are found in homes of higher socioeconomic levels. As for the apparent inferiority of twins, Howard suggests that they lack the necessary motivation, because they develop their own secret language of gestures, which, at the infancy stage, are substitutes for speech.

Bilingualism

The effects of bilingualism upon language development have been studied by several investigators, who have found that, generally, children from homes in which two languages are spoken are retarded in the rate and extent of their development in either language as compared with children reared in monolingual homes. Such findings may be the result of a normal tendency on the part of bilingual children to intersperse words from both languages throughout their speech and of the confusion of grammar and syntax between the one language and the other. Smith (1949) studied a group of bilingual children ranging in age from approximately three years to six and a half years who were given English and Chinese vocabulary tests in an effort to compare the development of bilingual and monolingual children. In spite of the fact that the parents of the bilingual children were slightly above the average with respect to occupational status, the vocabulary in neither language was near the norms for the monoglots of the same chronological age. When the vocabularies were combined for each child, the scores on the average were almost as high as the norms—two-fifths of the individual ratings exceeded the norms. When duplicate meanings were deleted, the group average fell to about eighty per cent of the estimated norm and only one-sixth of the individual children exceeded it. Furthermore, bilingual children are notably handicapped in their performance on intelligence tests. Since there is a close relationship between verbal ability and intelligence test scores, especially in group intelligence test scores obtained from school children, such results are to be expected. Smith concluded that parents would be unwise to start any but superior, well-adjusted children in learning two languages during early childhood or in the pre-school years.

LISTENING

At no time during the child's development of speech is listening unimportant to, nor even separable from, the acquisition of language. The child must be able to hear, identify, and interpret oral language before he will be able to speak it or to communicate effectively with others. Yet, in spite of its inseparableness from language development, listening as an independent subject has been given, in recent years, considerably more attention by students of speech, psychology, linguistics, and education. Hollow (1955) and Pratt (1956), utilizing control groups, conducted experiments which demonstrate that listening can be taught in the classroom; and some educators have introduced instruction in language arts on a sequence which provides for listening, speaking, reading, and, finally, writing in that order, because they have felt that such a program more nearly approximates normal language development.

Unfortunately, less is known about listening than about the other language areas. As is true with all areas of development, and language in particular, the total personality of the child is involved, and no one ability or characteristic functions in a separate and distinct way. Several studies, for example, have shown a significant relationship between intelligence and listening ability. In a study of sixth-grade children, Pratt found a correlation coefficient of +.42 between listening ability and reading ability and +.66 between listening ability and measures of intelligence. Hollow found a +.42 coefficient of correlation between measures of listening ability and intelligence in a fifth-grade group.

Up to a point, the child's ability to express himself is accompanied by a similar ability to understand and interpret the speech of others. During the elementary-school period, children improve their ability to follow oral language; but during the intermediate grades, listening ability fails to keep pace with speaking and reading achievements. Young (1936), who studied the language habits of approximately two thousand students, found that by the time the typical child attains the fifth grade his reading skills approximate his ability to listen. By the sixth grade, however, reading comprehension exceeds aural comprehension. In other words, listening ability appears to level off.

Possibly the mastery of reading skills results in the development of a more effective method of learning. Or, perhaps, the elementary curriculum and instructional practice places such a high premium on reading that listening ability is not nurtured at the intermediate-grade levels. Hopefully, additional research in this field will supplement our knowledge to the extent that the need for adequate listening comprehension will be universally recognized.

VISUAL LANGUAGE

Although emphasis has been placed on the importance to speech development of interpreting such visual language as gestures and facial expressions, prior to entering school almost all of the language which a child has mastered is oral. He has learned to discriminate between sounds and attach meanings to them. He has learned to reproduce them and to employ them for attaching labels to objects, places, persons, and situations. He is able to communicate many of his needs to others. During his elementary-school years, the child continues to expand his oral language; he learns many additional words, more polysyllabic words, and uses longer and more complex sentences. In addition, however, the child must learn the more advanced visual phases of language: reading and writing.

Reading

Like other types of language, reading is a form of communication, an essential language skill, and one which must be mastered by children if they are to succeed in school. The child's ability to master reading skills is dependent, developmentally, upon his vocabulary, general oral language attainment, mental age, and sex; culturally, upon his socioeconomic status and the educational level of his home; relatively, upon factors in his perceptual abilities, his social and emotional maturity, and hand-eye coordination. Although most of these factors function in an indirect way, the mastery of reading is so complex that it involves the total personality of the child.

Educators, after studying the problems inherent to reading instruction, have progressively recognized that instructional procedures must be correlated with the child's patterns of growth and development. They have devised what is commonly called "developmental reading" programs, which take into account the need for adjusting instruction to the developmental pattern and level of each child. Ilg and Ames (1950) have gone so far as to develop a theoretic "reading gradient," based on their observations of numerous children, which is suggestive of the various stages through which a child must pass before he can read easily and well.

The importance of adjusting reading instruction to the level of the child's development and to his individual patterns, abilities, and interests has led to considerable attention being given to "reading readiness." This term is a generalized one employed to describe a child's level of maturity and ability, with special attention devoted to those factors indicative of the likelihood that he can profit from instruction in reading. Typically, such measures include a sampling of the child's ability to perceive similarities and differences in printed symbols, his language capacity, and his ability to attach meaning to pictures, objects, or other ideographic forms.

As might be expected, educators have placed major emphasis upon evaluating the reading readiness of first-grade children. Although the degrees of relationship between measures of reading readiness and certain factors of development vary from study to study (depending in part upon the samples and types of instruments used), researchers have found positive and significant correlations between the reading readiness measures and such factors as mental age, chronological age, language capacity (including the extent of vocabulary), the ability to complete sentences, the length of sentences normally employed in speech, willingness to follow directions, motivation and desire to learn, and, as previously mentioned, the ability to perceive similarities and differences in printed forms. Slight sex differences occur in reading readiness, as in other forms of language development. Prescott (1955), for instance, found that when girls and boys were matched according to chronological age the test performance of the girls was somewhat superior. Similarly, reading specialists have observed that considerably more boys than girls encounter difficulty in mastering fundamental reading skills. Physical maturation, incidentally, appears to be of little significance. Karlin (1957), studying a group of first graders, found only a low positive relationship between measures of reading readiness or achievement and such measures of physical maturation as skeletal growth, height, and weight.

Despite the emphasis upon evaluation of first graders' reading attainments, educators have recently recognized the need for instruments to measure reading readiness at other grade levels, and instruments have been devised for that purpose. However, the development of reliable and valid tests has failed to nullify the importance of the classroom teacher's evaluations of her pupils. In a study of over three thousand first-grade children, Kottmeyer (1947) found that first-grade teachers' judgments were more accurate than either of two widely used standardized tests (available at that time) for the prediction of their pupils' progress.

Before the student decides that a certain age, or level of maturity, is requisite to reading readiness, he should consider that the materials and methods of reading instruction should be taken into account. The teacher as a person as well as the material used must, of necessity, be a factor in the child's success. Maya Pines (1963) has reported that O. K. Moore of Yale University has seen children of three and four years of age learn to read by using a "talking typewriter." The article reporting this is appropriately titled "How Three-year-olds Teach Themselves to Read—and Love It."

Writing

Handwriting is a motor skill that requires physical maturity, as manifested in the ability to coordinate and control the fine muscles in fingers, hands, and wrists. Havighurst (1953) denies that the child is biologically prepared for handwriting before the age of six. Thus, writing as a motor skill and writing as a form of language communication become almost entirely the responsibility of the school and are probably most directly influenced by it. If the child is expected to reproduce words ideographically, he must be taught how the sound system of his language is expressed in written form, and he must be taught the traditional and accepted forms of expressing his ideas. These tasks are usually left to the school teacher, ideally taking into consideration all the various personal and environmental factors which are related to the child's acquisition of oral language and his reading ability, since his attainments in these areas obviously affect his ability to communicate through written media.

Continued guidance and instruction in all phases of language is necessary throughout the school period. Both Ford (1954) and Harrell (1956) found a gradual development in the quality of oral and written language as children attain higher age levels. Ford analyzed the compositions of New Zealand children ranging in age from seven to twelve-thirteen and discovered advances in unity, continuity, clarity and complexity. He found no significant sex differences at the seven-year level, but later the amount written by girls was slightly greater than that written by boys. Moreover, girls at all ages portrayed less action than boys did, and their compositions contained more descriptive materials.

The younger children found straight exposition the most difficult type of writing, an excellent demonstration of the inability of this age group to select the essential facts and organize them in a logical manner.

Harrell's study analyzed both oral and written compositions from elementary and high-school students who had been asked to relate stories about movies they had seen. His analysis revealed that the stories increased in length as the children grew older and that at each age level from nine to fifteen years the oral stories were longer than the written ones. In both types of composition, the length of clauses increased with the child's age, and the older children used more adverb and adjective clauses in their writing and a greater percentage of noun clauses in their speaking. Complete maturity was not reached in either form by the age of fifteen, a finding that supports our original contention that persistent guidance and instruction throughout the school years is beneficial, even necessary, to good language development.

Drawing

A brief word must be said about drawing, a language for expression rather than communication, at least in its earliest stages. In his drawings a child expresses his ideas of objects and beings in his environment; he tells stories to himself; he even exercises a form of therapy for his own emotional disturbances. The stages through which a child travels in his art are amazingly analogous to the stages of oral language development (Kirkpatrick, 1930; Rand, Sweeney, and Vincent, 1953). A study of these stages combined with a study of the drawings themselves can reveal to the perceptive adult the child's relative position on the scale of physical and mental maturity, his emotional well-being, and other aspects of his personality.

The reader is directed to studies by Hildreth (1944) for an analysis of children's drawings as related to his development of concepts and as they relate to the developmental principle of progression from the general to the specific. The importance of this form of language is brilliantly expressed in two books by Lowenfeld (1952, 1954).

INNER LANGUAGE

Thinking is an inner language and so closely interrelated with oral and visual language as to make the study of one impossible without a consideration of the other. Yet, some authorities believe that thinking begins to develop long before the other forms of language. "Thinking begins," says Dewey (1933), "as soon as the baby who has lost the ball that he is playing with begins to foresee the possibility of something not yet existing—its recovery—and begins to forecast steps toward the realization of this possibility, and, by experimentation, to guide his acts by his ideas and thereby also test the ideas." Even before the young child develops language skills he gives evidence that he can react to "objects not present" through nonverbal representation, as may be noted in his early response to sounds or stimuli that bring forth a desire for his mother, frequently expressed by crying. This evidence of thought may also be noted in connection with his wanting something not within the realm of his immediate environment —something he cannot see, hear, or smell. As he matures and acquires language skills, his dependence upon nonverbal clues decreases, with a corresponding increase in his dependence upon language.

Thereafter, language becomes the child's chief vehicle for thinking and reasoning. By the means of language a child increases his understanding to include things not in his immediate environment and events that transpired many years ago. He is able to peer into the future and plan events that are to occur next year, or when he has grown into manhood. Through language, he is able to bridge both time and space in his search for meanings and relationships, to group together ideas that bear some similarities, and to develop concepts.

According to Piaget (1937), the child does not begin to grow conscious of his reasoning activities until after the age of seven or eight; nonetheless, the child's intellectual development serves at a relatively early stage to give him a better understanding of himself and the world he lives in.

Developmental Stages in Thinking

Reasoning, along with self-awareness, self-deception, and socialized speech, develops gradually from a feeble beginning in infancy (Dixon, 1957). Most attempts to state the stages of its development draw on the studies of Piaget; and, although most students of child development do not distinguish the different stages as clearly as Piaget did, they recognize that he made an important contribution to our understanding of the language and thought of children, which, according to him, are aspects of the cognitive process. Through a child's language and thought processes, his intellectual development can best be understood.

In his account, Piaget described three stages of development: (1) sensory-motor activity; (2) egocentric thought and language; and (3) rational thought. The first is the period during which the infant explores his world and comes to deal with it as something apart from his self. During this stage he learns that symbols are closely related to the objects and happenings in his world. He gradually learns that his world includes others and that he must learn to adjust to their activities. Language during this period is classified by Piaget as egocentric, since the child's world is still interpreted largely in terms of his self.

In the second stage, the child's speech includes elements of egocentricity, which were discussed earlier in this chapter.

The third stage, according to Piaget, emerges between the seventh and eleventh years. At this time, the child is capable of rational thought.

There is evidence that, with mental maturity and added experience, logical thought increases, while elementary and egocentric thought diminishes. However, attempts to separate the stages as clearly as Piaget separated them meets with many difficulties. Preschool children frequently display rational thought in their attempts to solve complex problems within their level of ability. Studies by Deutsche (1937) revealed that the different types of explanation of causal relations were used at various age levels—results which suggest that the child's thinking cannot be sharply distinguished from adult modes of thought. The best that can be said is that certain types of thinking predominate during childhood and decline during late childhood and adolescence, while other types of thinking, such as logic, increase during the school years.

Thinking as an inner language and its development as related to language has been touched upon in this chapter; thinking as an aspect of intellectual activity will be dealt with in the chapter on mental abilities.

SUMMARY

The development of language skills universally follows a pattern or sequence and each stage is closely interrelated with the previous one as new language patterns grow out of the old patterns.

A genetic study of speech development must begin with prelinguistic babblings, which the infant must be allowed and encouraged to exercise, both for the pleasure it gives him and for the salutary effect it has on the development of his vocal apparatus, hence on his vocabulary. The growth of the child's language involves both qualitative and quantitative changes at each age level. The quantitative growth of the child's vocabulary appears in the increasing amount of words he acquires; the qualitative changes appear in the changed percentage of different parts of speech making up his vocabulary.

The child's conversation has been classified into two large groups— egocentric speech and socialized speech. The early language of the child is markedly egocentric. Socialized speech increases with maturity and social experiences, although children of the same age vary enormously in the nature of their speech.

The number of words a child knows when he enters school determines in a large measure his school progress, and the size of his vocabulary is an indication of his intellectual development. Words are the means by which the child learns about his world. If his knowledge of them is grossly inadequate, the interpretation of his environment will be correspondingly so.

Although there is a close relationship between intelligence and language development, maturation and experience play important and influential roles in the child's acquisition of language. Girls tend to vocalize earlier and progress more rapidly in total language development than boys do. Children from homes in the lower socioeconomic levels progress less rapidly than children from the upper classes.

Given ample opportunity to experiment, a child will spontaneously acquire an expressive visual language by way of his drawings or other art work. However, the development of the communicative visual languages, reading and writing, is primarily a result of instruction and guidance in the schools. Progress is slower in these language forms because the strong urge to be understood is missing, depriving the child of the degree of incentive that led him to acquire oral language.

Language is not only our chief means of understanding things not in our immediate environment but also our chief vehicle for thinking and reasoning. Development of reasoning is directly related to development of language abilities; reasoning is, in fact, considered an inner language. The factors that have either direct or indirect influence upon the one form of language will have a comparable effect upon the other. Thus, as the child matures and progresses in his acquisition of oral, then visual, language, he makes greater use of inner language.

QUESTIONS AND PROBLEMS

1. Differentiate by definition and example *egocentric* and *socialized* speech. What are some of the different kinds of egocentric and socialized speech referred to by Piaget?
2. How would you account for the preponderance of egocentric speech among young children? What factors contribute to the development of socialized speech?
3. Observe children at different ages. What differences do you note in the nature of their language? Are your observations in harmony with the findings presented in this chapter?
4. Show how the child's language development is both qualitative and quantitative in nature.
5. Discuss the effects of each of the following factors upon language development: (1) maturation, (2) sex, (3) ordinal position, (4) bilingualism, and (5) intelligence.
6. How are oral language and listening ability related?
7. Why is reading so important to the child's educational progress? What are some barriers to the development of good reading habits?
8. Just what is meant by reading readiness? What can be done by the home to further reading readiness on the part of the child? To what extent does maturation limit any such attempts?
9. How is language related to thinking? Describe the developmental stages in thinking as presented by Piaget.

SELECTED READINGS

ANDERSON, JOHN E., *The Psychology of Development and Personal Adjustment.* Holt, Rinehart and Winston, 1961. Ch. 7.

BALLER, WARREN R., and DON C. CHARLES, *The Psychology of Human Growth and Development.* Holt, Rinehart and Winston, 1961. Ch. 11.

BRECKENRIDGE, MARIAN E., and E. LEE VINCENT, *Child Development*, 4th ed. Philadelphia: Saunders, 1960. Ch. 11.

HURLOCK, ELIZABETH B., *Child Development*, 4th ed. McGraw-Hill, 1964. Ch. 6.

JERSILD, ARTHUR T., *Child Psychology*, 5th ed. Englewood Cliffs, N. J.: Prentice-Hall, 1960, pp. 304–314.

JOHNSON, WENDELL, et al., *The Onset of Stuttering.* Minneapolis: University of Minnesota Press, 1959.

MCCARTHY, DOROTHEA, Language development in children, in *Manual of Child Psychology* (L. Carmichael, ed.), 2nd ed. John Wiley & Sons, 1954.

MILLARD, CECIL V., *Child Growth and Development in the Elementary School Years*, rev. ed. Boston: Heath, 1958. Ch. 7.

PIAGET, JEAN, *The Language and Thought of the Child.* Harcourt, Brace, 1926.

STRICKLAND, RUTH G., *The Language Arts in the Elementary School.* Boston: Heath, 1951; 2nd ed., 1957.

THOMPSON, GEORGE G., *Child Psychology*, 2nd ed. Boston: Houghton Mifflin, 1962. Ch. 10.

REFERENCES

ALLEN, I. M., Defect of the speech function in childhood, *New Zealand Medical Journal*, 1947, 46, 297–307.

CRAIG, R. S., *The Nature and Frequency of Speech Defects among First, Second, Third, and Fourth Grade Children in Four Negro Schools of Augusta, Georgia.* Ph.D. Dissertation, Northwestern University, 1951.

DAVIS, EDITH A., *The Development of Linguistic Skill in Twins, Singletons with Siblings, and only Children from Age Five to Ten Years.* Institute of Child Welfare Monograph Series No. 14. Minneapolis: University of Minnesota Press, 1937, p. 136.

DAVIS, EDITH A., Developmental changes in the distribution of parts of speech, *Child Development*, 1938, 9, 309–317.

DAVIS, IRENE P., The speech aspects of reading readiness, *Newer Practices in Reading in the Elementary School*, Seventeenth Yearbook, Department of Elementary School Principals, National Education Association, 1938, 17, 282–289.

DAWE, HELEN C., A study of the effect of an educational program upon language development and related mental functions in young children, *Journal of Experimental Education*, 1942, 11, 200–209.

DEUTSCHE, JEAN M., *The Development of Children's Concepts of Causal Relations.* Institute of Child Welfare Monograph Series No. 13. Minneapolis: University of Minnesota Press, 1937.

DEWEY, JOHN, *How We Think.* Boston: Heath, 1933, p. 89.

DIXON, J. C., Development of self recognition, *The Journal of Genetic Psychology*, 1957, 91, 251–256.

EVERHEART, RODNEY W., The relationship between articulation and other developmental factors in children, *Journal of Speech and Hearing Disorders*, 1953, 18, 332–338.

FITZSIMONS, RUTH, Developmental, psychological, and educational factors in children with nonorganic articulation problems, *Child Development*, 1958, 29, 481–489.

FORD, C. T., Developments in written composition during the primary school period, *British Journal of Educational Psychology*, 1954, 24, 38–45.

FREUD, ANNA, Nursery-school education—its uses and dangers, in *Our Children Today* (Sidonie M. Gruenberg, ed.). Viking, 1952, pp. 81–92.

GARRISON, KARL C., and DEWEY G. FORCE, JR., *The Psychology of Exceptional Children*, 4th ed. The Ronald Press, 1965, p. 189.

GENS, GEORGE W., Speech retardation in the normal and subnormal child, *The Training School Bulletin*, 1950, 42, 32–36.

GESELL, ARNOLD, and FLORENCE L. ILG, *Infant and Child in the Culture of Today.* Harper, 1943.

HARRELL, LESTER E., *An Inter-comparison of the Quality and Rate of the Development of Oral and Written Language in Children.* Ph.D. Dissertation, University of Minnesota, 1956.

HAVIGHURST, ROBERT J., *Human Development and Education.* Longmans, Green, (now McKay) 1953.

HILDRETH, G., The simplification tendency in reproducing designs, *The Journal of Genetic Psychology*, 1944, 64, 329–333.

HOLLOW, SISTER M. K., Listening comprehension at the intermediate-grade level, *Elementary School Journal*, 1955–56, 56, 158–161.

HOWARD, R. W., The language development of a group of triplets, *The Journal of Genetic Psychology*, 1946, *69*, 181–188.

HUGHES, MARIE M., and VIVIAN K. COX, The language of first grade children, *Elementary English*, 1949, *26*, 373–380, 406.

ILG, FRANCES, and L. B. AMES, Developmental trends in reading behavior, *The Journal of Genetic Psychology*, 1950, *76*, 291–312.

JERSILD, ARTHUR T., and RUTH RITZMAN, Aspects of language development: the growth of loquacity and vocabulary, *Child Development*, 1938, *9*, 243–259.

KARLIN, ISAAC W., Speech- and language-handicapped children, *Journal of Diseases of Children*, 1958, *95*, 370–376.

KARLIN, ROBERT, Physical growth and success in undertaking beginning reading, *Journal of Educational Research*, 1957, *51*, 191–201.

KIRKPATRICK, EDWIN A., *Fundamentals of Child Study*. Macmillan, 1930, pp. 285–289.

KOTTMEYER, WILLIAM, Readiness for reading, *Elementary English*, 1947, *24*, 355–366.

LOWENFELD, VIKTOR, *Creative and Mental Growth*, 2nd ed. Macmillan, 1952; 3rd ed., 1957.

LOWENFELD, VIKTOR, *Your Child and His Art: A Guide for Parents*. Macmillan, 1954.

MCCARTHY, DOROTHEA, *The Language Development of the Preschool Child*. Institute of Child Welfare Monograph Series No. IV. Minneopolis: University of Minnesota Press, 1930, p. 53.

MCCARTHY, DOROTHEA, Some possible explanations of sex differences in language development and disorders, *The Journal of Psychology*, 1953, *35*, 155–160.

MCCARTHY, DOROTHEA, Language development in children, in *Manual of Child Psychology* (L. Carmichael, ed), 2nd ed. John Wiley & Sons, 1954, p. 577.

MONCUR, J. P., Parental domination in stuttering, *Journal of Speech and Hearing Disorders*, 1952, *17*, 155–165.

MOORE, J. K., Speech content of selected groups of orphanage and non-orphanage pre-school children, *Journal of Experimental Education*, 1947, *16*, 122–133.

MURRAY, TONDOW, *A Study of the Oral and Written Language of Children in the Fourth, Fifth, and Sixth Grades in Various Social Situations*. Ph.D. Dissertaion, University of Southern California, 1953.

NOEL, DORIS I., A comparative study of the relationship between the quality of the child's language usage and the quality and types of language used in the home, *Journal of Educational Research*, 1953, *47*, 161–167.

PIAGET, JEAN, *The Language and Thought of the Child*. Harcourt, Brace, 1926.

PIAGET, JEAN, *Factors Determining Human Behavior*. Cambridge, Mass.: Harvard University Press, 1937.

PINES, MAYA, "How Three-year-olds Teach Themselves to Read—and Love It," *Harper's* (May 1963), *226*, 58–64.

POWERS, M. H., Functional disorders of articulation—symptomatology and etiology, in *Handbook of Speech Pathology* (L. E. Travis, ed.). Appleton-Century-Crofts, 1957, pp. 707–768.

PRATT, EDWARD, Experimental evaluation of a program for the improvement of listening, *Elementary School Journal*, 1955–56, *56*, 315–320.

PRESCOTT, GEORGE A., Sex differences in Metropolitan Readiness Test results, *Journal of Educational Research*, 1955, *48*, 605–610.

RAND, WINIFRED, MARY E. SWEENEY, and E. LEE VINCENT, *Growth and Development of the Young Child*, 5th ed. Philadelphia: Saunders, 1953, pp. 360–362.

ROE, V., and R. MILISEN, The effect of maturation upon defective articulation in elementary grades, *Journal of Speech and Hearing Disorders*, 1942, 7, 37–50.

RUSSELL, CATHINKA M., Personality factors in a motor speech delay case, *American Journal of Mental Deficiency*, 1944, 49, 171–176.

RUSSELL, HUGH K., *Articulation Profile of 209 Mentally Retarded Children*. Seminar in Special Education Report, San Francisco State College, 1952.

SAMPSON, OLIVE C., A study of speech development in children of 18–30 months, *British Journal of Educational Psychology*, 1956, 26, 194–201.

SEASHORE, ROBERT H., quoted in "A new light on children's vocabularies," *School and Society*, 1947, 66, 163–164.

SHIRLEY, M. M., *The First Two Years: A Study of Twenty-five Babies*. Vol. II: *Intellectual Development*. Institute of Child Welfare Monograph No. 7. Minneapolis: University of Minnesota Press, 1933.

SMITH, MADORAH E., An investigation of the development of the sentence and the extent of vocabulary in young children, *University of Iowa Studies in Child Welfare*, 1926, 3, No. 5.

SMITH, MADORAH E., Measurement of vocabularies of young bilingual children in both of the languages used, *The Journal of Genetic Psychology*, 1949, 74, 305–310.

SMITH, MARY K., Measurement of the size of the general English vocabulary through the elementary grades and high school, *Genetic Psychology Monographs*, 1941, 24, 311–345.

SOLOMON, ARTHUR L., Personality and behavior patterns of children with functional defects of articulation, *Child Development*, 1961, 32, 731–737.

STRAYER, LOIS C., Language and growth: the relative efficacy of early and deferred vocabulary training studied by the method of co-twin control, *Genetic Psychology Monographs*, 1930, 8, 209–319.

VAN RIPER, C., *Teaching Your Child to Talk*. Harper & Brothers, 1950, p. 86.

VIGOTSKY, L. S., Thought and speech, *Psychiatry*, 1939, 2, 29–54.

WEST, ROBERT, SEVERINA NELSON, and MILDRED BERRY, The heredity of stuttering, *Quarterly Journal of Speech*, 1939, 25, 23–30.

WYATT, GERTRUDE, *Mother-Child Relationship and Stuttering in Children*. Ph.D. Dissertation. Boston University Graduate School, 1958, p. 645.

YOUNG, FLORENCE M., An analysis of certain variables in a developmental study of language, *Genetic Psychology Monographs*, 1941, 23, 3–141.

YOUNG, FLORENE M., Language growth and development, in *Growth and Development* (Karl C. Garrison, ed.), 2nd ed. New York: Longmans, Green, (now McKay) 1959, p. 233.

YOUNG, WILLIAM E., The relation of reading comprehension and retention to hearing comprehension and retention, *Journal of Experimental Education*, 1936, 5, 30–39.

S E V E N

The Development
of Mental Abilities

THE PROCESS OF INTELLECTION

The mental life of an individual has its beginnings in the experiences he encounters through his senses—most of which are present before birth. A fetus responds to tactile stimulation (Bell, 1960, p. 474) and to sound. An infant reacts to light and to three dimensions of sound: pitch, intensity, and duration. And although opinion varies as to the presence of other senses in the neonate, the ability to distinguish between olfactory stimuli and between gustatory stimuli is certainly fairly well developed soon after birth. The normal infant, therefore, is structurally prepared to receive the sensations his environment offers.

> In the beginning the child's store of experiences and ideas is meager, but he quickly acquires skill in adapting himself to his environment. As his contacts with concrete reality expand and his understanding of this reality becomes clearer, he learns what experience means by seeing it as part of his own vital surroundings. Each experience is a richer addition to the one that preceded. Thus, his learning progresses by gradual, first-hand contact with objects or activities that lie within his range of comprehension. But these activities are not mere play or busy work, but are meanings dramatized, as it were, in action.

Those words by Hall-Quest and Kandel (1965, p. 592) imply that a wide range of experiences, both actual and vicarious, is essential for the development of the child's comprehension. Careful study of many similar and dissimilar objects, people, and situations is necessary if accurate meanings, or concepts, are to be accumulated.

The sensory impressions are carried to the brain where changes are produced leaving *memory* traces. No mental activity would be possible if the individual were unable to record and retain the impressions he receives and to later recall the ones necessary for comparison and association with new sensations. Forgetting, the fourth function of memory, serves to "purify" the storehouse of materials that have no meaning for the individual or have been ineffectively learned.

By comparison of stimuli, the child notices similarities and differences. He exercises discrimination, or differentiation. Generally speaking, this stage is about as far as the feebleminded person can go in his mental activity. Kounin (1943, p. 195), after analyzing tests in which his subjects were required to draw a man, observed: "The feeble-minded person includes as many, if not more, details (has the necessary differentiation and knows the various parts) but does not relate one part to another. This results in his drawing a man that is defective in proportion." Kounin's subjects failed to achieve the next step—the making of relationships, the application of new meanings to old experiences, old meanings to new experiences; the combining, associating, elaborating of old and new sensations in endless succession.

Having passed through these elementary stages of mental activity, the individual has reached a climax, the gateway to higher forms of intellectual life: He has formulated concepts, or ideas. He has organized his experiences into meaningful relationships. The achievement of this goal constitutes the beginning of true thought, or cognition, perception, understanding, intellectual—whatever term is used for what might be considered a plateau in the vertical and horizontal climb toward the peaks of reasoning, imagining, problem-solving, analyzing, generalizing, causal thinking, handling and using abstractions.

THE FORMATION OF CONCEPTS

As the child becomes increasingly aware of various objects, persons, and situations, he gradually develops an understanding of their natures and functions. He attaches to them meanings, both connotative and denotative, which are the result of their impact upon his needs, interests, and total personality. The quantity and quality of those meanings determine the nature of his various abilities and the degree of intelligence he manifests in them.

As the young person matures he is expected to differentiate between distances, judge relative sizes and weights, learn numbers and coin values,

Young thinker—Three is the age when children start to understand abstract concepts—such as time.

know and judge measures of time, including ages, hours and periods of the day, days of the week, seasons, and such abstractions as "past," "last week," "yesterday"; "present," "now," "today"; "future," "later," "tomorrow," etc. He forms ideas concerning life, birth, death, cause and effect, color and form combinations, himself, social relationships, and so forth.

Considering the staggering number of concepts a child must learn and the manner in which he learns them, one can easily see why a child's understanding is far different from an adult's, why it is immature and often erroneous, and why his explanations draw heavily on magic or the supernatural. Yet, the child's conception that seems amusingly illogical to an adult is not so to the child. The explanations he gives of phenomena are not only plausible to him but represent an unconscious pride in the ability to explain one event in terms of past knowledge and experience. For example, when one six-year-old child was asked why gas jets on a stove should not be turned on and left unattended, he quite happily explained, "Because big bunches of fire will keep going up to the ceiling, up to the ceiling, and when they all get together at the top they will start a fire." His answer was nearly identical to the simplified explanation he had been given of cloud formation and rain.

Patterns and Stages of Development

As with other phases of development, definite patterns appear in the acquisition of concepts. The understanding of individual properties and ideas proceeds from simple to complex, general to specific, vague to clear, and in an orderly sequence that is fairly stable from child to child. Weinstein (1957, pp. 171–172) studied the development of the concept of "flag" and a sense of national identity. He noted the different levels in the children's understanding. At ages five and six, the flag is a name for a class of objects with common physical characteristics. It "belongs" rather than identifies. At age seven, the flag identifies proprietorship. Countries are differentiated on the basis of geographical areas. The notion of multiplicity of flags appears at age eight, when the full extent of the symbolism associated with the flag begins to be understood. At age nine, the flag is understood as a conventional symbol; a country is regarded as both a geographical area and a particular form of governmental administration, with the group of people in the country having common purposes and allegiances.

Concerning life, the preschool child assumes that all moving things are alive and that everything in nature has human qualities. (The sun goes behind the clouds because it doesn't want to get wet. Clouds blow cold air on people.) The kindergartner or first-grader may recognize that an agent is required to move a bicycle and that it, therefore, is not alive. On the other hand, water might be included in his list of living things "because it runs." Similarly, plants, especially trees, are not included "because they don't move."

Through faulty perceptions and information, the young child "knows" that babies come from hospitals, or God, or the stork and that a mother goes to get one, or buys one, or prays for one, or has one given to her. With

*"Did you ask Daddy
if you can keep him?"*

maturity and more accurate information, the child is able to understand the mother's relationship to the birth process, but often he has reached adolescence before he is aware of the father's role.

As for the concept of death, a child's knowledge is largely dependent upon his religious training. Few children under the age of nine regard death as final: A youngster may ask, When will he come alive again? or, Will Rover still be sick in dog heaven? Nor do very young children understand that bodily processes cease with death. During the eulogies spoken at a funeral, one five-year-old asked why they didn't open the coffin so that the person could hear what they were saying about him.

Piaget (1932) assigned more or less specific ages to the developmental stages in a child's conceptions of living things, but, although Russell (1940, p. 364) agreed on the probability that "individuals pass sequentially through the series of concept stages with increasing mental and chronological age," he found it impossible to limit the age range for each stage as Piaget had done. Russell's conclusions appear to be much more logical when one considers that the growth curves among different classes of concepts are as varied as those for the different body parts. There are concepts that develop early and those that begin slowly and suddenly spurt toward crystallization. Some develop gradually over a relatively long period of time, and others do not begin to develop until much later than most. King (1961) studied the development of scientific concepts among children six to eleven years of age, presenting them with questions and problems involving (A) length, weight, time, direction; (B) volume and weight; (C) mechanical principles; (D) living things, seasons, etc. As shown in Figure VII–1, most of the ques-

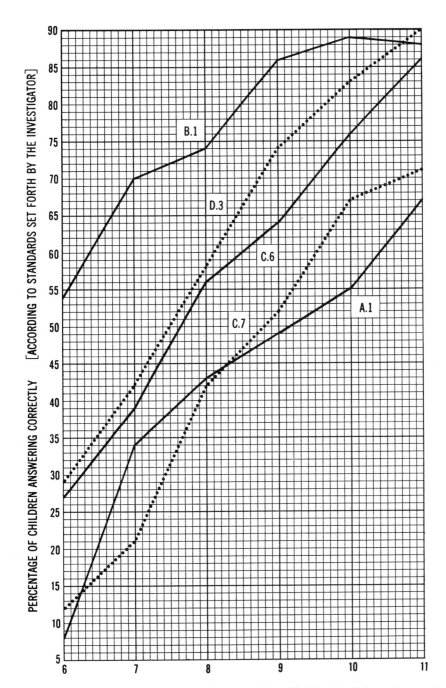

Figure VII–1. Growth Curves Showing the Nature of Growth of Certain Science Concepts.
A. 1. Estimation of time between two taps; B. 1. Is water level higher or lower when a stone is added to a jar of water?; C. 6. Direction of cogwheels; C. 7. Speed of cogwheels; D. 3. Are all things that move living? (After King, 1961, p. 20)

tions elicited a steady increase in correct solutions with age, although the increase was slower for the more complex concepts.

Furthermore, as the child becomes successful, interested, and more capable in one or more areas, he tends to specialize, resulting in an imbalance in concept maturity. He may, for example, be able to solve problems involving scientific concepts at an early age, yet, as an adult, be unable to enter into satisfactory social relationships because of immature social perceptions.

Misconceptions

Faulty concepts are difficult to eradicate or change and are just as cumulative as are the accurate ones, many being held throughout an individual's lifetime. Such faults of conception can be traced to various causes. Superstition is one. Transmitted through generations and centuries, many superstitious beliefs and practices create barriers to efficient action and the acquisition of precise knowledge. One of our most pervasive sets of superstitions involves the work *black* and its connotations of evil, death, sinister events, and sorrow. We speak of the Black Death, Black Friday, black cats, witches in black hats and robes, black mourning clothes, black crows, the black of night, black clouds, a black soul.

Misunderstanding of words is another cause of misconceptions. One child went all the way through high school wondering why the hero, or the "good guy," in a story should *heed* authority: she thought *heed* meant "don't pay attention to." Similarly, many adults believe the word *enervate* means exactly the opposite of "reduce vitality."

Faulty information and the making of incorrect relationships, as happened in the example of the child and the gas stove, are other causes of misconceptions. Sometimes, an individual makes too many relationships. A six-year-old who enjoyed watching a situation-comedy program featuring two carpenters was asked, what does a carpenter do? Her answer was, "He puts down rugs and moves furniture. Sometimes he baby-sits." At other times, children fail to make all the necessary relationships, as was evident in the case of the boy who could not understand why all the state highways didn't belong to his engineer father: "He built them, didn't he?" A perfectly logical reasoning for a child who is allowed to keep the things he makes in school!

BEYOND UNDERSTANDING: REASON AND IMAGINATION

If the mental activities that take place up to the point of misunderstanding are likened to the process of absorption, then inductive and deductive reasoning (or any of the higher forms of mental activity) can be analogous to a squeezing of the sponge. Or, we could say there is a passive and dynamic intellect. Many people, and most teachers, have come in contact with individuals who are extremely well equipped to remember material presented to them in one form or another—who have what are known as photographic or auditory memories and "total recall"—but who are unable to relate one item to another or the body of their knowledge to everyday behavior. They are ineffectual in social situations, seemingly incapable of performing, dressing, or speaking in accordance with the customs of any particular society. They fall just short of understanding; they lack a large measure of the dynamic abilities to reason logically, to make cause and effect relationships, to generalize, analyze, evaluate, solve problems, or handle abstractions.

In common practice, the highest orders of thinking are grouped into two major divisions: reasoning and imagining. Reasoning is frequently equated with problem-solving—the two being highly correlated—and is described as a rational organization of material or facts usually leading to the solution of a problem. Imagining is described as a search for uncommon relationships leading to a synthesis of original ideas.

Imagination

There is no doubt concerning the ability of children to indulge in feats of imagination. Childhood is often referred to as a period of fancy and fantasy, of magic and make-believe. With the utmost absorption and concentration, young people make up words, similies, metaphors, stories, dramatic skits, poems and jingles, jokes, songs, and dances. They create pictures and models from any available medium, whether it comes from nature, an art supply store, or a father's workshop. They design their own toys, make up their own games and rules, manufacture tools and instruments, including those for musical purposes. Creative imagination begins to show up early in infancy and, with encouragement, continues to manifest itself throughout a lifetime. According to the many studies made over the past decades regarding creativity, imagination is a property of every individual, it is not highly correlated with intelligence, it can be improved both in quantity and quality—through encouragement primarily, but also through training and guidance, and its effects are transferrable and useful to every field of human endeavor (Parnes and Harding, 1962).

Reasoning or Problem-Solving

Concerning the young child's ability to reason and the age at which he begins to do so, there is considerable difference of opinion. Anderson (1949) states: "Studies of the behavior of children in problem-solving situations reveal a complete range of behavior from random activity through to the immediate solution with ability to state the principle." Many investigators contend that the problem-solving behavior of preschool children is characterized almost exclusively by random activity, or trial-and-error methods to solution. These same authorities are of the opinion that reasoning, as it is equated with problem-solving behavior, does not appear with any consistency or identifiability until approximately six years of age. Heidbreder (1928), for example, concealed a small doll in one of two boxes and instructed the children to solve the problem by responding to clues. The three-year-olds were interested in nothing but obtaining the doll from the box, no matter how it was done. Four-year-olds were not particularly interested in either the doll or the problem. Children six to ten years of age recognized that there was a problem to be solved, and they solved it with the necessary objectivity.

Aside from the problem of semantics involved in defining *reasoning*, one difficulty that occurs when investigators attempt to ascertain the beginning ages for reasoning lies in the nature of testing, in the fact that the problem is an artificial one. Children's reactions when presented with a test which they know to be a test vary considerably and must necessarily affect the outcome of the analysis. Some children, for instance, will enjoy being tested, others will attempt to out-guess the testor. Some will view the problem with a fear of failing and will thus inhibit or cramp their thinking; others will self-consciously give silly answers. Instead of admitting any inadequacy in knowledge or ability, many youngsters will make up answers or tell the investigator what they think he wishes to hear.

Yet, in the dynamics of everyday living, children show evidence of reasoning, even though in elementary forms, long before the age of six. A nine-month-old baby who cannot reach an object on a table may pull the tablecloth in order to bring the object within his reach. Creative youngsters three- and four-years-old will solve the problem of "accidents," such as paint drippings on a picture, by verbalizing, "Oh, well, that can be the rain," by creating a new form in the drawing to conceal the splotches, or by changing the picture entirely in order to incorporate the mistakes. A six-year-old child wanted to make an apron from a piece of material that was several inches too short to tie around her waist immediately perceived the problem, found two pieces of string, and stapled one on each side of the cloth, after which she successfully tied the apron. Another six-year-old wanted to dig a hole, but the only tools available to him were a piece of broken glass and an old bent rod with a small, closed loop on one end. Rather than bear down on the jagged glass, which he knew to be dangerous, he wedged it into the loop and, using the bent portion of the rod as a handle, turned the tool in the manner of a hand drill. When there was an accumulation of loose dirt in the "drilled" hole, he removed the broken glass, gingerly used it as a scoop, and then resumed the drilling operation.

If we were to accept at face value the results of structured tests of children's problem-solving behavior, we should expect most children to begin reasoning on their sixth birthday. But it is inconceivable that this ability, any more than specific language or motor abilities, should arise overnight. Dixon (1957) and Dewey (1933), among others believe that reasoning and thinking begin in early infancy—when the child perceives a goal, concrete or abstract, and attempts to reach it despite obstacles. Upon encountering an obstacle, the goal-seeker takes the four necessary steps toward problem solution: He recognizes that he must surmount the obstacle (locates the problem), he studies ways in which it can be done (surveys possible solutions), he selects one of the methods (makes a decision), and he acts upon the decision (tries or evaluates the solution). Such a process is the essence of problem-solving behavior; and regardless of the extent to which the child's actions approximate a form of trial-and-error behavior, the elements of reasoning are present and become actuated the moment a child recognizes that something stands between him and his goal. The first time an infant climbs out of his crib, he has exercised an elementary form of reasoning.

Not that he continues to reason each time he climbs out, however! He soon finds that the action of climbing up, over, and down is satisfying in itself and henceforth will freely exercise the ability unless he meets another obstacle, such as a harness, to challenge and frustrate him.

Naturally, very young children will make errors in reasoning. Their attention span is too limited to enable them to keep a goal in mind for very long. Nor can they maintain concentrated thinking. As Rand, Sweeney, and Vincent (1953) have said: "They may have all the necessary facts for solution of a problem, but unless some progress toward solution becomes evident fairly soon, they are likely to lose sight of the goal, or are likely to become distracted by some trivial aspect of the problem."

Regardless of the age at which a child begins to reason or imagine, there is no denying that the abilities for causal, abstract, and logical thinking, analyzing, generalizing, creating, solving problems, and evaluating develop gradually rather than by stages and that the degree to which a child can perform those operations depends upon maturation, experience, training, and intelligence.

INTELLIGENCE

But just exactly what is "intelligence"? That is a question which perennially courses through academic circles and widespread discussions, the answers varying with each speaker and often being changed by any one speaker as he shifts his point of view or his audience. Scott (1963, p. 66) broadly defines *animal intelligence* as "the ability of animals to adapt to changes in environmental conditions through changes in behavior." He goes on to elaborate:

> ...In any species, intelligence reflects particular sensory, motor, and central nervous capacities, including the capacity for learning from previous experience, as well as the hereditary organization of these capacities. Thus broadly defined, some degree of intelligence is found in all animals that show behavior.

Brussel (1954) says: "Intelligence is the inborn capacity to cope with unexpected changes in the environment." Menninger (1961) calls it the capacity for using knowledge, but later adds that it is the ability to use the functions of memory "in facilitating the adjustment of the whole personality to the requirements of a situation." Kimble (1954, p. 2) breaks down all the definitions of *intelligence* into three general types: (1) what intelligence tests measure, (2) that which is manifested in certain specific abilities, (3) the capacity to engage in school work, or the individual's scholastic aptitude. Lastly, Thorpe (1962) gives us an excellent, all-inclusive summary of intelligence as a total concept:

> ...An individual is intelligent (at his age level) to the extent that he is able to think in the abstract, to discern relationships within difficult and complex problems or activities, to maintain a steady direction toward a goal with reasonable speed, to invent new solutions when necessary, to keep his activities within the range of normal social values, and to resist the pressures of emotional bias.

Most of the semantic arguments revolve around and are outgrowths of the fairly recent development of psychological tests, which measure *functional* intelligence and predict an individual's chances for academic success. Krugman (1952, p. 254), for one, deplores the use of the word *intelligence* for any measure of an individual's learning capacity. Speaking of psychological tests, he says:

> ...The result of a test of this kind is given a numerical value and called the Intelligence Quotient (I. Q.).[*] Statements in mathematical

------

[*] Intelligence test scores for children are usually reported in terms of mental age (MA) divided by chronological age (CA) and multiplied by 100 (to avoid decimals). If, on an intelligence test, an eight-year-old child makes the same score as an average ten-year-old, we say his mental age is ten. His intelligence quotient (10 × 100) would be 125. Whereas mental age indicates the rate at which the child is developing, IQ is an indication of the amount of intelligence.

The use of a single score may furnish a quick and easy way to classify children relative to intelligence, but it fails to furnish clues to the different mental abilities that characterize individual children, or to indicate the motivation to use the intellectual potential one possesses. Table VII–1, for instance, presents a comparison of two children with identical total scores on an intelligence test. The scores represent exactly opposite mental abilities, with Pupil A scoring high in memory ability and low in numerical reasoning, and Pupil B scoring just the reverse. Recording a single, unqualified score on a student's scholastic record, therefore, can mislead those persons responsible for his guidance.

terms seem somehow more "scientific" or exact; many people therefore accept the I. Q. without question. Actually the I. Q. measures only a part of the intelligence. It measures the ability to learn abstract and verbal subject matter in school. It does not measure practical or mechanical ability or the ability to deal with people, or musical ability, art ability, or any of the host of other types of functions that require intelligence of other sorts.

Furthermore, Krugman later reminds us (p. 261): "Intelligence tests do not measure the emotional or other personality factors that interfere with the utilization of one's abilities."

Nevertheless, despite their misuse, overuse, and fallibility, intelligence tests have provided us with a great body of knowledge concerning those facets of intelligence that can be measured. Also, they have furnished us with information relative to mental growth—its rate and constancy and variations—and the factors which have the greatest influence on it.

MENTAL GROWTH CURVES

Through data collected from intelligence tests of single individuals and groups of individuals over a number of years, investigators have been able to plot mental growth curves which furnish clues to the nature and rate

Table VII-1 Differences Between Two Pupils with Identical Total Raw Scores on the *California Test of Mental Maturity*, Grades 4–8 (Garrison, unpublished material)

Test Items	Possible Score	Actual Score Pupil A	Actual Score Pupil B
Memory	44	10	40
1. Immediate Recall	24	6	23
2. Delayed Recall	20	4	17
Spatial Relationships	35	24	30
3. Sensing Right and Left	20	14	18
4. Manipulation of Area	15	10	12
Logical Reasoning	60	54	38
5. Opposites	15	14	12
6. Similarities	15	14	12
7. Analogies	15	13	9
8. Inference	15	13	5
Numerical Reasoning	35	30	5
9. Number Series	10	7	3
10. Numerical Quantity	10	8	1
11. Numerical Quantity	15	15	1
12. Verbal Concepts	50	36	40
Total Raw Score	224	154	154

Tests can guide psychologists to understand the mental growth of children. Here the child is being given the opportunity to match pictures of familiar objects, a ball, a lamp, a moon, etc. The child picks up a small card—picture of the moon—and must find its mate on the large cards which have been set before him. You will recognize this problem in the object lotto games which are popular with young children.

of intellectual development among children. The curves show that there is a gradual and continuous growth in mental abilities from birth to maturity, with the various mental functions maturing at different periods. Most of the mental abilities that show a great deal of development during early childhood tend to reach their full power during adolescence.* Figure VII-2, for example, presents the growth curves for four of the eleven tests in the *Wechsler Intelligence Scale for Children.* These curves show roughly the proportion of fifteen-year old mental maturity attained at the different age levels. The mean score for digit span increases significantly until age eleven; thereafter little increase occurs. Vocabulary development follows a steadier, more gradual course.

The ability to memorize also improves rapidly until around the fourteenth birthday. The curves for memorizing poetry and nonsense syllables are similar and are roughly parallel to the curve for general intelligence.

Studies of individual curves reveal a wide variety of patterns, although they all follow the same "basic ground plan." Compared to the

* The reader must keep in mind we make a distinction between mental abilities and intelligence—the ability to use those abilities. Whereas the various functions generally reach their fullest powers coincidentally with physical maturity (between 25 and 30 years), intelligence continues to grow so long as one absorbs knowledge, or at least so long as one vigorously pursues learning as a full-time student. With the continued exercises of mental functions, people can learn more and can become wiser as they grow older (Duvall and Duvall, 1964).

later years, the preschool and early years are periods of rapid growth. Frequently a plateau shows up in the pattern, varying in duration from one individual to another. There may be periods of forging ahead, although there is no characteristic adolescent spurt as there is in physical growth curves. Rather, the curve during adolescence often flattens, forming a plateau, or sharply declines, after which the individual recovers and once again grows steadily, but at a slower rate, toward maturity. Some individual differences in growth rates and patterns may be observed in Figure VII-3.

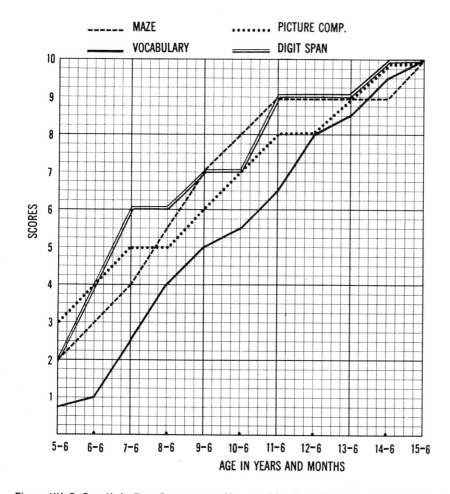

Figure VII–2. Growth in Four Components Measured by the WISC Test. Weighted scores at the mean of each age when base of comparison is the equivalent standard score of 15–4 to 15–7. (After Wechsler, 1950, p. 46)

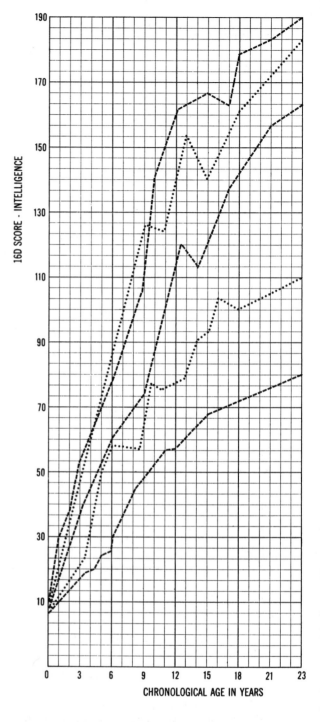

Figure VII–3. Individual Curves of Intelligence for Five Boys (Bayley, 1955, p. 814)

An observation that can be made from a study of Figure VII-3 is that, regardless of the overall rate of growth in intelligence, after the age of physical maturity (twenty-one) all the curves begin to flatten at approximately the same angle. In other words, such an observation would appear to support the contention of Freeman and Flory (1943, p. 159) that "children of mediocre ability continue to advance intellectually during the period of adolescence, as rapidly if not more rapidly than do bright children, and that they continue to advance to at least as late an age." Applying their findings to educational programs, the investigators continue:

> . . . In other words, children or youth of lesser promise may profit by continued education as much as if not more than their precocious and brighter comrades. If this is true, and we believe it is, it indicates that recent theories of development run the danger of doing serious injustice to children of mediocre ability by making too unfavorable prognosis of their attainment. Educational opportunity should be kept open to them into the college period if their interests and plans call for a continuance of education up to this period and if a suitable type of education can be provided. In advising students the course of their intellectual growth must be taken into account as well as their present intellectual ability; and the prediction of their intellectual growth must recognize the possibilities of growth at the lower levels as well as the variability of growth among individuals.

The predictability of mental growth spoken of by Freeman and Flory has become a rather controversial subject. Freeman (1936) found that the average mental growth curves for three groups of children (who had different degrees of mental abilities to start with) show that each group retains its relative position from one age to another. Thus, Freeman and many other investigators believe that an individual's overall rate of intellectual development is relatively constant. Such a belief is tenable only *if* we keep in mind that (1) we are speaking of the constancy of the IQ; (2) a child's score on an intelligence test is a measure of how many exercises and problems he can complete correctly and the number of items he can complete correctly depends upon hereditary characteristics, opportunity for learning, physical, mental, and emotional conditions, and motivation, among other factors; (3) the earlier the tests are administered, the greater will be the disparity with later test results (Bayley, 1955) *; and (4) the IQ is more likely to remain constant if environmental conditions in turn are relatively stable (Escalona and Moriarty, 1961). The latter point (4) should be emphasized, for there is substantial evidence that the IQ remains

* Honzik, Macfarlane, and Allen (1948) anticipated Bayley's conclusion in a presentation of correlations between intelligence test scores during the preschool years and IQ at ages ten and eighteen. As a child advances through the grades, his test scores become more predictive of later performance. Anderson (1939) has also maintained that accurate predictability is impossible if made on the basis of mental tests given to a child under two years of age.

constant precisely because an individual's environment tends to remain constant. Regardless of the child's *potential* intelligence, his IQ generally becomes stabilized at the same level as the environment in which he spends the largest proportion of his formulative years. (See pages 199–201.)

At the infant level, developmental tests and schedules are apparently reliable only in diagnosing extremes of intellectual ability. One reason for the disparity between the early and late scores is that the term *intelligence* seems to have different connotations at the various age levels, and the abilities are, of course, necessarily tested by different methods. Hofstaetter (1954), who analyzed the correlations obtained by Bayley from the California Growth Study into three statistically independent factors, found a rather definite age trend in the loading of the three factors, the first—sensorimotor alertness—being predominant during the first two years; the second—persistence—characterizing the ages from two to four; and the third—manipulation of symbols—accounting for the respective scores after the age of four.

FACTORS INFLUENCING MENTAL GROWTH

Chronological Age

As a child grows older he develops the sensorimotor abilities with which he expands his horizons and gains a multitude of experiences that enable him to form an increasing number of concepts. His language abilities develop with age, allowing him to form abstract concepts, behave symbolically, control his environment more adequately, and vary the quantity and quality of his social contacts. Most important, language enables a child to ask questions, an extremely valuable and continuing method of gaining knowledge.

With age, a child builds a richer vocabulary and gathers fuller and more exact meanings of words from hearing and seeing them in a number of concrete applications. Thus, his memory associations grow rapidly, and he exercises and improves the ability to retain and recall sensory material.

The older a child is, the better able he is to notice similarities and differences, and the better he can generalize. Terman and Merrill (1937), as part of their scale for measuring intelligence, test the ability to differentiate. At the designated ages, for example, the following questions are asked:

Year VII: In what way are wood and coal alike?
Year VIII: In what way are a baseball and an orange alike, and how are they different?

The test administrators point out that: "Giving similarities is fairly difficult at year VII, but too easy at year VIII. The increased difficulty of giving both a similarity and a difference (year VIII) is probably due to the necessity of keeping in mind the directing idea." They further note that comprehension of the words *alike* and *different* requires a level of maturity higher than the actual ability to perceive similarities.

If questioning should prove to be unfruitful in the child's search for information, he may turn to reading to satisfy his curiosity; but, again, reading is an ability that requires training and a certain level of maturity. Generally, not until the youngster is six years old does he begin to benefit from formal, scholastic instruction, which, if it did nothing else, would serve to call his attention to facts and experiences that he might not ordinarily come into contact with, notice, or be curious about. Schooling, then, not only adds to a child's knowledge as a matter of course, but also increases his means for obtaining knowledge in the absence of a tangible authority. Deutsche (1943, p. 144), speaking of causal thinking, has said that "the answers to specific questions are more closely related to school experience and whatever that implies in the way of direct or indirect instruction and training" than they are to maturation and innate factors.

Ausubel and Schiff (1954), also, found that the ability to learn a relevant causal relationship is a function of age. The older child is able to state a problem and verbalize its solution and the principles involved. Problem-solving, too, can be enhanced by practice and by training at appropriate ages. The older the child is, the fewer trial-and-error solutions he attempts; he deliberates longer and makes fewer mistakes.

Mental growth, the *"progressive behavior patterning of the individual"* (Gesell, 1952, p. 51), is a product of learning through an accumulation of sensory observations, motor manipulations, and symbolic meanings. Learning takes time, and time, therefore, is a major factor in the development of intellect.

Heredity ←——→ Environment

Time will never enable a dull child to learn his lessons or master his tasks as effectively (or what amounts to the same thing, as quickly) as the bright child. He may learn as much about some things, but it will take him longer. There is good evidence that the individual's maximum rate of development, the ultimate ease with which he may take any necessary step toward maturity, is established by heredity. However, one of the inadequacies of psychological tests is their incapability of showing us how fast an individual is *capable* of progressing. We can find out how fast he is progressing at present and predict how fast he is likely to progress in the future. We can determine and to some extent adjust the limits being set by environmental factors, but we can neither determine nor alter those limits established by heredity.

Furthermore, except insofar as intelligence is a functioning of neurological structures, there is not absolute surety that it *is* inherited, any more than are other forms of behavior. But considering the weight of evidence gathered from studies of correlations between IQ's and various degrees of genetic relationships, most authorities agree to the probability that individuals inherit a potential for intelligence. Burt (1958) found high positive correlations between the test scores of identical twins (see Table VII-2), and other investigators have discovered correlations in the .50's between parents and their children (Pearson, 1903; Jones, 1954).

Table VII–2 Correlations Between Mental Test Results and Different Degrees of Genetic Relationships (After Burt, 1958, p. 6)

	Group tests	Individual tests
Identical twins reared together	.944	.921
Identical twins reared apart	.771	.843
Nonidentical twins reared together	.542	.526
Siblings reared together	.515	.491
Siblings reared apart	.441	.463
Unrelated children reared together	.281	.252

Intellectual level of environment.   Parent-sibling mental correlations are found consistently whenever studies are made but are always recognized as being influenced by *both* heredity and environment. The mental capacity of parents affects not only the capacity of their children but also the mental level of the home—which in turn has an effect upon a child's intelligence. This fact is supported by numerous studies. Burks (1928) and Newman, Freeman, and Holzinger (1937) found that children placed in foster homes whose intellectual level was higher than their previous environment frequently made gains in intelligence test scores. Other environmental enriching, such as occurs when a child is placed in a nursery school, also appears to have a salutary influence upon IQ (Skeels, *et al.*, 1938).

Crissey (1937), also, has pointed out that the mental development of a child who has been diagnosed as a high-grade moron and placed in an institution designed for normal and dull-normal children is likely to show an improvement, whereas similarly diagnosed children placed in an institution designed for feebleminded patients register a loss in IQ. Similarly, the children of feebleminded mothers manifest a decided lowering of IQ scores if they are allowed to remain in their mothers' care (Speer, 1940), a finding that reaffirms the statement that the longer a child remains in a given environment the more his IQ assumes the level characteristic of that environment.

Restricted environment. Closely related to the studies of the effects upon a child of the intellectual level of his environment are the numerous studies of restricted environments and their influence upon an individual's ability to engage in various mental activities. There is no question but what the opportunity to experience is of prime importance to the development of intellect, and the restricted environment denies the child, in varying degrees, the situations and materials through which he expresses and fulfills his capacities. In general, children from low socioeconomic homes and those from rural areas score lower on intelligence tests than those from higher socioeconomic levels and urban areas. Such results are partly due to the manner in which the tests are culturally oriented, but the relatively impoverished environments must be taken into consideration when one attempts to explain the lower scores.

A unique study of the influence of an adverse environment upon the growth of intelligence was reported by Gordon (1923), who used a group of canal-boat children and a group of gypsy children as subjects. These youngsters led a very limited existence and most of the time were cut off from all social contact except with their own families. The average IQ of the canal-boat children was found to be 69.6, which is near the borderline for a classification of feeblemindedness. An interesting feature of this study was the decline in IQ with the increase in age. The age-group from four to six had an average IQ of approximately ninety, whereas the age-group from twelve to twenty-two had an average IQ of approximately sixty.

Asher (1935) has also indicated that a restricted environment has an adverse effect upon IQ and that this becomes more pronounced as the children spend more time in such an environment.

Physical Defects

Opportunities to experience are often severely limited by physical defects in a child. His ability to hear, see, feel, smell, and taste determines the things to which he will be able to respond. If hearing is impaired, there will be difficulty in associating sounds with written words. Those who are nearsighted miss much that happens at a distance; those who are farsighted have difficulty understanding relationships that depend upon the observation of minute details, such as those used in reading, writing, and number work. Both kinds of visual defects, as well as strabismus, astigmatism, and others, will naturally have an effect upon a child's competency to judge spatial relationships. Color blindness obviously robs the very young child of many pleasurable sensations and virtually blocks out an entire area of concepts.

Children born without a sense of taste or smell are, in a mild sense, isolated from the many social contacts that revolve around eating: picnics, congregating in the ice cream parlors, sharing candy bars. Sometimes, these children are considered "peculiar" by their peers because they choose all their food according to texture and colorfulness.

Not uncommonly, children are born who are unable to experience pain, tactile stimulation, heat, or cold. It could be said that they have no sense of feeling, and to them the world is a place of perpetual danger and restrictions, wherein they cannot be allowed to learn through experience that stoves and irons are hot, that flame burns, that knives cut deeply and quickly, and that hard falls can severely bruise, scrape, cut, or cause broken bones which, through a lack of pain, can remain undiscovered and thus be additionally damaging. Such a child is hardly less restricted than the hemophiliac who must be conscientiously protected from *any* blood-letting injury. These defects do, of course, hinder the normal development of motor abilities; and, as stated previously, motor development is a "handmaiden of mental development."

Emotional Climate

The dynamics of mental development are affected by the emotional climate of the home and the emotions that are stirred up in the individual as a result of the treatment he receives in his home, school, and society.

> ... For example, environmental deprivation of responsive human contact during the first several months of life can, if extreme, permanently handicap the individual's expression of his innate psychological potentialities. Such a lack of opportunity is not always, however, due to an impoverished human environment. Parental overprotection and overindulgence can contribute to lack of appropriate stimulation and so retard the child's expression of his naturally increasing capacities for physical, emotional, intellectual independence, and for self-control and self-direction.
>
> Milner, 1959

Neither child nor adult who is under tension from anxiety, fear of failure, self-reproach, jealousy, hate, or any of the stronger emotions, even excessive love with its distorting side effects, can be expected to behave efficiently, to maintain an attentive attitude toward new material, to concentrate for long periods of time, or to perceive with objectivity, thus with accuracy. Not unlike pain, excessive emotion is a parasite: No matter what activity the host attempts to engage in, the imbalance of excessive emotion and the resultant inner conflicts divert both his energy and his attention from the matter at hand.

Motivation

Eagerness to learn can be found in varying degrees among children, and it is apparently responsible for some of the differences to be noted in variability and direction of IQ changes. Sontag and his associates (1958) claim that a general accelerator-decelerator factor is always present, regardless of a child's own special competence. That factor has been called "learning to learn," eagerness to learn, or curiosity.

The degree to which a child possesses the motivation, or eagerness, to learn is dependent upon a number of factors, including parental expectations and the importance they assign to intellectual activities; the child's self-concept and his aspirations; and the successes, past and present, the child has achieved in mastering tasks and reaching goals. Without some measure of success, or progress toward a goal, the child becomes discouraged and his activities become tangential to the main course; he becomes "distracted by some trivial aspect of the problem."

There is, too, such a thing as overmotivation, which has a particularly adverse effect upon problem-solving, and presumably upon other behavior patterns. Scheerer (1963) cites a study by Birch, who found that if a chimpanzee were too hungry he would fixate on the goal—a banana—and strive in vain to reach it. A moderately hungry chimpanzee was able to think his way to obtaining the food by means of a less direct method. Scheerer added: "On the human level there is some evidence that strong ego-involvement in a problem makes for overmotivation and is detrimental to a solution" (p. 128). Thus, support can be found for the statement by Strong (1964) that inner motivation, made up partly of curiosity and partly of the desire for mastery over objects and events, is a feeling that needs preservation rather than stimulation.

SUMMARY

Through numerous experiences, both actual and vicarious, a child's sensory mechanisms record impressions of objects, people, and situations in his environment. The impressions are grouped into general categories and compared. The individual notes similarities and differences; he relates new and old sensations, attaching meanings to his experiences. In this manner, concepts are formed.

Every classification of concepts—the concrete, the social, the abstract —is formed by stages, but the timing varies with each category and each individual. The assignment of specific ages for the formation of particular concepts has been found to be impracticable, if not impossible. Misconceptions are common. Some are outgrown, others persist throughout a lifetime. They are caused by the transmission of superstitious beliefs and misinformation, by an inaccurate understanding of words, and by the making of faulty relationships.

Reasoning and imagining are the two most common activities of dynamic intellection. All normal children exercise these capacities to some degree, although imagination is more evident than reasoning in the early years, partly because imagining is more naturally spontaneous and partly because, semantically, there is some question as to the exact nature and manifestations of reasoning in youngsters.

Intelligence has been defined according to its two primary classifications: potential and functional. The former cannot be measured by psychological tests. Such tests indicate the amount of learning an individual has acquired and the rate of speed at which he acquired it; from these, intelligence is inferred. The scores from psychological tests are predictive of and positively correlated with academic success. Despite criticisms of their structures, uses, and interpretations, intelligence tests have furnished us with valuable information concerning mental growth and the manner in which it conforms to the principles of development.

Maturation is essential for the development of mental abilities. However, the rate and limit of mental development will be determined largely by heredity. Both the rate and the limit are further influenced by the opportunities to experience that are accorded the individual by the cultural and intellectual level of his environment and by his physical equipment; and those opportunities are grasped by the maturing child in proportion to his degree of motivation, or eagerness to learn.

QUESTIONS AND PROBLEMS

1. Give some examples of how vicarious experiences are interpreted through actual experiences. Considering the amount of vicarious experiences one absorbs in later life, through reading, for example, what is your opinion regarding the relative importance of the two types? Explain.
2. Describe how the child's concept of time or space follows an orderly process in development.
3. Describe how lack of experience may limit one's concept of gardening, or camping, or worship. How does lack of experience often present a barrier to a child's understanding of certain science concepts?
4. What are some common misconceptions that you have held or heard of? How do you think they occurred?
5. What particular mental abilities would be necessary for a diplomat? For an automobile mechanic? For an English teacher? For a critic?
6. Look up several definitions of intelligence. Do you find a common notion about intelligence in these different definitions? To what extent do you think that these definitions might reflect differences in point of view about the nature of child development?
7. Look up materials on "infant tests." What do studies indicate about the validity and usefulness of such tests?
8. What difference does it make if a teacher regards an intelligence test as a measure of potential ability rather than manifest or functional ability? Can you illustrate this in the case of her treatment of a third-grade child at school?

9. What are some evidences for the ill-effects of a restricted environment upon intelligence test scores? What criticisms would you offer relative to such evidences?
10. Describe what is implied by "eagerness to learn." How would you account for the relationship between "eagerness to learn" and IQ acceleration? What are the implications of this for education?

SELECTED READINGS

BERNARD, HAROLD W., *Human Development in Western Culture*, 2nd ed. Boston: Allyn and Bacon, 1966. Ch. 5.

BALLER, WARREN R., and DON C. CHARLES, *The Psychology of Human Growth and Development*. Holt, Rinehart & Winston, 1961. Ch 10.

DINKMEYER, DON C., *Child Development: The Emerging Self*. Englewood Cliffs, N. J.: Prentice-Hall, 1965. Ch. 8.

GARRISON, KARL C., ALBERT J. KINGSTON, and ARTHUR S. MCDONALD, *Educational Psychology*, 2nd ed. Appleton-Century-Crofts, 1965. Ch. 4.

HILGARD, ERNEST R., *Introduction to Psychology*, 2nd ed. Harcourt, Brace & World, 1957. Ch. 18.

HUNT, JOSEPH MCV., *Intelligence and Experience*. The Ronald Press, 1961.

THOMPSON, GEORGE G., *Child Psychology*, 2nd ed. Boston: Houghton Mifflin, 1962. Ch. 11.

THORPE, LOUIS P., *Child Psychology and Development*, 3rd ed. The Ronald Press, 1962. Ch. 9.

WANN, KENNETH D., *et al.*, *Fostering Intellectual Development in Young Children*. Bureau of Publications, Teachers College, Columbia University, 1962.

REFERENCES

ANDERSON, J. E., The limitations of infant and preschool tests in the measurement of intelligence, *Journal of Psychology*, 1939, 8, 351–379.

ANDERSON, J. E., *The Psychology of Development and Personality Adjustment*. Holt, Rinehart & Winston, 1949, p. 190.

ASHER, E. J., The inadequacy of current intelligence tests for testing Kentucky Mountain children, *The Journal of Genetic Psychology*, 1935, 46, 480–486.

AUSUBEL, DAVID P., and HERBERT M. SCHIFF, The effects of incidental and experimentally induced experience in the learning of relevant and irrelevant causal relationships by children, *The Journal of Genetic Psychology*, 1954, 84, 109–123.

BAYLEY, NANCY, On the growth of intelligence, *The American Psychologist*, 1955, 10, 805–818.

BELL, RICHARD Q., Relations between behavior manifestations in the human neonate, *Child Development*, 1960, 31, 463–477.

BRUSSEL, JAMES ARNOLD, Mental deficiency, in *Collier's Encyclopedia*, 1954, 13, 392.

BURKS, B. S., The relative influence of nature and nurture upon mental development: a comparative study of foster parent-foster child resemblance and true parent-true child resemblance, *Twenty-seventh Yearbook of the National Society for the Study of Education*, Part I, 1928, pp. 219–316.

BURT, CYRIL, The inheritance of mental ability, *The American Psychologist*, 1958, 13, 1–15.

CRISSEY, ORLO L., Mental development as related to institutional residence and educational achievement, *University of Iowa Studies in Child Welfare*, 1937, *13*, No. 1.

DEUTSCHE, JEAN MARQUIS, The development of children's concepts of causal relations, in *Child Behavior and Development* (Roger G. Barker, Jacob S. Kounin, and Herbert F. Wright, eds.). McGraw-Hill, 1943, pp. 129–145. Also, *University of Minnesota Child Welfare Monograph Series*, No. 13, 1937.

DEWEY, JOHN, *How We Think*. Boston: Heath, 1933, p. 89.

DIXON, J. C., Development of self recognition, *The Journal of Genetic Psychology*, 1957, *91*, 251–256.

DUVALL, SYLVANUS, and EVELYN DUVALL, "Let's Explore Your Mind," in *Long Island Press* (December 31, 1964), p. 26.

ESCALONA, SIBYLLE K., and ALICE MORIARTY, Prediction of school age intelligence from infant tests, *Child Development*, 1961, *32*, 597–605.

FREEMAN, FRANK N., Intellectual growth of children as indicated by repeated tests, *Psychological Monographs*, 1936, *47*, No. 212, 20–34.

FREEMAN, FRANK N., and CHARLES D. FLORY, Growth in intellectual ability, in *Child Behavior and Development* (Roger G. Barker, Jacob S. Kounin, and Herbert F. Wright, eds.). McGraw-Hill, 1943, pp. 147–160.

GESELL, ARNOLD, The child as a growing organism, in *Our Children Today* (Sidonie M. Gruenberg, ed.). Viking Press, 1952, pp. 49-56.

GORDON, HUGH, Mental and scholastic tests among retarded children, *Educational Pamphlet*, No. 44. London: Board of Education, 1923.

HALL-QUEST, ALFRED L., and I. L. KANDEL, Education, theories of, in *Collier's Encyclopedia*, 1965, *8*, 592.

HEIDBREDER, EDNA, Problem solving in children and adults, *The Journal of Genetic Psychology*, 1928, *35*, 522–545.

HOFSTAETTER, PETER R., The changing composition of "intelligence": a study in T-technique, *The Journal of Genetic Psychology*, 1954, *85*, 159–164.

HONZIK, M. P., J. W. MACFARLANE, and L. ALLEN, The stability of mental test performance between two and eighteen years, *Journal of Experimental Education*, 1948, *17*, 309–324.

JONES, H. E., The environment and mental development, in *Manual of Child Psychology* (L. Carmichael, ed.), 2nd ed. John Wiley & Sons, 1954, pp. 631–696.

KIMBLE, GREGORY A., Intelligence, in *Collier's Encyclopedia*, 1954, *11*, 2–4.

KING, W. H., I—The development of scientific concepts in children, *British Journal of Educational Psychology*, 1961, *31*, 1–20.

KOUNIN, JACOB S., Intellectual development and rigidity, in *Child Behavior and Development* (Roger G. Barker, Jacob S. Kounin, and Herbert F. Wright, eds.). McGraw-Hill, 1943, pp. 179-197.

KRUGMAN, MORRIS, What can we test?, in *Our Children Today* (Sidonie M. Gruenberg, ed.). Viking Press, 1952, pp. 253-265.

MENNINGER, KARL A., *The Human Mind*. Alfred A. Knopf., 1961, pp. 175, 191.

MILNER, ESTHER, *The Failure of Success*. Exposition Press, 1959, p. 150.

NEWMAN, H. H., F. N. FREEMAN, and K. J. HOLTZINGER, *Twins: A Study of Heredity and Environment*. Chicago: University of Chicago Press, 1937.

PARNES, SIDNEY J., and HAROLD F. HARDING, eds., *A Source Book for Creative Thinking*. Charles Scribner's Sons, 1962, *passim*.

PEARSON, K., On the inheritance of the mental and moral characters in man, and its comparison with the inheritance of the physical character, *Journal of the Anthropological Institute*, 1903, *33*, 179–237.

PIAGET, JEAN, *The Language and Thought of the Child*, 2nd ed., trans. M. Gabain. Harcourt, Brace, 1932.

RAND, WINIFRED, MARY E. SWEENEY, and E. LEE VINCENT, *Growth and Development of the Young Child*, 5th ed. Philadelphia: Saunders, 1953, p. 347.

RUSSELL, ROGER W., Studies in animism: II. The development of animism, *The Journal of Genetic Psychology*, 1940, *56*, 353–366.

SCHEERER, MARTIN, Problem-solving, *Scientific American* (April 1963), *208*, 118–128.

SCOTT, JOHN PAUL, Animal intelligence, in *The Harper Encyclopedia of Science*, 1963, *1*, 66–67.

SKEELS, H. M., R. UPDEGRAFF, B. L. WELLMAN, and H. M. WILLIAMS, A study of environmental stimulation: an orphanage preschool project, *University of Iowa Studies in Child Welfare*, 1938, No. 4.

SONTAG, LESTER W., CHARLES T. BAKER, and VIRGINIA L. NELSON, Mental growth and personality development: a longitudinal study, *Monographs of the Society for Research in Child Development*, 1958, *23*, No. 2.

SPEER, G. S., The mental development of children of feeble-minded and normal mothers, *Thirty-ninth Yearbook of the National Society for the Study of Education*, Part II. Chicago: University of Chicago Press, 1940.

STRONG, LYDIA, "When Children Don't 'Achieve,' " *The New York Times Magazine* (November 15, 1964), pp. 142, 156–157.

TERMAN, LEWIS M., and MAUD MERRILL, *Measuring Intelligence: A Guide to the Administration of the New Revised Stanford-Binet Tests of Intelligence*. Boston: Houghton Mifflin, 1937 p. 228. See also, *Child Behavior and Development* (Barker, Kounin, and Wright, eds.) McGraw-Hill, 1943, which summarizes the earlier work.

THORPE, LOUIS P., *Child Psychology and Development*, 3rd. ed. The Ronald Press, 1962, p. 381.

WECHSLER, DAVID, Intellectual development and psychological maturity, *Child Development*, 1950, *21*, 45–50.

WEINSTEIN, EUGENE A., Development of the concept of flag and the sense of national identity, *Child Development*, 1957, *28*, 167–174.

E I G H T

The Development

of Emotional Behavior

Because the development of the individual depends upon his ability to adjust to many situations, primarily social, the human organism needs special equipment to protect itself from physical and psychological harm, to foster social experiences and adjustments, and to motivate action at various physical and intellectual levels. Emotions serve these purposes. Without them, our sensations (and hence our mental abilities) would be severely limited. Without them, Man would have been unable to evolve intellect and will power, continuing instead, like the lower animals, to rely upon instinctual behavior as the sole means of survival. Niederland (1965, p. 332) has stated:

> By origin and nature man is not a rational animal. His attachments to people, to his parents, family, and friends, as well as his reactions to pain and pleasure, depend on what he feels, rather than on what he thinks. Even his actions are rarely the result of logical thinking alone. The most important and decisive early experiences of life are emotionally, not rationally, determined. This emotional element dominates the entire [mental growth] process during childhood, and it largely influences man's reaction to adult life. The influence of the emotional element is not limited to the mental sphere, but extends also to the functions of the organs and tissues. Emotions may stimulate or depress the functions of the heart, the stomach, the intestinal apparatus, the respiratory and circulatory systems, the skin, or the endocrine glands; they may interfere with the direction and absorption of food, with the functions of the sex organs, the muscles, or the blood vessels, or they may cause headache, insomnia, and other symptoms without apparent cause.
>
> Emotions are real and not imaginary, and their effects are experienced by every normal individual.

EFFECTS OF EMOTION

Physiological Reactions

Although the physiological effects mentioned by Niederland are under the control of the autonomic nervous system and are involuntary, they can be felt inwardly or observed outwardly, or both. With fear and anger, for instance, increased quantities of adrenalin are secreted and additional sugar, a source of quick energy, is liberated into the blood stream. The heart beats faster, the walls of the blood vessels contract, and the blood circulation increases, carrying the sugar more quickly to the different parts of the body. This series of events constitutes an internal "emergency reaction" which prepares the organism with additional energy for meeting excessively demanding situations. Many examples have been cited in popular literature of individuals who have accomplished astonishing feats of strength under conditions of extreme fright. During house fires in particular, both men and women have been known to lift and move, alone, large and heavy articles of furniture—items such as stoves, refrigerators, and overstuffed chairs which ordinarily require several men to move.

When one considers the usual behavior patterns of an individual who lacks emotion—who is apathetic or emotionally "flat"—the importance of emotions and their necessity for a healthy personality become quite clear. The apathetic person is generally described as inactive, aimless, silly, callous, indifferent, or shallow. Socially, they do not respond effectively to overtures of friendliness or love and are unaware of the finer nuances of social interactions. Physically, they may have extremely low tolerance for drugs and medications. They may "miss out" on the emotional responses commonly described as "my heart skipped a beat," "my stomach turned over," "my heart was in my mouth," "it sent shivers down my spine," "goose pimples," and "my scalp's all prickly."

Apathy as a more or less permanent state of being is sometimes "due to a lesion in physiological machinery of the organism—the basal ganglia of the brain, the endocrine glands, the autonomic nervous system . . ." but it may also be caused by "conflicts of emotional streams which neutralize each other . . ." (Menninger, 1961, p. 195).

Other physiological signs of emotion observed in or experienced by normal people are dilation and contraction of the pupils, blushing and blanching, prickling skin, erection of hairs, indigestion, muscle tension, "butterflies" in the stomach, "watery" knees, or fainting.

Strong Feelings

In addition to these internally controlled but externally stimulated reactions, emotion is also characterized by strong feelings whenever the organism experiences a departure from its normal, calm state. As the infant begins to differentiate the many bodily states that fall to his experience, he chooses some as being pleasurable, desirable, and satisfying. Other states he dislikes, finding them painful, uncomfortable, and otherwise disagreeable. The strength of his feelings is, of course, correlated positively with the degree of pleasantness or unpleasantness he assigns to any one situation. And, quite naturally, the strengths and degrees vary from individual to individual according to his constitution, or to the force with which the stimulus makes its impact. Indeed, the states chosen as pleasurable by one person at one age are not chosen by another person at the same age or by the same individual at a later age; what one person considers repulsive is desired by others; and the emotions that are suppressed in one society are encouragd in another.

Just as physiological reactions have two opposing directions—stimulation-depression or increase-decrease—strong feelings of emotion fall into two general categories—the positive and negative, or the pleasant-integrative response and the unpleasant-disintegrative response (Thompson, 1962; Hebb, 1949). Positive, integrative feelings, such as love, affection, happiness, elation, curiosity, joy, delight, and yearning, are elicited by the sensations an organism perceives as pleasurable. Negative, or disintegrative, feelings—fear, anger, disgust, jealousy, worry, grief, anxiety, hostility—are elicited by such disagreeable sensations as loss, pain, discomfort, frustration, conflict, strangeness, and threat. Some of the emotions classified as disintegrative have, in mild amounts, an integrative effect in certain areas. Fear operates as a protective mechanism, and anxiety, irritation, or apprehension stimulate learning when the organismic drive is at a low level (Hebb, 1955).

Impulse to Action

The third component of emotion, the impulse to action, is the true stepping off point for discussions of emotional behavior. Once the individual has classified a situation or condition as pleasant or unpleasant—has, in fact, built up a network of various states on the plus and minus side of comfort—he normally moves toward the retention, recall, or increase of the pleasurable states and the removal or decrease of the disagreeable. These impulses likewise can take a so-called positive or negative direction. The child who wishes to be cuddled may hold out his arms in the hope that he will be picked up, or he may throw a temper tantrum, having learned that the quickest way to get what he wants is to scream. The child who is afraid may drive away the stimulus, attempt to conquer it, or run away from it. A toddler may "love" his mother with kisses or with kicks. A jealous child may show excessive love for a sibling or attempt to cause it harm. Or, he may react to this threat to his self-importance by way of aggressive acts toward playmates, toys, authority, or himself.

Initially, the individual responds only to an external stimulus. The infant, for example, acts to maintain the experiences of stroking, rocking, moving colors, rhythmic sounds and to remove such discomforts as hunger, chafing, cold and heat, fatigue, lonesomeness—all quite tangible, or "real," stimuli. Later, however, the external stimulus-internal response relationship becomes a habit pattern to the extent that the response can be evoked by symbolic representation of the original stimulus. Most any parent is familiar with the case of a child who cries from pain and anger when a doctor (in a white coat) administers an injection; the crying raises the child's blood pressure, among other physiological changes, and later, the child experiences the same reactions accompanied by crying at the mere mention or sight of the doctor. Furthermore, a barber's white coat may cause the child to remember and react again. If the barber should then happen to brandish a pair of pointed shears or should inadvertently pull the child's neck hairs with dull clippers, the pattern of white coat = pain = internal reactions = overt behavior (crying) is reinforced. Further generalization may also occur, and, until the child is re-educated by experience, he may respond with fear to dentists, elevated chairs, and persons with characteristics (moustache, spectacles, etc.) similar to the doctor's or barber's.

To further complicate the subject of emotions and their responses, emotion can become its own stimulus. Love breeds love, fear breeds fear. Love can also arouse jealousy and fear can evoke anger. Moreover, the individual recognizes and responds not only to his own feelings but also to the emotions of others—and not always with consistency. He may feel genuine sympathy for the person who sobs with self-pity, yet be disgusted with himself for experiencing a similar state. He may be compassionate toward a cowardly friend, yet angered or ashamed at his own fears. And the anxious person may be anxious because he is anxious! As frequently happens, the anxiety-ridden individual may be aware of his state but not of what causes it—and that worries him.

EMOTIONAL HERITAGE

True emotions are a by-product of change, and change occurs only through maturation and learning. Emotions and their responses develop through the awareness, perception, memory, and differentiation of changes in external and internal environments and through the maturation of glandular and neural systems. Myelination and cortical development must occur before messages can be sent to muscles and glands, resulting in the increase and decrease of their activity which is such an integral part of emotional behavior. Most authorities are of the opinion that an infant under the age of three months is incapable of true emotion, although Bridges (1932), in a classic study which traced emotional development during the first two years of life, interpreted certain manifestations of general excitement as "delight." (See Figure VIII-1.) Delight, love, affection, and jealousy are dependent upon social awareness, a recognition of other people as having some special meaning to the observer. Fear requires anticipation (intelligence) of danger or some unpleasantness. True anger presupposes an awareness of "me" or "mine." When these elements of intellect are combined with the physiological changes that occur from hunger, thirst, crying, sucking, and the startle reaction, emotions are born.

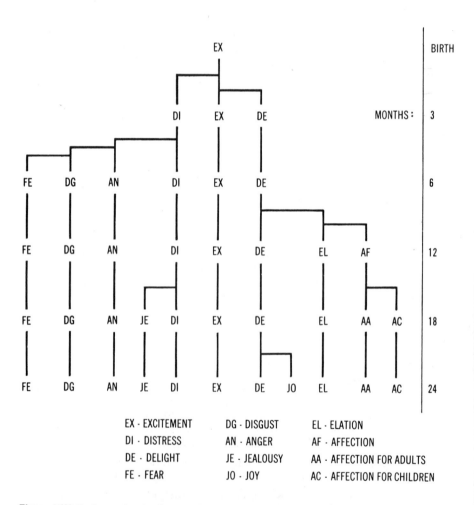

EX - EXCITEMENT	DG - DISGUST	EL - ELATION
DI - DISTRESS	AN - ANGER	AF - AFFECTION
DE - DELIGHT	JE - JEALOUSY	AA - AFFECTION FOR ADULTS
FE - FEAR	JO - JOY	AC - AFFECTION FOR CHILDREN

Figure VIII–1. Approximate Ages of Differentiation of the Various Emotions During the First Two Years of Life (Bridges, 1932, p. 340)

Thus, scientists lean more and more often toward the opinion that there are no *inborn* emotions. On the other hand, as stated in Chapter II, Jost and Sontag (1944) and Menninger (1961) believe that certain inherited physiological structures enable the individual to perform emotionally at a particular level—that, in other words, he inherits the potential for developing at one of the levels on the intensity continuum between depression and elation, is more or less sensitive to stimuli. Some persons live and perform their life tasks at a relatively high and stable level of elation; others are more passive; and yet others vacillate from one side of the scale to the other. *Apparently,* this "constitution," this "tempo," is inherited along with the pattern by which the endocrine glands function—at a "high," "low," cyclical, or erratic rate.* Levin (1965) cites three separate studies which add further information to our knowledge of hereditary factors. One team of five psychiatrists and psychologists observed 130 children in minute detail, she says, and they concluded (pp. 132, 134):

> '. . . . the characteristics of the child's behavior will be influenced by his primary reaction pattern as well as by his environment. In each new situation he faces his behavior will depend, in part at least, on whether his reactive style is primarily positive or negative, mild or of high intensity, rhythmic or arhythmic. . . . It follows, therefore, that there can be no universally valid set of rules that will work equally well for all children everywhere.'

The second study described by Levin consisted of detailed physical and psychological tests of the minute-by-minute behavior of 300 newborn babies. Results of the study "showed that a baby's response was likely to be consistent during the first few days of life. There were the intense reactors to sound and cold and the moderate ones indicating that the former might well be on their way to developing into taut, nervous, edgy individuals and the latter into serene, placid souls" (p. 134).

The third study highlighted by Levin concerns documentation of adult reactions to a baby of the "cuddly" type and to the type who is tense, rest-

---

* Once again science cannot be too dogmatic about this subject of hereditary functions because of its inability to separate and analyze with precision the interactive influences of heredity and environment. Although wide differences in reaction patterns are observable in newborn infants, there is an early, positive relationship between a mother's emotional attitudes as expressed in her child-care practices and the emotional makeup of her child. After studying thirty-three infants, Brody (1958, p. 366) has stated that:

> . . . mothers who were dominating had infants who were often noticeably passive or noticeably active; mothers who were generally elated had infants whose social maturity was advanced, sometimes to the point of too easy excitement; mothers who were steadily kind and affectionate had infants who responded with appropriate affect, but who sometimes lacked drive; mothers who spoke a great deal had infants whose vocalizations were superior in quantity and quality.

less and apparently uncomfortable in being held"; and the subsequent adjustments of those babies to the adult reactions elicited by their own personalities.

The terse conclusion made by Levin (p. 132) from all three studies is: "Babies are born with certain traits that directly influence their development as well as the way their mothers respond to them."

Constitution, or the emotional tone of the organism, determines the way in which he will perceive his environment and the degree to which the elements in it will make their impact. Some children are so acutely sensitive to emotional atmospheres that they will sense reactions an adult is trying to hide. Despite valiant efforts on the part of mothers to be nonchalant during electrical storms or while they are alone or in darkness, many young children gradually become uneasy under similar conditions. On the other hand, pain, conflict, or hunger may not be felt as strongly by the passive child, and his responses may more nearly approximate fussiness than anger. In later life, such a person may be erroneously described as a stoic, which implies fortitude under conditions of great stress, when in reality his "threshold of pain" is so high that some stimuli have simply not made an impact sufficient to cause a reaction. However, on this subject there is still a great deal of speculation and continuing research is needed.

Most of the disagreement and misconceptions concerning emotions in infancy and whether or not they are inborn arise from adult interpretations of children's reactions to various stimuli. A mother interprets a gas-bubble grimace as a social smile; a father says his son was born afraid of him because he cried in his presence, when in reality the inexperienced, oversolicitous father added a blanket or two, making the child too hot, or forgot to "burp" him.

At least two studies (Sherman, 1927; Taylor, 1934) have demonstrated that when the identity of the stimulus was unknown the responses of infants could not be classified. Students of psychology could not, in effect, interpret an infant's response in terms of their own reactions to specific stimuli. The mother who claims she can differentiate between the cries of her newborn is actually combining a bit of guesswork with a comprehensive knowledge of her child's schedule of needs. Yet, because her guesses are so often correct, she does in essence react to her child's experience: *She* responds to *his* stimulus. He, then, learns what is agreeable and disagreeable to her, and he imitates her responses.

Regarding emotional heredity, therefore, we can say that, in a sense, a child inherits the emotional climate and responses produced by his earliest, most intimate associates. He probably inherits a particular degree of sensitivity to stimuli (or emotional tone) through which he learns to identify and classify environmental conditions according to varying grades of pleasant-

ness and unpleasantness and develops an awareness of the many possible responses to those conditions.

EARLY RESPONSES

Homeostatic adjustments within the individual function to maintain
him in a calm, balanced state. The involuntary actions of bodily mechanics
permit the organism to realize a stable internal temperature, to ward off disease, to correct organic and nutritive deficiencies, and to supply certain elements necessary for meeting internal and external emergencies. The reflexes
and responses that later become differentiated into emotional behavior are
part of that homeostatic system. That is, an individual is born with reflexes
to protect him from overstimulation and harm and also to stimulate him to
exercise.

Crying

Generally, the first response to distress and violent stimuli is the birth
cry, which starts the infant breathing. Many months pass in the infant's life
before he substitutes other responses for this reaction to discomfort and tension and frustration. He also learns rapidly that crying brings relief through
some other person who delivers an amazing array of pleasant sensations.
Crying, then, becomes an effective way of gaining warmth, security, soothing motions, cuddling, and tactile stimulation, as well as protection and
lung exercises.

Sucking

The sucking response also is observable at birth, or within a few days of
it, although the stimulus is a much gentler one—a touch on the cheek. Aside
from its primary function of obtaining food, sucking is so powerful in its
ability to provide relief from all tensions that it virtually eliminates the sensation of pain. Stone and Church (1957) claim that the only anesthetic used
for circumcisions is a sugar ball in the infant's mouth. Many mothers find
that a pacifier prevents or relieves colic. For one reason or another, an infant
has its greatest need for sucking during the first three or four months of
life, and if the need is left unsatisfied, theorizes Spock (1957), the accumulated longings may produce a thumb-sucker who will be anxious to make up
for lost time when he is finally able to get his thumb up to his mouth (at
about three months).

The Startle Response

Sudden, violent auditory and visual stimuli, loss of support, and restraint precipitate physiological activity—an "emergency reaction" (Cannon,

1929)—that is exceedingly uncomfortable. In order to use up or burn off the excess energy released by the reaction, the infant (involuntarily) responds with generalized mass activity and gross motor movements, including a characteristic muscular flexion of the fingers, kicking, squirming, and crying. It is primarily through this startle reaction that the infant learns to fear, to be angry or cautious, and to appreciate equilibrium. On the other hand, the mass activity does its job of restoring internal balance and within a few months after birth substitutions can be noticed in the movements, such as smiling instead of crying, and this mass activity, this general excitement, is interpreted as delight. It would almost seem that the infant is reaching toward a new kind of balance, one that has been redefined in terms of more pleasure. At any rate, from the state of general excitement that involves the total organism all other emotional responses subsequently develop through the processes of differentiation and refinement.

DIFFERENTIATION AND CONTROL

Although students of child psychology still have a great deal to learn concerning the nature of emotions and the development of their manifestations, a summary can be presented that is based on the findings from certain genetic studies (Angelino, *et al.*, 1956; Banham, 1950; Vollmer, 1946; Wallis, 1954);

1. Differentiation of emotional behavior emerges early in life. This differentiation increases as the individual develops toward maturity.
2. Individuality of emotional behavior appears at an early age. This tends to increase as each individual matures and learns effective ways of meeting emotional situations.
3. The emergence of specific patterns of emotional behavior is closely related to the needs of the individual. Those forms of behavior which bring forth the greatest satisfaction tend to be repeated and to become part of the total behavior pattern.
4. There is a definite relationship between the stage of a child's maturation and the nature of his emotional response.

Typically, the young child's emotional behavior is characterized by a lack of gradation (Bousfield and Orbison, 1952): He reacts as strongly to trivial situations as he does to more serious ones. Also, his outbursts are generally frequent, brief, and transitory, unrestrained and of great intensity. Rapid recovery and sudden shifts of emotion are characteristic.

Just as a particular response becomes more appropriate to a situation, and a condition elicits a more appropriate response, so does the quality of a child's reaction become more appropriately graded. Some responses become weaker, while others become stronger. With training, children learn to express themselves less freely and less overtly and more in keeping with the expectations of society. These refinements increase at every age level as the child moves toward greater self-control. He experiences the meaning of growth and perceives the directions for self-improvement when he discovers that old patterns are no longer reinforced, are even discouraged or punished, and that new patterns elicit the sought-for praise, smile, favor, or other form of reward. Gradually, through the innumerable interactive agencies responsible for his maturation and learning, he achieves greater dominance and control over his emotions and his emotional responses. If those agencies are successful, the individual develops and maintains (1) the ability to meet conflicts in effective and acceptable ways and (2) a balanced realization of his fundamental needs and desires. The person who meets the standards for such development at his age level is considered emotionally mature.

The Role of Maturation

Before the individual is able to develop emotionally, his cerebral cortex, and especially the frontal lobes, must be able to function and continue to function with increasing efficiency (Russell, 1948). Glands and the autonomic nervous system are also important, and as they mature the organism becomes more sensitive and responsive to stimuli from within and without. Through maturing sensory capacities, he is better able to perceive and differentiate persons, objects, situations, and feeling and mental states as being threatening, unpleasant, or pleasurable; and as he develops his capacities for perception and understanding and learns to deal more effectively with a wider environment, he is able to anticipate and recognize the dangers, exciting events, and stimulating situations he finds around him.

With the development of imagination, a child's fears are directed more often toward intangibles and the supernatural—ghosts, gremlins, sea dragons, monsters, and Martians. As he begins to foresee natural consequences, he becomes apprehensive of accidents, illness, and death; but he also anticipates ridiculousness, incongruities, and surprises—thus, he can appreciate humorous situations.

With a growing awareness of self and social relationships, his affections are broadened and deepened but become more selective. Likewise, he develops a fear and dislike for personal ridicule and loss of esteem. He experiences and identifies injustices and indignities to himself and others, thereby laying the groundwork for the development of pity, sympathy, and compassion.

These various changes and maturing abilities affect the individual's behavior much the same as his organic functions are changed by physiological growth. Behavior creates conflicts, and so long as changes continue to occur, both behavior and conflicts become more complex. For example, once the frustrations incidental to acquiring locomotion disappear the toddler meets conflict in the form of a play pen, a harness, a watchful parent; in his attempts to climb, balance, and run; through falls, cuts, and fatigue; and so on, in an ever-widening circle. Through every maturational stage, specific frustrations are eliminated only to be replaced by others of a higher, more complicated order. Likewise, the complexity of responses grows. As the child begins to utter words, he finds that language is a more efficient way of communicating his needs and wants; thus, the elementary responses of crying and screaming are gradually replaced by the many nuances of words and vocal tones, inner language, fantasy, daydreaming, reading, and writing, all of which are used both to order one's thinking and as effective outlets for emotional expression.

The Role of Learning

The human infant inherits the drive and the mechanisms for maintaining a state of mental and physical equilibrium. Such a state normally exists without interruption from conception until birth. As soon as the infant enters the external environment, conditions operate to create imbalances to which he must adjust. He does, in effect, learn what equilibrium is by experiencing what it is not. On the other hand, he also learns to redefine *equilibrium* as it pertains to himself. That is, if we accept Maslow's hierarchy of needs theory (see p. 67), a continually hungry baby might need food and food alone to satisfy his requirements for equilibrium, whereas a well-fed child is able to add a need for love to his definition of mental and physical balance. Generally, the human animal in all its individual variations lives out its lifetime seeking to add rather than subtract pleasurable states, or at least to maintain itself more on the one side than on the other. Equilibrium becomes increasingly a matter of more pleasure (as the individual perceives it) and less pain, not a lack of both or a strict balance of one against the other.

Conditioning.   Through repeated experiences of comfort and tactile stimulation associated with the appearance and body of his mother, an infant is conditioned to enjoy her presence, to love her and be affectionate. As soon as he has associated a bottle or nipple with subsequent relief from hunger pangs and tension, he becomes excited at the sight of one. A newborn is completely indifferent to such matters as wet and soiled diapers, but he soon discovers that after successive changes he is slightly more comfortable. Thus, he is conditioned to prefer being dry. (We might suggest a reasonable but unproven theory that the more attention a mother pays to keeping her child dry and comfortable, the earlier the child will train himself to stay that way.)

Fear, apparently, is a direct result of conditioning through the startle response. Each time the infant is startled, he is conditioned to dislike his internal changes and, by association, the stimulus that caused them. Through further associative processes, he anticipates harm or threat from some of the stimuli, and he reacts with fear; with other sensations, he becomes enraged.

One of the earliest and best known studies of emotional conditioning was conducted by Watson and Rayner (1920). They showed a rat to an eleven-month-old boy who reacted without any signs of fear. Later, they produced a loud noise each time they presented the rat to the infant. The loud noise startled the boy. After a number of noise-rat presentations, the sight of the rat alone caused the child to react with fear.

As the environment of every child contains certain objects and conditions which are dangerous to his well-being, many parents employ conditioning techniques as the quickest way of training their children to behave safely. For instance, controlling the placement of a child's hand close to a hot stove or iron helps him to build a reflex action against not only the heat itself but also the word *hot*. Similar controlled experiences can be far less painful, traumatic, and dangerous than accidents. Conditioning, in a sense, is synonymous with discipline, instruction in consequences and the universal orderliness of Nature's responses. (See pp. 255–58.)

Imitation. Conditioning alone, however, does not explain all the types of emotional reactions manifested by children. Observation of the behavior of adults or siblings teaches a youngster what is fearful or pleasurable to others; imitation of that behavior helps him form a mode of response which —if he were capable of so reasoning—must be acceptable for him if it is for them. It is safe to assume that if an infant never saw a smile he would never respond with one; and, as a matter of fact, there is an aboriginal society which uses the smile as an anger response. Furthermore, when an older person interprets a child's facial expressions according to existing environmental conditions, reinforcements and refinements make themselves evident. There is, for example, a "blank" expression that frequently appears on the infant's face in response to new or unusual stimuli. An adult may interpret it as surprise and then open his eyes a bit wider and make his mouth round; or, he may smile with his mouth open and raise his eyebrows. If the adult interprets the expression as puzzlement, he may frown slightly. The infant notices these facial expressions, mimics them, and also associates them with certain stimuli or events.

Although psychologists cannot be sure how large a part imitation plays in the learning of emotional responses, they agree that at each maturational stage its role is considerable. Parents usually find themselves at one time or another coping with their children's use of familiar-sounding swear words in the face of some minor frustration. Or they observe in their offspring emotional acts equivalent to slamming down a newspaper, kicking a chair leg, or throwing a burnt pot in the trash can. The young ones have imitated both a method and a direction for "blowing off steam."

Absorption.   There is, too, a high probability that a large percentage of a child's emotional reactions and his attitudes toward conditions in his environment is developed during the times when his parents think he doesn't understand or hear what they are talking about. Gossip—or, for that matter, any discussion about religion, politics, race relations, or other emotionally charged subjects—generates a certain amount of emotional expressiveness. Even laughter is descriptive of an individual's state of mind, and what he laughs at is a reflection of his emotions, attitudes, and values. Adult vocalizations do not go unnoticed by children, as most parents eventually find out —sometimes to their acute embarrassment. The statement "Little pitchers have big ears" does not imply that children are maliciously intent on invading or spreading the adult's world of whispers. It merely calls attention to the subtle, continual, associative process that has such a direct bearing upon a child's personality development.

Training.   Direct and indirect training is responsible for many changes in a child's methods of responding to emotional situations. He is indirectly encouraged to use language for indicating his needs and directly discouraged from crying. Boys in the Western societies are taught early that "crying is for babies and girls. . . . Big boys don't cry." Even siblings and playmates jeer at boys who are "cry babies." Pragmatically, the boys discover that tears do not continue to gain them solicitude and sympathy from adults. Depending upon the family background, they are often encouraged to "stand up and fight," and such substitutes for crying as hitting, name-calling, kicking, sulking, and tattling are quickly found.

The adults in a child's society—including those responsible for the literature he reads and the television programs he watches—both directly and subtly, teach the desirability of suppressing emotions even in the face of pain and extreme fatigue, or they indicate the directions for expressing emotions constructively. Heroes, and most heroines, grit their teeth, square their shoulders, or otherwise control natural outbursts. Heroines (never heroes) are allowed to cry in sympathy for others, but rarely for themselves, although their sympathies are generally displayed less passively—by way of assistance, planned strategies, advice, etc. Fictitious characters are expected to love everyone, including their enemies, but they do not show it in the most natural way—through body contacts—but through the more indirect and abstract acts of kindness, consideration, loyalty, and understanding.

Furthermore, through every available media, children are given information about their world in order that they may be made aware of what is and is not dangerous and how to avoid or control something potentially dangerous. They are educated against fear of water and fire and heights, for example, by being taught to swim, use matches, and climb according to specific rules of safety.

At an early age, children are instructed by many adults to share toys and treats, to understand that others have desires and rights, to recognize that anger, jealousy, envy, and irrational fears are selfish, wasteful, undesirable—are, indeed, disintegrative emotions that work against effective action, both physically and mentally.

Love and Affection

The development of love and affection is "intimately tied up with satisfaction of body needs and appetites . . ." (Schlosberg, 1954). "Warmth and bodily satisfaction become equivalent to the love of the mother," states Ross (1952, p. 59), who further simplifies the equation: "Love equals Food." Spitz (1946, p. 108) also can be cited:

> . . . The first stage of relations between mother and child is, therefore, the stage in which the mother provides relief from discomfort. This is of cardinal importance during the first weeks of life. Insensibly, the relief from discomfort merges with the experience that the mother's presence ensures security, freedom from suffering. From here, it is only one step to the stage at which the child perceives the pleasurable quality of some stimuli offered to it by its mother's presence.

The attitudes and manner of the mother's feeding her infant determine the quality of his later affections. She provides her child with his first emotional climate; if she is happy, loving, and understanding, he feels secure, comfortable, friendly, and trusting; if she is impatient, hostile, and erratic in her behavior, it takes him longer—if he learns at all—to put his trust in others.

In a series of studies of infant monkeys, Harlow and Harlow (1962) have examined the infant-mother affectional bond, using in many experiments cloth mother-surrogates. Although the infants became strongly attached to the cloth substitutes, particularly in fright-inducing situations, their behavior several years later was no different from that of infants raised in cages without mother or mother substitute. The investigators described them as follows (p. 142):

> . . . They are without question socially and sexually aberrant. . . . The entire group of animals separated from their mothers at birth . . . must be written off as potential breeding stock. Apparently their early social deprivation permanently impairs their ability to form effective relations with other

monkeys, whether the opportunity was offered to them in the second six months of life or in the second to fifth year of life.

The infant's enjoyment of a mother's soft, warm body, the rocking motions, the smiles, and the soothing voices are the beginnings of his affection for her. Until he begins to differentiate between strangers and the people who care for him, everyone shares in the secure infant's delight. Generally, he will smile in answer to any smile. But during the second half of the first year, he regards strangers with a bland stare, sometimes with crying. Depending upon the child and the circumstances, once the infant has thoroughly scrutinized an unfamiliar face without being required to respond, he can be won over by the stranger. Some mothers have made it a cardinal rule to friends or relatives who are seeing a baby for the first time: "Don't look at him or speak to him for five minutes; after that you'll have trouble getting him off your lap."

Self-love, according to Banham (1950, p. 288), occurs much later than is commonly supposed. She states:

> During the second year, among the objects of the child's affections may be included himself. He clings to his toys, clothes, or chair, and collects small objects. He attracts attention to himself and cries at interference. From this phase, within the second and third year, he passes to one where affectionate behavior is shown largely to adults, but also to other children as well as himself.

In early childhood there is a display of affection for siblings and playmates. After he enters school, the child may become less demonstrative and show embarrassment when parents and older siblings hug and kiss him in front of other people. Boys particularly feel that such behavior is unmanly and that it hinders their growing sense of independence. Both sexes, however, show their love more often by doing things for others, by wanting to be with them, and, most importantly for the development of self-control, by wanting their behavior to resemble that of the people they idealize. "The ability to love constructively is in many senses simply the capacity to constructively identify oneself with other people" (Rand, et al., 1953, p. 396).

Although spontaneous expressions of affection can be observed among children of all ages, the nature and extent of the expressions will vary considerably with the emotional climate of the home, the sociocultural pattern of the family, and the sex of the child. If affectionate behavior is rewarding —as it generally is to girls, who are encouraged to be loving and lovable—it will be continued. If affection is rejected or not reinforced, the child learns to disguise or suppress his feelings. This latter situation is especially common in father-son relationships. Pitcher (1963) describes the intolerance of fathers to any signs of femininity in their sons; and flirting, cuddling, hugging, and kissing are among those signs.

Peer attachments. When the child comes into repeated contact with other people outside his home, he begins to form emotional ties with adults other than family members and especially with peers. Preschoolers frequently develop close friendships, but usually with one child at a time regardless of sex. Although the interest in playing with the friend may appear to be intense and all-consuming, there is rarely any jealousy displayed if one of the pair forms other attachments, or grief if the two are separated permanently by moving. (For one thing, they have no sense of finality at this age and phrases such as "You'll never see him again" have no meaning to the child.) New friendships are easily formed, and at this young age there is no apparent tendency to select a new friend with characteristics similar to an old one. Each friend seems to be chosen purely on the basis of his responsiveness.

Through the elementary grades there is a progressively greater tendency to form close attachments with like-sex peers as shown in Table VIII-1. As early as the first grade a girl may experience warm feelings and sympathetic reactions toward a single boy, but she generally hides her emotion even from her closest girl friend. A less covert interest in members of the opposite sex appears with the onset of puberty, followed by a period of "crushes," then "falling in love." The new interest between the sexes does not presuppose a break with like-sex peers. On the contrary, previous like-sex friendships become stronger because of the shared secrets concerning the biology of sex, emotions, the merits of one boy/girl over another, and strategies for making oneself more attractive, getting the desired attention, or bringing one boy and one girl into closer, more frequent proximity.

Table VIII–1 * Friendship Choices by Sex of Friend Chosen and by Grade [1]

Grade	Cross-Sex Choices	Same-Sex Choices	Total Number
Fifth	19.7	80.3	350
Sixth	16.0	84.0	256
Seventh	14.6	85.0	233

* See Table VIII–2.   [1] Each child has up to four choices

Pre-teen romance. A review of literature bearing on social-sex behavior of young adolescents shows the emergence in the later twentieth century of new norms in cross-sex relationships among boys and girls in the ten to twelve-year age range. The new pattern that is emerging has changed the traditional concept of an antagonism natural between boys and girls during the early teen years. Since the 1920's and 1930's, a remarkable thawing has occurred (Broderick and Fowler, 1961).

There has also been an increase in romantic interest. Heretofore, the twelve-year-old girl was very reluctant to admit that a certain boy was attractive to her, and the twelve- to thirteen-year-old boy preferred to pretend that girls were obnoxious to him, even when he had a covert interest in a particular girl. In a sample of data from the Broderick and Fowler study shown in Table VIII–2, the majority of children in each of the grades studied (fifth, sixth, and seventh) claimed to have a sweetheart. Responses to the question "Does your sweetheart like you too?" indicated that most of the sample expected reciprocation.

Table VIII–2 *   Frequency of Sweetheart Choice, by Grade and Sex

| | Per Cent | | | | Total Number | |
| | Have a Sweetheart | | No Sweetheart | | | |
Grade	Boys	Girls	Boys	Girls	Boys	Girls
Fifth	5.5	13.2	94.5	86.8	53	55
Sixth	2.9	13.6	97.1	86.4	44	35
Seventh	13.2	25.6	86.8	74.4	39	38

* Tables VIII–1 and VIII–2 from Broderick and Fowler, 1961, p. 28.

Experience with kissing was found to be quite common at this age, with 87.2 per cent of the seventh-grade boys and 86.8 per cent of the seventh-grade girls admitting to having been kissed by their opposite peers.

Probably the most convincing evidence of the growth in interest of young adolescents for the opposite sex was in the choice of friends for three activities; walking, eating, and attending movies. The pre-teenagers were asked to rank the desirability of a companion of the same sex, a companion of the opposite sex, or of no companion at all in the three activities. The results showed that the majority of sixth and seventh graders felt that when walking or going to the movies they preferred a companion of the opposite sex to none at all or to one of the same sex. Both boys and girls were more conservative when choosing an eating companion, although almost half of the seventh graders preferred to eat with a member of the opposite sex.

Several factors or conditions may be offered as explanations of the lessening antagonism. The trend toward overlapping and flexibility of sex roles makes it easier for boys and girls to plan, work, and play together. The increased amount of social interaction noted in schools, churches, and other community institutions has enabled children to gain a better understanding of each sex and has resulted in many common interests. The emphasis on equality between the sexes in social status, education, and opportunities subtly creates a situation in which a boy no longer feels such a great need to prove his superiority. Thus, when both sexes are working toward similar goals—as is happening more frequently in our middle-class culture—neither feels the need to be hostile and rejecting toward the other.

Happiness

Healthy, well-cared-for children are happy ones. They enjoy eating and feeling and living; running and jumping and climbing; sand and snow and tall grass; in short, they enjoy so much of their internal and external environment that it might be easier to list those relatively few situations that make them unhappy. However, Jersild and Tasch (1949) conducted a study to determine what children themselves considered happiness as indicated by their choices of "one of the happiest days of my life." Table VIII-3 summarizes the response percentages for some of the categories. (The table is abbreviated.) A very high percentage of elementary-school children choose holidays and other festive occasions as happy days. Apparently, such days as Christmas and birthdays are chosen for some special meaning other than the gifts received. Probably, the combination of gifts, visits, companionship, parties, special attention, and joyous spirits are responsible for placing those days so firmly in the young memories.

The most conspicuous change with age in accounts of happiest days is a decline in the mention of holidays. The oldest boys seem to enjoy camping and similar recreational activities; the oldest girls become concerned with facets of self-improvement. Significantly, girls of all ages are far more often happy in social relationships than boys are. (See Chapter II, p. 29.)

Laughter and Humor

Nearly all of the laughter of infants and preschool children occurs in social situations (Ding and Jersild, 1932; Kenderine, 1931). The infant's laugh, an extension of his social smile, may occur around three months of age, and is usually in response to some action by his mother—tickling, hiding-reappearing-hiding, ducking her head, bouncing him on her knees, and similar playing. Humor, likewise, apparently develops from "horseplay" situations, although it is difficult to tell exactly when humor begins to develop. Children generally are delighted to the point of open laughter when adults or other children engage in wild activity, running motions, head-shaking, silliness, pretending fright or surprise. Before they are able to talk clearly or understand many words, they will laugh at the laughter of other people. Certainly, the appeal of a television comedy program such as *The Three Stooges* is a product of these elements, plus the incongruities and contrasts inherent to the physical characteristics of the three men and the situations they become involved in. There is also the element of superiority and degra-

Table VIII–3   Per Cent of Children Giving One or More Responses in Each Category Describing "One of the Happiest Days of My Life" (Adapted from Jersild and Tasch, 1949, p. 128)

Category	Grades 1–3 Ages 6–9		Grades 4–6 Ages 9–12		Grades 7–9 Ages 12–15		Grades 10–12 Ages 15–18	
	Boys 363	Girls 331	Boys 309	Girls 343	Boys 282	Girls 290	Boys 159	Girls 171
Receiving or otherwise enjoying material things, gifts, toys, money, living quarters, etc.	8.7	8.1	10.4	7.2	10.1	4.5	5.6	3.1
Sports, games, swimming, hunting, bicycling, etc.	49.3	47.9	41.5	44.4	18.7	15.9	13.6	13.8
Holidays, festive occasions, birthdays, Christmas, etc.	39.1	40.5	32.4	38.9	6.3	10.1	0.6	6.5
Going to miscellaneous places of recreation, parks, camps, resorts, traveling	9.6	9.0	10.1	11.4	9.7	13.9	30.2	6.9
Self-improvement, success in school, educational opportunity, getting a job	2.4	2.3	2.9	1.9	4.8	4.1	13.6	15.9
Relationships with people, relatives, friends, companionship	7.7	15.9	8.0	15.8	10.5	22.0	8.7	19.9
Benefits for others (general or specific)	0.6	0.8	3.2	2.8	2.2	2.6	7.9	9.7

dation—another category of laughter-producing conditions (Jersild, 1954, p. 903).

Once the children have an elementary command of language they begin finding humor in words and word-play, especially plosive sounds, rhymes, and repetitions. Much of children's humor is suggestive of what might be called "silly humor," which, childish as it may be, appeals to the risibilities of all ages. They will laugh delightedly, for example, when first they hear the word *nincompoop* and will continue to use it on every occasion (for awhile) and with every variation. They also enjoy mimicking the neighborhood mothers, each of whom usually has a different way of expressing bodily necessities.

Unspoken concerns about sex differences may appear in verbal or dramatic forms of humor. Three youngsters, six, seven, and eight years of age, planned with hysterical laughter to exchange clothes one summer afternoon. (A five-year-old boy became upset with the idea and went home.) When an exchange was finally made, the two girls and one boy giggled and screamed with delight, clutching their stomachs and rolling on the floor. The exchange? Two summer T-shirts (or polo shirts) and two summer shorts. To an adult eye, the only observable difference in the items of clothing was in the position of the zippers—one in the front and one on the side. The children, however, were not openly aware of either the similarity or the difference in clothing. For them it was funny enough that Debbie wore David's clothes and David wore Debbie's.

As children grow older, their sense of humor becomes broader and more sophisticated, involving the same general categories already indicated but with a greater use of language. A precocious six-year-old, for example, thought that the description of a painting of peach blossoms as "unimpeachable" was extremely funny, as it was meant to be. Elementary-school children create jingles, repeat current jokes and riddles, play practical jokes, and generally exercise an increasing intellectual capacity for making humorous relationships and anticipating reactions.

Not until puberty does the basic content of children's humor change, when it may revolve around sly, subtle allusions to sex differences and sexual practices. At this time, however, jokes are more likely to be indications that the youngsters are truly curious about that which is "forbidden," "secret," or "shameful." Unfortunately, most of the "sex" jokes contain faulty information.

Anger

Anger and fear are closely related emotions, being two sides of the coin of threat. Anger is a protest against a situation to which the child cannot adjust. It is an outgrowth of frustration and is a normal, healthy response to physical or psychological restraint. Any condition which inhibits the gratification of a child's needs, as he perceives them, or the realization of his goals may elicit an anger response. Often, anger furnishes a significant clue to an individual's needs and to the nature of his emotional life.

The most systematic evidence concerning anger in young children is furnished by Goodenough (1931) in a study involving over eighteen hundred instances of anger outbursts recorded by mothers of children between the ages of seven months and seven years and ten months. One-fourth of all the outbursts recorded for children under one year of age arose in connection with routine care such as dressing and bathing. Minor physical discomforts accounted for almost another one-fourth of the outbursts. The highest frequency of responses to these particular frustrations occurred for both boys and girls at one and one-half years of age.

The major sources of anger in two-year-olds were in the establishment of routine physical habits, conflicts with authority, and social relations. After the age of two, boys consistently displayed anger more often than girls did.

Between the ages of three and four, irritations arising in social situations reached their maximum. Conflict with authority accounted for one-third of the anger displays.

By the age of three, the child has usually learned to substitute language for direct physical reactions. For the five- and six-year-old, language responses probably are the most important manifestations of anger. The primary-grade child, however, will continue to mix such physical responses as slapping, hitting, kicking, and pushing with crying, arguments, and name-calling (Gesell and Ilg, 1946).

Anger expressions after the age of eighteen months sometimes take the form of temper tantrums, which are characterized by head-beating, loud screams, infantile thrashing actions, breath-holding, or any such intense reaction. Because a child's tantrum is so unsettling, often embarrassing, and sometimes frightening to a parent, the angry child is quite likely to find it a rewarding method for gaining his own ends. For the child who is indulged during those moments, the temper tantrum may become a bad habit. Generally, however, this mode of expression declines after the age of three, although again boys display temper more frequently than girls. Macfarlane, Allen, and Honzik (1954) attribute the greater number of temper tantrums among boys to a higher energy level and the culturally accepted aggressiveness and mobility assigned to the male role. The difference is especially noticeable around age eight, when girls begin to substitute oversensitiveness for physical aggression. Temper tantrums among girls, therefore, may be more symptomatic of emotional disturbances than they would be among boys, particularly during the elementary-school years.

By the time he has reached school age, the child has developed an individual pattern of responses to anger. Some children will act directly and overtly against the threatening, frustrating person or object—hitting it, or screaming for help and thus frightening the stimulus away. Some will merely cry or have a temper tantrum. Others will smash a favorite toy, kick furniture, or throw something, blowing off steam against objects other than those that annoy. Some children rarely exhibit overt behavior, and their emotional responses are turned inward. They become negative and withdrawn, experiencing digestive upsets, loss of control over elimination, or anxiety. Feelings of anger, if they persist, can manifest themselves in various forms of disgust, resentment, rebellion, irritability, insubordination, or other aggressive acts against the individual, the stimulus, authority, or the world in general.

Ideally, the school functions to guide the child in trying out different ways of responding. In that way, he can learn to cope with his anger and direct his behavior into constructive channels. The child who withdraws from the angering scene must be guided first into displaying his anger overtly, and then into redirecting the forms he has chosen. (The child without the capacity to display anger is often a more serious mental hygiene problem than a child who occasionally lets loose.)

"The control of anger—that is, the preventing of wasteful emotional discharge in this form—is one of the aims and accomplishments of civilization. [It] depends organically upon the development of the highest centres of the brain . . ." (Menninger, 1961, p. 210). It develops out of experiences wherein a child's naturally chosen response fails to satisfy his needs, or creates further conflict. The boy who hits his father in anger and is punished in retaliation may smash a toy the next time. If he continues to lose toys in this manner, he may become irritable with his playmates and refuse to share. With guidance, he may learn to set aside a frustrating problem and return to it another time. Slowly, he learns and tries many methods of overcoming frustration and venting anger; and by the time he has entered the middle grades, only exceptional situations cause overt anger manifestations. The natural processes of growth, adult authority in the home and classroom, and the reactions of peer groups have served to help the child modify his behavior so that it more closely approximates the standards imposed by society.

Jealousy

Most often, jealousy is manifested by overt signs of hostility or negativism. Temper tantrums, destruction of toys, the deliberate breaking of well-learned rules, selfishness, excessive demands, sulking, and crying are typical signs. However, the child's *first* responses to envy and jealousy are usually concerted efforts to gain for himself whatever advantages he perceives another to have. If one child in the neighborhood has a bicycle or is allowed to walk to school instead of riding the bus or goes to the movies every Saturday, these advantages become of paramount importance to the "deprived" youngster. Without them, he expresses himself vehemently: "I never get anything!" "You never let me do anything!" "Why do I have to do that when she doesn't?"

When a new baby enters the family, a very young child seeks first to gain all of the mother's time and attention that is diverted elsewhere. Nor is a new baby always the catalyst! The jealous, envious child attempts to divert a mother's attention from everything and anything. One new mother who thought that the daily nursing periods would be ideal opportunities to catch up on her reading found that her three-week-old infant refused to suck, making plucking and patting motions on her face, whenever her eyes wandered from the child to a book. Even in later months, it became a standing joke in the family that the youngster had an uncanny sense of knowing when the mother was reading, for the child's demands for attention became excessive at just those times. Still later, although the child was of above-average intelligence, she refused to be interested in learning to read. Only when she realized how important this ability was to her teachers and peers did she master her jealousy of books enough to concentrate on the task.

The instances of sibling rivalry and jealousy are legion. Few children escape the feelings of rejection which follow the advent of a newcomer to the household, and few parents have the long-term patience necessary to prepare the child for sharing the love and care of a sibling or to help the child out of compounded emotional difficulties resulting from jealousy. A few admonitions are commonly presented, such as not sending a child to nursery school immediately after the new arrival, allowing the older to help care for the younger, scheduling the mother's time to include more activities shared with the older child, and particularly providing enough creative materials and doll-type toys so that the child can work off his aggression and hostility in ways that are not dangerous to the infant.

A certain amount of jealous behavior is natural in children, as occurs when older siblings are given special privileges—staying up later or attending movies. However, continued jealousy may indicate a fundamental insecurity or basic need that is not being satisfied. To a marked degree, jealous behavior is associated with oversolicitude, overindulgence, and inconsistent discipline on the part of the mother. Discord between parents, nagging, and comparisons with other children also threaten a child's security and his self-esteem. When we see jealousy in action, we must remember that its expression is a protective mechanism for the person involved. An outburst of anger, excessive affection, rejection, gossip, rationalizations, or any of the other faces that jealousy wears are expressions (and disguises) of intense, but conflicting, feelings. Granted, they are indications that he is learning to divert at least one of his more potentially dangerous emotions away from injurious acts of hatred, but his expressions are also indications that he needs assistance in feeling accepted.

When the child enters school, the possibilities for displaying jealousy increase, for he is faced with many new situations that threaten his sense of autonomy. Some children may attend school reluctantly, feeling that school is a means for "getting rid" of them. If a child has younger siblings, he may think that they are having more fun at home with mother, who obviously— to his way of thinking—must love them better because she keeps them with her.

[Within the classroom, the child has one of his first experiences with a large social group. He discovers that he must wait his turn and that he must share play materials and the teacher's attention with many other children]. If he has no core of self-confidence to rely upon, he becomes bothered by the fact that some of his classmates are larger or better coordinated or able to perform certain tasks which he cannot. When confronted by such realizations, the insecure child often displays jealousy. Competition, incidentally, points up such individual differences and, by breeding tension and failure as often as it breeds success, it encourages jealous behavior (Levy, 1937).

Although the knowing and experienced teacher tries to prevent excessive competition and sees that each child has an opportunity to succeed and lead, emotional outbursts of jealousy can be expected during the first school year. The teacher can greatly assist the child who demonstrates jealous behavior by providing him with many experiences and tasks in which he can be successful and by unconditionally accepting the child as worthy in his own right while showing him that other children deserve the same consideration. A teacher must rely on her own emotional maturity to support wholesome relationships of strength and tenderness which will feed the hungers of the jealous child. For jealousy is a kind of emotional malnutrition. It is starvation for confidence, esteem, and a sense of worth.

Fear

Although responses to fear are a product of conditioning and learning, they are more directly related to the startle response than are the other emotional reactions. Any sudden, unfamiliar occurrence in the life of an infant— a loud noise, quick movements, strange faces, the sensation of being unable to move freely or of being without support—in short, any quick disequilibrium or "departure from a calm state" will elicit the startle response, which has both internal and external manifestations. The involuntary, internal release of adrenalin is in itself a disequilibrium and is generally unpleasant, as is the accompanying rapid heartbeat and other physiological reactions. The infant learns rapidly to dislike this state, and later as he begins to anticipate certain events in his environment by means of association, he begins to show more signs of fearing specific things. Most of those things that a preschooler learns to fear are intimately related to his sense of security and the incidence of suddenness and strangeness. The unprotected, insecure child who has unsatisfied safety needs is quite likely to be afraid of anything that he himself cannot control—darkness, large dogs, bodies of water (especially the "roaring" ocean), strange situations or people. Likewise, he may develop fear of any situation in which he feels he must rely solely upon himself, such as being left alone or in a precarious position.

As children begin to understand the nature of various stimuli, their fear of them decreases. Meanwhile, they are also learning that other objects and conditions deserve to be feared or viewed with caution—moving automobiles, excessive heights, snakes. In other words, not until children become aware of conditions that are potentially dangerous—either physically or psychologically—do they develop emotional reactions to them. Jones and Jones (1928) revealed that children under the age of two showed no fear of a six-foot-long snake. By the age of three and one-half years, children showed caution. Those who were four years of age or older preferred to avoid close contact with the snake. The investigators concluded that "fear arises when we know enough to recognize the potential danger in the situation but have not advanced to the point of complete comprehension and control of the changing situation" (p. 143). This conclusion is given indirect support by Holmes (1935) who noted that the advanced, or precocious, child may display fears of things and conditions that do not bother other children of his age. Furthermore, as was pointed out in Chapter II, children in the lower socioeconomic groups are, quite naturally, more afraid of physical dangers having to do with poverty, lack of food, clothing, and shelter, etc. than they are about the school-related threats to personal security, self-esteem, success, academic achievements, and social relationships that are the primary concerns of the upper socioeconomic groups (Angelino, et al., 1956).

The typical school-age child develops or has developed fears relating to supernatural dangers, possible accidents, deprivations, failure, ridicule, security, and the like. Some fears result from the perception of real threats; some are products of faulty knowledge concerning natural phenomena; others have been absorbed from parents and older siblings. The wise teacher helps her pupils understand and deal with their fears. The child who is afraid of traffic can be effectively taught safety rules and ways of recognizing and avoiding dangerous situations, even to the extent of allowing him to share in the responsibilities of school-crossing guards. The child who is fearful of cooperating with other children can overcome his reticence when given opportunities to succeed in group activities.

Fears which are reasonable in the light of experiences and reality can be overcome with relatively small amounts of understanding and patience. Irrational fears are more difficult to handle. They must be studied carefully and understood in all of their ramifications before much assistance can be given. Sometimes parents, teachers, and other adults can help the child with fears of this sort by strengthening him and giving him opportunities to gain insight into his problems. Jersild (1948) has suggested four ways of accomplishing the strengthening: (1) By manipulating the child's environment, reducing tension and friction, so that he does not feel threatened by specific objects or people; (2) by letting him succeed at some task unrelated to his fears, thereby fostering a sense of security which is often transferrable; (3) by helping him to face the thing or condition he fears; and (4) by giving him the chance to talk about himself and his feelings.

One of the difficulties adults have in helping children overcome their fears lies in the method of response. When fear arises in some children, they make a determined effort to overcome the threat, usually by fighting, striking, or in other ways attempting to drive away the object. Other children, however, withdraw and run away from the problem. At a time of impending danger, this withdrawal pattern may be the best one to follow; however, as a consistent reaction to fear, it generally becomes a most serious problem to both the child and the adults who would help him, because it has a tendency to obscure its causes. Furthermore, adults frequently pay less attention to the shy, withdrawn child, who rarely presents the kind of discipline problems that must be solved immediately. For the teacher in particular, these latter problems are all too many. Thus, in many instances, the withdrawal behavior and its causes are compounded or fed by continued adult inattention to the child's needs. A persistent withdrawal pattern of behavior can, and often does, lead to various unhealthy patterns and characteristics, including escapism, timidity, submissiveness, introspection, feelings of inferiority, anxiety neuroses, phobias—all of which, if allowed to accumulate in the deeper emotional recesses of the individual, will eventually play a large part in neurotic distortions and mental disorders.

Anxiety and Worry

Ontologically, anxiety is preceded by fear. It is a function of fear, and like its predecessor is a learned response to threat. They are different in their manifestations. Whereas fear is associated with the release of adrenalin, anxiety is not. Fear dries the mouth; anxiety increases both salivation and gastric secretion (Cattell, 1963). Anxiety response patterns are not usually directed toward external objects or situations; indeed, the child frequently does not know just what causes his worry. That is, he may feel resentment toward another child or toward authority, but he may not be able to say exactly why. His responses are primarily internal, although he may be more nervous than other children, may frown and bite his lip or nails, because of his chronic uneasiness. Preschool children who are intensely anxious and emotionally immature oftentimes react with undifferentiated excitement.*

* Despert (1946), for example, found this or a similar manifestation of anxiety in every one of the seventy-eight preschool children she studied, although there were marked differences in the intensity and frequency of the responses.

Older children are observed to manifest anxiety through gastric disturbances, headaches, insomnia, constipation, irrational fears, tension, teeth-grinding, irritability, restlessness, inattention, learning blocks, rigidity in problem-solving, and underachievement.

Jersild (1954, p. 869) has summarized some of the criteria commonly used in describing anxiety:

> . . . Generally speaking, it is assumed that the danger or disaster which is involved in anxiety is subjective or internal in nature—it resides within the personality of the anxious person—there are conflicting tendencies and impulses, unfulfilled needs, strivings, obligations, "oughts" and "shoulds" within him that underlie the disturbance known as anxiety.

Sullivan (1948) maintains that anxiety is a reflection of warning of internally ordered discrepancies in the "self-system." To put it broadly, we could say that it is either a result of faulty adaptation to increasing demands or a combination of unsuccessful attempts to deal with elementary fears.

PROBLEM BEHAVIOR—OR IS IT?

Stress is an imbalance that the organism seeks to correct through two basic patterns of behavior, aggression and withdrawal, both of which serve to protect some facet of the physiological or psychological personality. In childhood, stress is synonymous with growing up. Certainly one does not occur without the other; and all the various reactions to stress are necessary to maintain the personality's equilibrium while it is assimilating experiences and to help it come in contact with more experiences. That is, both aggression and withdrawal are necessary for the development of personality over and above their functions as protective mechanisms. Initiative and ambition are forms of aggression, without which the individual cannot take an active part in learning. Sleep, seclusion, and introspection are forms of withdrawal required for good mental and physical health, spiritual growth, ordered thinking, and inner peace. However, when aggression approaches selfishness, lack of control, and lack of consideration for others, when withdrawal damages self-confidence and the ability to meet and search for intellectual and social experiences, trouble follows in the form of undesirable personality characteristics and ineffectual, destructive behavior.

In young children, most of the behavior that causes difficulties arises during periods of extreme stress, or disequilibriums in growth. "In a sense all children are problem children, because none can escape the universal problem of development which always presents some difficulties" (Gesell and Ilg, 1943). All new learning activities require intense concentration and exercise for mastery and are therefore generators of fatigue. Furthermore, Rand and her associates (1953, p. 389) state:

It is characteristic of learning that it reaches an apparently smooth, finished result on the surface before it has been practiced in the nervous system long enough to make it truly automatic. This unstable stage . . . is likely to come to light whenever the child is asked to make a new adjustment before given learnings are fixed. For example, children who seem to be trained for the toilet so that they no longer have accidents demonstrate this principle when they "relapse" if a baby is born into the family, or if they are entered in nursery school or if some other basic and demanding adjustment is required of them.

The behavior patterns that are only partially integrated into the nervous system become "jarred loose," Rand continues, when new demands are made shortly after a child has accomplished a task.

Hunger and breaks in routine also cause upsets in the child's system of balances, and the homeostatic adjustments brought into play are so strong as to make behavior appear exaggerated and "a problem." Sometimes the adjustments require a regression of behavior to the forms that previously brought security—as when a child entering school reverts to an overdependence upon his mother for the first few weeks or suddenly begins to suck his thumb again. At other times, the child may discontinue some activity whose mastery previously created anxiety—e.g., eating, bladder control, entering strange situations. That is, he may refuse to eat, may suddenly have more "accidents," etc. By and large, these behavior patterns are considered "growth phenomena" and are temporary, becoming fixed only if children are severely disciplined or nagged because of them. A sample of typical growth behavior problems among nursery-school children is presented in Table VIII-4, which the investigators compiled after a study of 555 children. These responses, they conclude, are products of their age—their necessary depend-

Table VIII–4   Behavior in Nursery School Children (After Hattwick and Sanders, 1938, pp. 40–46)

Per Cent of Children Showing the Behavior	Behavior	Peaks
80	Asks unnecessary help	2½–3 yrs.
90	Leaves tasks incomplete	2–3½ yrs.
90	Wastes time at routine tasks	2–4 yrs.
85	Ignores requests	2½–3 yrs.
85	Dawdles (at meals)	2½–3½ yrs.
75	Wriggles a great deal when sitting	2½–3½ yrs.
60	Resists at rest	2–4 yrs.
50	Fears strange people, objects, places	2–3½ yrs.
65	Laughs, squeals, jumps, around excessively	2–4 yrs. (consistent)
70	Slurs or speaks indistinctly	3 yrs.

ency on adults, high energy output, shifting focus of attention, assertion of independence (usually by negativism), and ego-involvement.

In other words, the most well-adjusted, emotionally healthy youngster has strong, conflicting emotions. "He may be very anxious if his parents are gone when he expects to find them home. He will be jealous of brothers or sisters and have quarrels with them. He will be enraged if someone hurts him or accuses him unjustly. He will be frightened by loud noises or furious adults . . ." (Wattenberg, 1964). As Auerbach (1952) has stated:

> . . . the behavior of children is meaningful. [It] is the expression of their normal needs—for physical well-being, for activity, for recognition, for satisfactions of many kinds. It is their response to the many complex factors of their physical and social environment. Trying and difficult though a child may be, he is not a "problem" if his behavior is appropriate to the circumstances [p. 217] . . . if, on the whole, his behavior is suitable for his age, appropriate to the situation in which he finds himself, and more or less in keeping with his temperamental make-up. These three concepts may serve as general yardsticks by which to judge the quality of a child's adjustment. [p. 212]

Truly maladjustive, or "problem," behavior is a *persistent*, inappropriate reaction that is damaging rather than protective for the child's personal-social integration. Some of its forms and treatments are discussed in Chapter XIII.

SUMMARY

Emotions involve the total human organism and may be viewed subjectively in terms of feeling or mental states, physiological disturbances, or impulses to action.

At one time it was generally believed that infants were born with definite emotions, a belief that may have resulted from the attempts of adults to interpret infants' actions in terms of their own reactions to the stimuli which they have assumed caused the infants' behavior. Most research workers today believe that emotional behavior is solely the result of maturation and learning and develops from the manner in which bodily needs are met or not met. However, there is a widely held opinion among psychologists that the individual inherits a sensitivity potential which determines the relative strength of the impact a stimulus has on the organism.

All the known behavioral manifestations of emotion have developed from the infant's reflex actions—among them, crying, sucking, and the startle response. The latter results in generalized mass activity, from which all the other responses are differentiated. Differentiation begins early in life and proceeds apace with maturing mental, motor, and social abilities. Control of behavior and the discrimination between more important and less important stimuli increase with age and are aided by the training insisted upon in a particular society.

Growing up is synonymous with stress—frustrations and conflicts, fears and anxieties. It also has its happy times, its laughter and humor, loves and affections. A child's constitution, his family relationships, socioeconomic status, personal experiences, mental age, and many other factors are instrumental in guiding him toward emotional maturity. He and his behavior become a "problem" only insofar as it is inappropriate to any one of those factors, or is persistently undesirable and harmful to himself and his community.

QUESTIONS AND PROBLEMS

1. Describe the emotional behavior of the infant. Look up additional materials bearing on the nature of the infant's emotional life.
2. Discuss various reasons why people might believe that infants are born with emotions.
3. Compare the emotions of preschool, primary-grade, intermediate-grade, and upper-elementary-grade children.
4. Explain the role that language plays in emotional behavior.
5. List the methods that a first-grade teacher could use to help a pupil overcome temper tantrums. What techniques might a sixth-grade teacher use if she were faced with the same problem?
6. Explain what we mean by emotional maturity.
7. List some of the methods you employ to conceal your emotions. Which emotions do you seek to hide and which do you show freely? Why?
8. Describe the ideal emotional climate which you think the classroom and the school should have.
9. What are the implications of emotional development for education?

SELECTED READINGS

BRECKENRIDGE, MARIAN E., and E. LEE VINCENT, *Child Development,* 4th ed. Philadelphia: Saunders, 1960. Ch. 3.

DINKEMEYER, DON C., *Child Development: The Emerging Self.* Englewood Cliffs, N.J.: Prentice-Hall, 1965. Ch. 9.

GARRISON, KARL C., *Growth and Development,* 2nd ed. Longmans, Green (now McKay), 1959. Ch. 14.

HUTT, MAX L., and ROBERT G. GIBBY, *The Child: Development and Adjustment.* Boston: Allyn and Bacon, 1959. Ch. 7.

JERSILD, ARTHUR T., *Child Psychology,* 5th ed. Englewood Cliffs, N.J.: Prentice-Hall, 1960. Chs. 11, 12, 13.

MOULY, GEORGE J., *Psychology for Effective Teaching.* Holt, Rinehart & Winston, 1960. Ch. 5.

OLSON, WILLARD C., *Child Development,* 2nd ed. Boston: D. C. Heath, 1959. Ch. 10.

THOMPSON, GEORGE G., *Child Psychology, Growth Trends in Psychological Adjustment,* 2nd ed. Boston: Houghton Mifflin, 1962. Ch. 8.

REFERENCES

ANGELINO, HENRY, JOSEPH DOLLINS, and EDMUND V. MECH, Trends in the "fears and worries" of school children as related to socio-economic status and age, *The Journal of Genetic Psychology*, 1956, *89*, 263–276.

AUERBACH, ALINE B., When children need special help with emotional problems, in *Our Children Today* (Sidonie M. Gruenberg, ed.). Viking, 1952, pp. 210–222.

BANHAM, KATHARINE M., The development of affectionate behavior in infancy, *The Journal of Genetic Psychology*, 1950, *76*, 283–289.

BOUSFIELD, W. A., and W. D. ORBISON, Ontogenesis of emotional behavior, *The Psychological Review*, 1952, *59*, 1–7.

BRIDGES, KATHARINE M. B., Emotional development in early infancy, *Child Development*, 1932, *3*, 324–341.

BRODERICK, CARLFRED B., and STANLEY E. FOWLER, New patterns of relationships between the sexes among preadolescents, *Marriage and Family Living*, 1961, *23*, 27–30.

BRODY, SYLVIA, Signs of disturbance in the first year of life, *American Journal of Orthopsychiatry*, 1958, *28*, 362–367.

CANNON, W. B., *Bodily Changes in Pain, Hunger, Fear, and Rage*, 2nd ed. Appleton-Century, 1929.

CATTELL, RAYMOND B., The nature and measurement of anxiety, *Scientific American* (March 1963), *208*, 96–104.

DESPERT, J. LOUISE, Anxiety, phobias, and fears in young children, *Nervous Child*, 1946, *5*, 8–24.

DING, G. F., and ARTHUR T. JERSILD, A study of the laughing and smiling of preschool children, *The Journal of Genetic Psychology*, 1932, *40*, 452–472.

GESELL, ARNOLD, and FRANCES L. ILG, *Infant and Child in the Culture of Today.* Harper & Bros., 1943, p. 295.

GESELL, ARNOLD, and FRANCES L. ILG, *The Child from Five to Ten.* Harper & Bros., 1946, pp. 287–294.

GOODENOUGH, FLORENCE L., *Anger in Young Children.* Minneapolis: University of Minnesota Press, 1931.

HARLOW, HARRY F., and MARGARET KUENNE HARLOW, Social deprivation in monkeys, *Scientific American* (November 1962), *207*, 136–146.

HATTWICK, LA BERTA A., and MOLLIE K. SANDERS, Age differences in behavior at the nursery school level, *Child Development*, 1938, *9*, 27–47.

HEBB, D. O., *The Organization of Behavior: A Neuropsychological Theory.* John Wiley & Sons, 1949.

HEBB, D. O., Drives and the C.N.S. [conceptual nervous system], *The Psychological Review*, 1955, *62*, 243–254.

HOLMES, F. B., An experimental study of the fears of young children, *Child Development Monographs*, No. 20, Pt. III. Bureau of Publications, Teachers College, Columbia University, 1935.

JERSILD, ARTHUR T., Children's fears, *NEA Journal*, 1948, *37*, 212–213.

JERSILD, ARTHUR T., Emotional development, in *Manual of Child Psychology* (L. Carmichael, ed.), 2nd ed. John Wiley & Sons, 1954.

JERSILD, ARTHUR T., and R. J. TASCH, *Children's Interests and What They Suggest for Education.* Teachers College, Columbia University, 1949, p. 128.

JONES, HAROLD E., and MARY C. JONES, A study of fear, *Childhood Education,* 1928, *5,* 136–143.

JOST, HUDSON, and LESTER W. SONTAG, The genetic factor in autonomic nervous system function, *Psychosomatic Medicine,* 1944, *6,* 308–310.

KENDERDINE, M., Laughter in the preschool child, *Child Development,* 1931, *2,* 228–230.

LEVIN, PHYLLIS LEE, "There Are Babies and Babies," *The New York Times Magazine* (September 12, 1965), pp. 132, 134.

LEVY, D. M., Studies in sibling rivalry, *Research Monographs of the American Orthopsychiatric Association,* 1937, No. 2.

MACFARLANE, JEAN W., LUCILE ALLEN, and MARJORIE P. HONZIK, *A Developmental Study of Behavior Problems of Normal Children between Twenty-One Months and Fourteen Years.* Berkeley: University of California Publications in Child Development, 1954, Vol. 2.

MENNINGER, KARL A., *The Human Mind.* Alfred A. Knopf, 1961.

NIEDERLAND, WILLIAM G., Psychoneurosis, in *Collier's Encyclopedia,* 1965, *16,* 332.

PITCHER, EVELYN GOODENOUGH, Male and female, *The Atlantic Monthly* (March 1963), *211,* 87–91.

RAND, WINIFRED, MARY E. SWEENEY, and E. LEE VINCENT, *Growth and Development of the Young Child,* 5th ed. Philadelphia: Saunders, 1953.

ROSS, HELEN, Emotional needs of the young child, in *Our Children Today* (Sidonie M. Gruenberg, ed.). Viking, 1952, pp. 57–68.

RUSSELL, W. RITCHIE, Functions of the frontal lobes, *The Lancet,* 1948, *254,* 356–360.

SCHLOSBERG, HAROLD, Emotion, in *Collier's Encyclopedia,* 1954, *7,* 261.

SHERMAN, MANDEL, Differentiation of emotional responses in infants, *Journal of Comparative Psychology,* 1927, *7,* 265–284, 335–351.

SPITZ, RENE A., The smiling response: a contribution to the ontogenesis of social relations, *Genetic Psychology Monographs,* 1946, *34,* 57–125.

SPOCK, BENJAMIN, *Baby and Child Care.* Pocket Books, 1957, p. 215.

STONE, L. JOSEPH, and JOSEPH CHURCH, *Childhood and Adolescence.* Random House, 1957, p. 9.

SULLIVAN, H. S., *The Meaning of Anxiety in Psychiatry and in Life.* William Alanson White Institute of Psychiatry, 1948.

TAYLOR, J. H., Innate emotional responses in infants, *Ohio State University Studies in Infant Behavior,* 1934, No. 12.

THOMPSON, GEORGE G., *Child Psychology, Growth Trends in Psychological Adjustment,* 2nd ed. Boston: Houghton Mifflin, 1962.

VOLLMER, HERMANN, Jealousy in children, *American Journal of Orthopsychiatry,* 1946, *16,* 660–671.

WALLIS, R. S., The overt fears of Dakota Indian children, *Child Development,* 1954, *25,* 185–192.

WATSON, JOHN B., and ROSALIE RAYNER, Conditioned emotional reactions, *Journal of Experimental Psychology,* 1920, *3,* 1–14.

WATTENBERG, W. W., *Your Child's Mental Health,* pamphlet no. 382–11652, National Education Association, Washington, D. C. Quoted in "Family Business in Brief" by Ann P. Eliasberg, *The New York Times Magazine* (May 17, 1964), p. 79.

N I N E

The Development

of Moral and

Ethical Behavior

The first thing that should be pointed out in a general discussion of morality and ethics is that the bare definitions of the words carry no inherent value judgment. *Moral* refers simply to right and wrong behavior and *ethical* refers to conduct in an individual or group; and both concepts are predicated upon the principles of such behavior that any one society, culture, or generation holds valid and valuable to the attainment of its goals. No matter how one may judge a society whose only goal is survival, one must acknowledge that its practices of sexual license and its placement of value on pregnancy before marriage are certainly in keeping with that goal. Its members have a code of conduct and a set of laws that would be considered immoral in another culture; but within the confines of their own social structure, they are moral. Nazi children were presented with the goal of racial purity and were taught a code of conduct which would assure them the attainment of that goal. To the extent that their behavior moved them in the proper direction and conformed to the code, they were ethical and moral *by Nazi standards*. But theirs was not a Christian morality. Nor did it approximate the Confucian, Buddhist, or Hebrew moralities. They had character—a complex of mental and ethical traits; moral excellence—but not the kind that is deemed desirable in either Western or Eastern societies.

Individuals who wish to understand the development of character in all children must first understand that the goals and values of a child's social milieu are the primary factors, for character development is more than the learning of ethical behavior. It is the construction and reconstruction of personal values and goals and the ability to conduct one's self toward those changing goals with good conscience and integrity of purpose. The evolution of character begins in early childhood and ends, according to modern philosophers, at the moment of death.

ACQUIRING VALUES AND IDEALS

Ideals, attitudes, and values are "soaked up" from the milieu in which a child lives. As his experiences accumulate and his horizons widen, he recognizes, absorbs, or learns about the objects, goals, characteristics, and behavior patterns that are considered worthwhile and valuable to the people in his environment. Berdie (1954), for example, sought to discover the differences in values between children who were and those who were not planning on attending college. Although the parents of both groups recognized the financial rewards of a college education, the parents of college-bound children emphasized the love of learning and the importance of higher education for one's personal development.

Along with the values learned from his social environment, the child develops some of his own, beginning with those involved in ego identity. The well-cared-for baby places a high value on those people who are responsible for his well-being at the same time he is recognizing his own value to them. As a person of importance, he finds those things which belong to him likewise of worth. He perceives no defects such as dirt, rips, breaks, rust, or missing parts. The entire value of an old blanket or toy is summed up in the word *mine*—one of the first words a child learns, along with *me* and *my*. In a sense, he establishes the meaning of *I* through the use of *my*. As an orphan child said to a psychiatrist, "How could I find out who I was when I never had anything that belonged to me, not even my clothing!"

This early identification with possessions is so strong that a major preschool task is the difficult one of learning to share. Ugurel-Semin (1952) has noted that selfishness is at its height among the four- to six-year-olds and only gradually diminishes thereafter. Children from large families are inclined to be slightly more generous than those from small families. Not only do these children get earlier practice in the art of sharing, but—we might speculate—they probably receive their sense of identity largely through intrafamily relationships.

As the child grows and his social contacts and experiences expand, his vocabulary changes to include the words *we* and *ours*, and he learns to value things outside of, but including, himself: friends, pets, cooperative play, money, and gifts. Only gradually does he discover such abstract values as beauty, peace, privacy, and the rights of every individual.

The Ideal Self

Socrates has said, "The shortest and surest way to live with honor in the world, is to be in reality what we would appear to be. . . ." Every individual has or has had a conception of the type of person he would like to be or to resemble. Havighurst, Robinson, and Dorr (1946) hypothesized that the ideal self may be developmental in nature, suggesting that it begins in childhood as identification with a parental figure. During middle childhood and early adolescence, it moves through a stage of romanticism and glamour, and culminates in late adolescence as a composite of desirable characteristics which may be symbolized by an attractive, real, and visible young adult, or perhaps by an imaginary person. By questioning a group of children about the people they would most like to resemble, the investigators were able to tabulate the answers (Table IX-1) and furnish valuable information regarding the types of people who influence children's conceptions regarding "ideal" or "model" behavior. The influences of parents and relatives, glamourous adults, and attractive, successful young adults are shown to be important to both boys and girls. The reader will also notice the effects that sex and sociocultural factors have on the choices.

By using this concept of the ideal self, some investigators have attempted to determine the values and the moral development of children through an examination of their self-aspirations. It has been found that the mature, well-integrated personality manifests a high degree of congruency between his ideal self and his self-concept (see Chapter X). Perkins (1958) further discovered that the self-concepts and ideal selves of children become increasingly and significantly more congruent with time. The findings of this study appear to lend support to the definition of *character* as a construction and reconstruction of personal values.

Value Systems

Lecky (1945) has classified values into six main categories as follows:

Theoretical—ideas, knowledge, learning, education
Aesthetic—beauty of form as expressed in the various arts
Economic—wealth, financial security, material possessions and comforts
Social—prestige, friendships, group welfare
Political—control, power, governing, administration
Religious—purposiveness, spirituality, life experiences, Supreme Being

Well-established value systems within and among each of these main categories furnish an individual with relative standards which not only determine his choices in different life situations but also give him a feeling of security for making those choices. Rather than flounder in trying to arrive at

Table IX–1   Classification of Persons Described as the Ideal Self, Percentage Distribution (After Havighurst, *et al.,* 1946, p. 247)

	Category	Group					
		A	B	C	D	E	F
	Boys						
I	Parents and relatives	7	23	11	–	16	7
II	Parent-surrogates	0	0	0	–	0	2
III	Glamorous adults	12	32	47	–	23	37
IV	Heroes	3	6	11	–	10	5
V	Attractive adults	53	30	23	–	21	15
VI	Composite or imaginary characters	25	6	8	–	28	28
VII	Age-mates	0	0	0	–	2	1
VIII	Miscellaneous responses (frequently, "myself")	0	3	0	–	0	5
	Girls						
I	Parents and relatives	6	32	14	6	11	7
II	Parent-surrogates	2	0	2	0	4	12
III	Glamorous adults	16	17	27	23	21	37
IV	Heroes	2	3	3	6	1	7
V	Attractive adults	36	13	25	18	25	18
VI	Composite or imaginary characters	33	22	23	29	35	18
VII	Age-mates	3	8	6	12	3	1
VIII	Miscellaneous responses (frequently, "myself")	0	5	0	6	0	0

Description of groups: A. Ten-, eleven- and twelve-year-olds in a typical midwestern community. B. Sixth graders (age 11–12) in an industrial section of Chicago. C. Fifth and sixth graders in a war industry community. D. Girls at a Chicago Settlement House, mostly Italian. E. Seventh and eighth graders in a war industry community. F. Middle-class Negro children (age 12–14) in Baltimore.

decisions, he is able to direct more attention and energy to the attainment of goals. Regardless of his capabilities, a child who values education as one of the most important forces in his life is likely to be more interested (and perhaps more successful) in school activities and academic achievement than the child who places greater value on physical prowess. The adolescent girl who values highly her relationship with the opposite sex (her "popularity") may find excuses for failing at school work, for dropping out before she graduates, and for eloping at an early age.

Values and Needs

Obviously, needs are fundamental to the development of values, and the manner in which an individual's needs are best served, by him, determines the direction of his values. The youngster who is interested in education and the girl who is interested in boys may have the same need for love, self-esteem, and self-realization; yet, each has a different way of achieving satisfaction. Perhaps the former was rewarded at an early age for acquiring correct speech, learning to read, and exercising his mind; whereas the girl may have been unrewarded for these activities, even though she may have succeeded to the same extent. It is conceivable, for instance, that the girl's achievements were accepted by her parents and teachers as a matter of course—which sometimes happens with bright children—and the rewards she received were for "unexpected" characteristics such as personal attractiveness, social adaptability, and femininity. Thus, her entire value system may have a social-sex orientation, and, by preferring to conform to her peers' concepts of popularity, she plays down her academic talents.

Need satisfaction also operates when children choose friends on the basis of similar values. One of the best ways a child has of exercising his capacities is through interaction with individuals having similar interests, habits, attitudes, and values. Myers (1950), for instance, noted that honor students generally chose their friends on the basis of good work habits, favorable attitudes toward school, and interests in things related to educational achievement. Apparently, there is also a relationship between a child's values and his position in the power structure of a group. Gold (1958, p. 59) concluded that "the values of the children do reflect a great deal of the situation in which they interact. Further, these values seem to play an important role in transforming certain properties of the children into resources which in turn determine the relative power positions of the children in classroom groups."

Community Institutions

The child is constantly bombarded with values expressed at home, church and school; on the street corners and playgrounds; in stores, recreational centers, and theaters; on television and radio; and in newspapers, comics, magazines, and books of every description. These values are an integral part of the child's environment as he progresses toward maturity. Some of the values are wholesome, some are not—depending upon the interpretation given them in a particular society. Many of them oppose each other; many are archaic, unreasonable, or unrealistic. In general, the community institutions having the guidance of children as their primary purpose attempt to teach boys and girls what attitudes and values are desirable for the preservation of their culture. They are successful only insofar as (1) their efforts are coordinated; (2) their teachings are related to life in a modern, complex society; (3) instruction by word and example is begun early in the child's life.

One of the primary purposes for the development of parochial schools is just such an integration of academic, moral, and spiritual experiences. The ecclesiastical administrators believe that the traditional separation of functions found in other American schools and churches may prevent the child from developing a well-integrated system of values. One experiment supports that belief to the extent that it shows a relatively early maturity of moral sense among parochial school children (Berkowitz, 1964).

We might also consider a fourth essential for the development of sound values in the youth of a community: the expression and establishment of goals, without which values have little meaning. Too many children learn by one method or another that people should or do value money or ideas or love or property rights without really learning *why* these things are valuable. Unless a boy can experientially equate the value of teamwork with "winning the game," it does little good to ask him to pass the ball. His desire for individual achievement—"star" status—may cause him to hold onto the ball or make an inefficient pass and, through inefficiency, lose both the game and the interest in it. He loses his goal—star status; the team loses theirs—a winning game; and, in theory, the community loses an individual who can cooperate in the establishment and attainment of similar group goals.

A value must have meaning for the child before it can become a working part of his character. It must be related to his needs and to his personality development, and its relationship to the various levels of human aspirations must be made clear to him. He needs a choice of directions for building a character and practice in choosing, analyzing, discarding, and following those directions.

MORAL CONCEPTS

Moral development begins when the infant first understands a reproving gesture, a negative facial expression, or a verbal admonition and first realizes that he himself is something to be valued (or not valued). As Hemming (1957, p. 77) has stated:

> At its simplest, the moral development of the child may be described in terms of the process by which the child acquires the values esteemed by his community, how he acquires a sense of right and wrong in terms of those values, and how he learns to regulate his personal desires and compulsions so that, when a situational conflict arises, he does what he ought to do rather than what he wants to do.

Understanding Rules

One of the most complete studies of moral development in the child is that by Piaget (1932). "All morality," he stated, "consists in a system of rules, and the essence of all morality is to be sought for in the respect which the individual acquires for these rules" (p. 1). From studies of the rules of play and the moral judgments pertaining to stories, Piaget presented two moral systems: (1) coercive pressure resulting from rules, and (2) free cooperation and respect for the rules based upon mutual understanding.

Through questioning children relative to a game of marbles and its extremely complex system of rules, or code of laws, Piaget distinguished four successive stages of moral development. The first stage is described as having "a purely *motor* and *individual* character, during which the child handles the marbles at the dictation of his desires and motor habits" (p. 16). Rules, at this stage, are not coercive. They are imitated, absorbed unconsciously, and are "regarded as interesting examples rather than as obligatory realities" (p. 18).

The second stage is termed *egocentric* and is closely parallel to the equivalent stage in speech development. The children, "even when they are playing together, play each one 'on his own' (everyone can win at once) and without regard for any codification of rules" (p. 16). During this second stage, whenever rules are encountered or imposed, they "are regarded as sacred and untouchable, emanating from adults and lasting forever. Every suggested alteration strikes the child as a transgression" (p. 18).

The third stage appears between the ages of seven and eight and is characterized by a desire to win. At this time, there is a form of cooperation in that a rule is regarded as "a law due to mutual consent, which you must respect if you want to be loyal but which it is permissible to alter on the condition of enlisting general opinion on your side" (p. 18).

Between the ages of eleven and twelve years, children enter the fourth stage: codification of the rules. All details relative to the game are fixed, and the actual code of rules is known to the whole group. And, whereas the previous stage brings forth a variety of interpretations of the rules, children at this later stage are remarkably in accord when asked about the game rules or their variations.

Piaget warns that these stages must not be considered as final. They are, however, convenient for the purposes of description and for showing moral growth as a continuum. In short, for the small child a rule is a reality to be followed in a strict manner; for the adult a rule is based upon mutual agreement between those involved. Moral realism—an absolute obedience to a particular person, code, or rule—is replaced by moral relativism—a respect for the feelings and desires of others and a cooperative (group) effort toward some goal.

A Sense of "Good" and "Bad"; "Right" and "Wrong"

The preschool child's conception of what actions are good and which ones are bad is closely identified with (1) objects or actions that produce pleasure or pain, and (2) behavior that parents either permit or forbid. Radke (1946) asked a group of preschool children to judge the behavior of hypothetical children. The frequencies with which the group reported various types of good and bad behavior are given in Tables IX-2 and IX-3.

In his study of moral judgments, Morris (1958) asked pupils what they should do and what they would do in fourteen problem situations of the following type:

> ... Someone in J's class at school has broken the school rules and the form teacher wants to find out who did it. He asks the pupils to own up; but no one does. Then he asks anyone who knows anything about it to come and see him afterwards. J. knows who did it. What should he do?

Table IX–2   Children's Standards of Good Behavior (Radke, 1946, p. 54)

Good Behavior	Percentage of Responses		
	Girls	Boys	Both
Helps mother (specific items such as dusts, washes, cleans, and performs other household tasks)	20	40	29
Takes care of own routine (i.e., dresses self, goes to toilet, picks up toys, cleans up his mess, etc.)	13	6	10
Plays (i.e., plays gently with dolls, colors, etc.)	28	6	18
Does nice, kind things (i.e., does good things, does things for people, etc.)	13	30	21
Obeys mother (i.e., does what mother says, etc.)	8	6	7
Doesn't destroy or break things (i.e., doesn't break records, etc.)	3	3	3
Stays out of mother's way (i.e., doesn't bother mother, etc.)	3	6	4
Miscellaneous and doesn't know	12	3	8

Table IX–3   Children's Standards of Bad Behavior (Radke, 1946, p. 54)

Bad Behavior	Percentage of Responses		
	Girls	Boys	Both
Doesn't do what mother asks	28	7	18
Doesn't do what other people tell him	0	14	6.5
Does overt acts of violence (i.e., spits, scratches, snatches, hits, breaks windows, throws mud, etc.)	47	55	51
Cries, says bad words, is cross, isn't nice	12.5	17	15
Makes mother sad	0	7	3
Miscellaneous and doesn't know	12.5	0	6.5

The pupil responses were tabulated and the following conclusions were drawn: (1) Marked discrepancies were found between what pupils thought should be done in the problem situations and what they thought would actually be done. On the normative level these increased with age. (2) There was a slow decline with age in judgments based upon self-interest, most marked on the level of actually expected behavior. (3) There was a decline in moral dependence upon authority and an increase in independence, both subject to marked fluctuations at the thirteen to fifteen age level.

A Sense of Justice

In the closely knit home, a young child associates right and wrong with statements from his parents. As he matures and becomes a member of larger groups, rules and moral judgments become less rigid and authoritarian. The feelings and needs of the group are given consideration. Also, with increased mental growth and understanding, the child is able to make a more critical analysis of rules which he earlier accepted without question. This movement toward maturity can be noted in the development of a sense of justice.

Like all other concepts, a sense of justice is a product of learning. It will vary with age, class structure, ethnic culture, family religion, and any of the other factors that influence learning. A study by Durkin (1959) dealing with this question involved second-, fifth-, and eighth-grade pupils. The children were tested by means of story situations and questions. The kinds of responses given to the question "What should a child do when hit by another?" are presented in Table IX-4. These results indicate a relationship between chronological age and a sense of justice. The older children showed more concern for mitigating factors in the situation.

Table IX–4   Question, "What should a child do when hit by another?" Kinds of Responses and Number of Subjects Giving Them (Durkin, 1959, p. 63) *

Kind of Response	Grade		
	2	5	8
Tell authority person	15	13	27
Return identical aggression	8	15	4
Other	5	10	4
Ignore aggression		6	1
Withdraw from situation	3		2
Have aggressor apologize		2	
Tell aggressor to stop		2	
Exclude aggressor from play	1		
Do nothing			1
Undecided	1		

* Reprinted by permission of the Society for Research in Child Development and the author.

Piaget (1932) also used stories involving a conflict between obedience to parents and a sense of justice. After studying the answers given by 150 children, he concluded that with advancing age there is a continuous and steady decline in the choices of solutions based on obedience. Whereas ninety-five per cent of the six-year-olds chose this as a solution, only five per cent of the eleven-year-olds favored that answer.

Likewise, Piaget lists examples of unfair behavior given by children. The youngest children frequently listed actions classified as "behavior forbidden by parents," while the examples mentioned by children in the nine- to twelve-year-old group most frequently fell under the heading "inequality of treatment." On the basis of a number of similar studies, Piaget (1932, p. 314) concluded that there are three significant periods in the development of a child's concept of justice:

> ... One period, lasting up to the age of 7–8, during which justice is subordinated to adult authority; a period contained approximately between 8–11, and which is that of progressive equalitarianism; and finally a period which sets in towards 11–12, and during which purely equalitarian justice is tempered by considerations of equity.

REGULATION OF CONDUCT: MORAL BEHAVIOR

There is evidence that teaching a child dogmas, creeds, or rules of conduct is insufficient (Hartshorne, *et al.*, 1930). Moral knowledge does not necessarily insure moral conduct consistent with it: Abstract knowledge of what is good and bad behavior may not keep children from doing wrong if particular conditions arise in which they are strongly tempted. The extent to which such knowledge functions as an inhibitor depends upon the nature of the child's insights and conscience, his opportunities to practice correct behavior under favorable, rewarding conditions, and the strength of temptation in terms of his needs and drives. For example, the child who feels accepted by his parents and peers does not usually have a compulsive need to gain attention, and therefore is less likely to use, with any persistence, such attention-seeking devices as stealing, bragging, fighting, or using profanity. There is evidence, too, that the bright child is more honest in the performance of educational tasks than the average or dull child—apparently because he does not fear failure (since he rarely fails) and does not need to cheat to be successful. He is not tempted.

If he is tempted in a situation—such as a test—wherein the outcome is important to him, the intelligent child learns quickly that cheating doesn't "pay off" for him. Either he is discovered and subjected to severe disapproval; or, he finds out that his own best guesses are likely to be correct more often than the answers submitted by a classmate of lesser intelligence. On

Cheating—When temptation is very strong even youngsters with high standards may yield.

the other hand, the bright child may have a better developed and stronger sense of justice which could easily lead him to cheat in reverse—by allowing the average or dull child who has a strong need for success to copy test answers or to engage in similar dishonest acts. Older children—and bright children are, of course, mentally older—are remarkably more indulgent of their peers' moral actions than they are of peculiarities of dress, for example. In a sense, the older child accords each of his peers the right to be responsible for his own morals.

Once the child has begun to develop moral concepts, he must be guided in the development of good moral habits. In order for behavior (good or bad) to become automatic and habitual, it needs to be practiced, and it will be practiced if it is rewarding. In their search for approval, children have a natural tendency to develop habit patterns similar to those practiced by their parents and other adults with whom they are closely associated. They may imitate the behavior of a favored sibling, of a teacher, or even of some character from the movies, comic books, or television. By accepting and practicing the early do's and don'ts of significant adults, the young child is able to satisfy basic needs—for love, acceptance, approval, safety—and to thereby establish a degree of security and self-confidence.

At first, moral habits and incidental acts function largely in specific situations in and about the home. A boy who faithfully helps his father wash the car every weekend may go off to throw mudballs at automobiles passing along a road. If his parents should happen to discover the activity and punish him, saying, "No more throwing mudballs at cars going along the street," the chances are he will stop throwing mudballs at passing cars. *But,* he may —and probably will—choose either to throw snowballs and rocks, or to throw mudballs at parked cars. Until maturation and a wider range of experiences enable children to expand their moral judgments from specific situations in the home to general situations outside the home, they accept and apply moral teachings literally. When the teachings conflict with each other and with historical facts, when discrepancies arise between the moral concepts of adults and their moral behavior, and when a conflict arises between moral values and ego integrity, character development is considerably slowed down. No child escapes the confusions inherent to these conditions. In the one ear he hears the doctrine of brotherly love and in the other he hears (or he experiences) racial violence, ethnic discriminations, and religious bigotries. Through every medium of communication he is told repeatedly that "honesty is the best policy"; then he reads attractively told tales of Robin Hood and Jesse James, or of America's early financial empires, which were built upon chicanery, dishonest practices, theft, and other forms of moral turpitude. The parents in whom the child has confidence exhort him to be truthful, while they in turn tell "white" lies—and some considerably darker. (Even the most conscientious parents find it extremely difficult to draw a distinct and understandable line between "truth" and "tact.")

In a study by Wolfenstein (1950) in which children were requested to tell a story about a "good" child, boys often expressed a theme of conflict between moral values and ego integrity. For example, there was confusion between maintaining masculine characteristics by obeying the directive "Stand up and fight; be a man" and suppressing those characteristics in obedience to the moral code against fighting or harmfully aggressive acts. Both sexes today must certainly have many doubts about the value of modesty, sexual continence, and respect for others, when our mass media make the opposite behavior patterns seem so commonplace (and attractive). Or, as Fleege (1945) states: "It would seem that too much emphasis has been placed on impurity and not enough on purity. The virtue has been left in the shadow while the failings have been paraded across the center of the stage."

The Emergence of Conscience

Psychoanalysts have referred to conscience as the superego, which represents in the person the mores and standards of his parents, associates, and the society in which he lives. In a more literary vein, W. Somerset Maugham has said, "Conscience is the guardian in the individual of the rules which the community has evolved for its own preservation."* In popular language, conscience is described as a self-directive or self-censoring agency. It is also the inner discipline of behavior that is extraneous to the individual's attainment of his ideal self.

Although the very young child controls his actions in order to obtain more rewards and fewer punishments, he continues to behave according to external standards, usually those of his parents. With practice, the behavior becomes automatic; he virtually adopts adult standards as his own. When

* From *The Moon and Sixpence.*

his thoughts or overt behavior are at variance with his newly internalized rules, he feels guilty—he anticipates the opinions of others and the shame he would feel if they knew of his failing. Such is the beginning of conscience. In harmony with changing needs and abilities, modifications appear which ultimately furnish him with a relatively sound, or reasonable, automatic, internal governing system.

Children at any particular chronological age will vary enormously in their notions of what is right and wrong, and at each age they will face varying degrees of temptation. Even within the same child, the application of rules will differ from situation to situation, depending in large part upon his present needs and values and the strength of the temptation. Children who would not think of stealing money from a coin box on the teacher's desk might have no scruples about stealing apples from a neighbor's yard. Honesty is not a unitary trait, rigidly applicable in like amounts to all experiences (Hartshorne, *et al.*, 1930). Many children, particularly the youngest ones, have difficulty understanding that an action is wrong even though no one else is present to observe it. Nor is the difficulty easily surmounted when parents consistently use phrases similar to "Don't let me *catch* you . . ." and "If I *see* you doing that again, you'll be punished." Parents who speak unthinkingly in such terms fail to realize how literally children take their remarks. One eleven-year-old girl who was admonished for tramping a neighbor's flower bed replied, "Oh, it's all right. It's nighttime and she can't see me." Not only had the girl never learned to value property rights, but her mother—despite reliable, eyewitness testimony—had never punished misbehavior that she herself had not observed! Each child in this mother's family is excessively silly, sneaky, inconsiderate, and a liar; and, of course, what consciences they can boast of are operable only under the opened eyes of authority. Perhaps it is also significant that the boys are overly dependent upon their mother and the girls are almost pathologically afraid of the dark, insects, heights, and strange situations. Such an observation could lend support to the theory that conscience and a sense of security have a close, reciprocal relationship.

The acquisition of conscience is an important stage in growing up. Without personal, internalized standards of behavior, an individual must depend upon others to guide him; and his independence and sense of autonomy are seriously cramped. By means of its laws, society forcibly penalizes adolescents and adults who have never developed adequate consciences, restricting them physically and psychologically to boundaries more tangible and more narrow than those which people normally devise for themselves and within which they experience their greatest freedom. Yet this fabrication of self-limits is by no means an easy one. The process is continuous from infancy through adolescence and one for which every environmental agency is responsible. The child must have good models, affectionate parents with whom to identify, and consistent but firm discipline at home and in the community in order for him to realize the orderliness with which the world reacts to his behavior patterns. At an early age he needs guidance in learning to share, to postpone gratification of desires for larger rewards, to be unselfish, to respect the rights of others, to cooperate in group effort, and to set realistic and worthwhile goals for himself.

THE GIFT OF DISCIPLINE

No area of living is without its disciplines. The potential ballerina must control unpicturesque movements; a student of the piano must repress his impulses to play after-school sports in favor of learning that scales are practiced with specific finger motions; the concert violinist found out at an early age that exquisite music never arises from an instrument whose strings are touched aimlessly by a bow. A teenage boy discovers that regardless of time, place, and his financial status an automobile runs out of gas if he neglects to fill the tank occasionally. Soon after registration day, a college girl painfully discovers the logical relationship between a full social life and unfinished essays.

Metronomes, clocks, calendars, and the laws of physics, chemistry, and biology are uncompromising and rigid disciplinarians. But, they are also impersonal. They neither threaten, bribe, frighten, nor force; they are neither rejectant nor overindulgent. Inexorably and consistently, they impose definite, sensible, unemotional penalties for infringements.

Society too imposes penalties for transgressions of its laws: disdain, ridicule, vituperation, fines, lawsuits, incarceration, and death. It places artificial limits on an individual's freedom or it works in subtle ways to show its disapproval of behavior that operates against the social welfare.

The Purpose of Discipline

Although the purpose of consequences is to help the individual learn a more efficient way of behaving in order to attain maximum freedom, there are many life situations in which people are not allowed to make a mistake— the first may be the last. Despite the advocacy of letting a child be free to explore and express himself in his environment, he must not be given the opportunity to make one of those fatal mistakes. As soon as he is old enough to understand the simple word *no*, he must be made to obey the elementary rules of safety concerning fire, poisons, traffic, sharp objects, and so forth.

But discipline is more than an insistence upon strict obedience. It is guidance. It is instruction by word and example in CONSEQUENCES. Under firm direction and kindly authority, a child can attain personality integration by feeling safe in a world that responds to his behavior in an orderly and systematic fashion. He cannot achieve control over any part of an internal or external environment that reacts unpredictably. He must know what to expect from it and what it expects from him. Geisel (1951, p. 11) suggests that a child has a need to live according to certain rules because:

> (1) He gets a feeling of security if he knows where his limits are and then lives according to these limits. (2) As he lives according to his limits and freedoms, he has less cause to feel guilty for having broken them, or for having been confused about them. (3) As he lives according to the rules and regulations, he gives parents many opportunities for praise, which in turn stimulates him to continue his orderly behavior. (4) It is ego-bolstering for the child to accomplish what is required of him.

To expect an inexperienced child with immature judgment and values to direct his own behavior, to make his own decisions, is simply asking too much of him. One might as profitably ask a five-year-old to drive the family car!

Discipline, then, is a developmental need, appreciated by the child, and often begged for. The parent who says to the child "You're asking for it!" usually does not realize how true the statement is and thus fails to follow through with the gift—which, ideally, discipline is.

Amounts and Methods

The problem of discipline is made difficult by the different reaction patterns found in children. For example, Chess, Thomas, and Birch (1959, pp. 799–801) have pointed out:

> . . . Babies with reaction patterns involving predominantly positive responses, easy malleability and/or quick distractibility can be disciplined easily. These are also children who respond well to a permissive approach but are most in danger of becoming inhibited and submissive if parental authority is put forward rigidly and with pressure. At the other extreme are the babies who have predominantly negative responses to new stimuli and whose patterns, once established, tend to be rigid and tenacious. Discipline is difficult to impose on such children and a permissive approach is unsatisfactory. Marked rigidity of parental approach, however, tends to produce negativistic reactions in these children.

The investigators present some conclusions which have an important bearing on child training:

> The majority of the children in our series show patterns involving clear-cut, consistent reactions of moderate and graded intensity, with the ability to form long-term responses in various areas quickly but without rigidity. It is our impression that within broad limits such babies could do well with differing child-care practices, as long as the parents are consistent in their approach. . . . What is perhaps more important, however, is that a sub-

stantial minority of babies show other types of reaction patterns which do not permit favorable responses to differing parental approaches. ... It is for such children that individualized approaches become important. However, for an individualized approach to be effective it must be based on knowledge of the particular child's specific reaction pattern.

Langmuir (1952, p. 127) has summed up the arguments and investigations concerning amounts and methods of discipline as follows:

> There is no doubt that discipline helps develop character. But it does not follow that the more discipline a child has, the more or the better character he will develop. We all know children who seem to have had little discipline (in the sense of coercion) and develop strong and excellent characters. Other children who are strictly brought up also develop strong and and excellent characters. Still others who are strictly disciplined have weak personalities. Obviously it is not primarily a question of strictness or leniency. Even the methods used do not guarantee definite or certain results.[*] Both punished and unpunished children can and do develop strong or weak characters, depending on many factors, and these apparent contradictions are confusing and perplexing.

Consistency

Havighurst (1952) also has found no relationship between severity of discipline and character development. But, in a longitudinal study of children, covering seven years of moral development, he computed correlation coefficients of .62 between moral competence and consistence of discipline.

Only through *consistent* discipline does the child learn that there is moral orderliness in the world—much the same as he learns the laws of gravity through repeated observations of falling objects. It is not enough to say to him, "What goes up must come down." He must see for himself, and after many trials he accepts the relentlessness of Nature. A child who is punished for an act on one occasion and not on the next is unable to predict what will happen to him. He becomes bewildered or frightened—or aggressively determined to find out whether he was punished because of the act or because of the conditions under which it was performed. Unfortunately, many children eventually make the assumption that lying is all right so long as it isn't done to "Father"; or that cheating and stealing are labels applied to acts against friendly individuals, not against "crabby" neighbors, insurance companies, government agencies, or supermarkets.

Adult consistency—whether it be in discipline, truthfulness, or the fulfillment of promises—provides the child with a faith in the future which is

* The "methods" referred to fall primarily into two categories: psychological discipline, based on reason, love, and the denial of privileges; and direct-attack, or physical discipline. Both Teevan (1955) and Berkowitz (1964) have concluded that children who are disciplined by psychological methods rather than by direct-attack methods have a tendency to develop stronger conscious moral standards.

necessary before he can set any goal for himself. He then directs his actions toward that goal, and when by trial and error he learns how it can be reached efficiently and quickly, he dramatically discovers the significance of self-control. He learns to resist temptation and to postpone pleasures in the hope of reaping higher rewards. Simultaneously, he maintains initiative and self-confidence and develops self-restraint. Such is the goal (and the value) of discipline.

INFLUENCES ON CHARACTER FORMATION

Modern conceptions of child training lay stress on the fact that morality is not developed solely by adherence to rules or by verbal teachings or by the establishment of specific amounts of discipline. These factors, although of value in training children, cannot be judged apart from the institutions, conditions, and emotional climates in which they appear. "Characters and personalities are developed over the years, not merely molded and shaped in early childhood. Children are influenced by all their experiences. . . ; they grow and they learn" (Langmuir, 1952, p. 126).

The Home

In order to determine whether events in early life are factors in moral development, the mothers of 113 junior-high-school boys were asked questions about weaning, toilet training, and disciplinary practices (Allinsmith, 1957). The overall results indicated a relationship between high guilt about aggression and early weaning, early bowel training, and psychological discipline. A strong sense of guilt over disobedience was associated with late rather than early weaning and bowel training.

There is also evidence that the psychological climate of the home has important effects upon the development of the character of children. Berkowitz (1964) states that, in general, hostile and aggressive children have imitated the hostile attitudes of their parents. Children who get into trouble with the law have, with few exceptions, internalized immoral standards and socially undesirable behavior patterns found in their homes (Coleman, 1956).

MacRae (1954) administered moral judgment tests and questionnaires about parents and peers to 244 boys between five and fourteen years of age. He found that the boys from strictly controlled homes were less likely to base their moral concepts on the welfare of the group or on loyalty and obligations to the group and to friends. Coleman (1956) also discovered that excessively severe discipline and overly high moral standards were frequently responsible for producing self-condemnation and self-devaluation in offspring, as well as fostering the development of rigid consciences, severe conflicts, and guilt.

Burton, Maccoby, and Allinsmith (1961) suggest that there is no simple relationship between "permissive" or "severe" child-rearing practices and resistance to temptation. Evidence of the effects of parental attitudes on character formation is less conclusive in studies of normal children from relatively favorable home conditions than in studies of children with markedly unfavorable home conditions. Apparently, home conditions classified as good cover a wider span than some studies would indicate (Roff, 1950). Studies of atypical children, especially those with delinquent characteristics, furnish more convincing evidence of the deleterious effects of unfavorable home conditions—lack of cohesion, family conflicts, rejection, neglect, and overindulgence (Koppitz, 1957). Conversely, significant correlations have been found between a family's affectional relations and scores obtained on character reputation tests for honesty, moral courage, friendliness, loyalty, and responsibility (Brown, *et al.*, 1947).

Social Class and Moral Growth

Some of the effects of social class status upon the moral development of children were discussed in Chapter II. The Kohn (1959) study in particular demonstrated the values and characteristics which are important to the mothers in various socioeconomic groups. Obedience and cleanliness are preferred by the lower classes; consideration, curiosity, and self-control by the upper classes. Middle-class families place a high value and a great deal of emphasis upon education and training for a fuller life; thus, Berkowitz (1964) has found that children from middle-class homes develop a mature system of moral values slightly earlier than poor children do.

Such disciplinary practices as have been shown to be influential in character development vary from class to class—the frequently detrimental punitive methods being prevalent in the lower classes, and the more effective psychological methods of discipline being characteristic of the middle and upper classes.

The socioeconomic status and cultural level of the home have an important influence upon the child's attitudes toward discipline, as observed by Dolger and Ginandes (1946–47) in a study of two selected groups of children who were interviewed concerning disciplinary measures appropriate for ten situations involving problem behavior. The children from low socioeconomic backgrounds were more inclined to hold an individual child responsible for his misbehavior, and they were more concerned with his punishment than were the children from the high socioeconomic and cultural backgrounds. The latter group of children seemed to comprehend an environmental basis for the conduct. For example, the low socioeconomic group expressed the opinion that a truant officer should see that the child who played "hookey" from school is punished; whereas the other group was inclined to account for the misconduct on the basis of an unhappy home, or unhappy school life, or some other factor largely beyond the control of the individual child.

The children from the low status group frequently referred to reform school, truant officers, and correction homes in the more serious offenses. The children from the high cultural levels did not reveal familiarity with these agencies of law enforcement.

Obviously, these differences have an important bearing on the needs of the two groups of children and on the nature of the guidance that should be provided for them.

Sex Differences in Morality

From early childhood, boys and girls are encouraged to adopt different values. Boys are expected to value independence, responsibility, and courage; and they are actively guided toward developing an inner strength for meeting difficulties. A girl, on the other hand, is taught that self-fulfillment lies in her potential role as wife, mother, and homemaker, dependent upon and submissive to the will of men. She is encouraged to develop interests in physically undemanding activities, creative and aesthetic pursuits, and social skills. Conformity to established mores is expected from girls to a greater extent than from boys.

When the shifts occur from moral judgments based on "obedience" to those based on "justice," there is a tendency for the girls to make the changes slightly earlier than the boys do. However, the discrepancies between "should" and "would" are apparently greater among girls (Morris, 1958).

Basic sex differences can be found in the views children hold concerning rules set forth at home. Boys consider them as restrictions on behavior that is likely to lead to trouble; whereas girls generally regard them as disciplines for directing and channeling energy. Douvan (1957) noted that more girls than boys felt that children might be able to manage their own lives. She also noted that twenty-five per cent of the boys in her study questioned parental restriction, not with hostility but with a freedom that implied the right to question. Only four per cent of the girls reacted in that manner. Boys are more inclined to break rules and justify such breaking; but the girls interviewed were more evasive about having broken rules, a fact which may indicate that purity, or conformity, is expected of them.

Religious Education

Swift (1952, p. 327) has called it the "judgment of history" that

... no nation can be truly united which does not deeply share among all its citizens a common core of faith, a joined awareness of a purpose greater than that of any single group, a sense of responsibility and duty to a righteousness and justice that transcend the nation itself and make of it one body of people. . . .

Such is the broad goal of the major religions—to instill in youth (and adults) a sense of purpose, and responsibility to a society larger than the self. Through examples, precepts, stories, parables, prayers, songs, rituals, and celebrations, the religions seek to lift character development toward progressively higher levels based on social responsibility, love and consideration for mankind, the perfectability of the human condition. They seek to develop an appreciation and reverence for the human spirit—man's hopes and dreams and all that sustains them.

The immediate goals of religious education lie in the presentation of abstract concepts of right and wrong behavior, including attitudes and beliefs, and in the guidance of children toward setting personal goals and values incorporating those concepts. Unfortunately, criticisms have been raised in recent years as to the effectiveness of teachings which are so far divorced from the everyday experiences encounterd by children. The youngsters are exhorted to discard personal pride in appearance and to eschew certain pleasures and the desire for possessions, but they are ridiculed by peers if they don't attend movies and dances, wear lipstick and appropriate clothing, kiss and pet, and contribute a bicycle, ice skates, a football, or various other items to the activities of the "gang." Many children develop guilt feelings and extreme anxiety neuroses because they are commanded to honor a mother and a father who are—to the children and to society at large—obviously unworthy of honor. At some time in their lives, most parents are hated briefly but intensely by their offspring. To insist that a child should feel guilty or that he will be severely punished for expressing his natural feelings hampers his emotional development. And, there is little evidence that it advances his moral sense.

Discrepancies also arise between concepts and conduct in ecclesiastical institutions, just as in families. The churches speak of the brotherhood of man and teach respect for the rights and opinions of others, yet individual denominations exercise varying degrees and kinds of discriminations against one another, defending claims to be the only, the best, or the true religion, and seeking converts, especially among young students.

At the verbal level, morality is expressed in stories, phrases, and proverbs that directly oppose each other in the literal mind of a youngster.* Re-

---

* Furthermore, Sunday-school teachers and other part-time instructors in religious education frequently do not realize that the ability to understand analogies and to paraphrase proverbs in modern language is a function of mental age and therefore beyond the powers of the youngest members of the church.

ligious instructors say "an eye for an eye" but "turn the other cheek"; love your enemies" but "remove the wicked"; "God loves—He is good and merciful" yet "God angers—He will punish you."

The confusions that arise from hearing such brief phrases out of context and not *apparently* related to the realism of modern living detract from the effectiveness of the moral teachings and all too often cause children to drift away from religion during adolescence—at a time when its stability and the sense of security it can engender could be of greatest value. Even earlier, children become tired of, embarrassed by, or rebellious against the idea of God as the Eternal Watchman. One story, which may well be a true one, is told about a little boy who had been quiet for so long that his mother was compelled to call out to him, "Johnny, what are you doing?" A resigned young voice answered her: "With you, Santa Claus, and God all watching me, what *can* I do?" Another child, a girl who was being taught rigid rules concerning modest behavior, became quite disturbed at the thought of a (male) God who could see through bathroom doors.

Despite the criticisms, however, one must realize that few, if any, other institutions are so dedicated to the character development of children. Within the confines of a religion or a single church, every act, example, word, story, pageant, celebration is devoted to teaching the moral and ethical behavior necessary for the attainment of man's highest spiritual goals. Insofar as the institutions are integrated with other forces in a child's life— his family and his school—they are effective. Berkowitz (1964), for example, cites an experiment showing that parochial-school children give mature responses to moral questions at an earlier age than public-school children, and he speculates that the earlier maturity may come about because the Roman Catholic Church requires a child over seven years of age to consider the difference between "accident" and "intent" in order that he may decide what should be confessed.

If maximum reinforcement is to result and if the core of human faith and conscience is to attain optimum strength, those persons responsible for the religious education of youth must conscientiously relate their ideas to the principles of learning set forth in educational psychology, to all facets of daily living, to society's standards of excellence, and, above all, to the ideas and goals of all other institutions which influence a child's character development.

SUMMARY

Character development is a continuing synthesis of personal values and goals and the internalization of society's standards for the moral and ethical behavior which will aid the individual in attaining those goals with a minimum of personal and social conflict. Through instruction and guidance (discipline) and maturing awareness of social interactions, a child learns what values, ideals, and attitudes are characteristic of his social milieu; and by a process of identification with possessions, parents, and significant people in his environment, the child seeks to reach perfection as he perceives it, attempting to maintain a balance between his system of values and his system of needs.

The child does not achieve moral maturity by himself. The home, school, and church take an active part in helping him to adopt appropriate values, set goals on ever-higher levels, and internalize the rules and regulations for efficient behavior. However, maturation of abilities also plays a role in determining moral growth. Strict obedience to rules is followed by an understanding of the purpose of rules, after which they can be analyzed, varied, reconstructed, and reapplied to changing conditions and goals. Thus, a sense of right and wrong is refined and incorporated with a sense of justice.

With practice, good moral habits become automatic; with maturation and experience, they are shifted from specific situations in the home to general situations outside the home. The stronger they are—the more sensibly they are in harmony with a child's needs—the less tempted a child will be to break the rules in the absence of authority, and therefore the less guilty, shamed, or fearful he will become for having exceeded known limits. He can pride himself on having independently behaved as he was expected to behave.

But, the limits must be known! The child must be shown where the lines are and what the consequences are for crossing them. True discipline is a process designed to teach a child the limits and consequences of behavior and to help him conform to the ways of living preferred by a society in order that he may retain a maximum of personal freedom. Discipline is a gift, but one that should be given for the benefit of the child's development toward self-control, not for the benefit of the giver's ego-satisfaction. Discipline should be as consistent and unemotional as the universal laws of Nature, which operates with both strictness and leniency—depending upon the objective or the viewpoint of the receiver. Thus, if adults are truly concerned with aiding the character development of children, they must take into consideration their individual reaction patterns; the quality of their home environment, including social class status; their sex; and the effectiveness of their religious education.

QUESTIONS AND PROBLEMS

1. Look up several definitions of morals. What are some different ways of regarding morals? How are they related to character?

2. List several moral concepts. How are moral concepts related to moral behavior? How are moral concepts acquired?
3. Discuss the role of rules, creeds, and dogmas in character development. What are some essentials if these are to be effective?
4. List some problems encountered in modern society that are likely to create conflicts with one's conscience. To what extent do you regard conscience as a relatively safe guide?
5. Describe how the teacher functions in the child's acquisition of moral standards.
6. Point out social-class differences in moral behavior. How would you account for any differences noted?
7. What are some nonconformity behavior patterns your community frowns upon? How are these related to the moral development of the child?
8. In what ways would you expect the morals of a child brought up in a religious atmosphere to be different from those of a child brought up in a nonreligious atmosphere?
9. Interview some boy or girl between seven and twelve years of age. Note the responses to see if the inferences of this chapter seem sound or valid. Note particularly what such youngsters tend to do that adults regard as wrong.

SELECTED READINGS

AUSUBEL, DAVID P., *Theory and Problems of Child Development.* Grune and Stratton, 1958. Ch. 12.

BARUCH, DOROTHY, *New Ways in Discipline.* Whittlesey House (McGraw-Hill), 1949.

CRONBACH, LEE J., *Educational Psychology,* 2nd ed. Harcourt, Brace & World, 1963. Ch. 18.

EDUCATIONAL POLICIES COMMISSION, *Moral and Spiritual Values in the Public Schools.* Washington: Educational Policies Commission, National Education Association, 1951.

GARRISON, KARL C., ALBERT J. KINGSTON, and ARTHUR S. MCDONALD, *Educational Psychology,* 2nd ed. Appleton-Century-Crofts, 1964. Ch. 12.

HURLOCK, ELIZABETH B., *Child Development,* 4th ed. McGraw-Hill, 1964. Ch. 12.

JONES, VERNON, Character development in children—an objective approach, in *Manual of Child Psychology* (L. Carmichael, ed.), 2nd ed. John Wiley & Sons, 1954. Ch. 13.

MARTIN, WILLIAM E., and CELIA B. STENDLER, *Child Behavior and Development,* rev. ed. Harcourt, Brace, 1959, pp. 406–410, 429–430.

PECK, ROBERT F., ROBERT J. HAVIGHURST, et al., *The Psychology of Character Development.* John Wiley & Sons, 1960. Ch. 5.

PIAGET, JEAN, *The Moral Judgment of the Child.* Harcourt, Brace, 1932.

THOMPSON, GEORGE G., *Child Psychology,* 2nd ed. Boston: Houghton Mifflin, 1962. Ch. 13.

REFERENCES

ALLINSMITH, WESLEY, Conscience and conflict: the moral force in personality, *Child Development,* 1957, 28, 469–476.

BERDIE, R. F., *After High School What?* Minneapolis: University of Minnesota Press, 1954.

BERKOWITZ, LEONARD, *The Development of Motives and Values in the Child*. Basic Books, 1964.

BROWN, A. W., J. W. MORRISON, and G. B. COUCH, Influence of affectional family relationships on character development, *The Journal of Abnormal and Social Psychology*, 1947, 42, 422–428.

BURTON, ROGER V., ELEANOR E. MACCOBY, and WESLEY ALLINSMITH, Antecedents of resistance to temptation in four-year-old children, *Child Development*, 1961, 32, 689–710.

CHESS, STELLA, ALEXANDER THOMAS, and HERBERT BIRCH, Characteristics of the individual child's behavioral responses to the environment, *American Journal of Orthopsychiatry*, 1959, 29, 791–802.

COLEMAN, JAMES C., *Abnormal Psychology and Modern Life*, 2nd ed. Chicago: Scott, Foresman, 1956.

DOLGER, LAURA, and JANET GINANDES, Children's attitude toward discipline as related to socio-economic status, *Journal of Experimental Education*, 1946–47, 15, 161–165.

DOUVAN, ELIZABETH, Independence and identity in adolescents, *Children* (September—October 1957). Published by the United States Department of Health, Education and Welfare.

DURKIN, DOLORES, Children's concepts of justice: a comparison with the Piaget data, *Child Development*, 1959, 30, 59–67.

FLEEGE, URBAN H., *Self-Revelation of the Adolescent Boy*. Milwaukee: Bruce Publishing Co., 1945, p. 286.

GEISEL, JOHN B., Discipline viewed as a developmental need of the child, *Nervous Child*, 1951, 9, 115–121.

GOLD, MARTIN, Power in the classroom, *Sociometry*, 1958, 21, 50–60.

HARTSHORNE, H. M. A. MAY, and F. K. SHUTTLEWORTH, *Studies in the Nature of Character*, 3 vols. Macmillan, 1960.

HAVIGHURST, ROBERT J., The function of successful discipline, *Understanding the Child*, 1952, 21, 35–38.

HAVIGHURST, ROBERT J., M. Z. ROBINSON, and M. DORR, The development of the ideal self in childhood and adolescence, *Journal of Educational Research*, 1946, 40, 241–257.

HEMMING, JAMES, Symposium: The development of children's moral values, *British Journal of Educational Psychology*, 1957, 27, 77–88.

KOHN, MELVIN L., Social class and parental values, *The American Journal of Sociology*, 1959, 64, 337–351.

KOPPITZ, ELIZABETH M., Relationships between some background factors and children's interpersonal attitude, *The Journal of Genetic Psychology*, 1957, 91, 119–129.

LANGMUIR, MARY FISHER, Discipline: means and ends, in *Our Children Today* (Sidonie M. Gruenberg, ed.). Viking, 1952, pp. 125–135.

LECKY, P., *Self-consistency*. New York: The Island Press, 1945 (Hamden, Conn., Shoestring Press, 1951).

MACRAE, DUNCAN, JR., A test of Piaget's theories of moral development, *The Journal of Abnormal and Social Psychology*, 1954, 49, 14–18.

MORRIS, J. F., Symposium: The development of moral values in children, *British Journal of Educational Psychology*, 1958, 28, 1–14.

MYERS, ROBERT C., The academic overachiever; stereotyped aspects, *Journal of Experimental Education*, 1950, 18, 229–238.

PERKINS, HUGH V., Factors influencing change in children's self-concepts, *Child Development*, 1958, *29*, 221–230.

PIAGET, JEAN, *The Moral Judgment of the Child*. Harcourt, Brace, 1932.

RADKE, MARIAN J., *The Relation of Parental Authority to Children's Behavior and Attitudes*. Minneapolis: University of Minnesota Press, 1946, p. 54.

ROFF, MERRILL, Intra-family resemblances in personality characteristics, *The Journal of Psychology*, 1950, *30*, 199–227.

SWIFT, ARTHUR L., JR., Childhood and spiritual values, in *Our Children Today* (Sidonie M. Gruenberg, ed.). Viking, 1952, pp. 323–333.

TEEVAN, RICHARD C., Standards of behavior as a function of social class, integrating setting and child-rearing practices, *Dissertation Abstracts*, 1955, *15*. Pt. 3, p. 1649.

UGUREL-SEMIN, R., Moral behavior and moral judgments of children, *The Journal of Abnormal and Social Psychology*, 1952, *47*, 463–474.

WOLFENSTEIN, M. T., A developmental study of children's fantasies about moral problems: II. Conceptions of "goodness," *The American Psychologist*, 1950, *5*, 304–305.

PART THREE

The Socialization Process

T E N

Personal-Social

Development

So far in this text, the physical and psychological aspects of personality
—physiological growth and health, motor abilities, language, intelligence,
emotions, and character have been examined. But personality is more than
a complex interaction of these components. There is also the social aspect.
Although at each stage of life a person's physical and psychological makeup
influences both the treatment he receives and the experiences he perceives,
by far the greatest number of life experiences and life adjustments are
brought about or made necessary by other people. The very word *personality*, despite its many scientific definitions, is commonly used to denote an individual's attitudes and actions toward other people and the effect he has
on them. These in turn have been determined by other people's attitudes
and actions toward him and the manner in which he perceives each social
relationship.

In other words, personality pertains to the *whole* individual, his physical characteristics, emotional tone, metabolism, reactions patterns, aptitudes, interests, temperament, attitudes, hopes—all that he is at any given
moment, plus that indefinable something, that "energy," if you will, produced when all the parts are added together. That whole individual, growing up as a unique source of unique energy in a community, is the subject of
the socialization process, which begins with the development of the individual as a *person*.

SELF-CONCEPTS

Any one individual has many concepts of himself—about his size; his sex; his physical appearance, constitution, and health; his relationships to mother, father, siblings, other adults, and peers; his trustworthiness, sense of responsibility, and moral behavior; and, of course, about each of his various abilities, especially the all-inclusive ability to master experience. The older the individual, the more complex his organization of concepts, although the organization is crowned and influenced by a total picture, an overall view, which is characterized on the positive side by self-confidence and initiative, and on the negative by insecurity, apathy, and anxiety.

Although self-concepts are changed (gradually) by new experiences, bodily growth, and the acquisition of different sets of values, an individual's behavior at any one level serves to maintain his organization of ideas, to allow him to continue developing comfortably along the lines of least resistance to that organization. Most human beings are highly resistant to radical changes, and the child behaves in harmony with his self-image in order to protect it from damage—even though that behavior may appear, to others, to be harmful and inefficient. Only through continuing growth and expansiveness are self-concepts altered—either for better or for worse.

Sometimes the alteration is drastic, as when the adolescent who has thought of himself as a short, fat, and slow-moving tenor—almost overnight —realizes that he is a tall, skinny, nervously energetic, and erratic baritone. Little wonder that the adolescent is anathema to his parents (and himself). Old ideas conflict with new experiences, and the old, familiar, comfortable, homeostatic behavior patterns are in violent turmoil: they no longer do the job, but they die hard.

A person's entire organization of self-ideas is determined by the models he chooses to imitate and resemble and his reactions to experiences, but it also determines what those models, reactions, and experiences will be. In short, the total behavior of children is greatly influenced by the concepts they have of themselves. "How *they* interpret the meaning of experiences sets the stage for readiness for new situations. They seek out or reject people, they volunteer or withdraw, they develop skill or resist learning depending upon their concepts of who they are, how well they like themselves, and where they think they are going" (Gordon, 1959).

How Self-Concepts Develop

Insofar as the infant is born with a physiological self—a particular pattern of reactions to environmental stimuli—he has a personality. However, the distinction between the self and environment is not clear during infancy, and true personality in all its aspects does not begin its lifelong process of formation until the child has learned to discriminate between the self and the nonself. Only then can he start developing those inner patterns of emotions, reactions, ideas, and experiences regarding himself and his relation to the world.

Probably the first concepts a child has are those of comfort and discomfort. The more often he experiences the pleasant states of comfort, the more significance he attaches to the person who causes those states. In the most elementary sense, the well-cared-for child calls and someone answers, he calls again and is answered once more. His world is controllable and he can control it.

As his calls are answered, he experiences more and more pleasurable states: He is rocked, cuddled, stroked, all with smiles, soft words, and soothing songs. He feels warm, secure, and friendly.

Other faces and bodies cross his horizon and each one seems to be smiling and crooning whenever he sees them. What are they looking at? He examines a hand, some feet, toes, fingers; he touches his toes and feels a sensation. He touches again with the same reaction. Not only does he discover the outlines of his body, but he finds that some of the pleasurable states can occur without "mother." He too can create them.

Sense of worth. In such a manner does the infant differentiate between "me" and "other," and to the extent that he is aware of and loves others he values what seems to be most important to them—himself. Thus is a child's sense of worth positively related to the pleasure a mother derives from caring for him, the time she gives to him, and the attitudes she displays toward his demands and needs. The well-cared-for child who is loved and wanted seeks, for the rest of his childhood (and beyond), to maintain that love and sense of worth. And he has a good start, because his concept of himself as a "worthy controller" works toward developing those qualities which will breed success for him—initiative, responsibility, independence, and self-confidence.

Feelings of adequacy. As the child's horizons expand, he needs reassurance that he can meet all the demands and pressures, the do's and don'ts, the expectations that are increasing and changing day by day. He wants to be important to all his social contacts and he works hard to adjust his behavior. Early in life, his ultimate value is the love and acceptance of his parents. If they praise him for academic achievements, he realizes both that this is something to value and that he has done something worthwhile in their eyes. As the praise continues he begins to see himself as someone who can do school work. If he thinks he can, he probably will—under normal conditions —even if he has to work harder than a brighter child. If in one instance he fails, he will be more likely to accept it philosophically, saying, "I can do it, but I didn't study."

If another child thinks he cannot do academic work (perhaps his parents expect the highest grades and fail to praise him for less), he will probably not be able to do school work as well as he could if his self-concept were better. The failure of a test, then, proves his point to himself. Academically, he is inadequate.

Later in life, the academic achiever of our example may place a higher value on peer acceptance, at which time other self-concepts may come to the fore. Maybe, besides his "I can get good marks" concept, he has always seen himself as the smallest member of his age groups and the "baby" of the family. On various occasions he has said to himself, "Everyone is bigger than I am," "Mother says I'm a big boy, but I'm not," and "I'm not like the other boys." However slightly, his sense of maleness suffers and the inadequacy he feels may create in him negative or passive attitudes of submission, strict conformity, or isolation. (Or he may become overaggressive and conceited, relying upon his accomplishments in school work to win him the favor of his comrades—which usually doesn't work.)

For a girl, the perception of herself as small might create concepts of "I'm cute and adored and protected; everyone likes to have me around; I like being a *girl*." A sense of importance and well-being are established, and she can meet her peers with confidence. (Obviously, self-concept behavior occurs in an endless variety of patterns.)

A number of investigators have shown that there is a relationship between self-acceptance and social adjustment. Taylor and Combs (1952) found that children who were better adjusted tended to see themselves in a more matter-of-fact manner than did those who were less well-adjusted. Walsh (1956) compared matched groups of low and adequate achievers and discovered significant differences. Low achievers consistently portrayed a boy doll as restricted, unable to express his feelings appropriately and adequately, and acting in a defensive manner. They also depicted the boy doll as being criticized, rejected, or isolated.

Goals and standards. The individual measures himself against the standards he perceives for any given condition or situation. If he does not "measure up," he feels inadequate, rejected, unwanted, or worthless, depending upon the importance he gives to success. He may set standards and goals for himself that are so high as to be impossible of attainment, and thus he retains his concept of unworthiness. He cannot, he thinks, master anything bigger than himself, he cannot do better than he has done, he cannot interact successfully with people he doesn't know because he has not done so with those he does know. He becomes timid, fearful, withdrawn, hostile; his attitudes toward experience are negative.

Feelings of adequacy are dependent upon the degree to which an individual's abilities are in harmony with standards for achievement. But unless he knows the limits and standards, by way of restrictions and expectations, he can achieve harmony only by trial and error—a gamble he cannot afford to take. All children, like many adults, require the knowledge that they have succeeded in meeting standards for approval. If those standards don't exist, abilities are useless, existing in a vacuum. If standards are too low, development of abilities is arrested and interest atrophies. The individual cannot succeed because he does not try. If standards are too high, failure results and the individual feels inadequate. Either way, he rejects himself, and his own goals and ideals—set too high or too low—reflect that attitude (Cohen, 1954).

Although the realization of abilities (e.g., learning to walk) brings a functional pleasure and a sense of accomplishment to the child, achievement in and for itself is not so important to the child as the reactions of others to that achievement. How he is received, how his behavior and abilities are received—these are the primary deciding factors in self-concept development. His reception is determined by the values, standards, attitudes, and practices of all those with whom he comes in contact, and those factors are in turn determined by each individual's social status, class membership, religious beliefs, sex, role in society, and his own particular self-concepts.

Sex-Role Behavior

One set of measures used by and for a child is his ability to play the roles his society expects of him. In Western society, he is expected to be a son to his father, a helper to his mother, a "good" Catholic or Protestant or Jew to his church, a leader or a follower in his peer group, a provider of playthings in his neighborhood, a monitor in his classroom, a "baby" to his grandmother, an obedient child to his maiden aunt, a potential delinquent to the community fathers, an audience and consumer to the television sponsor. He is many things to many people, and he is judged by his success in mastering the behavior typical of the various roles. However, the appropriateness of role behavior depends upon whether the child is a boy or a girl, because the standards against which children measure themselves vary from one sex to another with each individual, family, class, and society. For example, Ausubel and his associates (1954) found that girls perceived themselves to be accepted and valued by their parents more often than boys did. Apparently, the most positive perceptions of the girls reflect child-rearing attitudes and practices which differ with the sex of the child. Generally, both parents and teachers have different expectations for and exert somewhat different pressures on each sex.

A study reported by Rabin and Limuaco (1959) revealed that ten- and eleven-year-old Filipino children showed a higher degree of sexual differentiation than American children of the same ages. This finding may be accounted for by the differences in two cultures with respect to the clarity of sex-role differentiation in the families. The distinctions in the Filipino families are more clear-cut. On the other hand, American children are reared in an atmosphere characterized by a sex-role convergence wherein roles are not clearly defined. More and more frequently, American families are acting as a unit, with all members sharing routine duties, child care and discipline, recreations, and contributing to the family "treasury." This trend is more prevalent in the middle classes than in the lower; and, as might be expected, the lower-class child, whose models fill more well-defined roles, become aware of sex roles and sex-appropriate behavior earlier than the middle-class child. Differences are especially great between girls of the two classes (Rabban, 1950).

Long before they enter school, most children identify with their own sex, which is, of course, dependent upon their ability to discriminate sex differences. Katcher (1955) found that four-, five-, and six-year-olds easily assigned the correct sex to adults on the bases of clothing, hair style, genitals, and breasts, in that order. Rabban (1950) also studied the sex-discrimination ability of nursery-school and lower-elementary-school children from two different social classes, concluding (p. 141):

> (a) Three-year-old boys and girls of both groups show incomplete recognition of sex differences and as a group are unaware of any appropriateness of sex-typed toy objects. (b) The fourth and fifth years are periods of growth in clarification of sex rôle for working class boys, while the sixth year is particularly significant for middle class boys. (c) Working class girls accept the sex-appropriate pattern by six years of age, but middle class girls do not fully acquiesce to the definition of appropriate sex-patterning even by the eighth year, when all other groups have accepted the social expectations.

Brown (1957) dealt with the projected preferences of boys and girls for aspects of the masculine and feminine roles. A scale made up of thirty-six picture cards of objects and activities socially defined and generally identified with the masculine and feminine roles in our culture was administered to 613 children from the kindergarten through the fifth grade. The projective element in the scale is a child figure referred to as "It," which is used to facilitate the child's preference. Each child was asked to make choices for "It."

The results of the study, presented in Table X-1, indicate that boys show a predominantly masculine preference beginning at the kindergarten and first-grade levels with a mean score of sixty-six and continuing with greater scores throughout the rest of the grades. In sharp contrast, girls as a group do not show nearly the same degree of feminine role preference. At the kindergarten level, they show a mixed-role pattern, i.e., an approximately equal preference for both the masculine and feminine elements. Beginning at the

Table X–1   Group Scores, Variability and Differences by Grade and Sex in Masculinity-Femininity Preference (From Brown, 1957, p. 198)

Grade and Sex	N	Mdn*	M*	SD
Kindergarten				
Boys	44	72.50	66.18	19.29
Girls	46	41.16	42.50	27.93
First Grade				
Boys	55	77.00	66.04	25.39
Girls	73	72.00	52.07	33.72
Second Grade				
Boys	52	81.16	77.58	17.17
Girls	60	80.21	57.28	35.12
Third Grade				
Boys	56	81.46	77.93	18.70
Girls	58	79.97	59.02	32.92
Fourth Grade				
Boys	51	81.23	75.98	20.15
Girls	40	71.16	56.40	31.73
Fifth Grade				
Boys	45	80.87	76.73	17.05
Girls	33	12.00	22.15	27.92

* The scoring of the scale is such that masculine choices are credited with points
while feminine choices are not. A high score (84 is the highest) represents masculine
preferences; a low score (zero is the lowest) represents feminine preferences.

first grade and extending through the fourth grade, girls show a stronger
preference for aspects of the masculine role, reflecting perhaps not only the
influences of the customary coeducational school and playground activities
but also the girls' increasing love for and identification with their fathers.

In the fifth grade, despite a considerable preference for aspects of the
masculine role, a decided shift occurs in that the girls show a more pronounced acceptance of the feminine role, probably a result of (1) greater
segregation in playground competitions and (2) the beginnings of puberty
and the consequent instruction in sexual development.

The discrepancies in preferences between boys and girls and the lack
of strong preferences for the feminine role by girls are, as we have noted before, almost exclusively products of cultural demands and expectations
transmitted through parents, who begin establishing a specific climate of
sex-appropriate conditions, in many cases, before the child is born. Through
interviews with fathers and mothers, Pitcher (1963, p. 90) discovered a
"curious differential in parents' sex-typing." She observed:

> Both fathers and mothers allow what appears to be tomboyishness in
> girls during the early years, while they try to discourage what might be
> feminine behavior in their sons. Their attitude seems to reflect the general

pattern in America, where our culture tends to grant the female the privileges of two sexes: with impunity she can dress like a man; she can at will interchange the "little boy look" with cloying femininity. She can use any name—her own or her husband's—enter any job, any area of education, or she can make a career of motherhood. She can be independent or dependent, or both, as and when she pleases.

This cultural pattern, directly transmitted through parents by their attitudes toward each sex, is responsible for the many classifications and descriptions of maleness and femaleness by which the behavior of children and the success of their role mastery is measured.

Accuracy of Concepts

Generally, the child's experiences at home, in school, and in the community lead him to a *fairly* accurate insight into his abilities and achievements. Russell (1953), summarizing earlier studies of self-evaluations, observed that children tended to overestimate their standing on a variety of achievement and personality tests. However, studies by Amatora (1956), Green (1948), Webb (1952), and Wylie (1957) furnish evidence that the accuracy of self-evaluations is a function of the variables being evaluated. On those traits which furnish the subject with the most objective evidence for comparison with others (such as size or strength), a child is likely to make a more accurate evaluation than on those traits for which little or no tangible evidence is available.

Bledsoe and Garrison (1962) present evidence that self-overestimation is more common among children than self-underestimation (possibly a characteristic of most children in American culture) which held true for a wide variety of traits and persons. They also found consistent individual tendencies toward accuracy, overestimation, or underestimation across a variety of traits; and Amatora (1955) discovered consistent sex differences, with girls generally overestimating and boys underestimating themselves. The degree of underestimation for the boys was greatest at the fourth-grade level and tended to decrease thereafter.

THE SOCIAL SELF

Social responsiveness begins in the average infant at about four weeks, when he fixates on a transient face bent over him and changes his expression, indicating an awareness of the face as belonging to something different from the inanimate objects around him. During the next three months he gradually distinguishes the face of his mother or the person who cares for him from all other faces. He smiles or coos when she approaches, sometimes squirming vigorously in a state of general excitement. He responds similarly to strangers, particularly females. Other children will generally elicit expressions of curiosity or watchful interest rather than excitement, and the development of active responsiveness to other children is slower, becoming more evident after nine months of age. However, at this time the infant is starting the long processes of mastery over his body—gross motor control, standing, locomotion, bladder and bowel controls, self-feeding, and all those developmental tasks which give him an increasing sense of identity. He has little time or attention to spare for others, except insofar as they affect his needs and life activities. During this time, the cocoon of the home contains the only group to which he feels he must respond and adjust; nevertheless, it is from that group that he learns the responses and the sense of belonging that he subsequently attempts to transfer to groups outside the home.

Social Maturity

Doll (1947, 1965) has devised a useful test for evaluating the social maturity of children. After observing many youngsters over a period of years, he produced a well-defined list of functional activities incorporating significant social behavior graded by chronological age—the *Vineland Social Maturity Scale*. The following list contains some representative items from the *Scale* [see following page, 276].

These norms, however, were derived from conditions and social expectations in *average* environments, and one must expect to find wide variations in scores when the *Scale* is applied to individuals and to culturally separated groups. Werner (1957), for example, discovered significant differences in the scores attained by rural and urban children at both the kindergarten and fifth-grade levels. Urban children were generally more socially competent in kindergarten than those from rural areas; in the fifth grade, the rural boys and girls scored higher in self-reliance. Therefore, when the *Scale* is used for individual children, environment must be given adequate consideration. The rural child may be socially incompetent in comparison with his urban or suburban cousin but precociously mature for his own rural society. Similarly, it is conceivable that a child—from a large family, for instance—could accomplish easily all the tasks at the VIII-IX level but only one at the V-VI level. Lack of experiences, parental attitudes, and parental values, as well as other environmental conditions, may contribute to social "immaturity" at any one level.

A Sense of Responsibility

One of the best indications of emotional and social maturity is the ability to accept responsibility. The mature person is able to accept the conse-

Ages II-III

Initiates own play activities
Cuts with scissors
Eats with fork
Gets drink unassisted
Relates experiences
Avoids simple hazards

Ages III-IV

Washes hands unaided
Buttons coat or dress
Walks downstairs one step
    per tread
Plays cooperatively at
    kindergarten level
"Performs" for others

Ages IV-V

Dresses self except tying
Washes face unassisted
Goes about neighborhood
    unattended
Plays competitive exercise games
Uses pencil or crayon for drawing

Ages V-VI

Uses skates, sled, wagon
Prints simple words
Plays simple table games
Is trusted with money
Goes to school unattended

Ages VI-VII

Uses table knife for spreading
Uses pencil for writing
Bathes self assisted
Goes to bed unassisted

Ages VII-VIII

Tells time to quarter hour
Uses table knife for cutting
Disavows literal Santa Claus

Participates in preadolescent
    play
Combs or brushes hair

Ages VIII-IX

Uses tools or utensils
Does routine household tasks
Reads on own initiative
Bathes self unaided

Ages IX-X

Cares for self at table
Makes minor purchases
Goes about home town freely

Ages X-XI

Writes occasional short
    letters
Makes telephone calls
Does small remunerative
    work
Answers ads; purchases
    by mail

Ages XI-XII

Does simple creative work
Is left to care for self or others
Enjoys books, newspapers,
    magazines

Ages XII-XV

Plays difficult games
Exercises complete care
    of dress
Buys own clothing
    accessories
Engages in adolescent
    group activities
Performs responsible
    routine chores

quences and reap the benefits of his own decisions and actions; he is trusted to perform certain duties for his own welfare and the welfare of the group; he cooperates in the achievement of goals; he shares in the performance of routine tasks and in the development of purposes. The mature individual can "take care of himself" with varying degrees of efficiency. The better he is able to do so, the sooner and more efficiently he will be able to spread his abilities over any group of which he is a member. The kindergartner who can button his own clothes will usually help the child who cannot in order that the class can get to the playground more quickly. The eight-year-old boy who is adept with tools is willing to implement his "gang's" idea for a clubhouse; his nine-year-old brother may volunteer to be treasurer and to buy the nails. A twelve-year-old sister, whether she is a member of the club or not, may take it upon herself to organize and direct the members in the presentation of a circus, a puppet show, or a series of original dramatic skits for the benefit of the club treasury—or, as is being done more and more frequently, for the benefit of some worthy cause.

Habits of responsibility do not develop as a result of exhortations and formal teaching. First of all, the child must be trusted to take care of himself and to accept certain routine duties. In this complex age in which the individual is faced with many problems and hazards, many parents and teachers are likely to overprotect children. Some mothers will drive their children three or four blocks to school rather than have them cross one traffic-laden street, when in fact children are far more cautious away from the security of the home than they are in streets bordering the family property, which is precisely where the majority of child *vs.* vehicle accidents occur.

Yet, hazards at home, school, and on the streets must be recognized and dealt with accordingly. Inadequate protection that leads to fear or actual harm destroys a child's confidence in himself quite as quickly as does overprotection. He needs the assurance of adult help and protection along with the (controlled) freedom to satisfy his need for independence and status.

There is also the danger that a parent or teacher will expect too much of the child who displays a high degree of responsibility. They may expect him to operate at a peak level at all times, a feat that no child (or adult) can perform. Rather than face a reprimand or belittling, the youngster may drive himself into periods of extreme fatigue—and thus brings about what he fears, or worse. At best, his sense of trust suffers either before or after it has been established.

Training for responsibility should begin early in the child's life. He must gradually assume greater amounts of self-control and self-direction and must practice those activities that are important to socialization—sharing, compliance, cooperation. Experiences, however, must be adapted to the individual child. The demands made upon him should not be excessive *for him* or *for his age level.* The tasks need to be closely related to his life, and he should be able to perceive the importance of those tasks in relation to his world. In an emotional climate characterized by affection and security, the child can be guided toward bringing his interests and activities into closer harmony with those of others, usually adults. "Sharing in family planning," for example, showed the highest correlation ($r = .45$) with responsibility in

Table X–2   Averages of Teachers' Ratings in Response to the Question: How Much Responsibility Can Children Assume for Classroom Activities? * (Reed, 1957–58, *58,* p. 396) †

Activity	Grade IV	Grade V	Grade VI
Collect papers	4.6	4.5	4.8
Water plants	4.5	4.5	4.7
Keep bookshelves straight	4.4	4.5	4.6
Pass out supplies	4.3	4.4	4.6
Run errands for teachers	4.2	4.2	4.3
Dust furniture	4.1	4.3	4.4
Arrange furniture for group work	4.0	4.2	4.4
Check out library books	3.9	3.9	4.4
Drill one another on spelling	3.7	3.7	3.8
Take charge of the morning milk break	3.7	3.7	3.6
Notify those who have books due	3.5	3.9	4.5
Plan and take charge of opening exercises	3.4	3.4	3.7
Do recreational reading to the class	3.3	3.0	3.3
Answer classroom interruptions	3.3	3.2	3.5
Change room decorations	3.2	3.5	3.7
Take attendance	3.1	3.1	3.8
Plan and arrange bulletin boards	3.0	3.5	3.6
Check supplies in cupboard	2.9	3.3	3.6
Replace supplies after checking with teacher	2.9	3.4	3.7
Operate the phonograph	2.5	3.0	3.6
Write assignments and other information on board	2.4	2.7	3.0
Stamp and mark new books	2.4	3.1	3.6
Repair damaged books	2.4	3.1	3.2
Account for money collected for various organizations	2.3	2.4	3.1
Collect fines on library books	2.3	3.0	3.4
Make attendance report to central office	2.1	2.2	2.6
Collect lunch money	2.0	2.5	3.1
Account for lunch money	1.9	2.5	2.9
Operate the filmstrip projector	1.6	2.3	2.6
Operate the sound projector	1.4	2.0	2.5
Operate the duplicator	1.3	1.7	2.1

* Teachers' ratings were changed to numerical scores: "none"—1; "little"—2; "some"—3; "a great deal"—4; "all"—5.

† Reprinted from *Elementary School Journal* by permission of University of Chicago Press.

a study by Brown, Morrison, and Couch (1947) dealing with the relationship between parent-child interactions and character ratings.

The school setting offers a variety of conditions and tasks useful for aiding the development of responsibility, although teachers vary considerably in the opportunities they provide for children to assume various duties. A study by Reed (1957–58) illustrates the differences of opinion concerning responsibility held by a group of elementary-school teachers. Table X-2 gives the average ratings they assigned to certain classroom activities as related to pupils' ability to perform them. According to these teachers, fourth-grade children, *as a group,* can assume greater responsibility for some activities than fifth-grade children can; and, in many cases, sixth-grade children are hardly more responsible than fourth graders. However, we must take into consideration the fact that variations occur not only in teachers' opinions but also in individual children's abilities. The main point is that if the opinions are too low the teachers may neglect to provide the guidance and stimulation necessary for improvement.

Cooperation

Between the second and fifth years, the child feels the need for establishing relationships outside the family circle. He seeks to expand himself

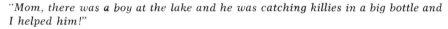

*"Mom, there was **a** boy at the lake and he was catching killies in a big bottle and I helped him!"*

by becoming a part of peer groups in his neighborhood, nursery school, and kindergarten. As he comes in contact with other boys and girls, it becomes increasingly important for him to obtain acceptance by his age-mates, and he adjusts his behavior to merit that acceptance. There appears an increase in the versatility of social interactions, which can be observed particularly in the development of cooperative behavior.

At first, the very young child watches other children play; then, he plays at the same time—parallel play. He shares neither himself nor his toys. He merely likes company. As he begins talking "to" instead of just talking "in the presence of" another child, he may engage in associative play that includes an elementary form of trading with the toys in sight, which amounts to putting down one item to pick up another, regardless of ownership, while the other child in turn picks up the discarded item. Naturally, many conflicts occur at this stage, for as often as not a toy is all the more attractive because it is being used by another child. (Strange as it may seem, this phenomenon is more closely allied to cooperation than it is to competition. Neither child has a strong desire to win for the sake of his ego strength; the efforts of each are turned toward gaining a common goal.)

Parten and Newhall (1943, p. 513) describe cooperative play as "the most highly organized group activity."

> ... In it appear the elements of division of labor, group censorship, centralization of control, and subordination of individual desire to that of the group. In the sandbox situation [nursery school], for instance, one child might suggest that they are all making supper. Soon the various family roles are assigned or adopted and the children speak of their shares in preparing the meal. Domination by one or more of the children occurs, one child being informed that he cannot cook because he is the baby. The group becomes closed to some children and open to others, depending upon the wishes of the leaders. The children are criticized by one another when they do not play their roles correctly. They are not permitted to leave the sandbox unless it is known what they are going to do next.

Although the investigators describe a nursery-school situation, most children of a similar age (three to five years) do not have the opportunity to play in such large groups. Before that age, they prefer to play in groups of two and only gradually, until they reach school age, do they increase the number (Parten, 1932–33). Frequently, the first year of school is quite a shock to a child who must suddenly learn to adjust to larger and more formal group situations. Few children will have experienced directed play activities; they will resist and attempt to prolong free play. Others shy away from group activities, either watching from the sidelines or playing by themselves. Generally, the first grader is fighting hard for independence; therefore, he finds it difficult to cooperate in games in which he must rely heavily on others.

The kindergarten or first-grade teacher concentrates her socialization efforts on creating a climate of friendliness in the classroom, where the children can become more relaxed and socially perceptive. At the same time, she gives them practice in following instructions and attempts to demonstrate the value of cooperative group activity, which, until the age of six or seven, the child rarely understands (Hirota, 1951).

Competition

Although many people believe that competitiveness is instinctive, research findings fail to support such a belief. Competitive behavior is a product of learning, occurring in increasing amounts as children grow older—*if* such behavior is culturally approved. Members of certain primitive tribes are strictly noncompetitive in their relations with each other (Mead, 1937); and, as might be expected, competition—an outgrowth of aggressive tendencies—is fostered and expected (thus is more intense) in groups from low socioeconomic origins more often than in those groups from higher statuses (McKee and Leader, 1955).

Rivalry appears among children in varying degrees, being intimately related to a child's self-concept and his needs. The youngster (or adult) who *feels* that he is important does not need to vie for attention or prove his superiority in order to gain acceptance, love, or respect; however, his sense

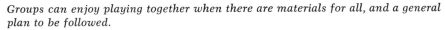

Groups can enjoy playing together when there are materials for all, and a general plan to be followed.

of importance may well vary from situation to situation. Whereas a boy may have no unsatisfied need for recognition in his home or in his academic achievements, he may feel an acute need for peer acceptance and recognition of skill in some area such as sports.

Competition as an outgrowth of teamwork, as the extension of a group's desire to demonstrate its skills, develops gradually and parallels development in cooperative behavior. Just as successful first-grade teachers recognize their pupils' immature ability to cooperate, so do they also know that the average six-year-old is not socially or psychologically ready for highly competitive games. Not only is he unable to fully understand and follow the rules of a game, but defeat (which must happen) is a threat to his self-concept. At this age, the desire to win is extremely strong. Learning to accept defeat gracefully and to compete without undue tension and anxiety is a long, slow process, and many authorities (particularly the American Academy of Pediatrics) feel that it is unwise to force any preadolescent into highly competitive sports. In other words, if emphasis in early childhood is put upon the enjoyment of the game rather than on winning, the necessary skills will be developed, practiced, and perfected to the extent that individuals and the teams of which they are a part will automatically desire to "show off" what they consider to be superior performances.

Leadership

Every organized group has at least one leader, one person who directs the activities of the others and furnishes most of the ideas, whose wishes dominate because the others in the group admire him and are willing to follow his lead. Sometimes the willingness to follow is unconscious, depending upon the quality of the leadership. The individual who rules by brute force, by bossiness, coercion, and aggressive tactics, may have a large following, but the membership of his group varies. One by one his followers become tired of intimidation and they drift into other, less fearful alliances. Their places are then filled by newcomers who have been bullied into joining or who have a temporary need to belong or to be dominated. The artful, diplomatic leader is followed more willingly and more constantly because he is resourceful, friendly, sympathetic, and original. The atmosphere he creates is one of accomplishment, success, and the harmonious freedom to be constructive.

The truly artful leader does not appear to lead: he hints and suggests and moves in such a way that another group member is unaware of having been directed. A leader might, for example, perceive a group member's need for a more efficient boring tool. He finds one, attempts to hammer with it, then lays it down, saying, "I guess that's better for making holes: what I need is a hammer." He goes off ostensibly to find a hammer; the other member picks up the new tool, examines it, and "discovers" its superiority as an instrument for boring. Unconsciously, he accepts the implanted idea as his own.

Obviously, leadership is not an inborn trait. It requires the desire to be a leader, plus a great deal of learning and experience and exertion on the part of the would-be leader. However, it is correlated with such inborn characteristics as intelligence and height. That is, leaders are superior in intelligence and above-average in height. (Parten and Newhall [1943] computed a mean IQ of 122 in the leaders they studied and found a .97 correlation with height—and age.) Leadership is also highly correlated with popularity and membership in the upper occupational classes, but in none of these cases is the reverse necessarily true: intelligence, height, age, popularity, and so forth, are not guarantees of leadership. Other characteristics and personality traits are essential. Hurlock (1956, p. 302) states:

> ... To be a leader, the child must be able to adapt his behavior to the needs of the group, must elicit positive reactions from the group, and must demonstrate his willingness and ability to carry cooperative tasks through to their completion. ...

Hurlock continues to list the traits commonly found in leaders: "dependability, sociability, responsibility, good naturedness, generosity, fairness, good work habits or efficiency, and good social and self-adjustments. ... They [are] self-confident, cooperative, [show] emotional stability, kindness, humor, and marked insight or awareness of the wishes of the group" (pp. 304, 305). It should be evident from this imposing list that leadership is concentrated in relatively few children.

Social Compliance

In a study by Crandall and others (1958), children's interactions with peers and teachers were carefully observed and rated on a scale entitled "Compliance with Commands and Suggestions from Others." An evaluation of each child's social behavior showed that the degree of social compliance between the ages of three and eight is not a function of either sex or intelligence. At the three to six age, significant correlations were obtained between children's compliance with their mothers while at home and their compliance with other adults. But the relationship did not extend to peers. The authority of peer groups—as expressed by acceptance or nonacceptance—has not yet become manifest in the child's life. Between the ages of six and eight, the magnitude of compliance becomes more generalized and consistent across situations (from home to school, or camp) and across people (from adults to peers).

Apparently, the attitude of the mother toward compliance is an important factor in the development of conformity, according to the investigators.

"By early grade school age, mothers' socialization attempts do seem to affect their children's general social compliance: before they do not—or at least there is no evidence in the present study that they do" (p. 441). The study also disclosed that, in general, maternal rewards for compliant behavior in the early years predicted the children's social compliance outside the home better than did maternal punishment for noncompliance. Later, the threat of peer punishment (nonacceptance) seems to be of equal importance in the maintenance of compliant actions.

Conformity to group mores and norms has often been associated with good emotional adjustment, and Langner (1954) tested the hypothesis by administering various clinical and social-psychological tests to six hundred school children. As expected, the correlation did exist. However, the study revealed that deviations were not necessarily indicative of maladjustment. Emotional maladjustments occurred mainly when the deviations separated the individual from the group, producing an "isolate." This action automatically cut off an important source for the satisfaction of an individual's needs. Those children who had friends but thought they had none were seriously disturbed. In other words, the *feeling* of isolation was a greater determinant of maladjustment than actual isolation, indicating further the importance of the individual's concept of self.

A number of discipline problems in the classroom stem from unsatisfied needs. Frequently, noncompliant behavior is the means that children take to express hostility or aggressiveness—whether it be disguised as defiance of mother in a form of negativism or an open protest against constriction of independence. The teacher who is concerned about nonconforming behavior should attempt to determine its function for the individual and thereby gain some indication of whether the pattern is temporary, easily remediable, or seriously maladjustive.

THE GROUP

The makeup of any one group* will, like a jigsaw puzzle, consist of interlocking parts forming an analyzable pattern: There will be leaders, who will—to some degree—take turns; there will be members who have little influence on the group activities; there will be the isolates and neglectees, the followers, the creative children—the latter often serving as "gadflies" or irritants (for both good and ill); above all, there will be the cliques. To study the pattern is to approach an understanding of the bases for social acceptance, which ideally will lead adults who are responsible for the welfare of children to understand the group "ins" and to aid the group "outs." Further-

---

* Like most child psychologists, we are primarily concerned with the group as it occurs in a single classroom.

more, the teacher who understands the power structure of her class can direct and guide the group more efficiently.

Determining the Structure

Scales have been developed for measuring the social structure of groups and for measuring social roles (Mussen, 1960). In the hands of a skillful teacher or counselor, they furnish useful information concerning the forces and conditions that contribute to the social acceptance of children by their peers. One of the most common sociometric methods for gaining such insight is the "guess who" technique. The teacher, or investigator, usually presents the class with a number of behavioral descriptions and asks the students to indicate the member of the group who fits the description. The following sample items are typical:

1. Here is someone who continually interrupts the classroom activities.
2. Here is someone who has lots of friends and is nice to everyone.
3. Here is someone who can lose at a game without getting angry.

The "guess who" method is easy to devise and administer. Items can be developed to include a variety of behavioral descriptions representative of all grade levels.

Another popular method for determining group structure requires pupils to indicate the children they prefer to associate with in varying situations. For example:

1. If you could choose any member of the class to work with in making an airplane or a boat, whom would you choose?
2. With whom would you like to go to a movie or a show?

The sociometric results are usually presented pictorially in a *sociogram,* which illustrates the interpersonal relationships in a group. Figure X-1 is the sociogram of a group of third-grade girls, each of whom was asked to select the two girls she liked best in her classroom.

The "Isolate"

Perhaps the greatest value of sociometric analyses comes from their spotlighting of social isolates. Studies by Gronlund (1951, 1955–56) reveal a significant consistency with which a certain percentage of isolates and neglectees appear in each group. Furthermore, the expectation and hope that acceptance on the playground would follow, or make up for, lack of acceptance in the classroom was not fulfilled. (Such variations in status as were found—between one activity and another—suggest that a particular ability or skill may have a large, though indeterminate, influence on the individual pupil's sociometric rating.) But, regardless of the reason for their isolation,

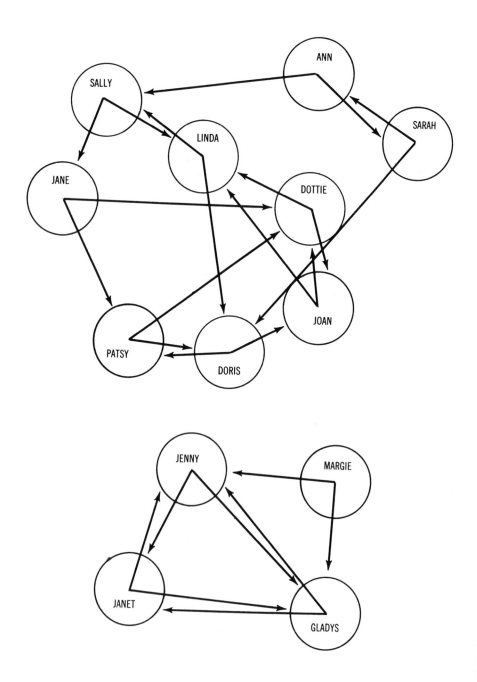

Figure X-1. One of the Simpler Kinds of Sociograms

these isolates often manifest adjustment difficulties which can lead to severe emotional problems. If the isolate—and hence his abilities, problems, and needs—is recognized early enough, remedial programs can be instituted which will produce outstanding improvements in his social adjustments.*

There are many reasons why a child is isolated from his peers, the most common being his own behavior, which often reflects personality disturbances of varying degrees of severity. That is, he may voluntarily withdraw from the group because he has little interest in its members or has a greater interest in other companions—pets, adults, himself, or, he may be rejected by the group because he is shy, introverted, and nondescript or aggressive, overbearing, and inconsiderate.

One of the primary differences between the two types of isolates is that the former is relatively indifferent to being an "outsider"—if he perceives himself as such. (Although such children may be personally well adjusted, they should be encouraged to take a more active social role in preparation for a fuller life which requires a reasonable amount of social participation.) The rejected child, however, has a strong desire to belong to the group and *knows* he is not accepted. He often develops further socially unacceptable forms of behavior which complete the circle of unpopularity. He perceives himself as "different," he acts "different," he becomes "different"; his behavior extends beyond a single peer group, disrupting not only the classroom but his family, neighborhood, and community.

Another value of sociometric analysis lies in the teacher's (or investigator's) ability to perceive any major fluctuations in a pupil's status. Minor fluctuations in choice status are to be expected, but when a sudden drop appears, or there is a decline over a relatively long period of time, the teacher should study the cause of such a change. Downward shifts may signify emotional problems resulting from home conditions, school activities, or community influences. Health or chronic fatigue may be other factors, or loss of status may result from value changes within the group as it advances toward greater maturity. Adolescent girls, for example, place a high value on clothing which may operate to the detriment of a girl from an underprivileged home, although prior to the shift in values the girl had been accepted in the group. Prejudice, too, begins to operate more strongly in the fourth grade, and members of minority groups who were accepted in the third grade may find themselves losing status in the following year (Moreno, 1953).

When considering the individual isolate, it is best to keep in mind that most of the problems—either the cause or the effects—are compounded rather than outgrown. The earlier they are detected and given assistance, the easier will be the task for both child and adult.

* See particularly the suggestions by Norman E. Gronlund on pp. 291–292 in his book *Sociometry in the Classroom* (New York: Harper & Brothers, 1959).

The Newcomer

Phillips, Shenker, and Revitz (1951) found that six- and seven-year-old newcomers to well-established "nucleus" play groups of unknown children their own age made strong efforts to become part of the group. At first, they offered very few suggestions, conforming to the interests and behavior of the group. Furthermore, members of the group made little effort to put the newcomer at ease or to get their suggestions relative to ideas and activities. Four sessions later the newcomers were actively engaged in initiating as well as carrying out activities.

The children who had known each other over a long period of time knew how to integrate, and each played a specialized role in the group. They had learned from experience what behaviors were rewarded. The newcomers, without the same background of experiences, foresaw only the attractiveness of membership. They were eager to be accepted but, at this age level, were forced to take the initiative. At a later age, a newcomer will find and attach himself to some youngster who gives him attention or displays friendliness toward him. Sometimes, this friendly one will be a neglected member of the group, or an isolate, who identifies with a new "isolate" or who seeks to gain acceptance from an untouched source; but usually, in any group of older children, there will be at least one child with that extra bit of sympathy necessary to help a stranger "belong."

SOCIAL ACCEPTANCE

A number of studies have shown that a relationship exists between the pupil's sociometric position within the group and his personal traits, achievements, and adjustments. Traits that contribute to a child's popularity will vary from age to age, group to group, from one socioeconomic status to another (see Chapter II, pp. 52–3), and from one sex to the other. Tuddenham (1951), for example, used the "guess who" technique to discover the traits closely associated with popularity in the first, third, fifth, and seventh grades. Central in the boys' constellation of values is athletic skill, predicated upon motor coordination, strength, size, and physical maturity. Thus, the boy who is advanced in his physical development during the elementary-school period generally has an advantage in peer status. The situation is quite different for girls. Traits connoting quietness, sedateness, and unassertive behavior are valued, while outgoing, dominant, assertive qualities are not, although there is an indistinct dividing line between the two categories. In summing up, Tuddenham states (p. 276) that

> . . . the problem of securing group approval for a boy is one of conforming to a clearly defined group of traits for which he may or may not

possess the requisite strength and motor skill. For a girl, the problem is more one of adapting to a continuously changing set of values which are never as clearly defined as they are for the boy.

Intelligence and Popularity

Of the many factors that contribute to social acceptance, the two which have apparently given rise to the most research are intelligence and academic achievement. Based on a rather complete review of pertinent literature, a conclusion was drawn by Lindzey and Borgatta (1954) stating that social acceptance is positively correlated with intelligence. Table X-3, also, shows a relation between intelligence test scores and the number of times a child was chosen by his classmates. Pupils with higher levels of intelligence

Table X–3 Average Number of Choices as Best Friend Received by 332 Pupils in Grades II–V According to Intelligence Test Scores (From Gallagher, 1958, p. 227)

Grade and Intelligence (T scores)	Number of Pupils	Number of Choices	Average Number of Choices
Grade II (79 pupils)			
70 and above	8	63	7.88
60–69	19	91	4.79
50–59	27	106	3.92
40–49	22	63	2.86
30–39	3	4	1.33
Grade III (76 pupils)			
70 and above	4	16	4.00
60–69	35	166	4.74
50–59	28	106	3.78
40–49	7	18	2.57
30–39	2	1	0.50
Grade IV (90 pupils)			
70 and above	4	29	7.25
60–69	26	131	5.04
50–59	46	218	4.74
40–49	13	60	4.62
30–39	1	2	2.00
Grade V (87 pupils)			
70 and above	2	6	3.00
60–69	15	75	5.00
50–59	46	187	4.06
40–49	19	79	4.16
30–39	5	24	4.80

tended to receive more friendship votes than those with lower test scores, a trend that was quite consistent from grade two through grade five, although not so marked at the later grade. (Incidentally, a further analysis of the choices by individual pupils showed that there was no pronounced tendency for the intellectually bright children to choose bright children as friends, or for intellectually average children to select their best friends from those within their range of intellectual ability. As previously stated, selection is more likely to be on the basis of interests, values, and habits.)

Gallagher and Crowder (1957) also concluded from a study of the adjustment of gifted children that superior intellect and popularity, as measured by sociometric tests, were directly related. Furthermore, children with higher intelligence had more social perceptiveness and were successful in predicting who would choose them as friends than were other children.

As for the opposite end of the intelligence scale, Johnson (1950) investigated the social acceptance of mentally retarded boys and girls in grades one to five and concluded that such handicapped children were rejected more often than were normal ones. Martin (1953) supports Johnson's conclusion by showing that average or above-average children in grades five through eight received significantly higher acceptance scores than mentally retarded children did.

Academic Achievement and Popularity

Buswell (1953–54) designed a study to determine whether or not those children who are accepted by their peers differ in certain achievements from those who are rejected. Its major conclusion was that, in general, those who are succeeding in school work are also succeeding in social relations with their peers. Feinberg (1963, p. 211) described a group of accepted boys (thirteen to sixteen years old) as follows:

> ... (a) Their marks were in the top 25 per cent of their class and they received prizes because of excellence in school grades. They felt that their academic achievements had been the result of hard work. (b) They received their best grades in arithmetic. (c) These boys have established good relationships with their teachers, most of whom they like and who they feel have had an influence on them, causing them, for example, to become very much interested in some particular subject.

Closely related to this question of correlative success is the nonacceptance of overage children. The results from two independent studies (Morrison, 1953; Perry, 1953) show to be true the supposition that the overage child has a significantly lower choice-status among his peers than do average and superior children. Out of the entire twenty-one overage children

in different elementary-class groups, none was found in the highest sociometric quarter of his class; eighty-six were found to be below the medians.

The facts of the Morrison and Perry studies should add further support
to promotion policies that attempt to keep children of the same maturational
level together in order to avoid harmful effects to personal and social development. Furthermore, all of these studies point out the importance of success to the child. If it is true that the boy or girl who achieves is more likely
to be accepted by his peers, the teacher should strive to help the nonachiever
succeed in at least one task, no matter how small it may seem. His self-
concept may be bolstered just enough to lead him to success in other efforts
or to try out new ways of gaining acceptance. Even small amounts of self-
confidence may diffuse across several areas of development and have a
salutary effect upon the individual as a whole.

Other Popularity Correlates

Sociometrically high and low children in the second grade were rated
by Bonney (1955) for giving praise, assistance, and sympathy. The high
group was more friendly, displaying better humor, and participating in the
different group activities. They were also much more involved in verbal
behavior, which, in view of the popularity experienced by the high groups,
bears out the general theory that facility in verbal behavior is an essential
aspect of socialization in our culture.

The high group of pupils showed evidence of greater personality balance, as evidenced by their social nature and their ability to occupy themselves alone. Dahlke (1953), also, found that the child who is well-adjusted
and thinks in terms of group activities is more popular than the child who is
poorly adjusted and thinks in terms of self. Some of the behavior problems
most common to the poorly adjusted child—cheating, temper outbursts, and
aggressive acts against others or their possessions—elicit definite, negative
correlations with power and popularity, as shown in Table X-4.

Table X-4 Correlations of Sociometric Ratings with Selected Behavior Ratings
(Echelberger, 1959)

Grades	N	Behavior Problems	Social Adjustment	Emotional Adjustment
1–3	64			
Power x		−.28	.26	.21
Popularity x		−.46	.26	.27
4–6	72			
Power x		−.31	.36	.41
Popularity x		−.29	.35	.38

Certain more or less specific factors such as health and good looks play a role in choice status. Popular children are more energetic and in better health than the less popular ones; and in elementary school many children are chosen as friends on the basis of their pleasing appearance. Proximity to the group is another factor: The child whose home is a place where others can gather or is located so that he can easily meet with the group has a decided advantage.

Elkins (1958) explored the factors related to choice status among eighth-grade children. (See Table X-5.) The importance, at this more advanced age, of such reasons for choice as "good natured," "sense of humor," "similar interests," "conforms to group mores," "helpful," "comforts," and "builds ego" is indicated by the fact that they constitute over sixty-four per cent of the total number of mentions.

Table X–5   Total Number of Mentions of Reasons for Choice and Percentages of Reasons as Given by Children in Three Choice Levels (Elkins, 1958, p. 224)

Reasons for making choices	Total number of mentions of reasons for choice	Percentages of reasons given by three choice levels		
		Most-chosen third	Average-chosen third	Least-chosen third
Is good natured	389	41	31	28
Has sense of humor	362	38	32	30
Has similar interests	352	40	37	23
Conforms to group mores	347	30	34	36
Is helpful	314	33	31	36
Comforts	264	44	29	27
Builds ego	201	38	30	32
Is generous	177	35	35	30
Accepts others	143	43	31	26
Is trustworthy	141	40	32	28
Is intelligent, skillful	123	40	31	29
Is friendly	113	31.5	21.5	47
Is attractive physically	77	25	27	48
Is popular	76	26	44	30
Protects others	75	44	24	32
Needs help	74	30	38	32
Has integrity	63	37	39	24
Is attractive to opposite sex	50	18	44	38
Is dependable	44	23	29	48
Demonstrates fondness	39	41	36	23
Exerts good influence	31	13	45	42
Has interesting personality	25	28	48	24
Total	3480			

A summary of the most commonly found correlates of social acceptance is presented by Elkins (p. 267) thus:

> ... (a) Children who were flexible in rôle-performance, who had the ability to meet the needs of others, who could further the goals of the group, who displayed certain acceptable behavior patterns, were among the highly chosen. (b) There was a slight tendency also for highly chosen children to elicit responses of satisfaction from parents, to find satisfaction in performance of rôles in the home, to be more intelligent, to be somewhat higher than others in socio-economic status, to achieve higher academic scores, and to be younger.

Stability of Acceptance Scores

The question may be raised, To what extent do children maintain a more or less stable status within their social group during the elementary-school period? In a series of rather complete studies, Bonney (1943) noted that the scores remained almost as constant from year to year as did the scores on intelligence tests and on achievement tests.

The stability of stars and neglectees in four sixth-grade classes was studied by Thompson and Powell (1951), who found that between sixty-six and one-hundred per cent of the stars maintained their high sociometric rating over one- and five-week intervals. The low sociometric rating of the neglectees ranged from fifty-nine to ninety per cent during this interval. However, the investigators did not feel that the stability of ratings would continue to be so great over a longer period of time.

PEER FRIENDSHIPS AND ATTITUDES

A striking characteristic of the personal-social development of the American child is an ever-widening circle of friends. During the preschool years, his social interactions are confined largely to members of his family and the children in his immediate neighborhood. Friendships are relatively stable. In the early stages of cooperative behavior, for example, quarreling and fussing are quite frequent but of short duration. Violent social conflicts are quickly dissipated in screams, cries, or fist-poundings, and play between belligerents is resumed after a brief interlude.

During the elementary-school years, a youngster becomes acquainted with children of the neighborhoods or communities served by the school, although his closest friends are generally from his own neighborhood or classroom (Seagoe, 1933). Fluctuations in friendships begin to appear at this time, becoming less pronounced with each succeeding grade level. (See Figure X-2.) According to Horrocks and Buker (1951), the most common reasons given by children for changing friends are lack of recent contact.

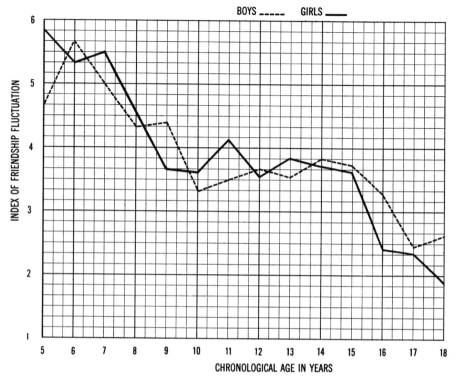

Figure X–2. Friendship Fluctuations of Boys and Girls at Different Age Levels (Horrocks and Buker, 1951, p. 139)

quarreling, replacement by another child, incompatibility, bossiness, conceit, and disloyalty.

As a child approaches adolescence, friendships become more important to him because of the security derived from peer acceptance. There is an accelerated dispersion of friends, with common interests, skills, and abilities, as well as social status, playing more important roles. (Spontaneous choices based on physical skills or intellectual status provide youngsters with opportunities for exercising their capabilities.) At this later age, friendships are characterized by intense loyalty and by jealousy if a friend forms other peer ties.

The early recognition of sex differences is accompanied by particular attitudes toward members of the opposite sex. Katcher and Levin (1955) noted that nursery-school children have a tendency to perceive members of the opposite sex as larger than their own. However, they make no discrimination when choosing playmates. Even as late as eight years of age, boys and girls play with either sex and display little self-consciousness in

their play behavior. The boy does not differentiate games culturally designated as masculine or feminine—he is as eager to jump rope as to play a
game of catch; and he is just as likely to fight with girls as with boys. The
girls are perfectly willing to play in groups composed entirely of boys, using
physical skills as readily as they do—and without concern for feminine
modesty (Campbell, 1939).

Beginning around the ninth year a notable differentiation appears as
each sex begins to show a preference for its own, both in attitudes and in

"I'll invite Kevin to my party for you, and you invite Erik so he won't know I like him
and Kevin will think you like Erik. Then we'll ask Donna to come with that creep Hugo
so she'll invite all of us to her birthday party week after next. Now, if we have my party
on Friday, we'll have to invite Maryanne, and Billy John says Erik likes her—so let's have
it on Saturday 'cause she's going away with her folks. We can always say we ... Do you
think I should wear my lavender bulky knit, or does it make me too yellow? What are
you going to wear? Did you see that hideous combination Betsy wore..."

selections for playmates. The "distance" between the sexes increases throughout the early elementary years and then decreases (Koch, 1944). Data from Koch's study also suggests that in the lower grades girls' preferences for girls exceeds boys' preferences for boys. These findings are borne out by Harris and Tseng (1957), who used the sentence-completion method for determining the attitudes of children toward their peers. The sentences were scored by evaluating the completions in terms of the positive, negative, or neutral affect of the responses. Curves were developed expressing the per cent of boys and girls who gave responses in a particular classification (Figures X-3 and X-4). Approximately sixty-five to seventy per cent of the boys gave positive responses to other boys at all grade levels. In the third, fourth, fifth, and sixth grades over eighty per cent of the girls gave favor-

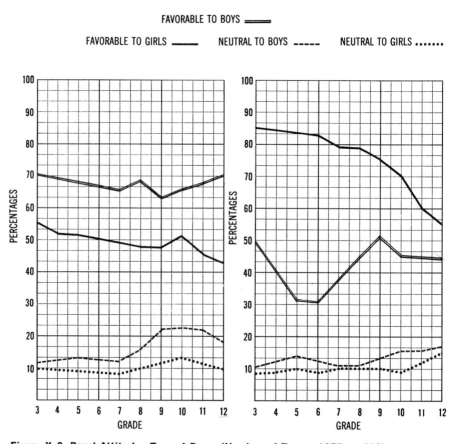

Figure X–3. Boys' Attitudes Toward Peers (Harris and Tseng, 1957, p. 403)
Figure X–4. Girls' Attitudes Toward Peers (Harris and Tseng, 1957, p. 403)

able responses to other girls. There was a distinct decline in favorable responses of girls to boys at the fifth- and sixth-grade levels followed by a rise of favorable responses. When neutral attitudes were taken into consideration, boys in the intermediate grades were found to be more favorably than unfavorably disposed toward girls. Concerning the data of this study, the writers concluded (p. 407):

> The data of our study are congruent with other findings, though not perhaps with the impression that boys go through an anti-girl phase in the elementary grades, followed by an increasing general interest in girls during high school. This cycle of events does appear to characterize girls. Boys change their affect less as they grow older and incline more than girls to neutral attitudes in peer relationships. In general, children are cordial rather than antipathetic or neutral in their attitudes toward peers.

After the age of twelve, a boy becomes sufficiently self-conscious not to join in activities made up entirely of girls. Should he find himself in such a group, he leaves. This self-consciousness in the presence of girls may continue into the fourteenth year.

During the same period of time, girls show an interest in what boys are doing merely because they are boys. However, a girl will not stay long alone in the presence of a group of boys. When given a choice, she will prefer to sit next to girls; and when choosing teammates for competitive games, she will be more likely to choose girls, unless physical strength and skill is needed to win the game. At the age of thirteen or fourteen, girls enter the stage of "whispering" among themselves. They become more shy around groups of boys and considerably more modest about the exposure of body and underclothing.

Between the ages of ten and fourteen, timorous adventures in romance are begun by both sexes, but almost universally the awakening interests in opposites strengthens the like-sex bonds already formed. (See pp. 223–24.)

INTERGROUP ATTITUDES

Of all the attitudes learned in and affecting the socialization process, perhaps the most important are the ones which children, as members of various social and minority groups, develop toward one another. Such attitudes determine the extent to which a child can work with others on common problems or toward a common goal.

At the preschool level, boys and girls pay little attention to differences in intelligence, physical characteristics, or sex. Sometimes age is equally unimportant, even at the extremes. The preschooler is ready to include everyone in his play activities and will gravitate toward anyone who will play with him. As he grows older, however, and enters nursery school,

During the early years of life, children are relatively free of race prejudice.

kindergarten, or first grade, he finds himself paired or grouped exclusively with children his own age. His powers of discrimination have a narrower social field in which to operate, but they operate under an increasing number of situations as the child becomes older and a member of several different groups simultaneously: the grade-school classroom, the Sunday school or church, confirmation class, dancing class, music class or band or orchestra, Scouts, YMCA, neighborhood playground, and so forth, not to mention that he is already a member of a race, ethnic culture, and family group.

In one way or another, all children become aware of what it means to be a member of a minority group, why one group is a minority and one is not, why one group is favored and another not. Particularly in elementary school do children become aware of racial, religious, and social-class differences. Socially perceptive first graders, for example, may observe that certain children are the tallest in the class, others are the smartest, one has many interesting possessions to share, another never has the money to pay for candy at snack time; that some children ride a bus to school, some are walkers, some are driven by their parents; that a neighbor goes to a different school, wears a uniform, has lots of homework, and always draws a heart with a cross in it.

There are few things missed by the eager and curious youngsters, and even though their observations have little meaning for them at the time, they accumulate into generalizations which are usually cemented or exaggerated by the attitudes and remarks of adults.

At least two studies have indicated that children in America become aware of racial differences at an early age. Stevenson and Stewart (1958) used tests on three- to seven-year-olds involving the discrimination of physical differences between Negroes and whites, which also elicited attitudes toward race. White children noticed differences slightly earlier than Negro children did. However, minority status and attitudes toward race are apparently felt earlier and more subtly by Negro children, because those of the study assigned negative roles to Negroes more frequently than whites did to whites. Radke-Yarrow (1953) also concluded from her studies of seven- and eight-year-olds that minority status begins to be felt in early childhood. Increasingly, with advancing age, children begin to see their affiliation with one group, while a gap is gradually developed between them and other groups. Radke and Trager (1950) found that part of children's concepts of race are based on such factors as occupations, clothing, and housing.

Friends share the pleasures of taking care of a pet rabbit.

Concomitants of Prejudice

No child inherits the prejudices of his parents through the germ plasm. Prejudice is learned by a process no different from other learning processes, although perhaps in more complex and subtle ways. There can be no doubt that (conscious or unconscious) parental attitudes are at least a beginning to the development of prejudices in children. Investigators have found that parents not only have little realization of their responsibilities in teaching children about cultural differences or about positive attitudes and values in human relationships, but they manifest their own attitudes toward ethnic groups by controlling their children's social relationships through the restrictions or encouragements given to the formation of friendships (Radke-Yarrow, *et al.*, 1952).

Although prejudice has roots in stereotyped concepts regarding the role and status of various subgroups, specific attitudes toward minority groups are part of more complex personality factors. One study disclosed that the children who were most fearful and suspicious, least confident and secure, displayed the greatest intolerance toward Jews and Negroes (Gough, *et al.*, 1950). According to the investigators, such personality traits seem to be most prevalent in authoritarian homes where parents demand strict and prompt obedience, and the circle is completed when we consider that children of authoritarian parents express more prejudice toward other groups of people than do children from democratic homes. Such attitudes are further reinforced by the parents of these children because, besides being authoritarian, the adults themselves have rigid attitudes, are highly prejudiced, and frequently are overly moralistic (Adorno, *et al.*, 1950).

Other personality patterns appear to be characteristic of prejudiced children, further illustrating the complexity of the subject. A study reported by Frenkel-Brunswik (1948) was designed to throw light on determinants of susceptibility to racial or ethnic prejudice and related forms of undemocratic attitudes. Boys and girls between the ages of eleven and sixteen were given tests to measure their attitudes toward Jews, Negroes, Japanese, Mexicans, and out-groups in general. A series of statements about these groups, some containing stereotyped accusations, was presented to the youngsters, and they were asked to express their agreement or disagreement with each of the statements. Other statements were made involving sharing activities, eating together, living in the same neighborhood, etc.

Comparisons between the 120 children scoring the greatest prejudice and the 120 scoring the least prejudice revealed a selfish orientation on the part of the prejudiced children. In consideration of other ethnic groups, such children agreed, for example, with the intolerant statement "Only people who are like myself have the right to be happy."

Other generalized attitudes typical of the prejudiced child but not of the unprejudiced were: rigid ideas of appropriate sex roles, intolerance of sex-role reversal, admiration of toughness and strength, rejection of weakness and things that are different," strong compulsion toward conformity and rejection of individuality, and a feeling of helplessness in a world full of chaos and evil. In general, their attitudes revealed a "narrow and rigid personality." (See also pp. 428–29.)

Future advances in our knowledge of prejudice will be made when the direct personality concomitants of community pressures are further isolated and better understood (Pettigrew, 1959).

Effects of Prejudice

As an influence on the child's development, membership in a minority group subjects him to barriers of acceptance, sometimes to outright discrimination, to identification by stereotype, and to being the victim of scapegoating. All of these things, of course, are reflected in the child's evolving concept of self and must therefore become powerful factors in his development. Certainly a healthy self-concept cannot grow in the soil of insecurity, unhappiness, friendlessness, and rejection. The child's need for acceptance is relatively unaffected (if anything, it is made stronger) by the accident of his birth; and neither child nor adult can accept with equanimity a devaluation of himself or his family because of conditions over which he or they have no control.

The child who grows up under such conditions may be unalterably marked by a lack of self-confidence, distrustfulness, and a lack of emotional security (Bledsoe and Garrison, 1962; Henton and Johnson, 1964). The manner and degree of manifestation depend upon the quality of the discrimination, which in turn depends upon how the larger society views the minority group to which a child belongs. The American Negro in the South, for instance, and the Untouchables in India have been relegated to a position of caste. Whereas social class is relatively flexible in nature (although there is little movement or interaction between members of polar classes), caste distinction carries rigid barriers to intermarriage or even contact between its members and those of any other group. It is a concept based on beliefs in hereditary inferiority, which, as noted in Chapter II, are scientifically untenable. Nonetheless, persons carrying the caste stigma are subject to the most acute forms of discrimination and are severely limited in their educational, cultural, and employment opportunities.

Other groups not placed in a position of caste are subjected to discrimination more subtle but just as insidious in their eventual effects.

Thus, it is inevitable that children who have epithets hurled at them consistently are ultimately hampered in their attitudes toward themselves and in their adjustments (Heaton, 1953). Whether he argues, fights, or turns away, the recipient may retain the nascent belief that such a frequently heard name, uttered like the nastiest of curses, lessens his importance as an individual, or makes him inferior to others.

Less evident than discrimination against skin color and nationality but at least as serious and extensive is the discrimination manifested in the school experiences of children from the lower social classes. Teachers, higher social class pupils, curricular offerings, and hidden educational costs all contribute to the maladjustment of these children who come to school already culturally deprived (Hodgkinson, 1962). Whether the discriminatory behavior is subtle, unconscious, or overt, within the lower social classes especially it causes serious problems in school behavior, motivation, delinquency rates, and incidence of mental breakdown (Havighurst and Neugarten, 1962).

Patterns for Change

Parents are deeply concerned about the effects of prejudice on their children, but the complexity of the problem leaves them at a loss as to what to do. Consequently, they do not adequately prepare the children beforehand and evade the issue when it is brought up (Weaver, 1955). Whether the lack of preparation is a product of oversight or foresight, such "protection" may make the child more vulnerable to prejudice when it is eventually encountered. Hence, Lewin (1940) advises, the child should be told early that he belongs to a minority group and that he may at some future time meet with marked prejudice.

The task of the schools in combating prejudice is not an easy one. Insofar as they reflect the community being served and the backgrounds and attitudes of teachers and administrators, the schools may naturally and unwittingly reinforce the prejudices children learn at home and in the community. There are, however, certain principles and methods that have been found effective in building desirable and healthy group attitudes in school-age children. Martin (1954) has set forth four principles which, if applied by the skillful teacher, should foster the development of desirable intergroup attitudes:

> Principle I: That program is most desirable which accepts the child as he is and provides recognition of accepting behavior on the part of each child toward every other child.

> • • • • •

> Principle II: That program is most desirable which leads to an understanding on the part of children of the reasons why different people live as they do.

> • • • • •

Principle III: That program is most desirable which fosters interaction among representatives of different groups, with every representative being given equal status.

•   •   •   •   •

Principle IV: That program is most desirable which makes it possible for each child to achieve success, but not at the expense of others.

Prejudice is no simple surface phenomenon. It enters into the perception and lives of children. Manipulations by psychological tricks can achieve limited ends and have their merits as small, cumulative steps, but, ultimately, there is no solution to the problem of minority group tensions except the inner growth of serene, confident, compassionate persons who seek their own security and integrity in common with their fellow man (Allport, 1952).

SUMMARY

The optimum development of the personality depends upon the individual's ability to interact successfully with members of his society. At birth the child does not recognize himself as an entity, but shortly after he distinguishes between the self and the nonself he begins the long, gradual process of forming concepts of himself in relation to his ability to meet and master experience. These concepts, crowned by a total self-image which in the mature individual converges with his ideal self, are developed through the child's sense of worth and feelings of adequacy. A sense of worth is directly related to the mother's attitudes toward the child and the methods of caring for him. Feelings of adequacy are developed through the child's perception of goals and standards of behavior. Many of those standards are based upon the individual's ability to perform his appropriate sex role, which he must perceive and conform to at an early age in order to attain satisfactory social adjustments.

Social maturity is generally measured by the degree to which a child is capable of caring for himself and assuming responsibiilty for his actions and the degree to which he can expand those capabilities to include larger groups of people. Through maturation, learning, and guidance, the child learns to assume greater self-control and self-direction and thus is able to broaden his social experiences and abilities by cooperating in group play. If his mother's socialization efforts have been successful, he may be socially compliant. If his society approves, he may develop a competitive spirit. If he has, among other factors, high intelligence, popularity, and above-average height, he may excel in leadership.

The various methods of determining group structure, e.g., the "guess who" technique and indicating companion choices, are valuable for understanding the purposes of any one group, for enabling the investigator to guide the group activities more effectively, and for pinpointing the isolates and neglectees who may need special help in overcoming behavior difficulties that work against peer acceptance.

When the child begins to broaden his social experiences, acceptance by his peers becomes important to his self-concept, his growth toward independence, and the general effectiveness of his social adjustments. Popularity has been found to be positively correlated with intelligence, academic achievement, and socioeconomic status. Other contributory characteristics are flexible role performance, good health, pleasant appearance, proximity to the group, and good social and emotional adjustments.

The attitudes of a child toward members of other groups affect his ability to work with others. Prejudice, particularly toward minority groups, is a *learned* attitude that operates to the disadvantage of both the giver and the receiver. Such an attitude is apparently more easily learned by insecure children with narrow, rigid personalities, especially those from authoritarian homes. They express a high degree of conformity to traditional behavior patterns and disdain all that is "different."

Those children who are consistently made to feel "different" through discrimination and stereotyping are severely hindered in personal development because of cyclical relationships between low ego concepts and poor performance.

The development of constructive group attitudes is the responsibility of every member of a community.

QUESTIONS AND PROBLEMS

1. Try to explain your *own* concept of self. What experiences have you had which might account for it?
2. Describe your ideal self in relation to your self-concept. In what areas do you find the greatest discrepancies? How would you account for them? How have these affected your social adjustments?
3. List the roles you have played in your life. What additional roles do you expect to play? How have these affected your personal-social development? Be specific.
4. Trace the development of cooperative behavior. What are some factors that determine a child's readiness for cooperative behavior?
5. What home conditions are conducive to the development of compliance? How do peers affect a child's compliance?
6. Describe the sociometric technique for gathering data. What are some kinds of data that can well be gathered by this method?
7. What are some factors that contribute to social acceptance among boys? Among girls?
8. Describe the background and some characteristics of some "isolate" of your acquaintance? What can be done to help the "isolate" to be better accepted?

9. Describe how social-class structure both helps and hinders personal-social development. (Refer back to Chapter II.) What are some problems encountered at school because of our social-class structure? What suggestions can you offer to help alleviate some of these problems?
10. Should legal desegregation of schools precede or follow changes in the predominant community attitude? Give reasons for your answer.
11. List a number of stereotypes you have used. What characteristics did you visualize when you used them?
12. To what extent do you believe a child becomes what he is perceived by others to be?

SELECTED READINGS

ANDERSON, HAROLD H., and GLADYS L. ANDERSON, Social development, in *Manual of Child Psychology* (L. Carmichael, ed.), 2nd ed. John Wiley & Sons, 1954.

BALDWIN, ALFRED L., *Behavior and Development in Childhood*. Dryden Press (now Holt, Rinehart and Winston), 1955. Chs. 8 and 9.

BRUCE, WILLIAM F., A teacher's theory of personality, in *Educational Psychology* (Charles E. Skinner, ed.), 4th ed. Englewood Cliffs, N. J.: Prentice-Hall, 1959. Ch. 4.

GARRISON, KARL C., and DEWEY G. FORCE, JR., *The Psychology of Exceptional Children*, 4th ed. The Ronald Press, 1965. Chs. 16–19.

GOODENOUGH, FLORENCE L., and LEONA E. TYLER, *Developmental Psychology*. Appleton-Century-Crofts, 1959. Ch. 17.

HUTT, MAX L., and ROBERT G. GIBBY, *The Child: Development and Adjustment*. Boston: Allyn and Bacon, 1959. Ch. 7.

JERSILD, ARTHUR T., *Child Psychology*, 5th ed. Englewood Cliffs, N. J.: Prentice-Hall, 1960. Chs. 9 and 10.

JERSILD, ARTHUR T., *In Search of Self*. New York: Teachers College, Columbia University, 1952. Ch. 3.

MCCANDLESS, BOYD R., *Children and Adolescents: Behavior and Development*. Holt, Rinehart & Winston, 1961. Ch. 6.

MARTIN, WILLIAM E., and CELIA B. STENDLER, *Child Behavior and Development*, rev. ed. Harcourt, Brace, 1959. Ch. 12.

OLSON, WILLARD C., *Child Development*, 2nd ed. Boston: D. C. Heath, 1959. Ch. 8.

ROE, KATHERINE H., Your child's self-picture, *Childhood Education*, 1962, 38, 333–336.

REFERENCES

ADORNO, T. W., ELSE FRENKEL-BRUNSWIK, D. J. LEVINSON, and R. N. SANFORD, *The Authoritarian Personality*. Harper, 1950.

ALLPORT, GORDON W., *The Resolution of Intergroup Tensions*. The National Conference of Christians and Jews, 1953, p. 45.

AMATORA, S. M., Comparisons in personality self-evaluation, *Journal of Social Psychology*, 1955, 42, 315–321.

AMATORA, S. M., Validity in self evaluation, *Educational and Psychological Measurement*, 1956, 16, 119–126.

AUSUBEL, DAVID, E. E. BALTHAZAR, I. ROSENTHAL, L. S. BLACKMAN, S. H. SCHPOONT, and J. WELKOWITZ, Perceived parent attitudes as determinants of children's ego structure, *Child Development*, 1954, 25, 173–183.

BLEDSOE, JOSEPH C., and KARL C. GARRISON, *The Self Concepts of Elementary School Children in Relation to Their Academic Achievement, Intelligence, Interests, and Manifest Anxiety.* Cooperative Research Project No. 1008, United States Office of Education, College of Education, University of Georgia, 1962.

BONNEY, MERL E., The relative stability of social, intellectual, and academic status in grades II to IV, and the inter-relationships between these various forms of growth, *The Journal of Educational Psychology*, 1943, *34*, 88–102.

BONNEY, MERL E., Social behavior differences between second grade children of high and low sociometric status, *Journal of Educational Research*, 1955, *48*, 481–495.

BROWN, DANIEL G., Masculinity-femininity development in children, *Journal of Consulting Psychology*, 1957, *21*, 197–202.

BROWN, A. W., J. W. MORRISON, and G. B. COUCH, Influence of affectional family relationships on character development, *The Journal of Abnormal and Social Psychology*, 1947, *42*, 422–428.

BUSWELL, MARGARET M., The relationship between the social structure of the classroom and the academic success of pupils, *Journal of Experimental Education*, 1953–54, *22*, 37–52.

CAMPBELL, ELSIE H., The social-sex development of children, *Genetic Psychology Monographs*, 1939, *21*, 461–552.

COHEN, LOUIS D., Level-of-aspiration behavior and feelings of adequacy and self-acceptance, *The Journal of Abnormal and Social Psychology*, 1954, *49*, 84–86.

CRANDALL, VAUGHN J., SONYA ORLEANS, ANNE PRESTON, and ALICE RABSON, The development of social compliance in young children, *Child Development*, 1958, *29*, 429–443.

DAHLKE, H. O., Determinants of sociometric relations among children in the elementary school, *Sociometry*, 1953, *16*, 327–338.

DOLL, EDGAR A., *Vineland Social Maturity Scale.* Minneapolis: Educational Test Bureau, 1947, pp. 3–8. Latest edition, Minneapolis: American Guidance Service, Inc., 1965.

DOLL, EDGAR A., The relation of social competence to social adjustment, *Educational Record*, 1948, *29*, 77–85.

ECHELBERGER, EDNA, *Relationship between Personality Traits and Peer Status.* Unpublished doctoral dissertation, University of Michigan, 1959.

ELKINS, DEBORAH, Some factors related to the choice-status of ninety eighth-grade children in a school society, *Genetic Psychology Monographs*, 1958, *58*, 207–272.

FEINBERG, MORTIMER, Relation of background experience to social acceptance, *The Journal of Abnormal and Social Psychology*, 1953, *48*, 206–214.

FRENKEL-BRUNSWIK, ELSE A., A study of prejudice in children, *Human Relations*, 1948, *1*, 295–306.

GALLAGHER, JAMES J., Social status of children related to intelligence, propinquity and social perception, *Elementary School Journal*, 1958, *58*, 225–231.

GALLAGHER, JAMES J., and THORA CROWDER, The adjustment of gifted children in the regular classroom, *Exceptional Children*, 1957, *23*, 306–319.

GORDON, IRA J., *Children's Views of Themselves.* Washington: Association for Childhood Education International, 1959, pp. 7–8.

GOUGH, HARRISON G., DALE B. HARRIS, WILLIAM E. MARTIN, and MARCIA EDWARDS, Children's ethnic attitudes: I. Relationship to certain personality factors, *Child Development*, 1950, *21*, 83–91.

GREEN, GEORGE H., Insight and group adjustment, *The Journal of Abnormal and Social Psychology*, 1948, *43*, 49–61.

GRONLUND, NORMAN E., The accuracy of teachers' judgments concerning the sociometric status of sixth-grade pupils, *Sociometry Monographs*, No. 25. Beacon House, 1951.

GRONLUND, NORMAN E., Generality of sociometric status over criteria in measurement of social acceptability, *Elementary School Journal*, 1955–56, *56*, 173–176.

HARRIS, DALE B., and SING CHU TSENG, Children's attitudes toward peers and parents as revealed by sentence completions, *Child Development*, 1957, *28*, 401–411.

HAVIGHURST, ROBERT J., and BERNICE L. NEUGARTEN, *Society and Education*, 2nd ed. Boston: Allyn and Bacon, 1962.

HEATON, MARGARET M., Feelings Are Facts. The National Conference of Christians and Jews, 1953, p. 19.

HENTON, COMRADGE L., and E. E. JOHNSON, *The Self Concepts of Elementary School Children in Relation to Their Academic Achievement, Intelligence, Interests and Manifest Anxiety.* Cooperative Research Project No. 1592, Department of Psychology, Southern University, Baton Rouge, La., 1964.

HIROTA, K., Experimental studies of competition, *Japanese Journal of Psychology*, 1951, *21*, 70–81.

HODGKINSON, HAROLD L., *Education in Social and Cultural Perspectives.* Englewood Cliffs, N.J.: Prentice-Hall, 1962, pp. 6–62.

HORROCKS, JOHN E., and MAE E. BUKER, A study of the friendship fluctuations of preadolescents, *The Journal of Genetic Psychology*, 1951, *78*, 131–144.

HURLOCK, ELIZABETH B., *Child Development*, 3rd ed. McGraw-Hill, 1956.

JOHNSON, G. ORVILLE, A study of the social position of mentally-handicapped children in the regular grades, *American Journal of Mental Deficiency*, 1950, *55*, 60–89.

KATCHER, ALLAN, The discrimination of sex differences by young children, *The Journal of Genetic Psychology*, 1955, *87*, 131–143.

KATCHER, ALLAN, and M. M. LEVIN, Children's conceptions of body size, *Child Development*, 1955, *26*, 103–110.

KOCH, HELEN L., A study of some factors conditioning the social distance between the sexes, *Journal of Social Psychology*, 1944, *20*, 79–107.

LANGNER, THOMAS S., *Normative Behavior and Emotional Adjustment.* Ph.D. Thesis, Columbia University, 1954.

LEWIN, KURT, Bringing up the Jewish child, *Menorah Journal*, 1940, *28*, 29–45.

LINDZEY, GARDNER, and E. F. BORGATTA, Sociometric measurement, in *Handbook of Social Psychology* (G. Lindzey, ed.). Cambridge, Mass.: Addison-Wesley, 1954.

MCKEE, JOHN P., and FLORENCE LEADER, The relationship of socio-economic status and aggression to the competitive behavior of preschool children, *Child Development*, 1955, *26*, 135–142.

MARTIN, SISTER MARY ALOYSE, *Social Acceptance and Attitude Toward School of Mentally Retarded Pupils in Regular Classes.* Ed.D. Dissertation, University of Southern California, 1953.

MARTIN, WILLIAM E., "Gee, I'm Glad We're All Different!": Some ways to develop desirable intergroup attitudes in children, *Journal of the National Education Association*, 1954, *43*, 219–220.

MEAD, MARGARET, *Cooperation and Competition among Primitive Tribes*. McGraw-Hill, 1937.

MORENO, JACOB L., *Who Shall Survive?* Beacon House, 1953.

MORRISON, IDA E., *Democracy and Interpersonal Relationships in the Classroom*. Unpublished Doctoral Dissertation, Stanford University, 1953.

MUSSEN, PAUL H., *Handbook of Research Methods in Child Development*. John Wiley & Sons, 1960, pp. 840–850.

PARTEN, MILDRED B., Social participation among preschool children, *The Journal of Abnormal and Social Psychology*, 1932–33, 27, 243–269.

PARTEN, MILDRED and S. M. NEWHALL, Social behavior of preschool children, in *Child Behavior and Development* (Roger G. Barker, Jacob S. Kounin, and Herbert F. Wright, eds.). McGraw-Hill, 1943, pp. 509–525.

PERRY, IDA E., *The Social Status of Overage Elementary School Children*. Unpublished Master's Thesis, Sacramento State College, 1953.

PETTIGREW, THOMAS F., Regional differences in anti-Negro prejudice, *The Journal of Abnormal and Social Psychology*, 1959, 59, 28–36.

PHILLIPS, E. LAKIN, SHIRLEY SHENKER, and PAULA REVITZ, The assimilation of the new child into the group, *Psychiatry*, 1951, *14*, 319–325.

PITCHER, EVELYN GOODENOUGH, Male and female, *The Atlantic Monthly* (March 1963), *211*, 87–91.

RABBAN, MEYER, Sex-role identification in young children in two diverse social groups, *Genetic Psychology Monographs*, 1950, 42, 81–158.

RABIN, A. I., and JOSEFINA LIMUACO, Sexual differentiation of American and Filipino children as reflected in the draw-a-person test, *The Journal of Social Psychology*, 1959, 50, 207–211.

RADKE, MARIAN J., and HELEN G. TRAGER, Children's perceptions of the social roles of Negroes and whites, *Journal of Psychology*, 1950, 29, 3–33.

RADKE-YARROW, MARIAN, Developmental changes in the meaning of minority group membership, *Journal of Educational Psychology*, 1953, 44, 82–101.

RADKE-YARROW, MARIAN, HELEN TRAGER, and JEAN MILLER, The role of parents in the development of children's ethnic attitudes, *Child Development*, 1952, 23, 13–53.

REED, CALVIN H., A sense of responsibility: are classroom activities nourishing it? *Elementary School Journal*, 1957–58, 58, 396.

RUSSELL, DAVID H., What does research say about self-evaluation? *Journal of Educational Research*, 1953, 46, 561–573.

SEAGOE, MAY V., Factors influencing the selection of associates, *Journal of Educational Research*, 1933, 27, 32–40.

STEVENSON, HAROLD W., and EDWARD C. STEWART, A developmental study of racial awareness in young children, *Child Development*, 1958, 29, 399–409.

TAYLOR, CHARLES, and ARTHUR COMBS, Self-acceptance and adjustment, *Journal of Consulting Psychology*, 1952, *16*, 89–91.

THOMPSON, GEORGE G., and MARVIN POWELL, An investigation of the rating-scale approach to the measurement of social status, *Educational and Psychological Measurements*, 1951, *11*, 440–455.

TUDDENHAM, READ D., Studies in reputation. III. Correlates of popularity among elementary-school children, *The Journal of Educational Psychology*, 1951, 42, 257–276.

WALSH, ANNE M., *Self-Concepts of Bright Boys with Learning Difficulties*. Bureau of Publications, Teachers College, Columbia University, 1956.

WEAVER, E., How do children discover they are Negroes? *Understanding the Child,*
    1955, *24,* 35–41.
WEBB, WILSE B., Self-evaluation compared with group evaluations, *Journal of Con-*
    sulting Psychology, 1952, *16,* 305–307.
WERNER, EMMY, Milieu differences in social competence, *The Journal of Genetic*
    Psychology, 1957, *91,* 239–249.
WYLIE, RUTH C., Some relationships between defensiveness and self-concept dis-
    crepancies, *Journal of Personality,* 1957, *25,* 600–616.

E L E V E N

The Role of the Family

The primary purpose in forming a family is the perpetuation of the species, and to that end parents are required to provide their children with the essentials for growth and development toward maturity and the assumption of appropriate father or mother roles. Aside from administering to the physical needs of a child for food, clothing, and shelter, responsible parents attempt to satisfy his psychological needs for affection, security, belongingness, status, models for behavior, praise, accomplishments, and, above all, a multitude of experiences, without which no learning can take place.

As a socializing agent, the family takes second place to no other influence in the child's life, because it is within this basic unit for human interactions, this miniature society composed of at least one man, one woman, and one child, that the young learn, or fail to learn, the fundamentals of cooperation and conformity with group standards through the acquisition of behavior patterns and attitudes similar to those of their parents and through the perception of intra-family relationships (Rosen, 1964). It is within the family group that a child forms concepts of himself as a person and begins to learn the essential skills for becoming an independent, responsible member of larger societies.

Thus, an individual's satisfactory adjustment to life situations—chiefly social—is directly related to the extent to which all of these basic needs are satisfied. But no simple equation exists wherein so many experiences, so much affection, or a prescribed amount of discipline will auto-

The family group establishes important relationships for the child.

matically produce a corresponding degree of adjustment. Needs and their satisfactions are partially dependent upon the perceptions of individuals, which are in turn products of age, sex, inherited potentials, culture, social class, occupation, geographical location, education, experiences, and the life adjustments of other persons in the individual's environment.

For example, almost all the experiences which fall to the lot of the preschool child are controlled and influenced by his parents.

The significance of this statement should not be underestimated. According to recent findings by Bloom (1964), half of all the growth in intelligence (as indicated by intelligence test scores) takes place during the first four years of life, and a full one-third of whatever the child will achieve academically is developed before he gets to school. Bloom and his associates were able to list thirteen specific environmental factors as having the greatest influence on this growth and development. All of them are related to family background and parent-child relationships.

> . . . Seven of these factors are process variables indicative of the parents' response to the child and his capacities—their intellectual aspirations for him, the rewards they offer for intellectual growth, the opportunities they provide for learning inside and outside the home (not including school); and the nature and amount of help they give to extend learning in a wide variety of situations. The other six factors tend to be more stable: they are characteristics of the parents and the home. Among them are the parents' use of language in a variety of situations; the opportunities in the home for enlarging vocabulary and the quality of the language used; whether there is emphasis on correct use of language; the availability of books, periodicals, and library facilities. These thirteen factors account for two-thirds of all intelligence development, a process that is completed before the child even enters school. [p. 3]

The toys and creative materials parents give a child, the television programs he is allowed to watch, the books they share with him, the places they take him—the zoo, public parks and beaches, Disneyland, historical points of interest, other cities and regions, supermarkets, department stores —all influence the child's concepts, helping him to gain knowledge of his world, to expand himself, and to develop independence and responsibility through a variety of socially oriented experiences. Such factors, both in quality and quantity, are affected by the family's socioeconomic status, the father's occupation, the mother's personality, the health of the parents, the size of the family, a child's ordinal position, the general pervasive attitudes and characteristics descriptive of the parents, and, perhaps of first importance, the child's perception of his relationship to the various members in his family.

The impact of social class, culture, and the family as a bearer of culture was discussed in Chapter II, and the reader should review that chapter in connection with the role of the family in the socialization process.

HUSBAND AND WIFE

Of first importance to the ability of parents to provide their children with need satisfactions is the emotional climate of the home, which is first and foremost a product of the relationship between a husband and wife. The personal adjustment of each to the other affects the general atmosphere of the home and determines whether it will be characterized by acceptance, affection, cooperation, and cohesion, or by constant discord, coerciveness, emotional turmoil, and inconsistency of behavior, values, and standards. As pointed out in previous chapters, it is this general atmosphere

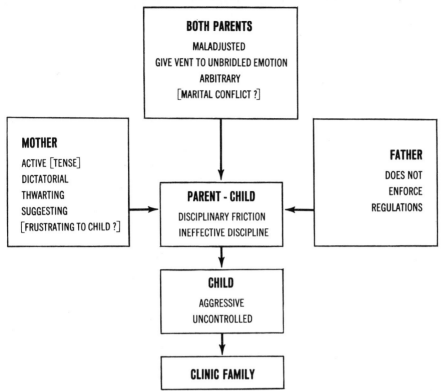

Figure XI–1. Family Relationships Which May Foster Conduct Problems in Children (Becker, et al., 1959, p. 113)

that is of greatest influence on the development of children. (See Chapter IX, in particular pp. 253–56 and the section on discipline.) Whether the child is weaned early or late, punished severely or not at all, well dressed or ragged, is of relatively little importance compared to whether or not he feels accepted, wanted, and loved by parents who worked well together. If, for instance, the child is to have a firm set of guiding values, he must perceive them expressed and endorsed by *both* his mother and his father.

Invariably, the attitudes and behavior patterns at the top of any social structure filter downward and permeate the whole unit. If the action patterns of an organization's president are discrete, disordered, and discordant, the organization and its other members are characterized by ineffectiveness, confusion, and unproductive, aimless efforts. Likewise, in many families where the children have behavior problems, investigators have found that both parents are maladjusted, unsociable, give vent to unbridled emotions, and are arbitrary and contentious in their relationships with their offspring * (Peterson, et al., 1959; Becker, et al., 1959; Adams and Sarason, 1963). Figure XI-1 illustrates some of these relationships.

* According to Speck (1964), even pets in a family may mirror the tensions, illnesses, phobias, and unsociable attitudes of their human masters. He cites one veterinarian who observed and reported "that peculiar and difficult clients have peculiar and difficult pets."

Other investigators point particularly to such characteristics as a child's sense of worth, and his honesty, loyalty, and responsibility as being functions of the quality of parental interactions and the consequent quality of affection among the family members (Farber, 1962; Brown, *et al.*, 1947).

∕ The relationship between the two parents and the personality of each is obviously important when one considers that parents interact with their children in ways that satisfy their own basic psychological needs. Thus, the patterns of child-rearing are closely related to the adjustment of parents, including their attitudes and biases, anxieties and inadequacies, and the degree to which they are able to reduce their own tensions and achieve security. Much of what a child thinks and does in his lifetime reflects these parental behaviors. Children of a neurotic father or mother, for example, absorb the fears, insecurities, and defense mechanisms of the parent with whom they identify the more closely. (See again Concomitants of Prejudice, pp. 300–01.) Also, the marital discord that is generally a product of faulty adjustments between parents frequently effects in the offspring such personality characteristics as anxiety, tension, insecurity, excessive jealousy, and fearfulness; if the discord is severe enough to result in separation or divorce, the children are likely to hold conflicting loyalties, feel isolated, and lack adequate models for sex-role behavior (Coleman, 1956). From inadequate parents, children learn to be inadequate parents. Or, as Terman and his associates (1938) have stated, marital happiness tends to run in families, not by biological inheritance but by repetitive learning milieus. The parent who has high hopes for his child's subsequent marital adjustment might well look *first* at the quality of his own.

Parents face problems of personal and social adjustment in any dynamic, changing society. In America, families are temporarily broken or depleted or upset because of the tendencies among the populace to be restless, mobile, and improvement-seeking. Parents who perceive the father's job-transfer as a challenge, an opportunity, and a broadening experience will likely have less trouble uprooting their children from a familiar school and community than will the rigid and insecure parents who are dependent upon old habits and long-term acquaintances for emotional stability.

Obviously, then, because world conditions promise no abatement of rapid changes, parents and educators should be concerned with the development of stable, adjustive individuals, a movement which must begin with the recognition and selection for marriage of one socially, mentally, and emotionally mature person by another. Ideally, such well-matched individuals should be able to demonstrate affection for each other and their children through the sharing of ideas, decision-making, responsibilities, recreations, and close emotional ties. Other desirable characteristics of parents are strength and vigor (for child-rearing is an arduous business), an understanding of childhood in general and each child in particular, and the willingness to help children explore their environments, successfully master developmental tasks, and set and achieve realistic goals. Probably above all, a husband and wife must be able to enjoy each of their children as he is rather than in egocentric terms of what they wish he were or hope he will be.

PARENTAL RESPONSIBILITIES

The interactions between a husband and wife are modified and made more complicated with the birth of a child. The responsibilities of parenthood are variously enumerated in the many societies of our world, but they are, in modern civilization, generally divided between the two sexes, with the male providing for the material care of the family and the female administering that care. Increasingly, the two roles are becoming indistinct, if not completely reversed in some cases. Middle-class America in particular has seen the rise of a society in which there is little sex-role differentiation, partly from necessity, partly from enlightenment (Babchuk and Bates, 1963). During World War II, society laid aside its oft-repeated adage, "Woman's place is in the home," and called for women to train as substitutes for the men who had left their occupations to enter the armed forces. After the war, when the cost-of-living index reached higher and higher levels, women found it necessary to supplement their husbands' earnings; and, under present conditions, automation, labor strikes, and erratic "lay-offs" in industries dependent upon government contracts have caused some women to seek full-time employment while their husbands temporarily take over the caring of home and children.

A century ago, such role-sharing would probably have been psychologically impossible for the men, who were anxious to retain whatever importance they seemed to have in the home. The old-fashioned concepts of a father as merely a necessary agent for the conception of a child and the economic provider for the home cast many doubts in the minds of both men and women about the importance of fatherhood. The men particularly often envisioned themselves as handing out either money or discipline, and little else. To them, the word *father* carried connotations of autocracy, sternness, sobriety, and financial responsibilities that permitted no "frivolous" manifestations of warmth and affection. However, just as investigators in child research were beginning to convince parents that the father's character and attitudes had more far-reaching effects than previously supposed, the war served to give fathers a new perspective—that of distance—which enabled them to view their roles, needs, and desires more objectively. As fathers, then, these "new" men with less emotionally rigid ideas returned home more eager and better able to subscribe to the popular idea of family "together-ness," which, for all its overuse, is a term that sociologists, psychologists, psychiatrists, and other experts in human relations find meaningful in the realm of child development.

Further role exchanges and balances have been facilitated by laws en-forcing a shorter work week. Many fathers now have more time to spend in the home and to devote to all aspects of child-rearing. Aside from the help and support a husband is able to give his wife in her homemaking, he is able to plan more vacations with his family, travel to new places, and take ad-vantage of public recreational facilities hitherto inaccessible because he lacked the time or because the facilities did not exist. Consequently, vast numbers of fathers no longer regard their roles simply as breadwinners. Tasch (1952) interviewed eighty-five fathers having a total of eighty boys and eighty girls and differing widely in nationality, religion, and occupa-tion concerning their roles in family life. The fathers felt that they were im-portant not only as economic providers but as companions, guides, and teachers to their children. Table XI-1 illustrates the distribution of activities which the fathers in the study reported having performed.

From the psychologists' point of view, the fusion of parental roles has proved generally beneficial to the children of the last generations. Slater (1961) has found that parental role differentiation contributes to emotional and social maladjustment among children; and although girls apparently

Table XI–1   Fathers' Reported Past and Present Activities Distributed According to Major Categories (From Tasch, 1952, p. 323)

Major Category	No. of Fathers	Per Cent of Fathers
Routine daily care and safety	80	94.1
Development of motor abilities, acquisition of skills, interests	74	87.0
Development of intellectual abilities and interests	74	87.0
Going to places of recreation	68	80.0
Development of social standards, conduct, and control	63	74.1
Emotional development	35	41.2
Moral and spiritual development	33	38.8
Maintaining family unity	32	37.6
Assignment of chores, work, allowance	31	36.5
Development of artistic interests	26	30.6
Development of personality characteristics	26	30.6
Radio, movies, comics	21	24.7
Giving material objects, presents	20	23.5

have some difficulty assuming appropriate sex-role behavior due to the fact
that the feminine role at best is not as clear-cut as the masculine role, fewer
maladjustments occur among youngsters from the middle classes, where
the sex-role differentiation is not so great as it is in the lower classes.

The Role of Mother

In the American societies, the tasks of satisfying the infant's needs for
food, cleanliness, and physical comfort are regarded, under normal conditions, as being the responsibility of the mother. As a rule, mothers spend
more time with their children than do other members of the family; therefore, any adequate study of children, particularly infants and the very
young, has been and must be concerned with the relationships between
mother and child. "The most important single factor influencing the survival
and welfare of infants appears to be the interest and ability of the mother
and the quality of care which she provides" (Stuart, 1963, p. 523). As Sears,
Maccoby, and Levin (1957, p. 15) have stated:

> . . . the mother plays a central part, for she is the most common element
> in her child's experience. She it is who decides what behavior is change-
> worthy, and she it is who does the changing—or tries to. In so doing, she
> must not only establish in her mind what new behavior is to be added to the
> child's repertory of acts, but she must devise ways of training him. Not all her
> interactions with him are purposefully designed to this end, of course. Much
> that she does, dayin and dayout, is simply caretaking or enjoyment of him
> as another human being whom she loves. Sometimes, too, she reacts to him
> as an annoying person, and she hurts or frustrates him.

Getting off to a good start in life consistently requires a process called
"mothering," which, during infancy, generates those forces that point toward later flexibility and durability. Lack of mothering fosters unalterability
and repetitiveness (Kubie, 1957). This mothering consists of responding to
the infant when he cries, feeding him when he is hungry, protecting him
from cold and excessive light and sound. Montagu (1963) has presented
evidence that physical contact—petting, patting, cuddling—has measurable
impact on degrees of contentedness, alertness, and vigor in the infant and increases the ease with which the infant's demands may be satisfied. Interestingly enough, much speculation about baby care has been stimulated by
Harlow (1959), who has reported that baby monkeys show a distinct need
for softness, warmth, and contact comfort.

Mothering is not some mystical force generated between the mother
and child during either pregnancy or the process of birth. It is a matter of
satisfying the needs of an infant and providing stimulation of his sense organs. Singing to him softly, telling him what a wonderful person he is (even
though he does not understand the words), rocking him, hugging him

showing true affection not only stimulate his sense organs but also teach him that he is an important, loved, accepted, and significant person. The danger of not providing this message in terms of mothering has been indicated repeatedly in studies by Spitz (1947), Bakwin (1949), and others. One of the more startling studies is that of thirty-eight adolescents who had been in an orphanage from the age of three weeks to three years. Sixteen to eighteen years later, of these thirty-eight, four were psychotic, twenty-one were deemed to have character disorders, four were mentally retarded, and two were diagnosed as being psychoneurotic (Beres and Obers, 1950).

The importance of the mother's personality and adjustment in relation to the adjustment of the child has been stressed by Koppitz (1957), who studied the relationships of parental attitudes and characteristics to the attitudes of children toward themselves and others. In her study, she used seventy-five boys with an average age of twelve years. On the basis of her findings she concluded that a child will be inclined to feel anxious and guilty and consider himself bad if his mother is unstable during his early years.

A fearful, resentful, irritable, impatient mother will probably encounter and create problems in all areas of child care. At least, in the Berkeley studies of parent-child relationships, Bayley and Schaefer (1960) have reported that the early warmth and affection of mothers is associated with calm, happy, and cooperative behavior from babies and children throughout the years prior to adolescence. Furthermore, if suddenly deprived of a mother's love, children who have consistently experienced security and well-being may feel unwanted and unloved, perceptions which are damaging to the child's ego.

Other evidence for the importance of the mother's attitudes toward her child can be found in the studies of Wyatt (1958) and Abbe (1958). The former, as cited in Chapter VI, theorizes that stuttering is often a symptom of some disturbance in the mother-child relationship at a time when the child is practicing speech. Abbe was able to show that restrictiveness, laxity, and overindulgence are in general more characteristic of mothers with disturbed children than of those with children who are making normal adjustments.

In connection with the increasing number of mothers employed outside the home, many studies have attempted to analyze and assess the effects of a mother's working on her children and on her child-rearing functions. A study reported by Peterson (1961) involving data from 616 adolescent girls indicated that mother-daughter relations were not adversely affected by the mother's part-time absence from the home. Roy (1961) also presented some significant conclusions:

> 1. The children of employed mothers seem to do more household chores than the children of non-employed mothers. . . .

·   ·   ·   ·   ·

2. The employment of the mother does not seem to have any adverse affect [*sic*] on the social activities of the children. . . .

3. The employment of the mother does not generally lower the academic performance or aspirations of the children. . . .

4. The general fear that delinquency would increase due to the employment of the mother was not borne out. . . .

As Duvall and Duvall (1964) have concluded:

> . . ."There is no evidence that maternal employment as such leads to devastating deviations from good parent-child relations." In some homes, the general family spirit improves when the mother gets a job and the children feel more a part of the total working team. Some women are good mothers and some are not. The fact of their working in itself seems to have little effect on their children.

In other words, it is the quality rather than the quantity of relationships that is most important. The *quality* of the mother-child relationship is generally based upon the *quantity* of consistent, loving care a child receives from his mother during his infancy and early childhood. The "maternal employment" studies cited involved adolescent children for the most part, and the assumption must be made that the qualitative nature of the relationships has already been established. It is doubtful that the same conclusions could be drawn from studies of relationships between children and mothers who had turned the daily care of their babies over to other women or agencies. Certainly one of the major problems faced by many fathers is the development of companionable relations with children they see for only a few hours a day, and usually at a time when both fathers and children are fatigued.

The Role of Father

If the mother's personality and adjustments are important to her ability to care for her children, the father's personality and his adjustments are important to the mother's happiness and to all other family experiences to which a child is exposed. Generally, it is the father's interests, educational background, occupation, socioeconomic status, and place in a community that determine the geographical location of the home, its size, its furnishings, and the amount and quality of play space, toys, books, playmates, and recreations available to the child. Even when the father does not reside in the home with his children, because of divorce, affiliation with the armed services, or an occupation that keeps him away from the family most of the time, the amount of financial support he lends to his wife determines the amount and quality of his children's earliest life experiences. What the absent father cannot adequately give his children is a model of maleness, without which they are subjected to undue difficulties in learning appropriate sex-role behavior; and, as we have indicated, this developmental task is one of the most important ones in the socialization of the child.

For a boy, his father is a primary source for much of his learning, not only of maleness *per se* but also of concepts related to male interests and occupations. From the father a boy learns about electricity, combustion engines, jet propulsion, carpentry, hunting, fishing, camping-out, and practical applications of the laws of physics, economics, biology, chemistry, and so forth. To both boys and girls, a father is the supreme authority on everything objective and factual. (Children generally turn to their mothers on subjective matters and the subtleties of social relationships.)

The influence of a father's maleness is exerted not merely through interactions between himself and his child but also through his attitudes toward other members of the family and his general behavior patterns. A boy will notice the gentleness with which his father treats elderly people, the politeness extended a woman, the protective attitudes toward girls in the family. One father, described by Pitcher (1963, p. 90), spoke—probably unconsciously—with a high voice when talking to his daughter but used a deep bass voice when speaking to his son.

This illustration shows the dependence of a child on the father.

If the father-son relationship is good and there is affection and understanding between them, the boy strongly identifies with his father and will notice and may copy some details of his behavior, his gestures, stance, phraseology, facial expressions, interests. Thus does the boy learn what society accepts and expects from his sex. The better he learns the appropriate behavior, the better his personal-social development. (See Chapter X.) Likewise, a favorable, or positive, self-concept is apparently related to the reinforcement a boy receives in the form of success or praise as he approaches closer identification with his father or a father figure (Helper, 1955; Bandura and Kupers, 1964).

For a girl, a father serves as an authority on factual matters, a disciplinarian, a love object, and a model for her concepts of male behavior. (One fatherless girl found herself at a considerable disadvantage in writing domestic fiction, which she subsequently gave up, claiming: "I couldn't write stories with fathers in them. I didn't know how they were supposed to act.") There is, too, a distinct possibility that girls reared without father may have a tendency to be less feminine, because, according to Pitcher (1963), it is the father more than the mother who encourages his daughter to assume behavior appropriate to girls through his notice of and expressed pleasure in such personality traits as "coyness," "lovableness," "flirting," "sweetness and gentle behavior." He verbally approves of femininity as displayed by styles that appeal to him. Fathers further accentuate sex differences in children by disapproving, however mildly, of aggressive behavior in girls while approving, even encouraging, similar actions from boys (Radke, 1946). All in all, fathers are less demanding of their daughters and give them considerable overt affection and protection.

Problems and Satisfactions

The role of parent, whether that of the mother or the father, is at best a difficult one. When all the various duties and responsibilities are counted, the list becomes long, complex, and awe-inspiring. At the beginning of the list is the satisfaction of a child's biological needs, which alone creates economic tensions on increasingly higher levels as our industrial society continues to reach new heights in living standards. Furthermore, the period of children's dependency has been extended by compulsory school laws, child labor regulations, and social pressures that advocate higher education. An increment in recreational opportunities and the availability of automobiles encourages children to range far from home, and the expansion of their experiences and social contacts, combined with the complexities of modern living, increases the worries of parents regarding the safety of their children, as well as their moral and ethical attitudes.

However, despite the difficulties encountered in the modern family, most mothers and fathers derive genuine satisfactions from their roles as parents. Tasch (1955) compiled various study reports of answers given by parents to questions concerning their greatest satisfactions and their greatest problems in child-rearing. The ten highest categories for each are presented in Tables XI-2 and XI-3. Generally, the differences in the rankings made by the fathers and mothers were interpreted to mean that fathers take a more personalized view of their relations with their children and that mothers are more concerned with the process of socialization.

PARENTAL ATTITUDES AND CONTROL PATTERNS

The lessons of life and how they are taught influence the child's self-concepts and his characteristic behavior toward others in general. Some parents dominate their children's lives to an excessive degree, exercising rigid control over their actions and experiences through authoritarian methods of child-rearing. Some parents submit to every demand made by an offspring. Others allow the child varying degrees of freedom to develop, to explore, to learn. Homes and parents are described in terms of overprotection,

Table XI–2 Comparison of Order in Which Ten Highest Categories of "Satisfactions" Are Ranked in Fathers' and Mothers' Reports * (Tasch, 1955, p. 61)

Brief description of major category	Rank in fathers' reports	Rank in mothers' reports
Companionship	1	2
Personality characteristics	2	1
Intellectual abilities	3	3
Fact of having	4	18
Child rearer	5	5
Endearing mannerisms, cute and cunning ways	6	23
Relatives' and other parent's relations with child	7	10
Motor ability, coordination, etc.	8	13
Growth; developmental progress	9.5	19
Artistic abilities, interests	9.5	11
Social relationships, adjustment	13	4
School progress, adjustment	15.5	6
Routines	15.5	7
Interests, hobbies	17	8
Relationships with siblings	11	9

* This list has been extended in order to accommodate the ten highest categories for both fathers and mothers.

Table XI–3   Comparison of Order in Which Ten Highest Categories of "Problems" Are Ranked in Fathers' and Mothers' Reports * (Tasch, 1955, p. 61)

Brief description of major category	Rank in fathers' reports	Rank in mothers' reports
Routine daily care: eating, sleeping, dressing, etc.	1	2
Relatives' and other parent's relations with child	2	7
Relationships with siblings	3	3
Parental convenience	4	15
Personality characteristics	5.5	1
Health	5.5	9
Companionship	7	24
Neighborhood	8.5	12
Reaction to authority	8.5	10
Child rearer	10	8
School progress, adjustment	14.5	4
Living quarters	11.5	5
Emotional behavior	14.5	6

* This list has been extended in order to accommodate the ten highest categories for both fathers and mothers.

rejection, democracy, autocracy, permissiveness, acceptance, indifference, casualness, neglect—with these and other patterns overlapping and interweaving within any one family. Probably nowhere do the attitudes approach a pure state: no parents are completely and constantly permissive, no child is accepted and loved unconditionally every moment of his childhood. Permissive parents are not always democratic; a democratic home may include one authoritarian or dominating adult; and overindulgence may be symptomatic of either extreme permissiveness or subtle rejection.

Nor does every rejected child become maladjusted or every "spoiled" child develop a weak character. There is no such thing as a one-to-one relationship between the attitudes and adjustments of parent and child. The behavior of youngsters is not a mere reflection of adult behavior; "each child reacts to his environment in a specific way, dependent upon a complexity of factors, internal and external ones, of which the child's emotional relationship with the parents reflected in the degree of his security is a most important one" (Sperling, 1951–52, p. 176).

At best, investigators have been able to find correlations between certain specific attitudes and practices on the part of one or both parents and similar behavior in their children. Lyle and Levitt (1955), for example, found a positive relationship between the punitiveness of parents and that of their children. (That is, a correlation can be found if the child's punitive-ness can be expressed without fear of retaliation, as in reaction tests contain-ing problem situations and incomplete sentences.) And, if a boy receives distinctive cues for male aggressiveness through punishment by a father with whom he closely identifies, he is quite likely to be highly aggressive. A similar correlation exists between a mother's punitiveness and her daugh-ter's aggression (Levin and Sears, 1956).

But, such correlations can be found between many specific behaviors, from a mother-daughter aversion to eggs to a father-son penchant for stamp-collecting. What we are primarily concerned with here when we speak of parental attitudes and control patterns is the prevailing, pervading atmos-phere that describes the child's home life in general and which has either a favorable or unfavorable effect upon his social adjustments. Some of the conditions often cited as favoring acceptable behavior patterns and opti-mum social adjustments are democratic homes, permissiveness, affectionate parents, warm and close parent-child relationships, tolerance, understand-ing—all of which could be put under the inclusive heading of "Acceptance." A list of conditions that characteristically produce unfavorable parent-child relationships and poor social adjustments usually includes authoritarian homes, possessiveness, overprotection, overindulgence, indifference, incon-sistent or severe discipline, dominating parents, lack of affectional relation-ships, high parental expectations, neglect—which could be summed up in the word "Rejection," denoting either the intention or the effect of parental behavior (Nurse, 1964).

Acceptance

Reflecting their neglect for the individuality of themselves and others, acceptant parents consider a child as unique, a developing personality who needs love, understanding, time devoted to him, and a reasonable amount of freedom, encouragement, and permission to develop his own potentials at his own rate. With emotional objectivity and genuine affection, these par-ents create a home atmosphere of rapport and democratic attitudes wherein no one member dominates or is given undue attention. If the parental atti-tudes of permissiveness do not cross the lines into neglect or indulgence, children reared in such a democratic climate are apt to have leadership qualities—to be resourceful, cooperative, persevering, responsible, and gen-erally well-adjusted emotionally and socially. Symonds (1938, p. 682) has pointed out that "good citizens, good scholars, good workers, good hus-bands and wives, and good parents come from homes in which the children are wanted and accepted." From homes so described come children who have happy relationships with parents, are closely identified with the par-ent of their sex, and show a marked quality of independence—traits fre-

Table XI–4   Comparison of Bright High-Achieving with Bright Under-Achieving High School Boys on the Family Relations Scales (From Morrow and Wilson, 1961, p. 506) *

Scale Title	Per Cent Above Median		
	High (N = 48)	Low (N = 48)	p
Family Sharing of Recreation	69	44	.02
Family Sharing of Confidence & Ideas	63	35	.01
Family Sharing in Making Decisions	60	44	ns
Parental Approval	73	33	.001
Parental Affection	60	42	ns
Parental Trust	60	25	.001
Parental Approval of Peer Activities	71	42	.01
Student Acceptance of Parental Standards	52	25	.01
Student Affection & Respect toward Parents	58	44	ns
Lack of Parental Overrestrictiveness	56	29	.01
Lack of Parental Severity of Discipline	69	42	.01
Lack of Parental Overprotection	52	56	ns
Lack of Parental Overinsistence on Achievement	63	46	ns
Parental Encouragement of Achievement	60	40	.05
Harmony of Parents (N = 40)	63	48	ns
Regularity of Home Routine	52	46	ns
Over-all Family Morale	67	33	.001

* Reprinted by permission of the Society for Research in Child Development and the authors.

quently found in achieving students (Gilmore, 1951). In fact, Morrow and Wilson (1961) compared and tabulated the descriptions of family life given by bright high-achieving and under-achieving students. (See Table XI-4.) The high-achievers, more often than the under-achievers, described their families as approving, trusting, affectionate, encouraging but not pressuring in achievement, and not overly severe in discipline. The overall family morale was high, and "sharing" seemed to be the byword for confidences, ideas, decision-making, and recreations.*

As a rule, acceptant parents are emotionally mature, and, regardless of the sacrifices involved, they work steadily (although not always consciously) toward the development of independence in their children. Porter (1954, pp. 176–177) has listed some of the characteristics by which the ac-

* This study supports the one by Brown, Morrison, and Couch (1947) mentioned in Chapter X: Responsibility is highly correlated with the democratic practice of encouraging "sharing in family planning."

cepting parent achieves his goal and then offers the following concise definition (p. 177):

> *Parental acceptance* may be defined as feelings and behavior on the part of the parents which are characterized by unconditional love for the child, a recognition of the child as a person with feelings who has a right and a need to express those feelings, a value for the unique make-up of the child and a recognition of the child's need to differentiate and separate himself from his parents in order that he may become an autonomous individual.

Rejection

Rejection occurs in many forms and for many reasons, most of the forms being products of emotional immaturity and self-centeredness on the part of parents.* Although a parent may not perceive his attitudes and behavior patterns as being rejectant (an overprotective parent is horrified at such a thought), his children will develop symptoms typical of the rejected child. They will perceive of themselves as being unworthy, unwanted, unloved, and inadequate. That is, so far as objective measurements are concerned, it makes little difference whether the child does not mature because he is retarded, will not mature because he resists authority, or cannot mature because he has never been allowed to learn how. Apparently receiving no support, sense of security, or sense of accomplishment from those closest to him, the rejected child becomes fearful, anxious, dependent, and perceives the elements in his environments as a threat to some portion of his existence —somewhat as though he were the sole target for the arrows of experience, and life a series of tests of his abilities and endurance. This self-centeredness manifests itself in inconsideration for the feelings of others and a tendency to compete for attention. Thus, the rejected child is likely to be inadequate in his social relations (Koppitz, 1957). Not having received affection, he is unable to offer it to others, not only because he has had no patterns to follow but also because he is—like his parents—too concerned with satisfying his own needs. One can hardly expect a starving youngster to share what food he has. Furthermore, neglect in any form destroys a child's confidence in himself and others.

Rejection is evident in many differing patterns of parental behavior. At one extreme there is outright rejection of the child manifested by physical abandonment by the parents, severe and inconsistent punishment, hostility, coldness, indifference, domination of his every action, insistence upon strict

---

* However, even intelligent, adequate parents will be likely to reject a mentally retarded child (Worchel and Worchel, 1961). The discovery that their child is thus handicapped seems to arouse anxieties, fears, and guilt which are not generally associated with the birth of a normal child. Children who are handicapped in other ways will be overprotected rather than rejected, but, as a rule, the effects are the same: dependency, insecurity, lack of initiative and responsibility, underachievement.

obedience, and so forth. Selfish and egocentric, the parent who rejects outright develops rigid standards of behavior designed to eliminate annoyances. Although the children may be docile, they are usually negativistic and unresponsive, resisting authority and learning. At the other extreme, a parent may be overindulgent and submissive to the whims of his offspring. If the acceptant parent understands his child's need for a reasonable amount of freedom to develop, controlling and channeling his curiosity and energy, the overindulgent parent—through self-centeredness, ignorance, laziness, inadequacies, fears, or a misguided sense of the meaning of permissiveness —allows the child more freedom than he is equipped to handle. Forced into an early independence, the child develops a rather shaky self-reliance. He feels self-important but not secure, and may meet experience with bluster, overassertiveness, excessive jealousy, and high aggression, or with anxiety-ridden withdrawal.

In between but overlapping both outright rejection and overindulgence is overprotection. It is perhaps the most common form of rejection in many societies, if only because it is so often unconscious, a characteristic of many well-meaning and conscientious parents. Japanese mothers coddle their children, creating for them an atmosphere of peace, quietude, and harmony. Frequently, women who were childless for many years throw themselves wholeheartedly into the role of motherhood and have no interests outside of their children. Parents of handicapped children also have a tendency to overprotect their offspring. Regardless of the reason for it—and many acceptant parents will overprotect their children from time to time or in certain situations—the overprotective parent attempts to shield a child from any emotional bruisings, frustrations, or conflicts. They are afraid to leave him for any length of time, they keep him close to the breast, the mother's bed, and the home far beyond the recommended time periods, they carefully screen and restrict his social contacts, they hover over him when he is ill, prolonging the recuperation periods, and, of course, they fulfill his excessive demands on their time, patience, and purse.

Kortlandt (1962), who made observations of chimpanzees in their natural habitats, noted that because of the forest dangers the mothers usually carried their young close to them for many years. In his descriptions of life in the wild, Kortlandt states (p. 138):

> . . . the behavior of the young chimpanzees . . . was markedly retarded in comparison with that of animals raised in captivity. The mothers' constant anxiety and close surveillance keeps the young dependent and must therefore act as a strong pressure against psychological development.

One mother, Kortlandt continues, apparently older than the others, allowed her two children much more freedom. "Both her children seemed more self-reliant than the other juveniles of corresponding ages."

A child reared in an emotional climate of excessive mothering, parental domination, and pampering learns to view himself in an unrealistic manner, to regard himself as the most important person in the world and one whose needs must always be satisfied even at the expense of others. He becomes autocratic and shows little consideration or respect for others. Disobedient and rebellious, he defies his mother, asserting at an early age an independence and a self-confidence that derive from an artificial set of circumstances —mainly, the child's belief that the sole duty of adults is to serve his important self. This belief suffers a rude shattering when the child enters the reality of life situations outside the home.

Pampering a child or dominating his every activity does not adequately prepare him for taking his place in the broader social milieu, for accepting disappointments and frustrations (Levy, 1943). When he enters school, he discovers that his teachers and classmates are unable and unwilling to give him the attention he selfishly demands or the help he needs for elementary acts of self-care. The faulty learning produced by overindulgence and the inability to perform preschool developmental tasks—because they have always been done for him—create in the child manifestations of chronic anxiety.* Lacking initiative and the experience for self-care, responding to new situations, directing his own activities, and assuming responsibilities, he has difficulty adjusting to larger groups, creates disturbances in the classroom, and often fails to benefit from instruction. Before he can function effectively in group situations and be socially successful, a certain amount of unlearning and relearning must be accomplished. Even in later school years, unless the child has learned the value of foregoing the immediate satisfaction of his pleasure impulses, he may find himself in academic difficulties, having never been forced to develop good study habits through application to tasks he may consider unappealing.

In many cases, overprotected and overindulged children can be assisted only when the attitudes of their parents undergo changes, which sometimes can be brought about once the parents understand the adverse effects of their relationships upon a child's independence, self-control, and self-direction.

Parental expectations. Probably the most characteristic feature of rejectant parents is inconsistency of thought, word, and action, and nowhere is this better shown than in the expectations they have of a child's attain-

---

* Pavenstedt (1964), attempting to explain the high incidence of stomach ulcers among Japanese, theorizes that the coddling of children and the constant harmony so prevalent in Japanese homes "may be rather dubious blessings." Also, as pointed out in Chapter VI, stuttering is frequently precipitated and aggravated by the nervous tension produced by overprotection, oversupervision, and parental domination (Moncur, 1952). Two other authorities, Reichard and Tillman (1950), suggest that when "parental rejection or overprotection is severe, it may account for the development of schizophrenia" (p. 257).

ments and behavior. The overprotective parent, for example, gives evidence on a large scale of his love for children—excessive fondling, attention, watchfulness, pampering, and coddling; yet, because the child is so obviously well "loved," the parent expects him to act and be just a little bit better than a less fortunate child. One mother was overheard giving her seven-year-old son an interminable list of expectations that included helping her get the girls in the family ready to go outdoors; being a big boy, the "man" of the house, when Daddy was away; going to school on the bus by himself (which he had never done); helping the teacher at school; not crossing the street; eating *all* of his lunch—and so on. And, all the while the mother spoke, she was *tying his shoelaces and brushing his teeth for him.*

In short, the overprotective parent with high expectations is paradoxical, requiring the child to achieve without giving him the incentive or the know-how. (See Figure XI-2.)

Another type of parent with unrealistic expectations is the one who would never consider forcing a child to eat food that makes him ill or to walk before his legs can support him, yet will in some form or other attempt to force upon him adult values, goals, and standards regardless of the child's particular aptitudes. Some of these attempts are direct and conscious, as when a dominating father actively prepares his son for entering the family business or profession—selecting his toys, school curriculum, college, and organizational affiliations. Other attempts are indirect and unconscious, as when a mother who missed the advantages of musical training expresses disappointment because her daughter displays no talent or inclination for playing an instrument.

Figure XI–2. The setting of high goals is a form of rejection. Under pressure, a child often rejects his goal, his parents' standards, and himself. The consequent self-concept of "non-achiever" may cause him to set his own unrealistically high goals so that he can maintain the idea of his unworthiness. Thus he becomes what he (and his parents) thinks he is. (New York Times, September 23, 1962, p. 100). Illustration idea courtesy of David Pascal.

In many ways, both subtle and overt, these parents fail to guide their children into analyzing their individual potentials, weaknesses, talents, and interests as a step toward setting their own realistic goals. Parents with high expectations, in fact, refuse to recognize weaknesses in their offspring's personality. Certainly they do not allow a child to be either a child or an individual (Medinnus, 1963). Through nagging and threats, they unwittingly bring about a child's will to fail, if only as a protest against pressure. At best, he becomes frustrated, anxious, lazy, critical yet unable to withstand criticism, unmotivated, sloppy, and underachieving. "Such a child bears not only the onus of his own strivings, but the weight of his parents' ambition as they use him to maintain or enlarge their own self-esteem" (Esman, 1962).

For its strength, the ego depends on constant recognition of real accomplishment; and when parental expectations are set too high, the child's ego suffers severe damage through lack of his recognition. (Expectations set too low deny stimulation to a child's abilities, ambition, and initiative through lack of encouragement and recognition of growth and development. The result is low standards of achievement and conduct.) Sometimes, too, the recognition of achievement is given by parents at the cost of creating further unrealistic expectations. If a child plays the role of the most responsible child in the family, he may be expected to be responsible in any and all situations and under all conditions. As he grows older, he may be expected to be correspondingly more responsible and independent than a younger sibling, when in reality, due to factors of intelligence, constitutions, sex, or environmental differences, the younger child may be more mature than the older.

Furthermore, as the child moves toward maturity, parents increase the number of their demands and expectations of him. He may be expected to assume more duties around the home, to contribute to the welfare of the family, to absorb in more detail the roles of homemaking he will eventually be expected to carry out. During adolescence particularly, these increased demands create conflicts between parent and child. Commonly, the parent treats the youngster as a child while requiring him to act as an adult; at the same time, while retaining many of the emotional behavior patterns of childhood and the interests of an earlier age, the youngster is experiencing bodily changes and additional independence that constantly remind him of the approaching adult status he is so anxious to attain. Seemingly, his own internal conflicts cannot stabilize themselves fast enough, and the external conflicts and pressures that he perceives as coming from his parents prolong, he thinks, the process of gaining equilibrium.

The importance of parental satisfaction with a child's behavior and development has been demonstrated by Elkins (1958), who noted that the eighth-grade children whose parents expressed the greatest satisfaction

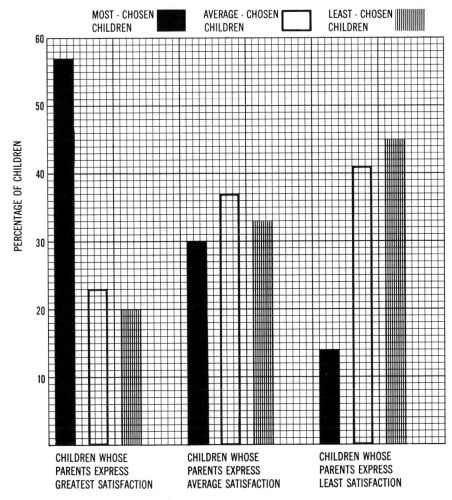

Figure XI–3. Relationship Between Childrens' Choice-Status and Degree of Parents' Expressed Satisfaction with Children (Elkins, 1958, p. 243)

were more frequently chosen by their classmates as friends—they were considerably more popular—than the children whose parents expressed the least satisfaction. Figure XI-3 presents the results of Elkins' study.

CHILDREN'S PERCEPTIONS OF PARENT-CHILD RELATIONSHIPS

No one method of child care, no single practice or technique, no amount of conscientious planning can assure parents of rearing the type of personality desired by them or by society. The individual reaction pattern and makeup of the child must be taken into consideration. In fact, it is the child's *perception* of his relationships that determines his adjustments, regardless of what the actual relationships are as perceived by other people (Serot and Teevan, 1961). Observers may shake their heads in dismay at a mother-son "apron-string" relationship, yet the *boy* may feel secure, well-loved, and adequate rather than cloistered or smothered. If the child feels loved, wanted, appreciated, trusted, and accepted, his emotional security is virtually assured and he is freed of the inner tensions that constrict social and intellectual expansion. The well-adjusted youngster, for example, perceives his parent-child relationship as warmly affectionate, relatively happy and close to the ideal; the maladjusted does not. Kagan (1958) found that stories told by aggressive boys—in response to pictures designed for story-telling purposes—frequently contained incidents of anger and hostility between children and parents.

Apparently, it makes a difference too which parent holds what attitudes, which one is dominant, and which is the punitive agent. Children will identify with the parent whom they perceive as being the more rewarding and affectionate (Payne and Mussen, 1956), and the relationships in turn are closer if a child sees himself as being similar to the parent of the same sex. This cycle of affection is extremely important to the socialization of a boy, particularly when one considers that peers are more likely to regard favorably the boy who sees himself as being like his father (Gray, 1959).

And yet, the majority of children examined by Kagan (1956) attributed positive attitudes to mothers more often than to fathers. They perceived her as being friendlier—less punitive, dominant, and threatening. (Table XI-5 lists the four questions asked by Kagan and the per cent of boys and girls

Table XI-5 Per Cent of Children Responding "Mother" to Questions About Their Homes (Kagan, 1956, p. 257)

	Per Cent	
Question	Boys	Girls
1. If you were in an argument at home with your mother and father, who would be on your side, your mother or your father?	60.9	73.6
2. Let's make believe you were bad and your mother and father were both home. Who would punish you, your mother or your father?	36.4	33.0
3. Who is the boss in your house, your mother or your father?	27.9	19.8
4. Who are you scared of more, your mother or your father?	16.7	29.2
Number	111	106

responding "Mother" to each.) Other studies, besides supporting these findings, report that children of both sexes consider the father as the authority or "boss," larger, stronger, more dangerous, and more commanding of respectful behavior (Hawkes, *et al.*, 1957; Harris and Tseng, 1957; Emmerich, 1961; Kagan, *et al.*, 1961).

It should come as no surprise, then, that boys report satisfactory relationships with parents less often than girls do (Hawkes, *et al.*, 1957), or that boys are the more aggressive sex (Levin and Sears, 1956). They would prefer to identify wholeheartedly with their fathers but feel closer to their mothers. Frequently, the ambivalence causes them to become highly aggressive, especially if the father is severely punitive; if the mother is perceived as the punitive agent whom the boy is most likely to obey, he may become nonaggressive and dependent. At least, Kagan (1958) found with relative frequency that this type of boy perceived his mother as the disciplinarian in the home.

Possibly the majority of children consider their mothers the more reliable of the two parents because she is available to them for a greater portion of the day and is therefore more actively involved in child-rearing. Or, such perceptions may reflect children's recognition of greater acceptance, tolerance, and understanding on her part.* However, even the most understanding fathers are handicapped in establishing good parent-child relationships because of their need to be out of the home during the largest part of a child's wakefulness. A schedule in the homes of modern surburbia— those within forty miles of New York City, for example—calls for a father to leave his home daily at seven A.M., arrive home again at seven P.M., and then attend a meeting of lodge brothers, a bowling league, a village planning board, a volunteer fire department, or a professional society some evenings. On weekends, he may spend a large part of his leisure time on a golf course, at a country club, involving hobbies and occasionally a second job— activities that do not or cannot include children. Relatively few of these commuting fathers are able to organize their interests and civic duties to include their sons, as in the case with scoutmasters and their assistants, church officers, Little League sponsors and coaches, and other workers with sports clubs or youth groups.

Although such conditions under which the father is rarely present in the home may have a deleterious effect upon girls, the boys suffer the most. During the years of their greatest growth and development, they are denied

---

* Burchinal (1958) found that at all levels of parental age, mothers showed a higher degree of acceptance than did fathers. Also, women who had had twelve or more years of formal education or whose husbands were business or professional men were significantly more accepting than were women with less education or with husbands employed at lower occupational levels. By contrast, the fathers' scores showed little variation according to either educational or occupational level.

a much-needed companionship, a male image. Poor social adjustments and delinquency are among the more disastrous results. At best, both sexes have lower and less stable self-concept ratings than children with fathers who accept them and devote time and attention to them (Silver, 1958; Tatum, 1957).

In studying parent-daughter relationships, Liccione (1955) showed twelve Thematic Apperception Test cards to fifty girls in each of the nine, eleven, thirteen, fifteen, and seventeen age brackets. Upon analysis, the story themes showed that mother-daughter tensions occurred more frequently than father-daughter tensions, the largest amount existing at the age of fifteen. Disequilibriums in father-daughter relationships were lowest at age thirteen and highest at seventeen. These findings may be accounted for by the fact that in middle-class families there is a widespread tendency for fathers to leave the early disciplining and counseling of girls to the mother; then, once the girls have reached puberty and begin asserting an increased independence and interest in dating, fathers' apparently fearing the possible effects of their daughters' diverse social contacts, become unwilling to permit them to grow up and face the difficulties, hazards, and decisions of life in the late teens.

On the other hand, most adolescents find that their parents are less comforting than formerly in times of stress or upset. As the child matures, parent-child relationships become more formal, with less apparent affection (as it deepens it becames less overt), less apparent understanding (adults have difficulty keeping up with the emotional shifts of adolescents), and less apparent empathy (because the children themselves draw away from adults as they become emotionally more dependent on peers).

THE ONLY CHILD

Traditional concepts of the only child as a spoiled darling, selfish, demanding, and unpopular with peers have undergone some gradual changes since the importance of parent-child and child-peer relationships has become accepted among modern adults. More and more only children are being sent to nursery schools in order to help them in the socialization process, and generally, because of the additional time and attention that parents are able to give them, they encounter a wider expansion of horizons and self, which facilitates good adjustments. When problem behavior occurs, it generally can be traced to home conditions. For example, the only child born in a rural community is necessarily isolated from social contacts, and it is this isolation that handicaps his personal-social development (Stott, 1945). Likewise, an only child may be a victim of maternal overprotection because the parents know for one reason or another that he is the only child they will

have. Another only child may be rejected by his parents because he was unwanted.

Parental attitudes, home setting, and family conditions, then, are more
important to the only child's adjustments than the fact of his loneliness. If
the home conditions are unfavorable, the child is at a disadvantage for being
the sole focal point of parent-child interactions. The shocks of a family
crisis cannot be shared with other children. If home conditions are favorable,
his advantages are immeasureably increased. His personality is not subjected to damage by sibling rivalries and jealousies, he is likely to have a
higher socioeconomic status, usually possesses more playthings, and enjoys
a greater amount of travel and broader educational opportunities. All in all,
the only child is less likely to be as "spoiled" as the child with one sibling
(Levy, 1939).

ORDINAL POSITION AND SIBLING RELATIONSHIPS

The interactions between two parents and the relationships they have
with their offspring affect and are affected by the size and composition of
the family unit, and the family interactions are codified with each new addition to it. In large families, the roles of the different members are likely
to be more complicated, with a greater tendency toward specialization resulting from the division of responsibilities and activities. Bossard and Boll
(1955, p. 71) point out that "very early in life, a child acquires a special personality role in the group life of the family, which comes to be recognized by
the family members as well as by other persons subsequently." Such role
specialization elicits from parents descriptions similar to "She's the mildest
one of them all"; "He's my helper—very responsible"; "She keeps the family
stirred up all the time, full of ideas and trouble and activity"; "Johnny was
a lot younger than the others—sort of an afterthought, and without knowing
it that's how we all treated him. Besides, he was so placid we just put him
down and forgot him. He never quite got over being 'last,' and he never tried
to be the first or the best in anything."

Obviously, role specialization is partly a result of variations in parental
behavior and attitudes which occur from one child to the next. Lasko (1954,
pp. 133–134), for example, summarized her investigation of parental behavior toward first and second children as follows:

> 1. Parent behavior toward first children as contrasted to second is on
> the average less warm emotionally and more restrictive and coercive. These
> differences are more apparent in the pre-school years than later. A similar
> differential exists between second and third children, though on a less dis-
> tinct level.
>
> 2. Parent behavior toward second children does not tend to change sys-
> tematically as the child grows older. Systematic changes do occur in the

treatment of first children, mainly in the direction of reduced parent-child interaction.

3. Parents tend to be consistent in their methods of handling children and in their policies of child-rearing as revealed by the correlations between the treatment of first and second children. However, the nature of the emotional relationship between parent and child is less predictable from one sibling to another.

4. The age difference between the siblings is an important contributor to the variation in parent behavior toward the two children. It appears that closely spaced children are, in certain respects, more advantageously treated than are widely spaced children. . . .

Various other studies have cited the tendencies of children in certain ordinal positions to have characteristics in common. To present just a few of the findings, first-born children are generally less aggressive than the youngest in a family (Sears, 1951). They are often adult-oriented, curious, self-confident, responsible, sensitive, and serious—more so than a younger child. Second-born children are likely to be peer-oriented, easy-going, and friendly (McArthur, 1956). The latter statement is generally borne out by Bossard and Boll (1955–56), who rated the adjustments of 879 children according to their ordinal position. The results of their study are presented in Table XI-6. In-between children—quite contrary to what many in-between children themselves think—show the highest ratings of good adjustment.*

Table XI–6   Adjustment, First-Born, In-between, and Last-Born by Sex and Percentages (After Bossard and Boll, 1955–56, p. 890)

Adjustment status	Males		Females	
	Number	Per cent	Number	Per cent
First-born:				
Well adjusted	17	58.6	16	55.2
Medium adjustment	8	27.6	7	24.1
Poorly adjusted	4	13.8	6	20.7
In-between children:				
Well adjusted	115	67.2	107	62.9
Medium adjustment	43	25.1	40	23.5
Poorly adjusted	13	7.7	23	13.6
Last-born:				
Well adjusted	19	54.3	13	56.5
Medium adjustment	13	37.1	8	34.8
Poorly adjusted	3	8.6	2	8.7

* We must point out that all of the children studied by Bossard and Boll were from relatively large families; and, considered collectively, the poorly adjusted children were from homes where the father was domineering or the mother was ineffective and irresponsible, and in which health problems were prevalent.

The process of socialization is apparently affected also by factors of sex and position and spacing. In one of her many studies of sibling relationships, Koch (1955, p. 48) stated:

> The interaction of the three variables, child's sex, ordinal position, and sibling's sex was significant in the case of the traits, leadership and exhibitionism, and near significance at the five-per-cent level in the case of jealousy. The first-borns in opposite sex pairs were rated higher in jealousy, exhibitionism, and leadership than were those in same-sex pairs, while among second-borns the differences were usually in the opposite direction, though less marked. The differences between boys with a younger sister and boys with an older sister were conspicuous. The former tended to be the more jealous, exhibitionistic, and inclined to lead. Boys with a younger sister also showed more jealousy, exhibitionism, and leadership than did girls with a younger sister or boys with a younger brother.

Among many other relationships noted in a remarkable set of studies published during 1956, Koch also observed that the range of interests widened as the differences in ages between siblings increased, that a boy with a much older sister tends to be more dependent, withdrawn, and tenacious than a boy with a much older brother, and that in general children with brothers were rated as being more competitive, ambitious, and enthusiastic than children with sisters. Boys with sisters only are, according to Brown (1956), somewhat more feminine in their preferences and activities than boys with all male or male and female siblings.

Intrafamily relationships are modified and made more complex as the size of the family increases or its composition is altered, whether such alterations occur because of additional children, the inclusion of adults other than the parents, such as blood relatives, servants, full- and part-time baby sitters, guests, or boarders, or the depletion of the existing household, which might occur for any number of reasons—death, illness, job transferrals, divorce, increased economic independence or marriage of the oldest children. However, further research into the characteristics of children from homes of varying composition is necessary before any valid conclusions can be drawn concerning the resultant atmospheres (Lehrman, 1962).

SUMMARY

Each home may be said to be unique. It has a "personality" all its own that includes the parent-child relationships, parental attitudes, parental authority patterns, and the close emotional ties of the different members of the family. The emotional tie to be considered of primary importance is the one between a husband and wife, for the degree of parental maturity and adjustments sets the tone for the entire family structure.

Although the responsibilities and roles of father and mother have been fairly well defined in past societies, middle-class America is finding itself increasingly a subscriber to the concepts of "togetherness" and "sharing." Parental roles are no longer so clear-cut as before, which apparently has a salutary effect upon the social adjustments of children as well as providing a wider range of satisfactions for parents, especially fathers.

Two major categories of parent-child relationships have been described, Acceptance and Rejection. Many attitudes and control patterns fall within each category—permissiveness, overindulgence, overprotection—and correlations can be found between specific child-rearing practices or attitudes and the social adjustments of children. However, although optimum growth and development occurs most often under the warm affection of acceptant, democratic parents, it is the child's perception of his relationship to them that is the determining factor in his socialization. The number, sex, ordinal position, and spacing of his siblings also have effects upon certain characteristics of a child; however, many of the effects are a product of role specialization and the attitudes of parents, which have a tendency to change slightly from one child to another, just as all the intrafamily relationships are modified whenever the composition of the family is altered.

QUESTIONS AND PROBLEMS

1. Compare your attitudes toward child-rearing with those of a close friend. Use the following questions for discussion purposes.
    a. At what age should a child be responsible for caring for his or her room?
    b. How old should the child be before he or she should date?
    c. How old should a girl be before she wears cosmetics?
    d. Should a child be forced to attend church or Sunday school?
    e. How should a parent react when a child refuses to obey?
    f. How should a child be disciplined?
    g. Should a child be allowed to eat what he chooses?
    h. How much allowance should a child receive at various ages?
    i. What kind of responsibilities should the five-year-old child have? The eight-year-old? The twelve-year-old?
2. Think back over your own upbringing. How would your parents have answered each of the above questions? If your attitudes are different from theirs, what do you think has caused the change?
3. What changes have taken place in your community during your lifetime which affect your family and the families of your friends?
4. What was your father's role in your family? What role did your mother play? In what ways did they or did they not work well together?
5. What do you believe are the major responsibilities of the mother in child-rearing? Of the father?
6. Describe the characteristics of an "ideal" family.
7. Discuss the problems which might result from the following types of families:
    a. A family where both parents are employed.
    b. A family where the father is absent much of the time.
    c. A family in which one or more grandparents reside.
    d. A family where the parents are divorced or separated.
    e. A family with either a stepmother or stepfather.

8. Just what do you understand the term *emotional climate* to mean? List the factors which help to provide a good emotional climate in a home.
9. What differences in social adjustment are faced by an only child? By a child from a large family?

SELECTED READINGS

ACKERMAN, NATHAN W., *The Psychodynamics of Family Life*. Basic Books. 1958.

BALLER, WARREN R., and DON C. CHARLES, *The Psychology of Human Growth and Development*. Holt, Rinehart & Winston, 1961. Ch. 13.

BERNARD, HAROLD W., *Human Development in Western Culture*, 2nd ed. Boston: Allyn and Bacon, 1966. Ch. 12.

DINKMEYER, DON C., *Child Development: The Emerging Self*. Englewood Cliffs, N.J.: Prentice-Hall, 1965. Ch. 13.

DUVALL, EVELYN M., *Family Development*, 2nd ed. Philadelphia: J. B. Lippincott, 1962. Chs. 2, 3, and 5.

GORDON, IRA J., *Human Development*. Harper, 1962. Ch. 7.

HURLOCK, ELIZABETH B., *Child Development*, 4th ed.: McGraw-Hill, 1964. Ch. 14.

JERSILD, ARTHUR T., *Child Psychology*, 5th ed. Englewood Cliffs, N.J.: Prentice-Hall, 1960. Ch. 8.

MARTIN, WILLIAM E., and CELIA B. STENDLER, *Child Behavior and Development*, rev. ed. Harcourt, Brace, 1959. Ch. 10.

OLSON, WILLARD C., *Child Development*, 2nd ed. Boston: D. C. Heath, 1959. Ch. 9.

SEARS, ROBERT R., ELEANOR E. MACCOBY, and HARRY LEVIN, *Patterns of Child Rearing*. Evanston, Ill.: Row, Peterson, 1957.

THORPE, LOUIS P., *Child Psychology and Development*, 3rd ed. Ronald Press, 1962. Ch. 4.

REFERENCES

ABBE, ALICE E., Maternal attitudes toward child behavior and their relationship to the diagnostic category of the child, *The Journal of Genetic Psychology*, 1958, 92, 167–173.

ADAMS, E. B., and I. G. SARASON, Relation between anxiety in children and their parents, *Child Development*, 1963, 34, 237–246.

BABCHUK, NICHOLAS, and A. P. BATES, The primary relations of middle-class couples: a study in male dominance, *American Sociological Review*, 1963, 28, 377–384.

BAKWIN, HARRY, Emotional deprivation in infants, *The Journal of Pediatrics*, 1949, 35, 512–521.

BANDURA, ALBERT, and CAROL J. KUPERS, Transmission of patterns of self-reinforcement through modeling, *Journal of Abnormal and Social Psychology*, 1964, 69, 1–9.

BAYLEY, NANCY, and E. S. SCHAEFER, Maternal behavior and personality development data from the Berkeley Growth Study. Presented at the Regional Research Council on Child Development and Child Psychiatry, Iowa City, Iowa, April 1960.

BECKER, WESLEY C., DONALD R. PETERSON, LEO A. HELLMER, DONALD J. SHOEMAKER, and HERBERT C. QUAY, Factors in parental behavior and personality as related to problem behavior in children, *Journal of Consulting Psychology*, 1959, 23, 107–118.

BERES, DAVID, and SAMUEL J. OBERS, The effects of extreme deprivation in infancy on psyche structure in adolescence: A study in ego development, in *The Psychoanalytic Study of the Child* (Ruth S. Eissler, *et al.*, eds.). International Universities Press, 1950.

BLOOM, BENJAMIN S., *Stability and Change in Human Characteristics.*: John Wiley & Sons, 1964, p. 78–9. See also review by Bruno Bettelheim, "How Much Can Man Change?" in *The New York Review of Books* (September 10, 1964), p. 1–4.

BOSSARD, JAMES H. S., and ELEANOR S. BOLL, Personality roles in the large family, *Child Development*, 1955, 26, 71–78.

BOSSARD, JAMES H. S., and ELEANOR S. BOLL, Adjustment of siblings in large families, *American Journal of Psychiatry*, 1955–56, *112*, 889–892.

BROWN, A. W., J. W. MORRISON, and G. B. COUCH, Influence of affectional family relationships on character development, *The Journal of Abnormal and Social Psychology*, 1947, 42, 422–428.

BROWN, DANIEL G., Sex-role preference in young children, *Psychological Monographs*, 1956, 70, No. 14 (Whole No. 421), 1–19.

BURCHINAL, LEE G., Mothers' and fathers' differences in parental acceptance of children for controlled comparisons based on parental and family characteristics, *The Journal of Genetic Psychology*, 1958, 92, 103–110.

COLEMAN, JAMES C., *Abnormal Psychology and Modern Life*, 2nd ed. Chicago: Scott, Foresman, 1956.

DUVALL, SYLVANUS, and EVELYN DUVALL, "Let's Explore Your Mind," in *Long Island Press* (December 7, 1964), p. 30.

ELKINS, DEBORAH, Some factors related to the choice-status of ninety eighth-grade children in a school society, *Genetic Psychology Monographs*, 1958, 58, 207–272.

EMMERICH, WALTER, Family role concepts of children ages six to ten, *Child Development*, 1961, 32, 609–624.

ESMAN, AARON H., "Case of the 'Underachiever,'" in *The New York Times Magazine* (September 23, 1962), p. 100.

FARBER, BERNARD, Marital integration as a factor in parent-child relations, *Child Development*, 1962, 33, 1–14.

GILMORE, JOHN V., A new venture in the testing of motivation, *College Board Review*, 1951, *15*, 221–226.

GRAY, SUSAN W., Perceived similarity to parents and adjustment, *Child Development*, 1959, 30, 91–107.

HARLOW, HARRY F., Love in infant monkeys, *Scientific American* (June 1959), 200, 68–74.

HARRIS, DALE B., and SING CHU TSENG, Children's attitudes toward peers and parents as revealed by sentence completions, *Child Development*, 1957, 28, 401–411.

HAWKES, GLENN, LEE G. BURCHINAL, and BRUCE GARDNER, Pre-adolescents' views of some of their relations with their parents, *Child Development*, 1957, 28, 393–399.

HELPER, MALCOLM M., Learning theory and the self concept, *The Journal of Abnormal and Social Psychology*, 1955, 51, 184–194.

KAGAN, JEROME, The Child's perception of the parent, *The Journal of Abnormal and Social Psychology*, 1956, 53, 257–258.

KAGAN, JEROME, Socialization of aggression and the perception of parents in fantasy, *Child Development*, 1958, 29, 311–320.

KAGAN, JEROME, BARBARA HOSKEN, and SARA WATSON, Child's symbolic conceptualization of parents, *Child Development*, 1961, 32, 625–636.

KOCH, HELEN L., Some personality correlates of sex, sibling position, and sex of sibling among five- and six-year-old children, *Genetic Psychology Monographs*, 1955, 52, 3–50.

KOCH, HELEN L., Attitudes of young children toward their peers as related to certain characteristics of their siblings, *Psychological Monographs*, 1956, 70, No. 19 (Whole No. 426), 1–41.

KOCH, HELEN L., Children's work attitudes and sibling characteristics, *Child Development*, 1956, 27, 289–310.

KOCH, HELEN L., Some emotional attitudes of the young child in relation to characteristics of his sibling, *Child Development*, 1956, 27, 393–426.

KOPPITZ, ELIZABETH M., Relationships between some background factors and children's interpersonal attitude, *The Journal of Genetic Psychology*, 1957, 91, 119–129.

KORTLANDT, ADRIAAN, Chimpanzees in the wild, *Scientific American* (May 1962), 206, 128–138.

KUBIE, LAWRENCE S., Social forces and neurotic process, in *Explorations in Social Psychiatry* (Alexander H. Leighton, John A. Clausen, and Robert N. Wilson, eds.). Basic Books, 1957, pp. 77–104

LASKO, JOAN K., Parent behavior toward first and second children, *Genetic Psychology Monographs*, 1954, 49, 97–137.

LEHRMAN, N. S., Anarchy, dictatorship and democracy within the family, a bisocial hierarchy, *The Psychiatric Quarterly*, 1962, 36, 455–474.

LEVIN, HARRY, and ROBERT R. SEARS, Identification with parents as a determinant of doll play aggression, *Child Development*, 1956, 27, 135–153.

LEVY, DAVID M., Maternal overprotection, *Psychiatry*, 1939, 2, 563–568.

LEVY, DAVID M., *Maternal Overprotection*. Columbia University Press, **1943**.

LICCIONE, JOHN V., The changing family relationships of adolescent girls, *The Journal of Abnormal and Social Psychology*, 1955, 51, 421–426.

LYLE, WILLIAM H., JR., and EUGENE E. LEVITT, Punitiveness, authoritarianism, and parental discipline of grade school children, *The Journal of Abnormal and Social Psychology*, 1955, 51, 42–46.

MCARTHUR, CHARLES, Personalities of first and second children, *Psychiatry*, 1956, 19, 47–54.

MEDINNUS, GENE R., The relation between parent attitudes and parental acceptance of the child, *The Journal of Genetic Psychology*, 1963, 103, 117–121.

MONCUR, J. P., Parental domination in stuttering, *Journal of Speech and Hearing Disorders*, 1952, 17, 155–165.

MONTAGU, ASHLEY, The awesome power of human love, *Reader's Digest* (February 1963), pp. 80–83.

MORROW, WILLIAM R., and ROBERT C. WILSON, Family relations of bright high-achieving and under-achieving high school boys, *Child Development*, 1961, 32, 501–510.

NURSE, SHIRLEY M., Familial patterns of parents who abuse their children, *Smith College Studies in Social Work*, 1964, 35, 11–25

PAVENSTEDT, ELEANOR, quoted by Ann P. Eliasberg in "Family Business in Brief," *The New York Times Magazine* (May 17, 1964), p. 79.

PAYNE, DONALD E., and PAUL H. MUSSEN, Parent-child relations and father identification among adolescent boys, *The Journal of Abnormal and Social Psychology*, 1956, 52, 358–362.

PETERSON, EVAN T., The impact of maternal employment on the mother-daughter relationship, *Marriage and Family Living*, 1961, *23*, 355–361.

PETERSON, DONALD R., WESLEY C. BECKER, LEO A. HELLMER, DONALD J. SHOEMAKER, and HERBERT C. QUAY, Parental attitudes and child adjustment, *Child Development*, 1959, *30*, 119–130.

PITCHER, EVELYN GOODENOUGH, Male and female, *The Atlantic Monthly* (March 1963), *211*, 87–91.

PORTER, BLAINE M., Measurement of paternal acceptance of children, *Journal of Home Economics*, 1954, *46*, 176–182.

RADKE, MARIAN J., *The Relation of Parental Authority to Children's Behavior and Attitudes*. Minneapolis: University of Minnesota Press, 1946.

REICHARD, SUZANNE, and CARL TILLMAN, Patterns of parent-child relationships in schizophrenia, *Psychiatry*, 1950, *13*, 247–257.

ROSEN, BERNARD C., Family structure and value transmission, *Merrill-Palmer Quarterly*, 1964, *10*, 59–76.

ROY, PRODIPTO, Maternal employment and adolescent roles: rural-urban differentials, *Marriage and Family Living*, 1961, *23*, 340–349.

SEARS, P. S., Doll play aggression in normal young children: influence of sex, age, sibling status, father's absence, *Psychological Monographs*, 1951, *65*, No. 6, Whole No. 323.

SEARS, ROBERT R., ELEANOR E. MACCOBY, and HARRY LEVIN, *Patterns of Child Rearing*. Evanston, Ill.: Row, Peterson, 1957.

SEROT, NAOMI M., and RICHARD C. TEEVAN, Perception of the parent-child relationship and its relation to child adjustment, *Child Development*, 1961, *32*, 373–378.

SILVER, ALBERT W., The self concept: its relationship to parental and peer acceptance, *Dissertation Abstracts*, 1958, *19* Pt. 1, 166–167.

SLATER, PHILIP E., Parental role differentiation, *American Journal of Sociology*, 1961, *67*, 296–311.

SPECK, ROSS V., quoted in "Illness of Owner Is Traced in Pet" by M. S. Sandler, *The New York Times* (July 19, 1964), p. 27. Speck's study can be found in the July 15, 1964, issue of *The Journal of the American Veterinary Medical Association*.

SPERLING, MELITTA, Psychoanalytic aspects of discipline, *Nervous Child*, 1951–52, *9*, 174–186.

SPITZ, R. A., Anaclitic depression: an inquiry into the genesis of psychiatric conditions in early childhood, in *The Psychoanalytic Study of the Child* (Anna Freud, ed.). International Universities Press, 1947, pp. 313–342.

STOTT, L. H., Research in family life in Nebraska, *Journal of Home Economics*, 1945, *37*, 80–83.

STUART, HAROLD C., and ROBERT J. HAGGERTY, Pediatrics, in *Collier's Encyclopedia*, 1963, *18*, 521–526.

SYMONDS, PERCIVAL M., A study of parental acceptance and rejection, *American Journal of Orthopsychiatry*, 1938, *8*, 679–688.

TASCH, RUTH J., The role of the father in the family, *Journal of Experimental Education*, 1952, *20*, 319–361.

TASCH, RUTH J., Interpersonal perceptions of fathers and mothers, *The Journal of Genetic Psychology*, 1955, *87*, 59–65.

TATUM, CARL D., The influence of parental acceptance on selected self factors in children, *Dissertation Abstracts*, 1957, *17* Pt. 1, 97.

TERMAN, LEWIS M., P. BUTTENWIESER, L. W. FERGUSON, W. B. JOHNSON, and D. P. WILSON, *Psychological Factors in Marital Happiness.* McGraw-Hill, 1938.

WORCHEL, TILLIE L., and PHILIP WORCHEL, The parental concept of the mentally retarded child, *American Journal of Mental Deficiency,* 1961, 65, 782–788.

WYATT, GERTRUD, Mother-Child Relationship and Stuttering in Children. Ph.D. Dissertation. Boston University Graduate School, 1958, p. 645.

T W E L V E

The Impact of Education

THE PURPOSE OF EDUCATION

Unlike the lower animals, Man must be *taught* if he is to live and live successfully in the physical and social world into which he was born. Education, therefore, is a prime condition for human life. Its purpose is to teach the young the skills necessary for attaining adulthood and to transmit the past history, traditions, experiences, and cultural beliefs and mores of society. Such is the purpose of even the most primitive and ancient societies in which a child's parents or relatives teach him ways of doing things—making and using weapons to hunt wildlife and to defend himself, preparing food, fashioning clothing and shelters—and whose elders, leaders, and priests are generally responsible for teaching tribal rituals and traditions, religious beliefs and superstitions, to the young boys. The primitive groups educate their children to live in the present. Ancient civilizations—exemplified in more modern times by India and China—educated their young to live in the past, emphasizing verbatim memorization of sacred writings and strict adherence to the ethical values of ancestors.

In the more modern, complex societies, such as those of Western civilization, the young child must learn a far greater variety of complicated skills and behaviors, and he must acquire a vast amount of knowledge in many areas. Furthermore, thanks to the Greeks, who recognized the dangers of a formal and rigid worship of the past, modern man looks to the future. One

344

might say that, in an educational sense, the Greeks invented progress. And, in America, one of the primary purposes of education is to unite the past and the present with the future. That is, having acquired the knowledge, skills, and standards of a culture, the young citizen is expected to contribute to the perpetuation or reconstruction of that culture.

Athenian education also recognized the needs of the individual and placed a heavy emphasis on mental development—a shift in viewpoint from the Spartan ideal of physical perfection. The democratic ideal, too, which America has borrowed from the Athenians, has as its central value respect for the individual and his freedom to make choices. However, as both Athenians and the American founding fathers realized, if a government based on popular vote is to operate effectively, those votes must come from educated people and the government must be administered by educated people. "Freedom imposes responsibilities on all; therefore all must be educated" (NEA, 1959, p. 6).

The central purpose of American education has come to be stated as the development of the ability to think. The Educational Policies Commission (NEA, 1961, p. 11) explains the purpose thus:

> The rational powers of the human mind have always been basic in establishing and preserving freedom. In furthering personal and social effectiveness they are becoming more important than ever. They are central to individual dignity, human progress, and national survival. . . . And the society which best develops the rational potentials of its people, along with their intuitive and aesthetic capabilities, will have the best chance of flour--ishing in the future. To help every person develop those powers is therefore a profoundly important objective and one which increases in importance with the passage of time.

THE SCHOOLS

While education has ever been the responsibility of parents, the clan or tribe has, from the outset, played an important role. The tribal elders and priests have been delegated to instruct the young in traditional beliefs and practices; and many savage groups today have what might be called schools, in which the youth are prepared for the elaborate tests of physical skill and endurance that constitute the formal ceremonies of initiation into tribal adulthood. As societies become more complex, the "initiation ceremonies" become more comprehensive and the training more intensive. Thus, in Western civilization, the major part of the socialization process, insofar as it pertains to an individual's mental, social, and moral development, devolves by design or coincidence upon the schools. The schools themselves have evolved from an orientation toward training youth for specific social or vocational roles (priesthood, monastic life, guild apprentice, knighthood, clerk, military life, statesmanship) toward equipping youth to be at home in the universe. By such training, the schools also serve society's needs. The National Education Association (1961, p. 1) states:

> . . . The political order depends on responsible participation of individual citizens; hence the schools have been concerned with good citizenship. The economic order depends on ability and willingness to work; hence the schools have taught vocational skills. The general morality depends on choices made by individuals; hence the schools have cultivated moral habits and upright character.

In short, schools are responsible for educating the uneducated. The definition and purpose of education in a particular school, state, or nation and the meaning of uneducated as it pertains to a specific individual determines the nature of the school and the type of clients it serves. The school may be vocational, teaching a child or adult the skills of a particular trade; it may be comprehensive, teaching academic and vocational skills to all the youth of a community; it may be parochial, emphasizing character development according to the principles of a religious denomination; it may be a private school emphasizing social skills. In the American single-ladder system of free education from kindergarten to the university, the public schools are commonly divided into segments geared for certain age groups—kindergarten, elementary, junior high, and high school. Adult education classes have been added to the top of the ladder, and nursery or prekindergarten classes may soon be universally added to the bottom.

The age requirements and the groupings for the various grade levels vary from state to state. Some states combine preschool classes, kindergarten, and first grade into a primary department; the remaining grades may be divided into elementary, intermediate, and secondary classifications. Some consider elementary school as consisting of grades one through eight; others make a relatively sharp distinction between sixth grade, and the junior high (seventh and eighth, or ninth) level. High school may constitute either the ninth, tenth, eleventh, and twelfth grades or just the last three. In this text, however, we are chiefly concerned with the influence of the elementary and pre-elementary schools *in general*. That is, we have for the most part limited the survey of childhood to the years prior to adolescence and to those environmental forces which have the greatest influence during that time.

Administration

Despite a certain uniformity of purpose, design, curriculum, and instructional methods, elementary schools in the United States vary according to the philosophy and economy of the cultural areas they serve. Any one school's government is truly "of the people, by the people, for the people."

At the top of the public school's organizational hierarchy is the local community, represented by the business and professional people (not educators) it elects as the trustees of educational policy, the members of the school board. Acting in the interests of community welfare, the board exercises near-complete control and authority over the whole structure. It establishes the broad outlines of social policy concerning education and dictates, directly or indirectly, the general direction a school will follow (Havighurst and Neugarten, 1962). Within its role, a school board screens and selects applicants for the chief administrative jobs (superintendent, principal, supervisor), appropriates funds, decides on school expenditures, approves salary schedules, and supervises projects (e.g., school construction) to which the funds are allocated. The board also maintains a continuous evaluation of the strengths and weaknesses of the academic program; it plans the curriculum and selects the textbooks to be adopted; it keeps itself and the community informed about state legislative actions concerning education, the progress of experimental programs, and other educational policies and programs throughout the nation.

Having selected an educational administrator, the local school board generally defers to him and his staff in matters of educational policy as it operates from day to day in the school system. Although in many instances the roles of educational administrator and school board overlap, the educator is usually responsible for hiring and dismissing teachers, handling teacher grievances, recommending textbooks for adoption, setting operational standards, reinforcing the authority of the teacher, and so forth. A principal in particular is primarily concerned with the teachers, the student body, and what he can offer them. However, as an educator, a principal can influence the board on educational policy; his suggestions as an expert are weighed carefully, and in many cases it is the principal who keeps the community and its school forward-looking and experimental-minded. A fearful, compromising principal, on the other hand, can—by the very nature of his personality—keep a school from moving ahead, holding to traditional, conservative, or rigid methods for fear that the influential citizens in the community will not approve of innovations.

By and large, however, the responsibility for a school's progress or lack of progress rests with the school board. It is these representatives of society who select the men most likely to fulfill the expectations and uphold the standards of the community.

Traditional and Progressive Schools

Philosophically, there are two major factions holding two polar viewpoints concerning just what the schools should accomplish. Traditionalists feel that the modern school should emphasize mental discipline through the acquisition of knowledge in a relatively rigid program of learning. The teacher in a traditional school covers a given amount of subject content daily by methods more often autocratic than democratic. Wholehearted recognition is not given to individual differences in motivation, potentiality, experiences, and maturational level among the various children in a classroom; nor is any great consideration given to the holistic approach to child development. Freedom in childhood is dangerous, the traditionalist might say, and discipline both mental and physical is the surest way to produce strength of character. Compliant, obedient behavior is considered most desirable.

Within the traditionalist group, there are two splinter groups, the perennialists and the essentialists. The former regards the learning process as an intellectual training and discipling of the mind; the latter conceives of it as instilling the proper response to a given stimulus. The purpose of the perennialist curriculum is to transmit the cultural heritage, train the mind, and foster the development of an intellectual elite; whereas the essentialist teaches the 3 R's to all and prepares the academically able for high school and college. Subject mastery is conceived of as an end in itself. Under both philosophies, a prescribed course of study is followed, with specific content outlines, although some enrichment of the program is proposed for the intellectually able child. The curriculum is organized on a subject-centered basis and is compartmentalized, with little correlation, except possibly between history and geography.

The progressive educator uses the holistic approach to children, believing that the child does not learn in a vacuum, that his mental development is intimately related to his personal-social development, and that the child himself is an active rather than passive part of the learning process. Instruction is oriented to the academic and social needs of the individual child, and teachers provide opportunities for group participation in the development of goals and objectives, encouraging cooperative achievement rather than competition. One branch of the progressivist group, the liberals, accepts no concept of the learning process as fully satisfactory or final. Their curriculum is conceived of as a means toward total human development in a rapidly changing culture; it is flexible, built around broad topics or themes. The other faction, the reconstructionists, conceive of learning as an ever-changing adjustment to new developments. The curriculum in a reconstructionist school stresses the changing of society and its reconstruction and is therefore oriented to radical change in content and method (Grieder, *et al.,* 1961). Tables XII-1 and XII-2 present representative schedules for children attending traditional and progressive schools.

Obviously, the classification of a school and its operational procedures are greatly dependent upon the economic assets of the school district. Progressive programs, because they are largely experimental, flexible, and individualistic, require a greater variety of instructional materials and a greater number of specialists. A wealthy community elects forward-looking board members who in turn hire a dynamic educator and, for the most part, leave the making of educational policy to him. If the community does not want or cannot afford innovations and experimentation with its children, it will not provide money for a progressive program, and the school board will hire an educator least likely to upset the status quo. A traditional school, for example, may have little or no provision for creative or vocational activities; the drama program, if there is one, may be a vestigial part of the English course; no industrial arts workshop would be provided for the boys; and the art and home economics courses may constitute superficial, hit-or-miss instruction in basic skills. In rural schools particularly, where the cost of education is generally higher on a per-pupil basis and the levying of equitable taxes on farm property difficult, the operational procedures and facilities of the school must necessarily be held to bare essentials.

Consider, for example, that the beginning salary for a rural school-teacher is approximately the same as her city colleague's; yet she may serve fewer children per grade level in comparison with the thirty or more served by the city teacher. Or, she may serve several grades as compared to the

Table XII–1 *

| Grade V   Traditional Schedule | |
Hours	Subjects
9:00--9:05	Inspection of hands, hair, teeth, etc.
9:05--9:20	Citizenship
9:20--9:35	Spelling
9:35--9:45	Penmanship
9:45-10:00	Oral or Written Composition or Reading
10:00-10:10	Recess
10:10-10:40	Arithmetic
10:40-11:00	Physical Education, including games
11:00-11:10	Recess
11:10-11:40	Reading
11:40-12:00	Language or Composition
1:00--1:05	Home Room with announcements
1:05--1:35	Art Education: Music or Drawing
1:35--2:00	Geography and Nature Study
2:00--2:15	Recess and Supervised Play
2:15--2:50	Reading
2:50--3:15	History or Civics

* The schedules in tables XII–1 and XII–2 were taken from Hall-Quest (1965a,b, p. 578–79)

Table XII–2

Grade V Modern Flexible Schedule				
Hour	Monday	Tuesday	Wednesday	Thursday	Friday
9:00 10:00	9:00–9:15 French 9:30–10:00 Music or Art	Work Period for various units	9:05–9:45 Auditorium Activity Music or Art	Work Period or French Library Guidance	Club Activities Creative Activities
10:00 11:00	Work Period for individual or groups and related to some unit Physical Education	10:00–10:30. Guidance in Reading 10:30–10:45. Physical Education 10:45–11:45. Work periods on units related to the program and emphasized guidance in learning			Unit activities Physical Education
12:00 1:00	Lunch and relaxation				
1:00 2:00	Art, creative writing, laboratory work				
2:00 3:00	Auditorium programs, creative work, conferences, reference work in library, home making activities, etc.				

city teacher's one. To put it another way, the responsibility for the rural teacher's salary may be divided among twenty-five families, the urban teacher's among several thousands of property owners.

As a rule, such "traditional" education based on a poverty of resources is inadequate and below the national standards (Wahlquist, 1954). However, the movement toward consolidation of administrative units or attendance districts in rural areas is tending to upgrade the educational level of the rural child. Among the benefits heretofore unavailable to him are library facilities, laboratories, up-to-date textbooks, guidance programs, hot lunches, transportation, and more uniform methods of teaching. He has the advantages of health examinations, remedial exercises, more and better teachers and equipment, better records of his progress in school, and the opportunity for advancement in his studies if so warranted.

The slum schools present other examples of the onerous tasks imposed upon educators by a community unwilling and unable to pay for education. In unattractive, ill-lighted, and cold buildings, teachers and administrative officials daily attempt to serve the needs of unkempt, hungry children cramped physically and emotionally with cold, fatigue, and too much personal freedom (Deutsch, 1964). Many of the youngsters do not have any sense of personal identity, there are astonishing gaps in all conceptual areas, and, like primitive peoples, they live in the here and now, grasping whatever they need for immediate survival while they can get it. Into this mass of unfulfilled needs, the slum educator must hammer the most basic skills. They attempt, often in vain, "to prepare a student for getting and keeping a job as soon as he leaves school and . . . to encourage those who have academic talent to aim at a profession through higher education" (Conant, 1961). This task, says Conant, is almost the reverse of the suburban educator's, which is to adjust parental expectations and ambitions to the abilities of their children.

Private and Denominational Schools

Until 1870, when the Education Act permitted the levying of taxes by school boards in order to build and maintain elementary schools, education in America was proffered by voluntary organizations, most of which were denominational. Most of these schools sought to protect the interests of the church sect with which they were affiliated. The other, private or "independent," schools have been maintained in order to provide a more specialized education for the children of specific communities and classes within a community—usually the wealthier ones (the upper and upper-middle classes)—or to serve the interests of children being trained for specific vocations and roles in society.

Although the states encourage private education (particularly through tax exemptions), they do not provide revenue for its support. However, in spite now of some state and federal aid, the principles of local freedom and local initiative continue to operate, and private and parochial schools are on the increase, as is the enrollment in them. The estimated enrollment in nonpublic elementary schools for 1961–1963 is 5,400,000 (IPA, 1964).

By far the larger percentage of nonpublic schools are parochial (parish) and private. The parochial school may be identified with the Roman Catholic Church, although some are found within a few Protestant and Jewish denominations. The group of educators connected with such schools believe that all branches of knowledge are grounded in moral law. They are maintained for the purpose of integrating religious instruction into the curriculum.

According to the 1963 summary by the Department of Education of the National Catholic Welfare Conference, there were 4,546,360 boys and girls enrolled in 10,775 Catholic elementary schools. They were taught by 77,113 religious and 38,355 lay teachers who were under the immediate direction of the pastor of the parish. He, in turn, is responsible to and guided by the Diocesan Superintendent of Schools. As with all private and denominational schools, the trustees are usually appointed by and out of the controlling groups within the church, denomination, society, or corporation concerned.

Nursery Schools

History. The movement toward group training of children below kindergarten, which has recently picked up great speed in the United States, began in England about fifty years ago. Shortly before World War I, nursery schools were established in the London slum districts for the purpose of improving the health and physical condition of the children there. In the United States, however, the first nursery schools had less immediate goals. At first, they were organized as laboratories—college or university workshops for the study of preschool children by potential teachers and research workers. In 1921, the University of Iowa established its play school as a laboratory in child psychology. Later, during World War II, play schools, nursery groups, and day camps were formed by individuals, corporations, or institutions as means for child care while parents contributed to the war effort. Still later, when the high cost of living led mothers to look for ways to supplement the family income, the nursery school was looked upon as a many-faceted blessing. For some middle-class families, the nursery school even became a means for gaining prestige or mobility toward the upper classes.

Regardless of the reasons for developing the schools and regardless of parents' reasons for sending a child to one, the national community gradually became aware that preschool groups such as the nursery schools were in many ways beneficial to society. As Hymes (1952, p. 71) has stated:

> For a half-century day nurseries had been showing that groups could help unfortunate children and families—where there was illness, death, poverty, great emotional stress. For a quarter-century scattered colleges had been showing that groups could help privileged children and families—the intellectually advanced, the only child of the wealthier famiy, the youngster in select urban centers.

Furthermore, new knowledge concerning the growth, development, and needs of children was gained from these groups, and educators, parents, and psychologists felt compelled to accept the evidence that good preschool groups could benefit all children and that preschool education was more often a necessity for optimum development of the child than a convenience for adults.

Goals. The young child needs activity, companionship, independence, self-expression, a "flowing-in of experiences." Above all, for good health and mental development he needs opportunities to *play*. As one teacher put it, "It is sometimes hard for parents to realize that playing with blocks and learning how to build are related to the development of the thinking process" (Hechinger, 1964, p. 61). Thus, the chief aim of the good nursery school is to provide the kind of environment that best serves the needs of the child: appropriate child-size furniture, toys and play materials, healthy playmates, proper food, clean air, and sunshine. More specifically, the goals have been set forth by Read (1955) as including programs to

1. Promote health.
2. Promote physical growth and motor development.
3. Increase independence—the ability to meet and solve own problems.
4. Increase self-confidence—add to feeling of being an adequate person.
5. Increase feeling of security with adults, with other children, in a variety of situations.
6. Increase liking for others and understanding of their needs.
7. Increase understanding of self and acceptance of reality.
8. Increase ability to handle emotions constructively.
9. Extend and enrich avenues of self-expression in art, music, rhythm, language.
10. Extend and enrich understanding of the world—broaden intellectual horizons.

Reading aloud can stimulate the imagination.

Values and effects.   In general, the broad goal of a good nursery school is well met: the child's social growth is positively influenced—he becomes more sociable than he might otherwise—and this trend is a wholesome one (Jersild, 1960, p. 164). Aside from that, a nursery-school environment provides space which is all too often lacking in our modern small homes and crowded communities, safety that cannot be assured in street playgrounds, toys in quantity and of quality beyond the ability of most parents to provide or to store, attention denied the children of busy mothers, and playmates for children deprived of sibling or peer interactions.

Other more specific benefits have been listed by various investigators. In the majority of cases, there is improvement in a child's initiative, self-reliance, curiosity, cooperation, independence, adaptability, self-assertiveness, and the establishment of routine habits of cleanliness, responsibility, and self-care. Van Alstyne and Hattwick (1939) found that nursery-school children were later rated more favorably by elementary school teachers in traits of leadership, independence, and ability to react in a constructive way to failure.

However, the effects of such preschool experiences, like those of all school experiences, are greatly dependent upon the individual child, the type of nursery school he attends, and his family background. Not all nursery schools are good ones. There is no universal standard by which one must be formed. Some are merely play groups supervised by untrained women; some are maintained as a part of church programs in religious education and housed in relatively cramped buildings; others are private institutions completely separated from the mainstream of educational thought; and still others have financial gain as their sole purpose. Furthermore, as Jersild (1960, p. 197) comments, if a particular school encourages the development of special talents, initiative, and spontaneous self-expression, all of its pupils cannot be expected to adjust easily to the established routines of a public school or to conform with eagerness to formal group situations.

As for family background, Hymes (1952, p. 80) reminds us that "nursery education is the widening out from the solid base of a comfortable family relationship." When a good relationship exists to begin with, it is improved in the sense that each member of the family lives more fully. If the family relations are faulty, there is apparently little improvement in the child's behavior patterns, although he may be aided by the alert nursery teacher who recognizes his behavior as indicative of later trouble and takes steps toward its correction.

One of the most frequently cited effects of nursery-school environment on a child is an increase in measurable intelligence. Again, family background is a deciding factor. If it is a culturally enriched one, no significant IQ increases are noted. Even a well-conducted nursery school can add little to the intellectual stimulation of children from privileged homes (Olson and Hughes, 1940). The majority of children from the upper classes may gain in skills and social adjustments, but they do not make the dramatic increases in IQ that are made by children from culturally restricted home environments (John, 1963).

The findings of such investigators as Skeels, Updegraff, Wellman, and Williams (1938) working with deprived orphanage children have given tremendous impetus to movements toward the establishment of pre-kindergarten schools for impoverished slum children.

> They do not know what a mirror is, or what an orange is. They do not know their own names. In slum schools across the U.S., normally intelligent children come to kindergarten and first grades innocent of the elementary knowledge and aspirations of their middle-class contemporaries. This mental poverty, caused by their parents' often shocking ignorance and inarticulation, starts the kids off in school so ill-equipped that they slip helplessly backward as they go on (central Harlem eighth-graders, for example, test almost three years behind other New York City students). Thus begins the vicious circle of slum birth to school failure to joblessness to slum adulthood.
>
> *TIME,* 1964

The significant words in the paragraph are *normally intelligent,* used in the broad sense of ability to use abilities. The accident of birth in an impoverished environment does not change a child's inherited potentials; it merely changes the realization of them. Curiosity and social friendliness are deadened in the cold, unstimulating atmosphere of ignorance, suspicion, ugliness, inadequate food and clothing, and ill health. Bruner (1964) maintains that "to make up for a bland impoverishment of experience early in life may be too great an obstacle for most organisms." Thus, in some thirty cities in the United States, nursery programs for the culturally deprived are being set up to provide children with the standard, elementary experiences that are the common lot of the middle-class child: shapes and colors and verbalizations; toys and sounds and motions; pictures and films and trips. Those schools which are modelled on the experimental classes directed by Dr. Martin Deutsch in New York City design their curriculums "to teach the youngsters the verbal and perceptual skills they need in order to learn to read, and also to bolster their sense of self. There is a great deal of emphasis on teaching labeling. . . . The physical arrangements of the classroom are planned carefully. The emphasis is on order, beauty, and clarity . . . because there is so little beauty and so little structure in the children's own lives" (Silberman, 1964, p. 40).

The "Early School Admissions Project" sponsored by the city of Baltimore, Maryland, and a grant of $155,000 from the Ford Foundation was scheduled to end in June 1965. If the successes noted thus far continue to be evident when the present pupils reach the third grade, there is a strong probability that Baltimore will be the first city to lower its entrance-age requirement for the public-school system, a policy that many educators believe is essential and inevitable for the entire nation. Project "Head Start," begun in the summer of 1965, represents a nationwide attempt to implement this type of program.

Kindergartens

History.   The idea of the kindergarten, a garden where children are unfolding plants, was brought into realization by Friedrich Froebel, who believed in the continuity of the child's life and that a child's capacities could best be unfolded by self-activity based upon the intelligent direction of the child's interests. Toward this end, Froebel emphasized play and self-expression through all the mediums available to the young child. Rather than learning through the passive absorption of reading matter, the child learns by doing.

The programs of directed activity devised by Froebel were enthusiastically accepted by educator Horace Mann, for one; and Mann encouraged his sister-in-law, Elizabeth Peabody, to open the first English-speaking kindergarten in the United States—in Boston. (Five years earlier, in 1855, Mrs. Carl Shurz had opened a kindergarten in Wisconsin for German-speaking children.)

The early kindergartens, which spread rapidly throughout Massachusetts but more slowly in the rest of the country, were private institutions, many of which used personnel trained in the psychologically sound educational methods introduced by Froebel. Other young kindergartens, somewhat like many nursery schools today, were formed by interested mothers. Not until 1913 did the state boards of education take action to establish kindergartens as part of the public-school system. At that time, California enacted an epoch-making law by which the boards of education were required to establish kindergartens and maintain them by taxation upon receiving a petition from the parents of twenty-five or more children.

Today, in most communities the kindergarten is considered an essential part of the school system and one which requires specially trained personnel and equipment to best serve the needs of very young children—much the same as can be found in the nursery-school environment. However, the individual differences in school districts are such that some communities are still not convinced of the necessity for providing such opportunities for their youngest members. Many rural areas either have no kindergartens at all, or the ones that do exist are run by untrained women. When, in other communities, the necessity for cutting down on educational expenses arises, the

kindergartens are generally the first part of the system to be dispensed with
—or at least the kindergarten issue is one often used as a threat to the community that balks at additional taxation. To many traditional-minded parents and businessmen, the kindergarten is still a progressive, experimental
program whose methods have not yet proven effective. In general, such
backward-moving communities hesitate to pay for what they cannot see;
and, of course, they cannot see the effects of what has never been bought.

Purposes.   Aside from the fact that kindergartens are more universally
standardized and publicly supported, there is little difference between them
and good nursery schools as we have described them. Through the detection of health defects and the encouragement of habits to maintain good
health, kindergarten teachers work toward the broad goal of self-realization
—hence, happiness—for all. For this, a child needs mental, physical, and social exercise in a variety of situations. "A good kindergarten helps a child
learn to get along with other children, use materials dexterously, express
himself confidently, listen intelligently, and follow directions. It teaches
him health and safety habits; it introduces him to school life" (NKA, n.d.).

The Association for Childhood Education International lists six major
purposes geared to the developmental needs of the child between the ages
of five and six. Table XII-3 was designed to show these basic aims, the corresponding needs, and the kindergarten practices by which they are satisfied.

The Doctrine of Interests

The name Froebel is a significant one for all educational theory, not
merely because he was the founding father of the kindergarten. As a theorist
he put into practice many of the ideas of Comenius, Rousseau, Pestalozzi,
and Herbart; and perhaps the most far-reaching philosophy, common to
them all, is contained in the doctrine of interests.

Traditional educational philosophies held that the school was required
to impart a fixed amount of knowledge, the teacher was required to make
the subject matter interesting by various external devices, and the pupils
were required to exert effort to learn by way of memory drill—whether they
understood the material or not. If the pupil did not learn, he was punished.
At best, he was a passive learner, sitting quietly and acquiring knowledge
through absorption.

Through a better understanding of the meaning of growth and development, the concept of interest and effort changed. The child, before he comes
to school, is exposed to a wide variety of experiences and has already acquired a number of personal interests. Froebel began with the interests a
child brings to school, expanded and enriched them through a meaningful
program that related school experiences to those outside the school. In this

Table XII-3 *

Purpose of Kindergartens	Need of the Child	Methods of Implementation
To help children feel adequate in school	Friendly adults; security	Homelike atmosphere with interesting materials; respectful, understanding, wise teacher
To help children live intelligently in their world	Exploration and understanding of their environment	Trips; pets; school gardening; blocks; paints; tools; dramatic plays; songs; story-telling; experiments
To facilitate sturdy growth	Maximum freedom; physical activity	Running; jumping; climbing; games; cutting; drawing; modelling in clay; working with tools
To protect children from hazards to health and safety	Protection; security	Rest; balanced schedule; snacks; hot meals; teaching rules of safety; outdoor play
To help a child find a comfortable, contributing place in his group	Help in learning to live with others	Practice in sharing and cooperation; communication of ideas and feelings
To teach children to manage themselves, their materials, the routines of the day, to take initiative in planning and doing things	To "act his age"	Practice in self-care; routine duties; making decisions and evaluations; suggesting projects; group planning

* Adapted from materials in ACEI pamphlet, n.d.

way, the pupil is made an active rather than passive participant in the learning process, his interest becomes intrinsic, and the academic material becomes more meaningful. With an increasing number of experiences which have meaning for him, the pupil develops a wider range of interests. The learning effort, then, is put forth voluntarily, without the need for external discipline. The child learns to discipline himself.

In actual practice, the modern teacher attempts to relate what the child must learn to what he already knows. Because most children are interested in and curious about objects and situations in their immediate environment, the teacher teaches arithmetic with coins or buttons or balloons and simulates marketing experiences during play periods. She trades on a child's interests in animals and nature to read stories about them, which stimulates the child's desire to read about them by himself. Some children will "specialize" and concentrate, for example, on birds, collecting birds nests or eggs or coloring pictures of the different varieties. Other forms of nature intrigue other children—plants, seeds, flowers; marine life; rocks, seashells; insects. The idea of collections expands to include stamps, which the teacher relates to history and geography; foreign dolls, often related to customs of other countries; and puppets and marionettes, which can lead to interests in any one or all of the activities involved in presenting dramatic productions. The various forms of drama in turn provide myriad opportunities for a teacher to present material that might otherwise be difficult or uninteresting, as well as allowing for the development of aesthetic appreciation of literature and music. The value of dramatic activities for instructing and motivating children is well illustrated in a 1963 news item from *The New York Times*:

CHILDREN IN SLUM RESPOND TO ARTS
12 PHILADELPHIA VOLUNTEERS ESTABLISH EXPERIMENT
PHILADELPHIA, Sept. 1 (UPI)—Children in one of Philadelphia's toughest, most culturally bankrupt neighborhoods were exposed to the arts this summer through the vision of a slum-district teacher and the talents of volunteers from several states.

The Philadelphia Theatre for Children started as a bold experiment in dramatics. Its twelve-member staff, unpaid volunteers from Pennsylvania, Ohio, New York and Michigan, also taught their students writing, reading, poetry, and dancing. More than 100 children participated in the program.

The theatre's productions were Jean Cocteau's modern play "Orphée" and Sophocles' "Oedipus Rex."

The lead in "Orphée" was played by 10-year-old Arthur Purnell, who was a member of a class for retarded children in the Philadelphia School District before Christopher Speeth of Cleveland, director of the theatre, took him in hand. Mr. Speeth teaches in one of the slum district's schools.

Arthur has a reading level several grades above the sixth grade, which he enters this month. Like the other members of the cast, he memorized within a week all his own lines in the forty-page play. For fun, Arthur also memorized the rest of the play.

The teacher uses a child's interests in the objects of his environment in order to teach prescribed subjects. For example, coins and other forms of money are useful for teaching economic concepts, simple arithmetic, fractions, history—even elementary metallurgy.

Mr. Speeth, with Ross Gelbspan of Chicago, talked the African Methodist Episcopal Church into donating a vacant six-story building in the area for the theatre.

The place was a wreck. Members of the theatre's staff scraped walls, painted and did all the work necessary to open the building.

Neighborhood businesses contributed glass for the windows, paint for the walls and other items. Churches raised money and offered their services. The artistic staff were also the carpenters and painters.

It wasn't easy to keep the eager children out of the building until the refurbishing was finished. They walked in and tried to help. The staff found many who were scheduled for early sessions staying for afternoon classes.

Through such devices the child is motivated to a more active exploration of his environment, including the objects, people, and processes he observes in it.

The doctrine of interests also serves both a teacher and a child in the socialization process when a problem arises in group dynamics. If, for instance, a teacher should recognize that a particular child is an isolate in the group because of shyness or lack of self-confidence, an examination of the child's talents, interests, hobbies, or accomplishments may reveal to the teacher several means of drawing out the child and bringing him to the attention of the group. Gradually, the teacher will guide a pupil experiencing difficulties into sharing his special assets. She thereby encourages him to participate in group activities and helps him gain the success and self-confidence he needs to interact more effectively with his peers.

Quiet contemplation can be as important as formal study in the development of thinking.

Academically, of course, the interested pupil is more highly motivated to learn than the disinterested one. What, then, are the subjects preferred by boys and girls? Amatora (1960) noted that when children freely expressed interests in academic subjects arithmetic was the first choice of both boys and girls. Geography, reading, spelling, and religion were the next highest in order, the major difference between the two sexes being the more frequent expression of interest in music and art by the girls and the greater consistency with which boys chose arithmetic and sports. Chase and Wilson (1958) studied the preferences of almost twenty-thousand fifth-grade pupils and found considerable variation in their choices. Table XII-4 illustrates the per cent choosing each subject.

Table XII–4 Rank Order of Preferences for School Subjects, First Choices Only, of 19,135 Fifth-Grade Children in 1957 (Chase and Wilson, 1958, No. 4, p. 3)

Rank Order of Subjects	Number Choosing	Per Cent
1. Arithmetic	4,098	21.42
2. Reading	3,759	19.64
3. Art	2,895	15.13
4. Spelling	2,288	11.96
5. Social Studies	2,080	10.87
6. Science	1,645	8.60
7. Music	1,236	6.46
8. Health Education	494	2.58
9. Penmanship	487	2.54
10. Language	153	.80
	19,135	100.00

In brief summation, the influence of the kindergarten method permeates every educational level. As Hall-Quest (1954b, p. 600) has written:

> . . . The activity program, progressive education, workshops, socialized school and class management, individual differences, units instead of textbook assignments, the various types of guidance, character and personality education—all are direct or indirect outcomes of the . . . methods introduced by Froebel in opposition to the traditional and regimented type of schooling which had prevailed for centuries.

Elementary Schools

History. The United States government has encouraged education from the time of its earliest formation: under the Articles of Confederation a Land Ordinance required that a small section of each township be set aside for the support of schools. Even as early as 1647, a colonial legislature passed a law requiring certain towns to provide an instructor for the children.

However, elementary education remained a private responsibility. Either the parents paid the teacher, exercising their right to send the children to "school" or keep them home, or the churches set up their own schools and meted out an education that was primarily religious. So strong was the belief that education was the responsibility of church and home that the idea of a public, tax-supported school system, which began around 1850, took hold slowly; and even after the passage of the Education Act in 1870, public opinion had to be continuously educated. Such leaders as DeWitt Clinton, Horace Mann, Lyman Beecher, and Calvin E. Stowe worked zealously throughout the nineteenth century to overcome opposition to the secularization and state control of education and to the levying of taxes for its support. The development of elementary education as we know it today is still relatively new, even though some of the greatest, most far-reaching educational advances have been made at this level.

Purpose. The National Education Association (1959, pp. 7–8) delineates the purpose of the elementary curriculum as follows:

> The program of the elementary school provides the basis on which all later schooling rests. It should emphasize reading, writing, arithmetic, speaking, and listening—the basic skills of the civilized person and the foundation of further intellectual growth. It should help pupils to acquire ideas, information, understanding, and skills in the social studies, science, music, and art. It should promote understanding of the importance of learning and of intellectual values. It should teach pupils that people live, think, and speak in various ways.
>
> The superior elementary-school program seeks to develop initiative and to promote concern for accuracy, reasoning, progress, and beauty. It teaches the essentials of safety and personal health and promotes physical coordination and skill. It helps the child learn to care for resources, both human and natural, to use simple tools, and to look after his possessions.
>
> The superior elementary program, by carefully organizing experiences in which the children work together in groups, fosters their ability to get along with others and thus helps lay the base for social responsibility.

Values and effects. Stendler and Young (1950, pp. 254–255) interviewed the mothers of children entering the first grade to discover the effects of school upon their children. The findings were summarized thus:

> 1. In general, children look forward to beginning first grade with a high degree of favorable anticipation. According to what mothers tell us, they look upon the experience as a very important stage in the process of growing up. . . .
> 2. In general, beginning first-graders show evidences of change in self-concept in the direction of feelings of bigness and importance. . . .
> 3. In general, children's behavior improves with respect to such traits as responsibility, helpfulness, good humor, independence and the like following school entrance. . . .

4. With regard to attitude toward the mother's authority and importance as compared with the teacher's, most mothers report no change. . . .

5. In general, first-grade children like school very much. Their greatest task of adjustment is in the area of social relationships. They find it hard to take the aggressiveness of other children . . . and to understand the behavior of children when it differs from their standards of goodness and badness.

The child's attempts at social adjustment are the trial and error methods by which he learns cooperation, teamwork, compliance, leadership, and all the varying degrees of conformity to a group. He gains practice in social perception, in playing different roles, and in relating to a wide variety of personalities. His classroom experiences stimulate his curiosities and help develop them into sustaining interests—usually through the efforts of a teacher who strikes responsive chords with new material, but also through a child's admiration for a teacher or another pupil who happens to be enthusiastic about a particular subject.

A school playground can provide opportunities for development of control and coordination, with fun and excitement.

For many children, particularly those reared in one of the American "pockets of poverty," school gives them their first contact with books, magazines, pictures, toys, paints, crayons, and other creative materials (Goodenough and Harris, 1950; Merry and Merry, 1950; Elkish, 1952). In many cases it is also their first contact with swings, seesaws, and similar playground equipment so valuable in helping them develop muscular control, skill, and coordination. What a frightening place it must be, in a sense, where thousands of new sensory impressions are forced upon these children whose senses have never been stimulated! When one considers the fact that small children cannot adapt to frequent, rapid changes in their environment, it seems unlikely that even the calm, steadying influence of a highly skilled teacher can do much to aid slum children in the tremendously difficult adjustments they have to make (Deutsch, 1965). The fact that some slum pupils do make a better than average adjustment to school life is a tribute to both the individual child and the school he attends.

The importance of the school situation as a means for peer contacts, creative expression in groups, play activities, and contact with toys should never be underestimated. Sullivan (1965) reports that in a recent meeting of the American Association for the Advancement of Science, Dr. Gordon D. Jensen told an international symposium that "pigtail monkeys raised with their mothers but without playthings were retarded in development and overdependent on their mothers. Those with toys were close to normal. . . .'" Sullivan continued:

> . . . This fell in line with other findings, reported at the meeting, showing that the development of human infants raised in slum conditions tends to be impaired unless they are stimulated by companionship and play.

A study by Harlow and Harlow (1962) supports these discoveries: infant monkeys raised in total isolation were found to be aberrant in every respect in later social behavior. The second most retarded group consisted of monkeys who were put into isolation with their mothers; that is, they were denied peer interactions. The only groups in which every infant was regarded as normal or "probably normal" were those raised with peers but without mothers. Even more than mothering, therefore, play with peers seems necessary to the development of effective social relations among monkeys; and, in the case of motherless infants, the "opportunity for optimal infant-infant interaction may compensate for lack of mothering" (p. 146).

Throughout the period of adjustments to the social situations of the school, the child is expected to meet demands of a more academic nature. These too are important aspects of his general development, as listed by the National Education Association in describing the purpose of the elementary curriculum. But the child also needs to achieve academically for other, perhaps less functional, reasons. Achievement at school profoundly affects a child's self-concept and his relations with peers (Bledsoe and Garrison, 1962); it allows him to think of himself as growing up and to fulfill the expectations of adults, which in turn enhances his ability to meet challenges successfully. Thus, a certain amount of academic success is necessary if a child is to broaden his social experiences and make optimum social adjustments.

Perhaps influenced by the rapid increase in the number of parochial schools throughout the nation, many parents raise the question as to whether or not their children are being taught moral and spiritual values in the public schools. According to Bernard (1966), there is widespread agreement that the schools do stress character development as evidenced in moral and ethical behavior, and without dependency upon sectarian doctrine. He lists those values being taught in the schools as they have been set forth by the National Education Association (1951):

   (1) Respect for human personality
   (2) Responsibility for one's own moral conduct
   (3) Belief that institutions are the servants of man
   (4) Belief that common consent and voluntary cooperation are superior to rule by physical strength and violence
   (5) Devotion to truth as the opportunity and obligation of free men
   (6) Respect for differences and personal excellence
   (7) Equality of men before the law and judgment by the same moral codes
   (8) The brotherhood of man as opposed to selfish interests
   (9) Right to pursue happiness if the pursuit does not interfere with the same right of others
 (10) Belief that emotional and spiritual experiences should complement the materialistic phases of life

THE TEACHER'S INFLUENCE

The task of the schools could not be carried out without teachers. "Teachers stimulate minds and hearts to that creative self-effort which alone gives significance to the term education" (Lambert, 1954, p. 86). Furthermore, as the National Education Association (1959, pp. 9–10) states:

> The quality of the teaching in a given classroom largely influences whether a pupil learns a subject or learns instead to dislike it; whether he learns to interpret, evaluate, and use subject matter, or merely to memorize it; whether he comes to appreciate the value of learning, or learns to seek knowledge only in response to authority; whether he learns to respect others or to disregard others, to lead or to conform.

It is the teacher who must guide each pupil into learning all he must know, interrelating him with his environment, and for that job the teacher

Interests grow out of satisfying experiences. Note the freedom of the children in their work, which is accompanied by guidance and help, while studying the atom in an elementary school in Eugene, Oregon.

must know a great deal. When society held primarily to the concept of a teacher as one who imparts information, conducts memory drills, and sees to it that pupils absorb a prescribed amount of knowledge in a rigid program of studies, teacher training was a simple matter of seeing to it that a trainee had enough knowledge to keep ahead of the students and certain skills in imparting the lessons. However, with the trend toward the progressive type of education, teacher training has become more intensive and comprehensive, an education that demands a longer period—perhaps a lifetime—of professional study. In addition to the specialized subject or subjects a trainee elects to teach, the prospective teacher is expected to acquire a general cultural education. Beyond that, as Kandel (1954, p. 68) states:

> . . . The teacher must have an appreciation of the social meaning and purpose of education. . . . He must know more about the psychology of the child as a growing personality, his growth, and the learning process. Since there has been a shift of emphasis from mental training to education of the whole person, he is expected to know something about the health of his pupils, and the effect of physical condition on intellectual progress as well

as about their particular abilities and even disabilities, and about their environment and social background. Such preparation is essential if the current trend toward individualization of instruction is to become established in practice.

In an experimental study, in which he summarized classroom practices, Jackson (1953) observed that teachers were mainly concerned with the academic growth of their pupils. However, most elementary teachers today show greater insight into the personal-social needs and the behavioral problems of their children than did teachers of previous years. Both clinicians and teachers appear to be more in accord in their attitudes toward the severity of behavior problems (Schrupp and Gjerde, 1953; Sparks, 1952). Slobetz (1951) presented 280 elementary-school teachers with forty behavior-problem situations related to classroom decorum, to authorities or school regulations, to application to school work, to aggressive and antagonistic behavior, to morality and integrity, and to withdrawing and recessive behavior. An analysis of the figures shown in Table XII-5 indicates that the teachers regarded behavior which was related to morality as the most serious, and that relating to classroom decorum as the most annoying. The investigator concluded that in meeting behavior problems the teachers operated from a constructive point of view and that there was some evidence to indicate that the teachers searched for reasons for the behavior. A number of experiments have shown that the perceptions of teachers can be improved

Table XII–5 Percentage Distribution of 280 Elementary-school Teachers' Ratings of the Three Most Serious and the Three Most Annoying Situations Classified by Types of Situations (Slobetz, 1951, p. 350)

Types of Situations	Most Serious	Most Annoying	CR
Situations Related to Morality and Integrity	50.4	3.0	14.8
Situations Related to Aggressive and Antagonistic Behavior	17.1	24.9	2.2
Situations Related to Withdrawing and Recessive Behavior	16.1	5.6	4.0
Situations Related to Application to School Work	13.1	26.5	4.0
Situations Related to Authorities or School Regulations	2.1	4.3	1.4
Situations Related to Classroom Decorum	1.2	35.7	17.0
Total Per Cents	100.0	100.0	

by proper guidance and training. Perkins (1958) found that teacher participation in child-study programs resulted in their obtaining greater understanding of children. Ojemann and his colleagues (1955) studied four teachers and their pupils in grades four, five, and six. Each group was matched with a control group. The teachers participated in a special training program designed to help them to understand child behavior. Various objective measures showed significant gains in comparison to the pretraining results and in comparison to the control groups. These studies furnish clues as to how individual teachers or schools can secure assistance in improving their competencies.

The character of a teacher as evidenced in her behavior is subjected to continued scrutiny by a community, and for good reason. Research abounds with evidence of the impact of a teacher's personality on the personalities of children (Torgoff, 1961). If the thesis is accepted that all of the child's experiences combine to form him into what he ultimately becomes, then the teacher's influence cannot be disregarded just because it is a transitory one.

"What the teacher is is more important than what she teaches or how she teaches it. Attitudes are more important than the method . . ." (Menninger, 1961). In essence, a teacher teaches attitudes: She teaches that certain people (exemplified by herself) hold certain opinions, place emphasis on certain values, and have, despite themselves, particular attitudes toward ideas, subjects, institutions, and other people. The more well-liked a teacher is by a pupil, the more likely the child is to emulate the aspects of her behavior to which he is most sensitive—and admiration sharpens those sensitivities!

A teacher's attitudes, opinions, and viewpoints impinge upon the child during the day. Interactions with specific children and with other teachers, attitudes toward parents and school administrators, the enthusiasm or indifference with which lessons are imparted and activities organized are observed or sensed by pupils and often set the tone for the child's reactions under similar conditions. Even the attitudes displayed by children toward school are often reflections of their attitudes toward a current teacher. It is here that the affective, personal, and human factors of the teacher's personality deserve consideration (Soloman, et al., 1964). If a child in the lower grades does not like his teacher, generally he does not like school; and the reasons often given by children for disliking a teacher are meanness, unfairness, or bad temper as these traits are revealed in personal relationships, not as shown by grades given. On the positive side, children like a teacher who exhibits fairness, smiles, good humor, and warmth. Leeds and Cook (1947) and Amatora (1952) also found that children are in considerable agreement as to which teachers are liked and which are disliked, and for what reasons a teacher falls in one or the other category.

Whether a child likes his teacher or not, he spends the largest part of his day with her. As an authority and parent-substitute, she exerts a subtle pressure on him to conform to her demands and expectations. In order to gain her acceptance and approval, a child not only modifies his behavior but engages in active competition with other children to gain her favor.

In general, children are easily influenced by authority in any form, just as many adults are. To youngsters, apparently, conformity and acceptance have a close cause and effect relationship. Ausubel and his colleagues (1956), for example, sought to determine whether fourth- and fifth-grade children were responsive to influence by adult opinion concerning preferences for artistic works. Forty children were shown pairs of slides representing paintings. One picture of each pair was a conventional type of painting while the other was an abstract painting. The children were asked to indicate their preferences for one of each pair. Later, one of the experimenters was introduced as an expert in art. The pictures were reshown and the "expert" made favorable comments about the abstract paintings and disparaged the conventional pictures. A second polling of the children revealed a significant change in opinions: the majority now indicated a preference for the abstract pictures.

Similar experiments have been conducted by Asch (1955) and Barron (1958) on older subjects. Barron, in particular, identifies highly creative individuals by testing their independence of judgment—or, in other words, their lack of conformity to the opinions of others.

By the standards imposed, the opportunities furnished for social interactions and variations in role-playing, and the degree of good will toward children, teachers construct an atmosphere to which a child must adjust. It may be a completely strange one to the child. If he has been reared in a democratic home and his teacher is dominating and autocratic, he will probably experience adjustment difficulties. Likewise, the overprotected child who attempts to establish a similar dependent relationship with his teacher will quite likely feel rejected under her more dispassionate attitude. The only child may find that he is not the center of *all* adult attention, and even the child from a large family discovers that his behavior is no longer judged on the basis of a family role as the youngest or oldest or the only boy in a family of girls, and similar situations.

The lower-class child probably has the greatest number of difficulties adjusting to the personality of a teacher because of the difference in social-class backgrounds.* Especially in the case of slum children, the teacher is

_____

* Sims (1951) employed a Social Class Identification Scale with a group of 726 public-school teachers and found that the majority of both men and women associated themselves or identified with the middle and upper-middle classes. Although Havighurst and Neugarten (1962, p. 465) caution against the overgeneralization that teachers come predominantly from middle-class origins, they do offer evidence that teachers

not a representative of their society, and her values are often drastically at variance with the great majority of adults in the slum areas.

Among other problems faced by the lower-class child and his teacher, his motivation toward school instruction is low (Milner, 1951), he lacks language facility and commonplace cultural experiences, he usually receives no parental encouragement or reinforcement as he progresses through the school program, and he is generally more aggressive than his middle-class peers (Griffiths, 1952). As a result of these and other factors, the lower-class child is less popular with his classmates, his self-concept is lower, and his achievements are below the average. The consequent academic and social failure that results from an inability to adjust to the middle-class nature of the schools is one reason why the lower-class child does not continue to take advantage of public education. In fact, for him, it is not education at all because that which he learns within the school milieu does not fit him to take a place in *his* society. As bad as it may be described by other societies and other classes, it is still the only atmosphere in which the child feels comfortable and secure and successful as *he* measures comfort, security, and success.

Suggestions have been made that the school faced with excessive disciplinary problems and a large number of truancies or drop-outs can increase its effectiveness by helping its teachers to become better acquainted with the problems of children from lower subcultures, by securing more teachers who are themselves from lower-class backgrounds, and by developing greater flexibility in standards.

Boys are apt to experience more difficulties adjusting to teacher expectations than girls are, if only because boyish behavior is more observable and teachers, therefore, can and do deal with problems more immediately. That is, girls tend to deal with problems on an intrapsychic level (Ullmann, 1957), manifesting adjustment difficulties by internal upsets—poor digestion, allergies, headaches, fatigue; whereas boys, under similar conditions, are more likely to stutter, develop nervous habits, or become overaggressive. Because the latter trait especially upsets cassroom decorum, it might seem that a teacher is more often annoyed with boys than with girls. And perhaps they are. As Beilin (1959, p. 18) has stated:

> ... Whatever the *ultimate* reasons (whether biological or social), the temptation is to say that the differences, in an *immediate* sense at least, result from different *expectations*. It is evident ... that boys and girls are expected to act in prescribed ways in our culture. The reasons girls are

---

"represent in substantial number all but the extremes at the upper and lower ends of the socioeconomic range." When speaking of the lower-class child, then, it is the lack of representation at that crucial lower level with which educators today are concerned.

considered better adjusted by teachers is that teachers have certain expectations of what good adjustment *in school* should be and the prescription for girls' adjustment is more consistent with these expectations than the prescription for boys' good adjustment.

A child is particularly influenced by the characteristic manner in which the teacher controls and interacts with her pupils—by the emotional climate of the classroom. The influence of the classroom atmosphere upon a child's learning and behavior, although again subject to extreme variations among individuals, is as profound as the home atmosphere, sometimes for better, sometimes for worse, hopefully supplementary, often complementary (Kelly and Stephens, 1964). Many investigators have examined the effects of a teacher's personality as it determines the autocratic or democratic nature of the classroom situation. Generally, when a teacher uses domination—imposing rigid standards of conduct, such as raising hands to speak, asking permission to leave seats, and paying strict attention—nonconforming behavior results (some pupils may be docile, others hostile), and instances of good mental hygiene are fewer. Anderson, Brewer, and Reed (1946) noted that a greater number of nervous habits were manifested among pupils who studied under dominative teachers than were observed among pupils who had democratic teachers. In the socialization process, the dominating teacher who holds herself aloof from the group, setting up formal relationships geared to academic tasks, creates barriers which limit the type and extent of interactions between her and her pupils and between one pupil and another.

The more permissive, democratic teacher does not impose rigid standards; she is usually a friendly, interested, and understanding person who encourages her pupils to interact freely with her and among themselves. In a democratic classroom, children often talk in low tones to each other while comparing work or seeking help from each other; emphasis is on the classroom as a group in which the tasks at hand are approached with cooperative efforts. The teacher facilitates the personal-social development of her pupils by creating situations in which individual children can experience success and can participate in developing and setting their own goals, both as group members and as individuals.

There is evidence that the freer atmosphere of the group-centered class produces greater conformity to the norm of the group than does the teacher-centered class (McKeachie, 1954). There is also an atmosphere of greater friendliness and cooperation and more individual satisfaction; moreover, the structure of the group remains more stable and tends to produce more constructively original work-products (Lippitt, 1940a, 1940b).

Directions, suggestions, and regulations given by an affectionate, acceptant teacher are more readily accepted by children (Winterbottom,

1953), a fact that becomes especially important in the teaching of abstract concepts of moral behavior. And, even at the nursery-school level, frequent, warm, friendly interactions between teacher and pupils have been shown to be more beneficial to the children than attitudes of detachment. Active teacher guidance is apparently instrumental in fostering leadership, creativity, and good emotional adjustments (Thompson, 1944).

These, of course, are overall findings, and we must point out again that the effects of one type of class or the preference for one type of class over another depends in large measure upon the personality of the individual concerned. Some pupils are better suited psychologically to the one than to the other.

Many of the influences a teacher has on her pupils are not immediately perceived in the child's home, but even a child's overt imitation of a teacher's mannerisms, voice inflections, phraseology, verbal expressions, and general behavior cause concern (as well as amusement) among parents as to the effects of the teacher's personality and character upon their children. Carrying the imitative capacity of a child to its logical, long-term conclusions, parents develop expectations for the "proper" behavior of members of the school faculty. Often, the expectations are unconscious, even ridiculous. One teacher reluctantly gave up lunching with her husband in a public cafeteria after repeatedly being asked by friendly mothers why she wasn't at the school. Both parents and children evince great surprise whenever they observe a teacher engaging in any activity outside an academic context.

Parental concern for teacher behavior and personality culminates in the standards set by a school board and an educational administrator for the selection of a faculty. Good mental health and personal adjustment are important criteria. The teacher who is insecure, depressed, or fraught with anxieties has difficulty assisting pupils who have problems. Overdependent adults, for example, become frustrated by overdependent children. A restrictive, compulsive-obsessive teacher imposes unrealistic standards—particularly of orderliness and cleanliness—and creates a situation at which pupils rebel by deliberately upsetting her.

Unfortunately, because demand for teachers far exceeds the supply, school officials cannot afford to be so selective as they would like to be (Leonard, 1959). Resnick (1954) has suggested that almost one out of five teachers is maladjusted and that the maladjusted teacher frequently is depressed, sarcastic, and fault-finding. A study by Stendler (1949) indicated that, in spite of the trend for elementary teachers to have good insight into the dynamics of child behavior, many have a tendency to view behavior from the moralistic viewpoint or as a threat to their authority. (See Table XII-6.)

Until more money, more teachers, and better teacher-training programs

Table XII–6 Percentage of Responses in Each of Six Categories for 25 Items on a Problems of Child Behavior Test Taken by 157 Elementary Teachers in a Mid-western Public School System (Adapted from Stendler, 1949, pp. 494–495)

Hypothetical Problems in Child Behavior: How would you treat the child who.... Items	Categories of Recommended Action						
	1. Take Punitive Measures	2. Talk to him; Moralize	3. Send him to a Doctor	4. Adjust the Work	5. Praise or Encourage	6. Study to Find Cause of Behavior	7. No Answer
1) never finishes on time	12.1	13.4	1.3	44.0	17.2	10.8	1.3
2) fights with other children	15.9	42.7	2.6	10.8	.64	26.8	.64
3) steals	7.0	49.0	1.3	3.2	0	38.2	1.3
4) bites his finger-nails	1.9	16.6	34.4	18.5	3.2	22.3	3.2
5) daydreams	1.9	17.2	7.6	55.4	2.6	10.8	4.5
6) relies on the teacher too much	3.2	22.9	0	54.8	17.8	.64	.64
7) does his work over and over until it is just right	1.3	49.7	0	17.8	27.4	1.3	2.6
8) won't work up to his capacity	9.6	20.4	3.2	36.9	19.8	8.3	1.9
9) doesn't pay attention	24.2	19.1	7.6	27.4	1.3	8.9	11.5
10) is always late	30.6	22.9	.64	9.6	0	33.8	2.6
11) lies	10.8	58.0	1.3	5.10	0	18.8	6.4
12) talks back to the teacher	14.7	58.0	0	5.10	0	17.2	5.1
13) is easily discouraged	0	7.6	0	33.8	57.3	1.3	0

Table XII-6 Continued

14) shows off in class	22.3	25.5	0	36.3	.64	7.6	7.6
15) feels everyone is picking on him	1.3	37.6	1.3	15.9	15.3	22.9	5.7
16) loses temper when he doesn't get his way	29.3	52.9	0	4.5	0	8.3	5.1
17) uses vulgar language	19.1	65.6	0	3.2	0	8.3	3.8
18) tries to cheat on exams	12.7	58.6	0	19.1	0	5.1	4.5
19) is unhappy and moody	0	10.2	6.4	34.4	16.6	29.9	2.6
20) plays truant	12.7	20.4	0	24.8	.64	36.9	4.5
21) is a bully	38.2	25.5	0	22.9	.64	7.6	5.1
22) wastes school materials	38.9	52.9	0	3.8	0	.64	3.8
23) disobeys	38.9	39.5	0	2.6	0	11.5	7.6
24) is disliked by other children	0	46.5	0	15.3	7.6	28.0	2.6
25) is timid and shy	0	2.6	0	56.7	39.6	.64	.64

are made available in the nation's educational systems, the influences of in-adequate teachers should be carefully examined and counter-balanced by the home environment if the purpose of education is to be fulfilled.

SUMMARY

The role of the schools in the socialization process of the child has al-ways been one of fitting him to maintain life and effective action within his community. As transportation and the arts of communication have brought all societies into closer contact, the purpose of the schools has broadened to include education toward self-fulfillment in the world community. However, a child's parents and other representatives of the immediate society into which he was born are still responsible for administering to his individual needs for instruction and practice in the various human skills. The economic assets of the community and the philosophical viewpoints of its representa-tives determine the manner in which that instruction is meted out—whether it transmits academic essentials or adapts itself to dynamic changes in a to-tal social organism.

Depending upon their values, social status, and aspirations, parents send their young children to various types of schools—nursery or preschool groups, kindergartens, and private, parochial, or public elementary schools. In spite of wide variations among the schools in a particular category, ob-servers have cited significant effects on the social development of children at each age level.

There is little doubt that within the school milieu the teacher has the greatest influence on the subsequent adjustments of children. By the charac-teristic manner in which she controls a class and interrelates the individual child with his environment, by her standards, attitudes, and values, by her general behavior and personality, she plays a role in the social order which leaves profound and lasting impressions on the children in her classroom. For this reason, parents and educators attempt to select well-trained teach-ers from the ranks of well-integrated personalities.

QUESTIONS AND PROBLEMS

1. Discuss the ways in which play activities assist children in making social adjustments.
2. Do you think that prekindergarten education should be compulsory? Why or why not?
3. What would be some of the problems faced by a first-grade teacher in a school that has no kindergarten?
4. List some elementary schools you are familiar with. Explain how they are similar and how they differ.
5. The educational-aid policies of Lyndon Johnson are based on the principle that the poorest school districts should receive the greatest monetary support.

The educational policy of James Conant maintains that the poorest (underprivileged) students should have the best teachers rather than the inexperienced ones. Discuss the social implications of these "most to the least, best to the worst" policies from the standpoint of your own agreement or disagreement with them.

6. How can the school help children develop interest in academic study?
7. What interests do you have that you can trace directly to the influence of a particular teacher?
8. What are the personal characteristics of the teachers you liked the most? Of those you disliked?
9. List the child behavior problems you think teachers encounter in schools located in a section which is lower class. Which of these problems do you think will also be encountered by teachers who work in a school where the patrons are largely middle-class children?
10. List examples of child behavior which you feel are indicative of social maladjustment. Which do you consider are the most serious?

SELECTED READINGS

BERNARD, HAROLD W., *Human Development in Western Culture*, 2nd ed. Boston: Allyn and Bacon, 1966. Ch. 13.

CONANT, JAMES B., *Slums and Suburbs*. McGraw-Hill, 1961.

DINKMEYER, DON C., *Child Development: The Emerging Self*. Englewood Cliffs, N.J.: Prentice-Hall, 1965. Ch. 12.

HAVIGHURST, ROBERT J., and BERNICE L. NEUGARTEN, *Society and Education,* 2nd ed. Boston: Allyn and Bacon, 1962.

HUTT, MAX L., and ROBERT G. GIBBY, *The Child: Development and Adjustment*. Boston: Allyn and Bacon, 1959. Ch. 7.

MARTIN, WILLIAM E., and CELIA B. STENDLER, *Child Behavior and Development*. Harcourt, Brace, 1959. Ch. 11.

SMITH, HENRY P., *Psychology in Teaching*, 2nd ed. Englewood Cliffs, N.J.: Prentice-Hall, 1962. Ch. 4.

STONE, L. JOSEPH, and JOSEPH CHURCH, *Childhood and Adolescence*. Random House, 1957. Ch. 9.

THORPE, LOUIS P., *Child Psychology and Development*, 3rd ed. The Ronald Press, 1962. Ch. 11.

YOUNG, KIMBALL, Social roles of teachers in the classroom, in *Education and the Social Order* (Blaine E. Mercer and Edwin R. Carr, eds.). Rinehart (now Holt, Rinehart and Winston), 1957. Chs. 1, 4.

REFERENCES

ACEI: *What Are Kindergartens For?* (pamphlet). Washington, D.C.: Association for Childhood Education International, n.d.

AMATORA, S. MARY, Can elementary school children discriminate certain traits in their teachers? *Child Development*, 1952, 23, 75–80.

AMATORA, S. MARY, School interests in later childhood, *Education*, 1960, 81, 32–37.

ANDERSON, HAROLD H., JOSEPH B. BREWER, and MARY F. REED, Studies in teachers' classroom personalities, *Applied Psychology Monographs*, 1946, No. 11.

ASCH, SOLOMON, Opinions and social pressure, *Scientific American* (November 1955), *193*, No. 5, 31–35.

AUSUBEL, D. P., F. DEWIT, B. GOLDEN, and S. H. SCHPOONT, Prestige suggestion in children's art preferences, *The Journal of Genetic Psychology*, 1956, *89*, 85–93.

BARRON, FRANK, The psychology of imagination, *Scientific American* (September 1958), *199*, No. 3, 150–166.

BEILIN, HARRY, Teachers' and clinicians' attitudes toward the behavior problems of children: a reappraisal, *Child Development*, 1959, *30*, 9–25.

BERNARD, HAROLD W., *Human Development in Western Culture*, 2nd ed. Boston: Allyn and Bacon, 1966, p. 410.

BLEDSOE, JOSEPH C., and KARL C. GARRISON, *The Self Concepts of Elementary School Children in Relation to Their Academic Achievement, Intelligence, Interests, and Manifest Anxiety.* Cooperative Research Project No. 1008, United States Office of Education. College of Education, University of Georgia, 1962.

BRUNER, JEROME, quoted. See Silberman, 1964, p. 39.

CHASE, W. LINWOOD, and GILBERT M. WILSON, Preference studies in elementary school social studies, *Journal of Education*, 1958, *140*, No. 4, p. 3.

CONANT, JAMES B., *Slums and Suburbs.* McGraw-Hill, 1961, p. 2.

DEUTSCH, MARTIN, Social and psychological perspectives on the development of the disadvantaged learner, *Journal of Negro Education*, 1964, *33*, 232–244.

DEUTSCH, MARTIN, The role of social class in language development and cognition, *American Journal of Orthopsychiatry*, 1965, *35*, 78–88.

ELKISH, P., Significant relationships between the human figure and the machine in the drawings of boys, *American Journal of Orthopsychiatry*, 1952, 22, 79–85.

GOODENOUGH, FLORENCE, and DALE B. HARRIS, Studies in the psychology of children's drawings. II. 1928–1949, *Psychological Bulletin*, 1950, 47, 369–433.

GRIEDER, CALVIN, TRUMAN M. PIERCE, and WILLIAM E. ROSENSTENGEL, *Public School Administration*, 2nd ed. The Ronald Press, 1961.

GRIFFITHS, W., *Behavior Difficulties of Children as Perceived and Judged by Parents, Teachers, and Children Themselves.* Minneapolis: University of Minnesota Press, 1952.

HALL-QUEST, ALFRED L., Curriculum, in *Collier's Encyclopedia*, 1965a, 7, 578.

HALL-QUEST, ALFRED L., Kindergarten, in *Collier's Encyclopedia*, 1965b, *11*, 579.

HARLOW, HARRY F., and MARGARET KUENNE HARLOW, Social deprivation in monkeys, *Scientific American* (November 1962), *207*, No. 5, 136–146.

HAVIGHURST, ROBERT J., and BERNICE L. NEUGARTEN, *Society and Education*, 2nd ed. Boston: Allyn and Bacon, 1962.

HECHINGER, GRACE, "Who's For Nursery School?" in *The New York Times Magazine* (March 1, 1964), pp. 61, 63.

HYMES, JAMES L., JR., The beginning of education, in *Our Children Today* (Sidonie Gruenberg, ed.). Viking Press, 1952, pp. 69–80.

IPA: *Information Please Almanac.* Simon and Schuster, 1964, p. 346.

JACKSON, JOSEPH, The effect of classroom organization and guidance practice upon the personality adjustment and academic growth of students, *The Journal of Genetic Psychology*, 1953, 83, 159–170.

JERSILD, ARTHUR T., *Child Psychology*, 5th ed. Englewood Cliffs, N.J.: Prentice-Hall, 1960.

JOHN, VERA P., The intellectual development of slum children: some preliminary findings, *American Journal of Orthopsychiatry*, 1963, 33, 813–822.

KANDEL, I. L., Theories of education, in *Collier's Encyclopedia*, 1954, 7, 64–68.

KELLY, RICHARD, and M. W. STEPHENS, Comparison of different patterns of social reinforcement in children's operant learning, *Journal of Comparative and Physiological Psychology*, 1964, 57, 294–296.

LAMBERT, ASAEL C., Education in the United States, in *Collier's Encyclopedia*, 1954, 7, 79–87.

LEEDS, CARROLL H., and WALTER W. COOK, The construction and differential value of a scale for determining teacher-pupil attitudes, *Journal of Experimental Education*, 1947, 16, 149–159.

LEONARD, GEORGE B., The truth about the teacher crisis, in *The Great Debate: Our Schools in Crisis* (Cecil Winfield Scott, Clyde M. Hill, and Hobart W. Burns, eds.). Englewood Cliffs, N.J.: Prentice-Hall, 1959, pp. 121–127.

LIPPITT, RONALD, *An Analysis of Group Reaction to Three Types of Experimentally Created Social Climates.* Ph.D. Thesis, State University of Iowa, 1940*a*.

LIPPITT, RONALD, An experimental study of the effect of democratic and authoritarian group atmospheres, *University of Iowa Studies in Child Welfare*, 1940*b*, 16, No. 3, 43–195.

MCKEACHIE, WILBERT J., Individual conformity to attitudes of classroom group, *The Journal of Abnormal and Social Psychology*, 1954, 49, 282–289.

MENNINGER, KARL A., *The Human Mind*, 3rd ed. Alfred A. Knopf, 1961, p. 425.

MERRY, F. K., and R. V. MERRY, *The First Two Decades of Life.* Harper, 1950.

MILNER, ESTHER, A study of the relationship between reading readiness in grade one school children and patterns of parent-child interaction, *Child Development*, 1951, 22, 95–112.

NEA: Educational Policies Commission, *Moral and Spiritual Values in the Public Schools.* Washington, D.C.: National Education Association, 1951, pp. 18–30.

NEA: Educational Policies Commission, *An Essay on Quality in Public Education.* Washington, D.C.: National Education Association, 1959, booklet, pp. 31.

NEA: Educational Policies Commission, *The Central Purpose of American Education.* Washington, D.C.: National Education Association, 1961, booklet, pp. 21.

NKA: National Kindergarten Association, *About Kindergartens*, pamphlet. National Kindergarten Association, n.d., p. 3.

OJEMANN, RALPH H., EUGENE E. LEVITT, WILLIAM H. LYLE, JR., and MAXINE F. WHITESIDE, The effects of a "causal" teacher-training program and certain curricular changes on grade school children, *Journal of Experimental Education*, 1955, 24, 95–114.

OLSON, W. C., and B. O. HUGHES, Subsequent growth of children with and without nursery-school experience, in *Intelligence: Its Nature and Nurture*, Thirty-ninth Yearbook, National Society for the Study of Education, Part II, 1940, pp. 237–244.

PERKINS, HUGH V., Teachers' and peers' perceptions of children's self-concepts, *Child Development*, 1958, 29, 203–220; and Factors influencing change in children's self-concepts, *same source*, pp. 221–230.

READ, KATHERINE H., *The Nursery School.* Philadelphia: Saunders, 1955, pp. 77–78.

RESNICK, JOSEPH, Classroom maladjustment can be reduced, *Educational Administration and Supervision*, 1954, 40, 489–493.

SCHRUPP, MANFRED H., and CLAYTON M. GJERDE, Teacher growth in attitudes toward behavior problems of children, *The Journal of Educational Psychology*, 1953, *44*, 203–214.

SILBERMAN, CHARLES E., Give slum children a chance, *Harper's* Magazine (May 1964), pp. 37–42.

SIMS, VERNER M., The social-class affiliation of a group of public school teachers, *The School Review*, 1951, *59*, 331–338.

SKEELS, H. M., R. UPDEGRAFF, B. L. WELLMAN, and H. M. WILLIAMS, *A Study of Environmental Stimulation: An Orphanage Preschool Project*. University of Iowa Studies in Child Welfare, *15*, No. 4. Iowa City: University of Iowa Press, 1938.

SLOBETZ, FRANK, How elementary-school teachers meet selected school situations, *The Journal of Educational Psychology*, 1951, *42*, 339–356.

SOLOMAN, DANIEL, W. E. BEZDEK, and LARRY ROSENBERG, Dimensions of teacher behavior, *Journal of Experimental Education*, 1964, *33*, 23–40.

SPARKS, JACK N., Teachers' attitudes toward the behavior problems of children, *The Journal of Educational Psychology*, 1952, *43*, 284–291.

STENDLER, CELIA B., How well do elementary-school teachers understand child behavior? *The Journal of Educational Psychology*, 1949, *40*, 489–498.

STENDLER, CELIA B., and NORMAN YOUNG, The impact of beginning first grade upon socialization as reported by mothers, *Child Development*, 1950, *21*, 241–260.

SULLIVAN, WALTER, Animal talk, *The New York Times* (January 3, 1965), p. 6E.

THOMPSON, G. G., The social and emotional development of preschool children under two types of educational program, *Psychological Monographs*, 1944, *56*, No. 5.

TIME (November 27, 1964), p. 73.

TORGOFF, IRVING, Personality and social development: societal influences, *Review of Educational Research*, December 1961, *31*, No. 5, 475–486.

ULLMANN, C. A., *Identification of Maladjusted School Children*, rev. ed. Public Health Monograph, No. 7. Washington, D.C.: Government Printing Office, 1957.

VAN ALSTYNE, DOROTHY, and LABERTA A. HATTWICK, A follow-up study of the behavior of nursery school children, *Child Development*, 1939, *10*, 43–72.

WAHLQUIST, JOHN T., Rural education, in *Collier's Encyclopedia*, 1954, *17*, 194–197.

WINTERBOTTOM, M. R., *The Relation of Childhood Training in Independence to Achievement and Motivation*. Ph.D. Thesis, University of Michigan, 1953.

T H I R T E E N

Children With

Adjustment Problems

The very young child lacks the cortical development, experience, accurate information, and special knowledge necessary for coping with his emotional and social environment. Through maturation and learning, he acquires these essentials in varying degrees, and in his own individual, usually immature, manner, he attempts to adjust his potentially dangerous or destructive impulses to the demands and standards of his social milieu. Conflict, frustration, tension, disappointment, and failure are normal occurrences. No vigorous, fun-loving, curious, and adventuresome child can live and grow without facing them. Nor would it be good for him if he could. To a certain degree, adjustment problems are normal *and* desirable.

However, generally when a person speaks of "adjustment problems," he refers to those difficulties which threaten an individual's ability to master future challenges and which are of such a degree of seriousness that they are not readily resolved. This concept, if not semantically correct, is certainly practical and justifiable as a point of distinguishing problems that warrant more than passing attention. In the present context, the phrase "adjustment problems" refers to those behavior difficulties which are intense or chronic enough to set a child apart from the majority of his age-mates. The child with adjustment problems is, therefore, one of that minority* who seriously disrupts the continuity of group processes around him.

---

* Vaughan (1961) estimates that some ten per cent of the child population is in need of professional help for maladjustment.

At one time children who had trouble adjusting to life situations were referred to as problem children, a terminology which seemed to place all the blame on the child. However, evidence from scientific research has made it clear that adjustment results from *learning* through meaningful, active experiences in a variety of situations; and, of course, the bulk of these external agents are controlled by adults. They can unwittingly teach a child ineffective ways of adjusting as well as effective ways; they can curtail his experiences, his expansiveness, and thus foster his destructiveness; they can, singly or as a total society, express unrealistic demands and standards. Lawrence Kubie (1952, pp. 139–140) has written:

> As the child by about the eighth month begins to acquire the ability to feel and primitively to express disappointment, to discriminate between known adults and strangers, and to express his feelings through his voice, through the movements of his trunk and limbs, and through the expulsion of his body products, these controls make possible the first effective expression of aggressive feelings toward the outside world. Here he encounters for the first time the resistance of the greater forces of the adult and inanimate world. They can oppose him, force their will on him, and hurt him. This rouses his anger; and as his rage mounts, his internal conflicts increase until nightmares are born in him. What we call "self-control" in the young child becomes an aggressive act toward himself, which is expressed partly as a passive gesture of submission out of love for some adult, and partly out of fear. If the love component in the relationship is too seriously distorted under the influence of the terror, then the aggressive reaction becomes excessive and at the same time is driven underground. It may take the form of blindly compulsive rebellion, of diffuse and lasting bitterness, or of excessive inhibition of elementary physiological functions. It may inhibit the development of all motor activities of speech. Thus primary aggression pendulates between internal and external targets.
>
> The acquisition of positive, self-assertive, commanding, and demanding attitudes in the first two years of human life is an essential step in the development of every child. Aggression must occur in this primary sense; in which *ad* means *forward, ahead;* and *gress* means to *move.* Otherwise there would be no possibility of either physical survival or psychological development.
>
> A point soon comes, however, in which these forward-moving, self-serving, aggressive impulses bring the child into a cumulative series of conflicts, partly within himself and partly with external realities. This is the beginning of a critical new phase, because out of those conflicts, unresolved but rendered unconscious through repression, begins a neurotic distortion of human aggression. These conflicts arise about everything which the toddler has to learn to do for himself. They arise merely about the process of bodily growth, about the fundamental processes of eating, sleeping, and toilet functions, and in the competitive struggle for the love of parents.

Although Kubie emphasizes the effects of adult-controlled stimuli, he also implies that the individual's heredity is not to be discounted. Those persons who have attempted to place most of the blame for children's behavioral disturbances on the family, especially on the mother, have failed to take into consideration the individuality of the child's reaction pattern. As was pointed out in Chapter IX in connection with discipline, parental behavior which is considered undesirable for one child may be constructive and desirable for another. Chess, Thomas, and Birch (1959), who investigated eighty-five children in a longitudinal study of behavioral responses, were able to analyze reaction patterns in terms of nine categories:

1. Activity—Passivity
2. Regularity—Irregularity
3. Intense Reactor—Mild Reactor
4. Approacher—Withdrawer
5. Adaptive—Nonadaptive
6. High Threshold—Low Threshold
7. Positive Mood—Negative Mood
8. Selective—Nonselective
9. Distractibility—Nondistractibility

In other words, as Rand and her associates (1953, p. 392) have pointed out:

> . . . Some personalities absorb the emotional repercussions of new learning in their stride, showing, in periods of strain, little more maladjustment than slight extra fatigue. Other personalities take each of the new learnings required by life so hard that they seem constantly upset emotionally. Such children require a longer time in which to integrate or stabilize learnings before new demands are made upon them. Almost every person has some areas of learning in which integration comes more easily than in others.

Attempts to assign blame for maladjustments, then, are relatively academic and serve only to illustrate once again the inseparableness of environmental and hereditary operations. Studying the maladjusted children themselves, however, has more useful purposes. For one, much can be learned about meeting the needs of all children from a study of those whose needs have not been met. For another, the child with problems merits, like others, an acceptance and understanding that will reduce the hazards which he is unable to master without help.

One further introductory note: Babies and children are gratifyingly and surprisingly tough. To make them into children with adjustment problems requires rejection, condemnation, and mishandling in considerable amounts. Therefore, needless to say, once a child has learned a maladaptive kind of behavior, time, effort, and understanding in considerable amounts must go into reconditioning or re-teaching him.

CLASSIFICATIONS OF ADJUSTMENT PROBLEMS

Classification by Levels

Buhler and her associates (1952) have suggested a three-level classification of adjustment problems. Level one consists of problems that can be dealt with on a behavioral level; i.e., successful correction of the behavior can be accomplished without understanding the causes. The child is reprimanded, told to stop, or advised to substitute an approved behavior.

Level two problems may involve the same kind of behavior as level one, but the problems are more serious because the behavior is repetitious. Repeated, unacceptable behavior is indicative of disturbances deeper and more chronic than those that create the tension being released by the one behavior episode at level one. Thus, the child who refuses to eat on a specific occasion presents a less serious problem than the one who refuses routinely. Nor is the normally courteous pupil who speaks impudently once in the same category as the pupil who seldom acts with respect.

A single serious disturbance may also be included at level two. A two-year-old, the youngest of four children by several years, was left with friends while his parents and siblings went on a long weekend trip. He sat for three days, clutching his teddy bear, without playing, crying, or talking; and he ate only one meal. As was clearly evident, he sorely missed his doting and affectionate family. The one episode was serious enough to indicate that the child could be "farmed out" again only at the risk of warping his personality.

Level two problems may also be indicated by a succession of different disturbing behaviors—restlessness on one occasion, regression to soiling or wetting on another, and alternations between aggressive and withdrawal behaviors at still other times. These behaviors can, however, be reduced or eradicated by specific environmental changes or by altering child-rearing or teaching methods.

Level three problems are serious or chronic enough that professional intervention is essential to their remediation. The actual behaviors may be the same or quite similar to those shown at levels one and two but their persistence is much greater. Typically, a restructuring of the child's relationship with his parents is required, in which case the parents should receive therapy with or parallel to that given the child.

The case of a boy seen at an out-patient psychiatric clinic can serve to illustrate a level three problem. At fourteen, the boy appeared to be smaller than the average ten-year-old, except for his more mature facial features. His response to questions was apathetic and hesitant. Asked why he had been brought to the clinic he at first pretended he did not know and then said, "I guess it's for messing around with gasoline." The questioner learned that whenever the boy could get hold of gasoline, cleaning fluid, or paint thinner he drank it. This action, of course, worried his grandmother, who would verbally and physically attack him and then "protect" him by locking him in any available room or closet. Her hostility toward the boy was evident in both the manner and wording of her responses. Furthermore, the father had, a year after the child was born, abandoned him and his mother; three years later, the mother went her independent way. The ultimate result was a boy who was suspicious of people and thought so little of himself that he simply shrugged and *smiled* when the psychiatrist suggested that by drinking gasoline a person could kill himself. Because careful supervision of the boy in his home setting while his grandmother received treatment (if she would consent—and she was not convinced that it was really her problem or business) was a course thought to be fraught with danger, custodial treatment was the recommended course.

Levels of problems cannot be clearly distinguished. The boy who drank gasoline could just as easily have responded to his problems by exaggerated aggressive tendencies which would make him a threat to his peers rather than to himself. In contrast, a less aggressive child who shoves and grabs now and then may be less of a problem to his peers than he is to his embarrassed parents. The temporary absence of the two-year-old's family is one point in a continuum of behaviors that ends with permanent abandonment, as in the case of the gasoline drinker. Thus, behaviors are distinguishable on levels in terms of degrees rather than kind—picky eaters and children who resist going to bed may be on the low end of the self-destruction continuum that includes drinking gasoline at the other.

Classification of levels is particularly helpful in suggesting treatment. Level one problems can be treated by correcting the behavior—verbally establishing some do's and don'ts. Level two requires the manipulation of the environment by teachers, parents, and other key persons. Level three problems are serious enough to require psychiatric or psychological intervention.

Classification by Types

Adjustment problems may be classified by the general pattern of behavior without regard for the degree of seriousness; i.e., each group could include levels one, two, and three problems (Griffiths, 1952). This classification, also, has the weakness of overlapping: Aggression may merge with withdrawal as is the case of aggression against oneself, where one "gets even" by self-destruction—the ultimate in withdrawal. The same cause may eventuate in the types of responses indicated in the following pages.

Aggressive responses.   When the child encounters need deprivation or frustration he may strike back either directly or obliquely at persons or objects around him; he may kick his mother, his toys, or his pet cat. Aggression is probably the most common and noticeable of adjustment problems because of the disruption it creates in the lives of others. It may run the gamut from talking back, throwing things, and breaking toys to vandalism and the use of lethal weapons.

Although aggression is quite irritating to those around the offender, it is, at least in a clinical sense, a more fortunate response to frustration than are withdrawal and psychosomatic disturbances. The aggressive child has not given up the battle to bring about adjustment, although his mode of solution will, in the long run, not be productive. Furthermore, his responses are generally overt, and redirecting extroverted behavior is easier than reversing introvertive responses (such as withdrawal) and then providing direction.

Despite a long history, the use of punishment and retaliation for aggressive wrongdoing finds no justification, even at the adult level, in terms of results (Hollister, 1962). The fallacy of punishment is that it not only provides the child with no clues to a better attack on life's problems but also runs the danger of forcing him to "bottle up" his emotions wherein they will ferment and subsequently be given an even more violent release. Kubie (1952, p. 146) cites the risks and offers a prescription:

> The bitterness, the hatred, the envy, and the jealousies of the earliest years can rarely be wholly eradicated if we wait to begin their eradication until many years after the original cause has disappeared. If we are ever to lessen the neurotic distortions of human aggression, then it seems clear that the anger must be allowed and encouraged to express itself in early childhood, not in blindly destructive acts but in words, so as to keep it on the highest level of conscious awareness. Furthermore, such conscious ventilation of feelings must be encouraged in the very situations in which they have arisen, and toward those adults and children who have been either the active or the innocent sources of the feelings. Only in this way can we lessen the burden of unconscious aggression that every human being carries from infancy to the grave. Therefore as parents, educators, pediatricians, teachers, clergymen, or psychiatrists, we must dedicate ourselves to the Fifth Freedom—the child's Freedom and Right to Feel, and to know what he feels by helping him make his feelings articulate in words. Thus his conflicts and confusions and misconceptions can be corrected as they arise, instead of being subjected to such repression that they must be dealt with entirely in the dark of the unconscious. Only in this way can we avoid the process of neurotic distortion which turns normal aggressiveness into a blind, insatiable, destructive force.

Kubie's advice accords with the postulations of Dollard and his associates (1939), who propose the hypothesis that frustration always leads to some form of aggression. While punishment or the threat of punishment may immediately inhibit the revelation of frustration, it does not remove or mitigate the source. Thus, the child with adjustment problems of the aggressive type cannot be substantially helped at the behavioral level. Causes must be discovered, analyzed, and remedied.

Near-delinquent behavior. The concept of delinquency is an extremely complex one involving place, time, age, seriousness, frequency, and individual personality* (Kvaraceus, 1954; Kvaraceus and others, 1959). Certain manifestations in early childhood behavior are forerunners to increasingly disturbing and more serious misbehavior at a later age. Among the symptomatic behaviors must be included disinterest in school work (despite ability for doing it), tardiness and truancy, resistance to authority, and inability to get along with parents, siblings, peers, and teachers. The children who chronically reveal these behaviors are unhappy, insecure, worried, and critical of others.

Detection of the potential delinquent is complicated by the fact that well-adjusted, exuberant, and experimental-minded children show these symptomatic behaviors *occasionally*; and, of course, there are always those about whom adults should be concerned who are between the seriously disturbed and the merely exuberant. Resolution of the dilemma may be approached by the use of formal instruments such as the *Delinquency Proneness Scale* and the *Haggerty-Olson-Wickman Behavior Rating Scales*. Such instruments must be cautiously used because they are subject to the usual limitations of inventories and observational records (Rothney, *et al.*, 1959). In addition, children sometimes do change their patterns of response and "straighten up and fly right." To identify a youngster as being difficult or as a problem child, and to let it be known to him by some careless or unthinking adult, may cause an insecure child to give up his struggle for a kind of equilibrium (which misbehavior is) and live out the expectation—that is, to continue to misbehave in accordance with what adults expect from a so-called problem child. If the instruments are regarded as tentative and suggestive, they will be more likely to direct attention to the environmenal factors that are creating the problem behavior. Moreover, consideration must be given to the fact that two children, both undergoing like amounts of stress, may differ markedly in overt behavior (Kraus, 1956). One appears calm and confident but the other is explosive and defensive.

---

* Carr (1954) states:
    In the United States, the laws generally define a juvenile delinquent as any child under a given age (14 in a few states, 15 to 18 in others, 21 in Arkansas and California) who violates any local ordinance or state or Federal law, or whose behavior, leisure-time associations, or living conditions are such as to indicate the need for public supervision.
He further cites many of the investigators who have traced the causes of delinquency to three sets of factors: "(1) personality maladjustments; (2) antisocial influences, or 'deviation pressures,' in the environment; and (3) various combinations of these two."

A further difficulty in classifying behavior lies in its relation to environmental setting. Thus, the Gluecks (1952) have built a series of predictive weights for probability of delinquency based largely on environmental factors, which they narrowed to five: family cohesiveness, paternal discipline, maternal supervision, and paternal and maternal affection. Such an emphasis directs attention to where it should be—on causes. These causes of delinquency, to a remarkable if not frightening extent, turn out to be lower social class characteristics. (See pages 49–51.) Broken families (lack of cohesiveness), for instance, are *much more frequent* in the lower classes (Havighurst and Neugarten, 1962).

Near-delinquent behavior is an individual's response to deprivation of needs. Need deprivation must be remedied by altering situations so that greater need satisfaction may be obtained, a large task which means seeking for slow improvement in the total environment—homes, neighborhoods, schools. The individual's perception of and response to his situation cannot be ignored, because the first deviant behaviors usually alienate key adults, who then respond with irritation and rejection, thereby intensifying the child's abortive behaviors. For example, a boy may respond directly to the very real situation of poverty by stealing money—a natural, though socially unacceptable, response. If, because of this behavior, his parents become irritable and rejectant, the boy may continue to steal because he unconsciously resents feeling unwanted. Stealing, then, becomes not a natural response to a real situation but a neurotic response to emotional imbalance. The boy's problem, and therefore his rehabilitation, is much more complicated.

Social withdrawal. Some years ago Wickman demonstrated that teachers regarded lying, stealing, and fighting as being the most serious kinds of behavior. On the other hand, child specialists, psychologists, and psychiatrists viewed shyness, recessiveness, and social withdrawal as being those behaviors of greatest concern (Wickman, 1928). Today, the views of teachers and psychiatrists are in closer accord, but teachers have the practical difficulty of dealing with the immediate and disconcerting overt behavior and being thankful for the shy, quiet, and retiring pupil (Beilin, 1959; Hunter, 1957).

The reason for the greater concern of child specialists for withdrawing behaviors is of interest to the student of child psychology. The aggressive child is (1) continuing his battle for recognition and autonomy and (2) his behavior so disturbs others that he calls attention to himself and is recognized—even if in an unfavorable manner. The withdrawn child, on the other hand, has given up the struggle—he has shut himself in his own closet; and, if he is to be helped, the helper must not only get him out into the light of an interactive society but also aid him in establishing acceptable overt responses. The first part of the process alone requires a great deal of patience and understanding on the part of the adult lest the social situations force the fearful, shy child into deeper retreats. Secondly, the withdrawn child is likely to be overlooked and his injuries remain to fester and intensify. At best, the personality that habitually retreats from situations to which it cannot adjust itself may develop undesirable character traits such as suspiciousness, timidity, fearfulness and anxiety. Or, the flights "may appear as such dodges as inefficiency, 'passing the buck,' refusal to accept responsibility, and depending upon luck, tricks, routine, or rules of thumb instead of intelligent solutions" (Menninger, 1961, p. 33).

Although the causes of withdrawal cannot be differentiated sharply from those generating the more overt and immediately disturbing behaviors, some tendencies are worth noting. Parents of withdrawn boys often are rejecting; they discourage both aggressive and dependent behavior; and their forms of punishment are guilt-producing (blaming, censoring, and belittling) rather than punitive (Bandura, 1960).

There is some indication that body build may influence the response to stress. Stocky, heavy boys show more self-confidence and aggressive behavior than boys who are below average in size and muscular development (Davidson, *et al.*, 1957). Children who engage excessively in wishful thinking and daydreaming (autistic thinking) often have fathers whose personality problems are so serious that they are unable to assume normal parental functions (Eisenberg, 1957).

There is no single simple explanation for withdrawal. An explanation that would include most cases would be low self-regard, frequently caused by rejection or belittling treatment by parents. Simply inviting such a child to play more with his peers or encouraging him to speak up in class is not enough. He needs to have steady, continuing assurance that he is liked and accepted. Recognition of, and praise for, minor manifestations of outgoing behavior may help him build a stronger self-concept. Obviously, above all, he needs love and time to find self-confidence.

Psychosomatic Disturbances

In this text frequent note has been made of the fact that wide variations exist in individual reaction patterns. Some of these patterns fall into a category referred to as the "intrapsychic level." For example, a person under stress may characteristically become hypertensive. No matter what adjustment is required or what tension-producing stimulus is met, such an individual tends to react inwardly, with a rise in blood pressure, increased pulse rate, flushing or blanching, and similar evidences of organic imbalance. For those persons who react to conflict on this inner level, chronic stress or persistent maladjustment often lead to symptoms of physical illness, to an aggravation of a physiological weakness which produces organic malfunctioning and disease, or to a dysfunction in the autonomic nervous system which constitutes a physical disease. From one-third to one-half of all the patients seen by general practitioners suffer "more conspicuously from emotional pathology than from physical pathology" (Menninger, 1961, p. 36; see also Krapf and Moser, 1962).

Let us consider briefly the distinctions between the three groupings of "psychosomatic" disturbances.

Symptoms of physical illness. Disturbed individuals may experience severe chest pains, headaches, paralysis, or indigestion (among other complaints), which, although disabling, disappear when the stressful situation is resolved. This is not to say that these patients are not ill. They are. Chest pain is a reality to be dealt with whether it is caused by worry or a heart attack; paralysis of the lower limbs means crutches or a wheel chair to both the emotionally disturbed individual and the accident victim. The difference lies in the treatment. When no physical basis exists for a symptom, the physician attends to his patient's psychological health.

Aggravation of a physiological weakness. The particular manner in which psychological stress shows itself in somatic symptoms is believed to be a matter of the weakest organ in the system (Lazarus, 1961). This is often in the digestive system. Obesity is sometimes a symptom of digestive-system malfunction caused by psychological factors. (See pages 117–18.) The respiratory system is also a common center for psychosomatic illness, as has been noted by Miller and Baruch (1956). Chronic stress is dangerous to the person subject to epileptic seizures; high blood pressure caused by emotional upsets may considerably shorten the life-span of the individual with a heart defect. In treating an individual with tendencies toward specific physical malfunctioning, the physician attempts to control his patient's health by ensuring his mental-emotional well-being.

Dysfunction in the autonomic nervous system. Migraine, asthma, and stomach ulcers are disorders falling within this category. Both the etiology and the therapy of such illnesses are tied to psychological factors. The physician treats the illness with medication and/or surgery *and* attempts to control its recurrence and severity through advice concerning the emotional climate in which the patient lives. Cases of allergy, for instance, are often described in terms of rejection, threats, anxieties, and affect hungers which characterize the milieu of children suffering from this form of psychosomatic disorder.

Among children, psychosomatic troubles are common. In some cases, the illness becomes a form of defense against environmental conditions. Guilt and anxiety may be relieved through sickness, a need for dependence and attention may be satisfied, even an unconscious desire for punishment may be satisfied by pain or by undergoing surgery (Thorpe, 1962). As Menninger (1961, p. 37) has stated:

> ... The unconscious wish to be sick may be expressed in mental symptoms, but it is very frequently expressed in physical symptoms and actual physical diseases. Such a wish is, of course, "abnormal," but that does not mean that it is illogical or reprehensible. It is the only thing that some personalities can do because of previous experiences and pre-existing drives, conflicts, fears, and frustrations.

Referral Problems

The behavior problems encountered in child guidance clinics furnish a guide to the incidence of behavior disorders and to the varieties of child behavior patterns regarded as undesirable in our culture. Gilbert (1957) reported the results of a survey of referrals to two types of child guidance clinics—two community orthopsychiatry clinics and two school psychoeducational clinics, or guidance bureaus. The composite distribution of ten referral-problem categories, broken down by age and sex, is shown in Table XIII-1. Although the subjects are often referred for more than one reason, the leading cause for referral to school clinics was academic difficulties; to community clinics, aggressive and antisocial behavior. In all age groups and for all problem categories, more boys than girls are referred for guidance, the overall ratio being about 2.5 to 1.

SYMPTOMS OF MALADJUSTMENT

Children with adjustment problems, whether the manifestations are in terms of social or somatic disturbances, are giving evidence that their needs are not being met. Those needs, as well as the determinants and symptoms of emotionally disturbed and socially maladjusted behavior, fall into three integrated and overlapping categories: biological, psychological, and social. Psychologists and psychiatrists have had to force a separation of the three categories in order to understand and effectively treat the pathological behavior pattern. They must decide first whether the disturbed behavior results from chronic nutritional deficiency or from emotional deprivation during the period of infancy and early childhood. Obviously, the treatment in each case is quite different. On the other hand, such a separation of causes sometimes lulls the casual investigator into assigning a single causative factor to the maladjustment, thus failing to take into account all of the forces affecting the child.

Recognizing symptoms and determining causes is further complicated by the fact that children do not react in the same manner to the same factors;

Table XIII-1 Composite Distribution of "Referral Problems" in Four Metropolitan Child Guidance Centers (N = 2,500 Children; Average 1.9 Complaints per Child) (Gilbert, p. 40)

Referral Problems	under 6 M	under 6 F	6 to 10 M	6 to 10 F	10 to 14 M	10 to 14 F	14 to 18 M	14 to 18 F	All Ages M	All Ages F	All Ages Total	Total as % of N	Percent of all cases in 2 community clinics	in 2 school clinics
Academic Difficulties	3	0	358	126	322	117	146	54	829	297	1,126	45	27	56
Mental Retardation	16	9	166	94	180	123	50	35	412	261	673	27	6	40
Aggressive and Anti-Social Behavior	45	12	242	65	192	39	115	45	594	161	755	30	45	20
Passive, Withdrawn, Asocial Behavior	38	15	174	74	110	50	60	25	382	164	546	22	32	14
Emotional Instability and Anxiety Symptoms	45	16	205	86	108	46	49	25	407	173	580	23	34	16
Hyperactivity and Motor Symptoms	24	12	139	59	69	24	20	5	252	100	352	14	22	8
Sexual Behavior Problems	6	1	12	10	13	6	6	6	37	23	60	2½	4	1
Toilet Training	27	7	50	25	36	14	0	2	113	48	161	6½	12	1
Speech Defects	25	9	62	19	26	9	10	1	123	38	161	6½	6	7
Miscellaneous	14	17	90	38	71	51	34	29	209	135	344	14	20	9

and identical symptoms may arise for different reasons. Rejectant parents, for example, may find that one of their children is withdrawn, another is aggressive, a third has a persistent bed-wetting problem, and a fourth is asthmatic. Likewise, a teacher may observe four instances of excessive crying amongst her pupils, yet subsequently discover that one child is overly dependent and emotionally immature, the second is suffering from fatigue, the third is abnormally fearful of failing, and the fourth has a glandular imbalance.

Some cases of maladjustment arise as a result of needs that the teacher and school situation can easily satisfy, while others may require the services of a psychiatric social worker, a clinical psychologist, or a psychiatrist. There are many signs indicative of emotional and social maladjustments, but they are so interrelated that no clear-cut classification can be presented, although different investigators have classified them in various ways.* The authors of this text have attempted a three-fold classification involving (a) physical signs, (b) behavior deviations, and (c) emotional manifestations. These are presented in Table XIII-2.

Aggression as Symptomatic

Among psychologists there seems to be agreement that aggression is a response to frustration. One form of the response commonly found among children is belligerency. In the small child, it often appears in temper tantrums. When a toy is taken from a two-year-old, he is likely to resort to crying, kicking, biting, or some other form of aggressive behavior, which becomes a bad habit if the child is not trained to respond otherwise. Such anger responses during childhood—if frequent—may be associated with illness, sleep disturbances, constipation, and certain psychosomatic reactions, notably gastrointestinal.

The child who fails is frustrated in his desire to achieve. The force of the "norm" is one of the most important sources for feelings of insecurity, resulting from failure. These feelings, which may be accomplished by violent outbursts, are often encountered by those people who work with mentally retarded and brain-damaged children. Goldstein (1939) observed in his work with brain-injured soldiers that temper outbursts frequently occurred in connection with frustrations, an observation that also lends support to Menninger's statement that the control of anger depends upon the adequate development and functioning of the highest centers of the brain. (See Chapter VIII, p. 229.)

The child who is frustrated may resort to a form of projection in which

---

* Topp (1951–52) has presented a list of forty behavior patterns indicative of emotional maladjustment. These, when combined with other evidences, should point to those children who are in need of careful study and help.

Table XIII–2   Symptoms of Maladjustment (Garrison, Kingston, McDonald, 1964, p. 475)

Physical Signs

facial twitching	rocking feet
nervous spasms	drumming with fingers
stuttering	twisting hair
biting nails	restlessness
scratching self	fidgeting
vomiting	rapid, nervous speech
enuresis	crying easily
digestive disturbances	

Behavior Deviations

aggressiveness	retiring
negativism	easily embarrassed
night terrors	sleep disturbances
bullying	walking in sleep
lying	masturbation
voluntary mutism	stubbornness
poor school work	regression
oversensitiveness	

Emotional Manifestations

given to excessive worry	disposition to hate
feelings of inferiority	resentful
abnormal fears	temper tantrums
pouting	extreme timidity

he blames other persons or things for his troubles. Or, he may use aggressive displacement by breaking street lights, damaging public and private property, when frustrated by adult reactions (or, more commonly, the lack of reactions) to his failure or misbehavior. Attempts to handle conflicts and frustrations through regression, displacement, and related devices are rarely entirely satisfactory, because such methods do not actually solve the causal problem.

Goal-setting on the part of the child may be a form of defense. According to the results of a study by Cohen (1954), both very high and very low goal-setting reflect self-rejection. This conclusion is in harmony with the results of a study by Sears (1941) who noted that the setting of a high goal was for some children the goal itself; for others the setting of a low goal was a means of protection. Both groups of children were insecure and uncertain of their own abilities.

The extent of aggressive behavior observed among elementary-school children has increased during the past two or more decades (Redwin and

Wainwright, 1955), quite likely a result of the increased permissiveness in the American home and the emphasis upon competition in so many aspects of children's lives. Children can be aided in the acquisition of friendliness and cooperative behavior if parents and teachers will guide them in the development of their abilities and in the pursuance of useful activities that will help them secure social approval and thus feel worthwhile. The advocacy of such a program is well illustrated in the case of Philip, which is described by Franklin (1952–54, pp. 372–373).

> Philip was referred to the social worker by the classroom teacher when he was in the second grade because of his overly aggressive behavior. He would frequently become so angry that he had to be removed bodily from the classroom to prevent him from physically harming other children. The social worker conferred with the mother and with the child. It became evident that the boy had strongly exaggerated fears. He felt that people were "mean." This was a threat to him, and he was sure that adults wanted to hurt him. When these feelings were explained to the teacher, she immediately made every effort to assure him of her friendly attitude and found opportunities to praise him for any constructive classroom activities. He was admitted to an after school club. His first few weeks in the club were marked by frequent fights with the other children. The group teacher discovered he had ability in dramatics, and was skillful in handling puppets. This won him recognition from the other children in the club. His presentation of a puppet play developed after school helped to establish him both in the club and in the classroom. As his need for aggressive behavior diminished it was evident that he had a better than average mental ability. With the friendly attitude of the teachers and the administrative staff he was gradually able to mobilize his aggression into greatly improved accomplishment in academic skills.

Restlessness and Irritability as Symptomatic

When children become fatigued and disturbed because of difficulties in their environment that lead to frustration and tension, restlessness and irritability are likely to result. Failure in reading or other important learning tasks often leads to such forms of behavior. On the other hand, emotional disturbances may also cause these particular behavior patterns, and the child may be unable to concentrate in school, being generally inefficient in the performance of his school activities, especially reading. Cummings (1944) found from a study of school children that restlessness, anxiety, and lack of concentration are closely associated with a high incidence of emotional symptoms. Specific fears were found in over one-fifth of the children, with eight per cent showing fear of animals.

Restlessness is not so poorly received by other children as it is by the teacher. This trait is often observed among children generally classified as nervous. In a study of the peer status of sixth- and seventh-grade pupils,

Laughlin (1954) obtained a correlation of -.484 between restlessness and social acceptance among sixth-grade pupils and a correlation of -.535 at the seventh-grade level. Correlations between restlessness and other personality traits are presented in Table XIII-3. A high correlation was obtained between restlessness and both talkativeness and attention-seeking. The negative correlations obtained between restlessness and friendliness, enthusiasm, cheerfulness, good-lookingness, and likableness indicate that this particular trait is more likely to be associated with undesirable traits than with desirable traits. The correlations bear out the theory that emotional maladjustment interferes with the total adjustment of the child.

Table XIII–3   Correlation Between Restlessness and Other Personality Traits (Laughlin, 1954, p. 27)

Personality trait	Correlation with restlessness	
	Sixth grade	Seventh grade
Talkativeness		
(6th grade)	.747	.489
(7th grade)	.489	.640
Initiative		
(6th grade)	−.086	−.084
(7th grade)	−.044	−.143
Enthusiasm		
(6th grade)	−.227	−.217
(7th grade)	−.140	−.192
Cheerfulness		
(6th grade)	−.104	−.151
(7th grade)	−.068	−.139
Good-lookingness		
(6th grade)	−.315	−.275
(7th grade)	−.226	−.331
Likableness		
(6th grade)	−.320	−.330
(7th grade)	−.221	−.376
Interest in dating		
(6th grade)	.045	.002
(7th grade)	.130	.093
Ability to take a joke on self		
(6th grade)	−.138	−.136
(7th grade)	−.095	−.171
Attention-seeking		
(6th grade)	.508	.414
(7th grade)	.513	.579
Friendliness		
(6th grade)	−.382	−.357
(7th grade)	−.240	−.412

Evasion as Symptomatic

Aggression and withdrawal are reaction patterns simultaneously present in every child. Only when they appear in an exaggerated form are they indicative of a relatively serious disturbance. Furthermore, these exaggerated behavior patterns develop out of similar circumstances. The child's constitution and his early childhood experiences will largely determine the preponderance of aggressive or withdrawal behavior patterns exercised in different environmental settings. Evasion or withdrawal may be observed in the growing child's world of fantasy—in the amount of time he spends escaping reality, which disturbs him. He then seeks satisfaction in daydreaming, reading books, or watching television, which he can control. When the child turns to these agencies more and more often as need satisfiers or substitutes for normal relationships with parents and peers, his fantasies begin to control him—and they engender situations even more difficult than those from which he originally attempted escape, partly from adult pressures against such evasions and partly from the frightful exaggerations conjured by his imagination when it was in control.

Emotional Immaturity

Emotional immaturity is a rather loose term which usually implies that an individual's reactions to a frustrating situation, or his behavior in a social situation, is not typical of his age level; it is more typical of a younger person. The emotionally immature child is handicapped in his social and educational development, because he is unable to participate effectively in the school and out-of-school activities of his age groups.

Using the *Rorschach Ink Blot Test*, Robbertse (1955) obtained a record of significant differences in the personality structure of socially adjusted and socially maladjusted pupils ten to thirteen years of age. The socially adjusted surpassed the socially maladjusted in such characteristics as willingness, desire, and ability to establish harmonious relations with their environment. The maladjusted gave more responses indicative of emotional immaturity, such as irritability, impulsiveness, depressive moods, and inability to adjust normally to outer reality. Successful children, in comparison with children in a state mental hospital, have no difficulties making friends (Baker and Holzworth, 1961).

Emotional immaturity seems to arise primarily from an atmosphere of overprotection, a condition that frequently accrues to children during periods of protracted illness. Apparently, continuous and healthy peer relations are important enough to merit the following statement from Harlow and Harlow (1962, p. 138) as one of the conclusions for a protracted study of infant monkeys:

... Our observations sustain the significance of the maternal relation, particularly in facilitating the interaction of the infant with other infants. But at the same time we have found compelling evidence that opportunity for infant-infant interaction under optimal conditions may fully compensate for lack of mothering, at least in so far as infant-infant social and heterosexual relations are concerned. It seems possible—even likely—that the infant-mother affectional system is indispensable, whereas the infant-infant system is the *sine qua non* for later adjustment in all spheres of monkey life.... Our experiments indicate that ... social deprivation, particularly deprivation of the company of its peers, irreversibly blights the animal's capacity for social adjustment.

Obviously, then, emphasis upon the human child's participation with peers in a variety of experiences will be helpful in the development of emotional maturity comparable with his age level and cultural surroundings.

Stuttering as Symptomatic

"The motor control which regulates speech is the finest in balance of any motor control in human behavior; it is the most easily disturbed.... Any tension, shock, self-consciousness, fear of ridicule, or fear of failure may upset this balance ..." (Rand, *et al.*, 1953, p. 337). Stuttering, therefore, seems to have its basis in difficulties faced by the individual that provoke emotional manifestations. (See also Chapter VI, pp. 162–63.) In a study reported by Moncur (1955), a group of stutterers consisting of forty-two boys and six girls (the incidence of stuttering is considerably higher among boys than among girls) was compared with an equivalent group of non-stutterers. On the whole, the young stutterers displayed a number of symptoms of maladjustment other than stuttering itself, averaging more than twice as many symptoms as the non-stutterers. According to the parents, "young stutterers characteristically appear to be very nervous, are enuretic, have nightmares and night terrors, display aggressive behavior, are 'fussy' eaters, and need to be disciplined often" (p. 96).

Educational Retardation and Maladjustment

Earlier, in Chapter X, it was indicated that overage children are not accepted by their classmates. Unable to achieve status and satisfy his need for achievement through some endeavors in (or out) of school, the educationally retarded child is likely to be maladjusted. Using the *Rosensweig Test* to assess adjustment, Spache (1957) made a study of 125 elementary-school children with reading disabilities. The cases studied were children retarded from one to two years in grade placement. He found that these youngsters could be classified into five groups: the aggressive or hostile children in conflict with authority, the adjustive children who sought only to be inoffensive, the defensive children who were sensitive and resentful, the solution seekers or peacemakers, and the autistic who were characterized by blocking or withdrawal.

McCarthy (1954), after considering the clinical treatment of approximately fifty cases of language disability, identified just two behavioral syndromes associated with poor readers—the aggressive personality syndrome and the submissive syndrome of infantile behavior. Those children who gave evidence of the aggressive syndrome usually suffered from marked parental rejection, harsh discipline, and unfavorable comparisons with siblings, while those classified under the submissive syndrome seemed to be severely overprotected. The latter group appeared to receive little expression of real love and affection during illness. McCarthy further found that the overprotected child was more amenable to psychotherapy and remedial treatment than the rejected child.

In considering the educationally retarded child, the important point is that he is not necessarily dull. As in the case of Philip, described earlier, his emotional problems may keep him from showing his potential mental and educational abilities. It is one of the criticisms of intelligence tests that they do not differentiate between the truly dull and the apparently dull, between those who cannot achieve beyond a certain level and rate and those who can if given the proper aid.

Anxiety Neurosis in Childhood

Anxiety *per se* during childhood is not abnormal. After studying seventy-eight unselected preschool children, Despert (1946, p. 9) concluded:

> Anxiety . . . is commonly observed in young children, and it can be said that not one of the 78 children was totally free from anxiety manifestations. There are, however, marked differences in frequency and intensity among the different children.

Normal anxiety is concerned about things which warrant concern. Only when anxiety becomes excessive or inappropriately directed should it be regarded as damaging to personality integration. The child is limited in his ability to withstand frustration and threats to his sense of security; and, particularly in the early years when ego involvement is so important, the continuous experience of defeat or rejection inhibits self-expression and produces varied symptoms of behavior disorders, such as temper tantrums, destructiveness, acts of mischief or violence, and running away.

The etiology of childhood anxiety neurosis, first described by Freud in 1894, frequently is related to a rejecting, hostile attitude in the family environment, one which may be unconscious and which may also take the form of overprotection as a compensatory reaction. Parental pressures, tension, outright rejection, high expectations are all contributory factors to anxiety states in children. The boy whose father is disappointed in his son's "soft-ness" or unmanly interests may try in vain to do something that will cause a spark of admiration in his father's eyes. With each succeeding failure, the boy loses interest in everything—even in life.

METHODS OF TREATMENT

Child-guidance clinics are the best known and most extensive agencies for dealing with seriously disturbed children. "For the most part," states Witmer (1965, p. 227), "such clinics do not accept as patients children who are feeble-minded or those whose difficulties require the attention of a neurologist. . . . The patients of the clinics are largely children who display behavior or personality disorders that are traceable to environmental strains, usually the result of adverse parent-child relationships." Most large cities have such clinics which are supported by tax funds or community chest resources. Typically, the child-guidance clinic is notable for its team approach to the solution or mitigation of children's problems. One member of this team is the social caseworker who has the responsibility for gathering data on (1) the home and social life of the subject, (2) the history of his physical development (medical history), and (3) his school life. Another team member is the psychologist who evaluates the child's mental abilities —his talents and disabilities—and his characteristic emotional responses. Standardized tests, projective techniques, and interviews are the psychologist's commonly used tools. The other member of the team is the psychiatrist who seeks to discover the dynamics of the child's disturbing behaviors. The psychiatrist's job is to understand the child's emotional responses to parents, siblings, other relatives, and friends, as well as to know his interests, aversions, and daily pattern of life (Lippman, 1956). In some clinics there is a fourth team member who conducts group therapy sessions. His emphasis is on the study of ways in which the child conducts himself in the presence of peers and on an attempt to get the child to understand and improve his peer relationships. As these investigations continue, his work as diagnostician and therapist become indistinguishable. In many instances, the caseworker and especially the psychologist will conduct some or all of the therapeutic sessions. An important aspect of the work of the child-guidance clinic is the case conference at which the findings of the team members are presented and discussed and at which the method of treatment is outlined. Periodically, the case conference is then used to evaluate and recommend continuation or alteration of the method of treatment.

Play Therapy

Youngsters aged nine or ten, with the help of an attentive, accepting therapist, can express themselves quite clearly; but inability to verbalize does handicap the younger counselee in achieving catharsis (ventilating his feelings) and getting others to understand just what his problem is. For these very young children, play therapy provides therapists with a means of gaining tentative insights into the client's thought processes.

Play therapy may be thought of as a situation in which a child may freely express his attitudes and feelings. He treats the toys, dolls, and other objects in the play situation as he would like to treat the furniture, adults, siblings, and such things as water, pets, or food in his home if he were free to do so. The important aspects of the play situation are not the equipment, however, but the basic attitudes of faith, acceptance, and respect as expressed by the therapist (Moustakas, 1953). In describing the therapeutic stages, Bernard (1961) implies the importance of establishing these basic attitudes:

> Typically the therapeutic process progresses through definite stages. At first there is hesitancy and doubt. As he gains confidence that he will not be reprimanded, his feelings of hostility, fear, and anxiety are given generalized expression. He will attack toys indiscriminately and express hostility to people in general. Then the expressions are focused more sharply and superficially—toys substituted for parents and teachers whom he dislikes are attacked and destroyed. This victory may then lead him to attack the therapist or some other person. . . . Finally, negative feelings begin to diminish and there is a more consistent display of positive feelings which are in accord with reality.

Play therapy, like other forms of therapy and like personality growth in general, is a slow process and requires both time and patience. But, as children gradually see themseves being accepted by the therapist they begin to accept themselves and can then accept others. Their actions become less irritable, obnoxious, and defensive; and their parents and siblings can live with them more comfortably—thus giving rise to fewer crises.

Treatment of Parents

Quite often the parents are much more in need of help than the child is. Unless the child can be returned to a more salutary home situation than that from which he was referred, he will quickly regress to his maladjustive patterns of behavior. In such cases, the parents too need therapy. In fact, some therapists refuse, others are reluctant, to treat children unless parents receive treatment concurrently. Their reason is rather obvious: Because it is usually a poor home situation which causes the child's behavior, treating him will have little long-term effect if, after treatment, he has to remain in, or return to, the same situation. Once in a while, especially among older children, one can be made to understand that his parents "are not well" and he can learn to live with them. Usually this is too much to hope for.

A healthy person has difficulty understanding why parents object to treatment. Actually, there are several reasons. Immature or unstable persons are reluctant to accept the thesis that it is they who need help. Even if there is a tentative acceptance of the idea, therapy is often a painful process which immature parents tend to avoid. This same immaturity obscures their perception that this temporary discomfort may lead to much greater, if delayed, satisfactions over a long period of time. Impatience with slow gain (also an evidence of immaturity) discourages continuation of therapy, even if there has been an acceptance of its desirability.

As to the methods which are used to bring about personality growth on the part of parents, they are about as varied as the reasons for concern and as the therapists who deal with the cases. The fact that the cause for referral—neglect or abuse of children—differs from other causes for concern makes little difference in the manner of treatment (Patterson, 1959).

Family Group Counseling

Most, but not all, child behavior problems spring from defective relationships within the family. Therefore, the utilization of family group counseling can be advantageous. The Portland Continuation Center of the Division of Continuing Education of the Oregon State System of Higher Education has conducted several such groups with reported satisfaction on the part of the participants, and there is now a steady demand for an increase in such services. Although no claim is made that participants have their difficulties removed, they do learn to live with them and they do learn to communicate with each other.

Parents in these sessions learn that their ways of influencing children do not look the same to others or to their children as they appear to themselves (Fullmer and Bernard, 1964). Thus, a parent may say, "I keep reminding him of the big opportunity he has for attending Ivyland College— especially when his father was not able to." This seems like a reasonable urging until the youngster turns to the therapist early in the sessions (later, directly to his father or mother) and says, "All I get at home is yak, yak, yak, nag, nag, nag about what a grand college Ivyland is. I'm sick of it before I get there. If I go to college, I want to go to State."

Saying something before others in a group and hearing how it comes out when those not emotionally involved are listening often causes the reporters to evaluate immediately, "I guess I've been too demanding," "I have failed to show affection," "I've tried to impose my way of life on my youngsters even though I fought my mother like fury on the same deal."

Institutional Treatment

Occasionally a child reacts so markedly, either by withdrawal or attack, to the pressures and frustrations he experiences that removal from his normal environment is necessary. His parents and his teachers lack either the ability or the understanding to deal fruitfully with him. Usually, constant treatment under close supervision is clearly desirable.

Institutional treatment is no single, standardized procedure. In some states there is no separate institution for children, and the disturbed child may be sent to the state mental hospital, where, typically, there are wards for children of various ages. Care in state hospitals varies from highly efficient and effective places where there is adequate staff with both time and proper training for the work, to institutions where the contribution is simply custodial. There are a few "half-way" institutions—hospitals, homes, or wards where the child may spend part of his time, with the rest of the time being spent in his normal school and home environment. The ideas behind the "half-way" institution include (1) providing the comfort which comes from associating with others who have problems, (2) giving the client a chance to ventilate his feelings to a therapist immediately after the occurrence of an incident, (3) reminding both parent and child of the possibility of greater separation.

Removing the child from his home environment is usually done with considerable reluctance (Flato, 1962). There is a deep-seated conviction in many people that almost anything is preferable to separating a child from his parents. The fallacy of this belief is indicated in the recidivist rates of delinquents. A boy who has been put into a home for juvenile delinquents will appear to be making good adjustments in school work, with his peers, and with adults whom he contacts. He may occasionally have a very satisfactory weekend at home, and progress is so evident that he is returned to the custody of his parents. But the burden of living with them continually is too much; the frustrations and temptations of his community are too great. He repeats his delinquent acts, and is, of course, returned to the institution. Ideally, his next release will be only to capable and understanding foster parents.

Foster home placement is perhaps the most widely used method for removing a child from an undesirable home. As is the case with state hospitals, there is a great variation in the interest and capability of foster parents. In some cases, the care provided is financially oriented, and both the remuneration and the rewards are nominal. Other foster parents, however, have taken most-difficult cases and patiently lived with their foster children through crises, discouraging regressions, and encouraging progress.

Emotional adherence to faith in home and motherhood, regardless of their conditions or suitability, simply leads to the neglect of children, particularly disturbed children who are likely, in the majority of cases, to repeat in some form the inadequacy of their parents. Well staffed and well supported institutions can break the recurring pattern. Thus, the sensible approach to the problem of parent-child separation is a rational, open-minded evaluation of the situation and of the available institutional facilities.

School Adjustments

Children develop and behave as a unitary whole. They bring their problems to school, and their ability to acquire facts is inseparably related to their degree of socialization and the quality of their personalities. The schools, in fact, despite criticism, have been placing more emphasis on "life adjustment" education. And while some people apparently feel that schools should teach facts and leave personality and adjustment to adults other than teachers, many communities have fostered the expansion of school guidance and counseling services beyond a merely vocational orientation. In turn, some members of school staffs extend the controversy by advocating a "hands off" policy for seriously disturbed pupils. Arbuckle (1962), who has described the issues, advises that until the pupil is so disturbed that he is unable to live without institutionalization he must be dealt with at school.

Some schools are charting the way. In many communities, the work begins in the preschool years by providing nurseries for disturbed children. Much use is made of play therapy techniques, not only as a means of understanding the child but also as a means of emotional release, easement of tensions, and structuring of thoughts. In the primary and higher grades, one can occasionally find "opportunity" or remedial classes. Hence, the emphasis is quite as much on learning to live harmoniously with self and others as it is on correcting deficiencies in reading, language, or arithmetic. In the upper grades and high school, the approach is even more direct. In classes in human relations pupils are led to discuss their reactions in various situations and to evaluate the probable results, especially in terms of the impact of their behavior on other pupils. Others in the group describe their feelings about the actions being discussed. While these classes constitute only a small part of the pupil's total environment, there are enough positive results in terms of improved school work and better attitudes that continuation and expansion of such classes warrant recommendation.

School counselors who go beyond the routines of assignment to classes and vocational orientation realize how frequently the pupil's uppermost need is for guidance in daily living. In periodic counseling sessions, the pupil is led to describe his feelings—about parents, peers, and teachers. He is encouraged to formulate, at first on the verbal level and later at the action level, improved patterns of behavior. Numerous reports attest to the value of such counseling. Improved school grades are typically the goal most sought in experiments and the last to appear as results. More readily achieved are a by-passing of the pupil's determination to leave school, clearly perceivable ability to get along with peers, less frequent reports of clashes at home, and verbal expression of faith in self. Without belittling the contribution of a well-educated and skilled counselor, we can make the observation that a problem child's contact with one person who will take a real interest in him, devote time to him, and treat him as a worthwhile individual gives considerable impetus to his willingness to keep trying.

In all of these approaches—preschool classes, special classes, counseling—human relations can play a vital role in improved patterns of adjusting. There seems to be no one way that is clearly superior for all disturbed pupils. What is central is the mature help given by an understanding and accepting person. Such persons have faith in children which they communicate to the extent that children develop faith in themselves. They are persons who have achieved the goal of maturity, who are so much at one with the world that service to others is a means of self-fulfillment.

SUMMARY

Adjustment problems may be viewed from several orientations. They may be classified by levels in terms of the difficulty of treatment—demanding a change in behavior, requiring treatment by the adult concerned (teacher or parent), or requiring professional intervention. They may be classified by types—aggressive, near-delinquent behavior, social withdrawal, and psychosomatic illness.

The classification of needs is helpful in adult communication. The important thing for children is to be understood and treated appropriately. Understanding is facilitated by the concept of needs. It is when needs are not satisfied, or are approaching satisfaction, that the child, in abortive efforts to adjust, encounters problems of adjustment. Needs have been stated in terms of physical, status, and integrative needs—in terms of achievement, recognition, physical and emotional satisfactions and other similar statements.

When children's needs have been consistently denied for a prolonged period it is often necessary to bring about a marked change in environment to effect improved behavior. Play therapy may serve both as a diagnostic method and a therapeutic technique. Individual or group therapy for parents is often regarded as the most essential feature for effecting improved child behavior. Family group therapy which includes the children has been used in a few places with good results. In some cases, where parents refuse therapy or fail to respond to it, the child may have to be taken from them and placed with foster parents or in an institution. In between treatment of parents and removal from them the child may be given help in clinics at school and in individual counseling. Here the ultimate goal is to help him see his circumstances from a more objective viewpoint so that he may consequently change his own behavior patterns.

QUESTIONS AND PROBLEMS

1. Do you think that classification of adjustment problems by type or degree of seriousness is the more helpful?
2. How would you account for some children becoming excessively withdrawn and others becoming disturbingly aggressive?
3. Do you feel that the term "near-delinquency" is a helpful category of behavior? Why or why not?
4. Why is social withdrawal often considered to be a more alarming symptom of maladjustment than aggressiveness?
5. What is your opinion of those who are, under most circumstances, unwilling to recommend that a child be taken away from his parents?
6. What are some advantages of institutional treatment of problem children?
7. Name several ways in which teachers might help to reduce the tensions which contribute to maladjustment.

SOURCES OF MATERIALS IN THE AREA OF MENTAL HEALTH

American Orthopsychiatric Association
    1790 Broadway, New York, New York
Child Study Association of America
    132 East 74th Street, New York, New York
Child Welfare League of America, Inc.
    24 West 40th Street, New York, New York
Mental Health Materials Association
    1790 Broadway, New York, New York
New York Committee on Mental Health
    105 West 22nd Street, New York, New York

SELECTED READINGS

BERKOWITZ, PEARL H., and ESTHER P. ROTHMAN, The Disturbed Child. New York University Press, 1960.

GARRISON, KARL C., and DEWEY G. FORCE, JR., The Psychology of Exceptional Children, 4th ed. The Ronald Press, 1965. Chs. 16, 17, and 18.

HARING, NORRIS G., and E. LAKIN PHILLIPS, Educating Emotionally Disturbed Children. McGraw-Hill, 1962.

HOLLINGSHEAD, AUGUST B., and FREDRICK C. REDLICH, Social Class and Mental Illness. John Wiley & Sons, 1958.

HURLOCK, ELIZABETH B., Child Development, 4th ed. McGraw-Hill, 1964. Chs. 9 and 15.

LICHTER, SOLOMON O., and others, The Drop-Outs. Free Press of Glencoe, 1962.

LIPPMAN, HYMAN S., Treatment of the Child in Emotional Conflict. McGraw-Hill, 1956.

MILLER, HYMAN, and DOROTHY W. BARUCH, The Practice of Psychosomatic Medicine as Illustrated in Allergy. McGraw-Hill, 1956.

O'NEAL, PATRICIA, and LEE N. ROBINS, The relation of childhood behavior problems to adult psychiatric status: A 30-year follow-up study of 150 subjects, *American Journal of Psychiatry*, 1958, *114*, 961–969.

RIESSMAN, FRANK, *The Culturally Deprived Child*. Harper & Bros., 1962.

REFERENCES

ARBUCKLE, DUGALD S., A semantic excursion, *The Personnel and Guidance Journal* (September 1962), *41*, No. 1, 64–66.

BAKER, JOHN W., and ANNETTE HOLZWORTH, Social histories of successful and unsuccessful children, *Child Development*, 1961, *32*, 135–149.

BANDURA, A., Relationship of family patterns to child behavior disorders, *Progress Report*, United States Public Health Service, Project No. M–1734. Stanford, Calif.: Stanford University, 1960.

BEILIN, HARRY, Teachers' and clinicians' attitudes toward the behavior problems of children: a reappraisal, *Child Development*, 1959, *30*, 9–25.

BERNARD, HAROLD W., *Mental Hygiene for Classroom Teachers*, 2nd ed. McGraw-Hill, 1961, pp. 388–389.

BÜHLER, CHARLOTTE, FAITH SMITTER, and SYBIL RICHARDSON, *Childhood Problems and the Teachers*. Holt, 1952.

CARR, LOWELL JUILLIARD, Juvenile delinquency, in *Collier's Encyclopedia*, 1954, *11*, 487–488.

CHESS, STELLA, ALEXANDER THOMAS, and HERBERT BIRCH, Characteristics of the individual child's behavioral responses to the environment, *American Journal of Orthopsychiatry*, 1959, *29*, 791–802.

COHEN, LOUIS D., Level-of-aspiration behavior and feelings of adequacy and self-acceptance, *The Journal of Abnormal and Social Psychology*, 1954, *49*, 84–86.

CUMMINGS, J. D., The incidence of emotional symptoms in school children, *British Journal of Educational Psychology*, 1944, *14*, 151–161.

DAVIDSON, MAY A., R. G. MCINNES, and R. W. PARNELL, The distribution of personality traits in seven-year-old children: a combined psychological, psychiatric and somatotype study, *British Journal of Educational Psychology*, 1957, *27*, 48–61.

DESPERT, J. LOUISE, Anxiety, phobias, and fears in young children, *Nervous Child*, 1946, *5*, 8–24.

DOLLARD, JOHN, L. W. DOOB, N. E. MILLER, O. H. MOWRER, and R. R. SEARS, *Frustration and Aggression*. New Haven, Conn.: Yale University Press, 1939.

EISENBERG, LEON, The fathers of autistic children, *American Journal of Orthopsychiatry*, 1957, *27*, 715–724.

FLATO, CHARLES, Parents who beat children, *The Saturday Evening Post* (October 6, 1962), *235*, pt. 5, 30–35.

FRANKLIN, ADELE, Teachers—not therapists, *Nervous Child*, 1952–54, *10*, 368–377.

FULLMER, D. W., and H. W. BERNARD, *Counseling: Content and Process*. Chicago: Science Research Associates, Inc., 1964, pp. 207–227.

GARRISON, KARL C., ALBERT J. KINGSTON, and ARTHUR S. MCDONALD, *Educational Psychology*, 2nd ed. Appleton-Century-Crofts, 1964, p. 475.

GILBERT, G. M., A survey of "referral problems" in metropolitan child guidance centers, *Journal of Clinical Psychology*, 1957, *13*, 37–42.

GLUECK, SHELDON, and ELEANOR T. GLUECK, *Delinquents in the Making*. Harper & Bros., 1952.

GOLDSTEIN, KURT, *Organism: A Holistic Approach to Biology*. . . . American Book Company, 1939.

GRIFFITHS, W., *Behavior Difficulties of Children as Perceived and Judged by Parents, Teachers, and Children Themselves*. Minneapolis: University of Minnesota Press, 1952.

HARLOW, HARRY F., and MARGARET KUENNE HARLOW, Social deprivation in monkeys, *Scientific American* (November 1962), 207, No. 5, 136–146.

HAVIGHURST, ROBERT J., and BERNICE L. NEUGARTEN, *Society and Education*, 2nd ed. Boston: Allyn and Bacon, 1962, p. 106.

HOLLISTER, HAL, An ex-convict's scheme for more practical prisons, *Harper's Magazine* (August 1962), 225, 14–20.

HUNTER, E. C., Changes in teachers' attitudes toward children's behavior over the last thirty years, *Mental Hygiene*, 1957, 41, 3–11.

KRAPF, E. E., and JOY MOSER, Changes of emphasis and accomplishments in mental health work, 1948–1960, *Mental Hygiene*, 1962, 46, 163–191.

KRAUS, PHILIP E., *A Longitudinal Study of Children*. Board of Education, 1956, mimeograph.

KUBIE, LAWRENCE S., The child's fifth freedom, in *Our Children Today* (Sidonie M. Gruenberg, ed.). Viking Press, 1952, pp. 136–146.

KVARACEUS, WILLIAM C., *The Community and the Delinquent*. Yonkers-on-Hudson, N.Y.: World Book (now Harcourt, Brace & World), 1954, pp. 57–60.

KVARACEUS, WILLIAM C., and others, *Delinquent Behavior: Culture and the Individual*. Washington: National Education Association, 1959.

LAUGHLIN, FRANCES, *The Peer Status of Sixth and Seventh Grade Children*. Bureau of Publications, Teachers College, Columbia University, 1954, p. 27.

LAZARUS, RICHARD S., *Adjustment and Personality*. McGraw-Hill, 1961, p. 348.

LIPPMAN, HYMAN S., *Treatment of the Child in Emotional Conflict*. McGraw-Hill, 1956.

MCCARTHY, DOROTHEA, Language development in children, in *Manual of Child Psychology* (L. Carmichael, ed.), 2nd ed. John Wiley & Sons, 1954, pp. 492–630.

MENNINGER, KARL A., *The Human Mind*, 3rd ed. Alfred A. Knopf, 1961.

MILLER, HYMAN, and DOROTHY W. BARUCH, *The Practice of Psychosomatic Medicine as Illustrated in Allergy*. McGraw-Hill, 1956.

MONCUR, JOHN P., Symptoms of maladjustment differentiating young stutterers from non-stutterers, *Child Development*, 1955, 26, 91–96.

MOUSTAKAS, CLARK E., *Children in Play Therapy*. McGraw-Hill, 1953, pp. 2–9.

PATTERSON, CECIL H., *Counseling and Psychotherapy: Theory and Practice*. Harper & Bros., 1959.

RAND, WINIFRED, MARY SWEENY, and E. LEE VINCENT, *Growth and Development of the Young Child*, 5th ed. Philadelphia: Saunders, 1953.

REDWIN, ELEANORE, and LETITIA WAINWRIGHT, The development of a power contest, *The American Journal of Individual Psychology*, 1955, 11, No. 2, 172–177.

ROBBERTSE, P. M., Personality structure of socially adjusted and socially maladjusted children, according to the Rorschach test, *Psychological Monographs*, 1955, 69, No. 19.

ROTHNEY, JOHN W. M., PAUL J. DANIELSON, and ROBERT A. HEIMANN, *Measurement for Guidance*. Harper & Row, 1959.

SEARS, PAULINE S., Level of aspiration in relation to some variables of personality: clinical studies, *Journal of Social Psychology*, 1941, *14*, 311–336.

SPACHE, GEORGE, Personality patterns of retarded readers, *Journal of Educational Research*, 1957, *50*, 461–469.

THORPE, LOUIS P., *Child Psychology and Development*, 3rd ed. The Ronald Press, 1962, p. 511.

TOPP, ROBERT F., Preadolescent behavior patterns suggestive of emotional malfunctioning, *Elementary School Journal*, 1951–52, *52*, 340–343.

VAUGHAN, WARREN T., JR., Children in crisis, *Mental Hygiene*, 1961, *45*, 354–359.

WICKMAN, E. K., *Children's Behavior and Teachers' Attitudes*. New York: The Commonwealth Fund, Division of Publications, 1928.

WITMER, HELEN L., Child guidance clinics, in *Collier's Encyclopedia*, 1965, *6*, 217.

F O U R T E E N

The Child As an

Integrated Personality

Adults have many hopes and ambitions for the younger generation. Some wish the young might find the way to world peace, others that they will be successful in business and attain wealth and prestige, some hope for achievement in the arts, sciences, or humanities. A great many parents will simply say, "I want my children to be happy." Whatever the hopes of the parents for their children might be, progress toward the realization of that hope will be facilitated if during childhood one can be referred to as an integrated personality—if the forces within and about him are such as to foster that integration.

THE MEANING OF PERSONALITY

In modern psychiatry, the term *personality* refers to the psychological, physical, chemical, and social aspects of the individual as they combine at any given instant, a process that is continuous from birth to death. First, according to Menninger (1961), there is the nucleus of inherited physiological and psychological potentials. Next, this nucleus is powerfully influenced by

> ... the teaching, training, and example of the parents, and the reactions to brothers and sisters; there are climate and weather, the architecture of the home, the food, fashions; there is the influence of the school, church, newspapers, playmates, society in general. Economic laws and social laws are brought to bear and modify behaviour patterns. Then come the accidents

of life, physical and mental, the illnesses, the wounds, the griefs, the disappointments, the shocks of all kinds that come to all people. All of these
mould the personality. All of these things go to make up a personality.

In other words, as Menninger defines it, personality pertains to "the individual as a whole, his height and weight and loves and hates and blood-
pressure and reflexes; his smiles and hopes and bowed legs and enlarged
tonsils. It means all that anyone is and all that he is trying to become."

THE MEANING OF INTEGRATED

The word *integrated* also brings to mind the idea of a unity. Psychologically, integration refers to the processes by which organic, mental, emotional, and social forces are combined into a complex but organized unity,
the parts of which are working together in a harmonious manner. Balance is
an important component of integration. If one is engrossed in meeting his
physical needs to the neglect of developing intellectual potential or social
skills, his behavior is not integrative. Even if we take one of these, intellectual development, integration is still a central issue. Until knowledge is
weighed, organized, interrelated, and made personally meaningful it is of
little use. If a child has simultaneous desires which are not compatible—retaining personal possession of his toys and having a good time with his peers
—integration cannot be achieved until a compromise is achieved.

Personality integration does not imply either a meek bowing to the demands of society or an abject surrender of one's self. Neither does it mean
the absence of anxiety or conflict. Rather the integrated person is one who
can handle his anxiety and keep it within the bounds of reality. He is a realistic person. Moreover, his behavior is flexible, productive, and foresightful;
he has many, diversified interests; and he has no difficulty making friends
(Baker and Holzworth, 1961).

Integration and Mental Health

Having good mental health and being an integrated personality are
very closely related. This may be made clear by citing a White House Conference (1930) definition of mental health:

> Mental health may be defined as the adjustment of individuals to
> themselves and the world at large with a maximum of effectiveness, satis-
> factions, cheerfulness, and socially considerate behavior, and the ability
> of facing and accepting the realities of life.

The highest degree of mental health, therefore, might be described as
that which permits an individual to realize the greatest success which his
capabilities will permit, with a maximum of satisfaction to himself and the

social order, and a minimum of friction and tension. This description implies a stage of such well-being that the individual is not conscious of unsatisfied tensions, does not show socially inadequate or objectionable behavior, and maintains himself intellectually and emotionally in any environment under any circumstances (White House Conference, 1930).

The phrase "socially acceptable behavior" might possibly mark a debatable distinction between integration and mental health. It is possible to conceive of an individual who is "at one with himself"—an integrated person —yet whose goals are in conflict with society. A criminal who firmly believes in his right to a larger share of the nation's wealth is such a person. His conscious purposes, his internal desires, and his external actions do work together harmoniously (Cattell, 1950). But he does not achieve integration in his society and thus does not experience mental health as defined by the White House Conference. This larger concept of integration, the one which considers the individual in society is the one employed herein. That is, we are here concerned with the whole individual growing up in and moving out into his community.

Personality integration is promoted in an atmosphere that helps the individual satisfy his need for self-realization.

Forces of Integration

In this book we have looked microscopically at many aspects of child development. We have described specific forces which contribute to the shaping of the child's life—heredity, organic factors, intelligence, parental behavior and parental handling, peer groups, the school, socioeconomic factors, and ethical standards. As these factors combine and coalesce in dynamic life patterns, we recognize the importance of need-satisfaction and culture as motivating forces. We recognize the importance of the individual and the holistic approach to understanding him. But, what should be glaringly obvious is the necessity of treating a child as a person with certain rights, without which he is handicapped in his movement toward integration of his self elements and subsequently of his self and society. The International Federation of Teachers Associations formulated, in 1950, a "Charter of Rights for Children," and, by using the ten points in the Charter as section headings, we can summarize some of the more potent forces of integration operating throughout a child's life.

THE CHARTER OF RIGHTS

1. The Child Has a Right to Be a Child Without Discrimination as to Birth, Sex, Language, Color, or Opinions

The development of the individual results partly from an intrinsic maturing of abilities, characteristics, and structures, partly from experience. Through these agencies a child acquires competence in using his resources and develops an awareness of himself as a personality. However, the acquisition of competence and awareness are considerably slowed down if a child is expected to be anything more or less than what he is at any given age. Treating him as "better" or "worse" than another denies him the opportunity to develop his own ego as it operates in his surrounding environment. Treating him as a valued *possession* smothers his initiative and keeps him from developing a concept of himself as he relates to others. That is, if a mother (by giving him everything) expects nothing from her child, he gives nothing and becomes so dependent upon her support and help that the apron string becomes an extension of the umbilical cord.

Any form of rejection—high expectations, overprotection, neglect, ignorance, authoritarianism, parental egocentricity—denies the child his right to be a child. In practice, the patterns of rejection are infinite and the reasons for discrimination range over a wide area. Unwanted pregnancies, parental immaturity, sibling rivalry, internal resentment of the child and external overacceptance, disappointment in the sex of the child, stereotyping minority-group members—any one of these conditions can cause an atmosphere in which the child is made to feel guilty about sex, intelligence, looks, or even existence.

Other conditions also prevail. Generally, too much is expected of a child with a low IQ. And even the bright child is often pressured in terms of adult conformity, although he has as much right to such growth phenomena as temper tantrums, daydreaming, and moral lapses as does any other child. Likewise, a young boy is not a man with emotional self-control: he should have the same right to shed tears of frustration as a girl has; and a young girl should be allowed to exercise her large muscles through rough-and-tumble play similar to the kind indulged in by boys.

Parents, in fact, act as though they would be much better satisfied if their children were just two years older. (Only upon reaching adulthood does one begin hearing the phrase "Act your age.") There is too often an urgency to dress oneself, to learn to walk and to read, to be properly groomed at all times, to learn to dance, to act like a man or behave like a lady. This constant hurrying conveys to the child the impression that he is not quite so successful as he should be. He is not recognized quite so much for what he is as what he might become.

Both parents and teachers should realize that success is a strong and positive motivator. Hence, the child should be guided into those pursuits, and at an appropriate speed, that will allow him a reasonable expectation and experience of success. Moreover, these key persons should know enough about the capacities and potentialities of the individual, and of children as a group, that appropriate progress will be recognized and sincerely appreciated. Integration is promoted because children can think well of themselves and because their feelings of success in growth gives them confidence in attacking their next developmental tasks.

Each child is an individual and should be treated as an individual child. Unless he is accepted with patience, respect for his individuality, faith in his developmental processes, and tolerance for his inevitable errors, the child has difficulty accepting himself and consequently experiences conflicts from within and without whenever he attempts to meet life situations. If he feels the meaning of warmth, understanding, acceptance, and success in his efforts to master his environment, he can give of himself and broaden his horizons with confidence.

In short, the child has a right to assimilate, integrate, and adjust to new learnings at his *own* rate—not in comparison with another's rate or in accordance with adult expectations for individuals of his sex, intellectual status, physical makeup, or culture. The demands made of him should be reasonable—in accord with his ability to perform.

"It is time," states LeShan (1964, p. 106), "we once again shared with our children some of the privileges of adulthood—our right to find our own way at our own pace and to have a sense of personal worth and success despite imperfections."

2. The Child Has a Right to Develop in an Atmosphere of Liberty and Dignity

The child's right to liberty implies freedom from parental overprotection and the overorganization of his activities, freedom to explore his environment (within the bounds of safe conduct), freedom to develop his own interests and to satisfy those which have already been developed, without the pressures of parental expectations and adult exploitation. In the realm of interests alone, many adults impose their own ideas upon children, choosing the toys, academic subjects, books, and activities which the adult thinks the child *should* want. (See also the eighth right in the Charter.)

Emotional liberty implies permission to express strong feelings toward the objects and people causing them. Such freedom can obviate guilt and may encourage the free expression of the more integrative feelings of love, affection, and brotherhood. Emphasis placed on the disguise and suppression of one type of emotion, particularly before the discriminating abilities of a child are developed, may lead him to withdraw from all displays of emotion or seek to hide his feelings in devious, disintegrative ways.

The child's right to dignity is implicit in the prevailing concepts of individual privacy. Youngsters have the right to discover themselves and to form their sense of identity with a minimum of adult interference, nagging, and belittling. For this they need adult models of "ideal" behavior, and possessions and space they can call their own. Ardrey (1961) has developed the thesis that man's struggle is not one for power or prestige, but for territory—space. Where space is limited maldevelopment occurs with greater frequency than otherwise, as attested by the high incidence of delinquency in crowded areas. When youngsters of all ages are crowded together for play in inclement weather and for sleeping, the frequency of norm-violating behavior is increased. Sometimes this crowding involves closer physical proximity with parents or other adults. Whether because of crowded conditions or overprotectiveness, many children sleep with their mothers, and, contrary to the belief of some people, such a practice does not promote secure childhood personalities; it more often creates poor self-adjustment, lack of personal freedom, and sleep disturbances (Sewell, 1952, p. 157).

The right to dignity also implies the necessity of being educated to earn a livelihood and the need for community efforts to eliminate substandard housing and poor living conditions.

> . . . The neighborhood in which young people live and form their most important associations is perhaps the most decisive phase of community influences, though it reflects too the broader influences of the society and culture. The factors which shape character derive largely from these com-

munity influences as they operate through the family, the school, the church and other social institutions. Community action to prevent juvenile delinquency is to a great extent a matter of organizing the variety of community resources so as to provide, on the one hand, an environment in which children may develop without abnormalities of character and in which . . . those who are in danger of becoming delinquent may be discovered and guided toward conformity to normal standards.

United Nations, 1956

The responsibility for creating atmospheres of liberty and dignity rests with all adults and organizations in a community, not the least of which are the churches and the manner in which they operate to help families share the experiences and ideals of religion. "Fortunate is the family that finds acceptable and ready to its hand the . . . beliefs and devotions of one of the great historic faiths" (Swift, 1952, p. 332). Ultimately, however, spiritual dignity, like church affiliation, is a product of the family group; and regardless of what parents believe or disbelieve or by what medium they express their beliefs, there is a great need of children to develop a sense of worth in relation to purposes beyond the tasks of self-development. As Swift (p. 333) prescribes:

> . . . let no family with children fail to share the sense of a unity of devotion to whatever in that family's experience is highest and noblest and most significant—be it found in music, in art, in literature, in science, in religion, or in a combination of these, or in some other area of man's high adventuring.

3. The Child Has a Right to the Benefits of Economic and Social Security

In a wealthy nation reaching toward new heights of civilization, indifference to the welfare of children in slums and other culturally barren areas is a crime against the future of that nation. Whether aid to deprived sections comes from national, state, and local governments, from philanthropic organizations, from groups of citizens, or from private individuals, the move toward insuring economic security for the underprivileged enhances the present and future dignity of every citizen. The child whose most basic needs are not met cannot assume a contributing role in society, if only because the energies he needs for developing his rational powers are dissipated in his drives to obtain food, clothing, and shelter. The natural assumption must also be made that if the child does not have the essentials for attaining good physical development he does not have the necessities for good mental development—toys and books and other means for turning his curiosities into interests. The possibilities for exploring his environment are soon exhausted.

Unsurprisingly, the deprived child lacks self-confidence, which in turn produces unfavorable attitudes toward life experiences: they are exhausting struggles, not exciting challenges. Friendships are formed in proportion to the amount of self-confidence and security a child feels; and there is little doubt from the evidence presented in previous chapters that peer relationships and acceptance are essential to the development of an integrated personality. Lack of free, abundant, and educative peer contacts leads to various forms of aberrant behavior.

Social security also inheres in consistency of demands and expectations, and especially of discipline. Key adults must administer discipline that holds a balance between autocracy and license (Radke, 1946). Sensible discipline fosters security by keeping anger, humiliation, guilt, and anxiety at a minimum while teaching that the world reacts to behavior in an orderly fashion. Insensible, emotionally administered discipline keeps a child from developing self-confidence and self-control. For example, the practice of withdrawing love, or threatening to, is one form of discipline that most psychologists feel is extremely harmful to a child's social security. Even physical punishment is preferable to this type, because the child can feel that he has paid for his misdeed and does not suffer guilt feelings. (Even adults at times experience the need for overt or verbal punishment, as when an errant husband says to his overpatient wife, "If you'd only *yell* at me, I'd feel better.")

4. The Child Has a Right to Healthful Food, Clothing, Recreation, and Games

The benefits of economic and social security include medical care, health programs, adequate food, clothing, or shelter, which few people would consciously deny a child. Generally, adults are not greatly concerned about a child's colds, headaches, low-grade and temporary fevers, and tooth decay. Nor does research show a retarding influence of frequent minor illnesses on the total growth pattern (Hardy, 1938; see also p. 113); but the child who does not have robust health may find himself unfavorably compared with his peers because he lacks the energy for sustained application to developmental tasks. The added burden of not feeling well makes him cross and irritable; those about him often respond in kind; and he comes then to view himself as inadequate and unloved. This chain of events makes his problems of adjustment the more difficult.

The personality impact of "delicate" health is not so easy to prove; but as one of the factors contributing to one's self-concept, minor illnesses must not be too quickly discounted. As Coleman (1960) asserts, the importance of nutrition, health, rest, and exercise cannot be sidestepped by the occasional securing of medical care during acute illness. Personality integration of necessity must include optimum and cooperative functioning of mind and body as social interaction is pursued.

Youngsters who are physically strong and well-coordinated enjoy games, contests, and sports which allow them to exercise their capacities.

Very young children reveal an almost frantic desire for exercise of capacities in their running, babbling, and apparently ceaseless activity. The child who is mentally alert enjoys reading, conversation with older persons, playing chess, checkers, or other social games; and he reveals curiosity which extends beyond the school curriculum.

Clinical studies show that disintegration (maladjustment, mental illness) may sometimes be explained in terms of an individual's having to function in areas that do not stretch, or even exercise, his capacities (O'Connor, 1941). Sufficiently varied opportunities for recreation and games should be provided in the home and school so that the child may learn what his capacities are, exercise them, and choose the pursuits that interest and satisfy him. Thus, play in childhood is important business. It furthers his individual physical and mental development through the exercise of large and small muscles and through the acquisition of knowledge, such as the properties of many different materials, including the material of his imagination, his fantasies, and dreams. It helps him structure his thinking. Play activities further enhance these aspects by allowing the child to test newly acquired knowledge and to practice recently developed skills. More knowledge and a refinement of skills follow.

Play activities also facilitate a child's social and emotional adjustments. Through recreation and games, a child learns teamwork and cooperation, leadership and followership; it provides him with acceptable emotional outlets and increased social contacts. One of the most beneficial types of learning accrues from the kinds of play in which children try out various roles which society expects them to play as they develop. Thus, the young girls who play with dolls are actually practicing the role of motherhood. The boy who plays soldier and cowboy is absorbing the principles of protection, tactical maneuvers, responsibility, discipline.

Play activities reflect the maturation, physical growth, language, knowledge, interests, and personality development of the child. They reflect the child's ideal of the world in which he lives and the way in which he sees himself. This concept is one of the bases of the play therapy technique employed by specialists who seek to diagnose and treat children who have manifested special difficulties in integration.

Parents who consciously or unconsciously exert excessive pressure on a child to achieve academically often ignore this right of the child to play and in so doing deny him the opportunity to grow soundly, to attain optimum physical fitness, emotional control, and intellectual fulfillment.

5. The Child Has a Right to Grow Up in a Friendly Atmosphere of Affection and Understanding

Birth in an emotionally secure and harmonious home environment is one of the prerequisites for good character formation (Garrison, *et al.,*

1964). Well-loved and well-fed babies move more rapidly from one stage in the hierarchy of needs to the next; they show a greater interest in the world around them. Because such interest stimulates all the sensory equipment of the infant, which hastens his intellectual development, we can add it to all the other necessary ingredients for a healthy personality. Obviously, then, to achieve integration the growing child needs mothering, parental felicity, consistency of demands and expectations, well-trained and emotionally mature teachers, adult understanding of the principles of growth and development, and "all the emotionally constructive experiences (of joy, rest, peace) possible" (Rand, *et al.,* 1953). Above all, we must not forget the child's need for TIME! Time to grow, time to integrate new learnings, and *time devoted to him by his parents.* Hechinger (1964) cites one of the causes of children's emotional difficulties as being a lack of close companionship between parents and their children.

Ego strength and moral stability are positively correlated with mutual trust and respect for differences within a family (Peck and Havighurst, 1960). In contrast, the higher incidence of delinquency in children from broken homes indicates the child's need for friendly adult contacts—for stable parents who can give affection (Monahan, 1960). One understanding and successful teacher of primary-grade pupils even observed: "A great need of children is for a friendly voice."

The major benefits and the implementation of this right of children is made explicit throughout chapters XI and XII, the one in regard to the family role and the other as it affects the school atmosphere.

6. The Child Has a Right to Peace

Those who drafted the statement regarding a child's right to peace were thinking of military and political peace, the desirability of which need not be documented. However, youngsters also have the right to the peace of mind and body that comes from security, routine, orderliness, good health, and consistency. These concomitants of peace are especially important during infancy, according to Escalona (1952), who has observed that:

> . . . other things being equal, those babies whose experience has a definite rhythm and sameness to it, especially with respect to vital situations such as feeding and bathing, may somewhat earlier and somewhat more easily acquire a sense of themselves as entities to whom things happen and who can make things happen.

Another, all too often overlooked, need of the child is the peace that comes from solitude. The rapid pace of twentieth-century progress makes itself felt among youngsters through pressures to learn more and to learn it faster; to be constantly active; to join dance and swimming and music classes, church groups, Scouts; to study school lessons; to "go out and play" or "find something to do instead of just sitting there." Apparently, adults are

The child brought up in an atmosphere of affection and security perceives the world and the people in it in a favorable manner.

afraid that to be idle is to fall behind, or that an idle child is a bored child who is fomenting mischief. Yet some of the most spiritually wholesome, integrating elements of personality are assimilated during the moments when a child finds time to be by himself, to indulge in fantasies and daydreams, to discover and examine the core of his own uniqueness.

The satisfaction of a child's need for peace inheres in the peace kept by his parents. Few things are so shattering to the child as to see the two persons who are the center of his universe and upon whom he must depend at odds with each other—quarreling, silently distant from one another, openly avoiding contact and conversation, or threatening separation and divorce. When children hear their parents quarrel, they worry about one of the parents running away, fear the outbreak of violence, or are torn by ambivalent loyalties (Moustakas, 1953). Even when parents realize the impact their own unhappiness has upon the developing emotions of the child, they find it difficult to mask the underlying mood, and an attempt to compensate for lack of marital harmony often leads to overprotection or overindulgence for the child (Miller and Baruch, 1956). Under conditions of parental disharmony, a child cannot feel that the world is a trustworthy, secure, orderly place.

When a child is nagged and belittled, when the pressures from adults are too strong or unrealistic, emotional peace disappears. The child is likely to become overanxious and his feelings of adequacy may suffer damage. Small amounts of anxiety, especially in situations over which he has some control, incite him to action, experience, learning, persistence, and mastery. But, anxiety caused by situations in which the child's world appears to be an obstacle course devised for (and by) adults operates to the detriment of his mental and emotional health.

7. The Child Has a Right to Receive an Education for Complete and Harmonious Development

The seventh right of a child includes his needs for a wide variety of experiences under the guidance of adults responsible for teaching him moral and ethical behavior, imparting social attitudes, cultural values, and ways of putting knowledge together sensibly. Most of these experiences (the foundations for all later learning) are begun in the home through the care he receives as an infant; the quality and quantity of the language he hears from his parents; the kinds of toys and mediums of expression he has; the variety of his peer and sibling interactions; the books, pictures, magazines, radios, television, and recreational activities provided in the family group. Through the everyday, informal sharing of knowledge and experiences, parents stimulate a child to become aware of his environment and guide him toward a mastery of it.

Through more formal methods, the community reinforces and supplements the learnings a child acquires at home, and it is the community that is responsible for the quality, the vitality, of a youngster's formal education (Bernard, 1966). Without community interest and support, education becomes static, substandard, highly inadequate; and youth, through lack of practice in active *thinking*, sublimates its creativity in the passive absorption of knowledge, developing disinterested, often rigid, attitudes toward change: They are unable to force a change in existing conditions and they cannot adapt readily to changes that occur as a result of cultural forces broader than those in their surrounding environment. Thus, the attitudinal circle is reinforced.

Unfortunately for the young, too many adults rigidly believe that what was good enough for them is good enough for their children. Earl Kelley (1962) has expressed this idea more poignantly:

> . . . The conflict between age and youth is one of the saddest aspects of our culture. And the saddest fact is that age always strikes the first blow.

. . . .

A good measure . . . of our attitudes toward youth may be gained by the money we are willing to spend for them. The young have many needs, but a good place to start would be to provide them with good schools taught by well-educated, competent, well-paid teachers. This would not answer all of youth's needs, but it would be a good beginning. On the whole, however, we seem to be unwilling to do even this much. I do not know, except by inference, how the schools are faring in other parts of the country, but in Michigan we are in a continuous uproar about getting the voters to approve taxes for our schools. Many of the proposals turned down by the voters are most niggardly to begin with. In many cities of this state schools are being operated on half-time schedules. Parts of the curriculum enjoyed by youth are being cut out, leaving only the parts young people dislike. The building of new schools is being discontinued. Old buildings are being left to deteriorate. One community has two new buildings already finished which are standing idle because there is no staff for them. . . .

We cannot educate children to live happily and successfully if we continuously look toward the past or persist in believing that our present world is the best possible. Perhaps it is; but we cannot be sure. One thing is certain, for better or for worse, the world will be different tomorrow. The only aspect of all cultures and societies, of all animal species and natural phenomena, that has never ceased to exist, that has never become extinct, is Change. Thus, effective education must be education for change, and the major requirement for every educational system and its trustees, administrators, and teachers is continuous experimentation, adaptation, and improvement. Speaking of the elementary-school teacher alone, Diekhoff (1962, p. 63) has said: "If he has some of the characteristics of a walking and talking encyclopedia, he must be a loose-leaf edition, in which current knowledge is inserted and from which outmoded pages are discarded."

If this right of every child to be educated for a complete and harmonious development is to be implemented, attention must be concentrated on adapting procedures to the individual learner. Nowhere is this need more imperative than in the "educational disaster areas," where malnourished children from unstable homes or homes of low moral character are often expected to respond to educational opportunities in the same way that healthy, ambitious children commonly do. (See Silberman, 1964.) Fortunately, a great deal of time, talent, and financial aid is being poured into these areas through the Economic Opportunity Act and the Community Action Program. Stress is or will be laid upon preschool education, after-school study centers, cultural enrichment, summer programs, week-end instruction, and other means of supplementing the currently existing school programs. Emphasis is upon getting youth back to school, creating lasting work habits, interesting young people in fields they had not considered open to them, and especially educating girls and women to become better homemakers, wives, and mothers.

Within the public schools themselves, new methods of educating lower-class children are being tried, similar to those suggested by Conant (1961): placing the best teachers in schools serving slum areas, providing a curriculum which fits the perceived needs of the lower-class child, trying to instill the concepts of self-worth in children by exposing them to goals commensurate with their ability rather than with their current community status, and by continuing cultivation of varied talents.

8. The Child Has a Right to Be Protected from Neglect, Cruelty, and Exploitation

Although this right of the child would rarely be questioned in modern societies, many adults might argue the operational definitions of the terms. Cruelty, for example, is not always manifested in some form of physical stress or punishment, nor is neglect necessarily abandonment. A kind of cruelty and exploitation frequently found in child guidance clinics and juvenile courts stems from parental ignorance or inadequacy (Becker, 1960), and takes the form of belittling the child, constantly shouting and yelling at him, invidiously comparing him with siblings, or insisting on achievement standards which, at the time at least, are unrealistic. Exploitation of the child as a means of getting even with an unloved spouse probably precipitates more mental illness than does starting to work at an early age (a practice no longer prevalent in America since the child labor laws were enacted). This type of exploitation sometimes occurs when parents are divorced and one or both parents seek to win the favor of the child by indulgence. It occurs less frequently in the unbroken home.

Inconsistent discipline, based on parental convenience, is neglect to teach a child that the world reacts to his behavior in an orderly fashion. Inconsistency of demands and expectations is cruelty to the child who needs to find his own successes, assess his own abilities, and develop his own core of judgment.

"Smother" love, or overprotection, constitutes, in its effects, both neglect of a child's inclination to gain independence and thoughtlessness in the sense of crippling his need to exercise his capacities.

Overorganization of a child's activities denies him the right to make his own choices; and in the struggle for prestige and upward mobility, many middle-class parents exploit their children by dictating what games they will play, what toys and friends they shall play with, the books they should or should not read, the interests they should pursue, and so on. Keeping up with the Joneses applies to child-rearing practices and parental expectations of child behavior equally as often, if not more so, as purchasing automobiles, refurnishing homes, and attending cultural events.

Highly concentrated efforts are applied to the development of a vocabulary equally as precocious as a neighbor's child. Toys designed for five-year-olds are considered too young for a four- or five-year-old; and the mother of a ten-year-old despairs openly when her child takes a sudden fancy to a stuffed toy.

Identical patterns of expectations occur within the academic community. Overdependence on intelligence test scores, in many cases, denies children the right to slow up, to fall behind temporarily, to have "unacademic" interests, or to "overachieve." One teacher gave up "wasting her time" on a pupil with an IQ of 164 who was failing all his subjects because his only interest was in playing the clarinet. Another pupil who scored 100 in IQ consistently produced work higher in quality than might be expected from such a score; yet a counselor attempted to discourage her from attending a four-year university. From the standpoint of both society and the individual, the seriousness of overdependence on IQ scores and academic achievement as criteria for success in adulthood is implicit in a study by Strauss (1956), which analyzed the backgrounds and traits of sixty scientists.

> . . . Drive was the most apparent factor in successful achievement among the scientists studied. . . . Only a few subjects were outstanding students while in high school. Their college experiences played a greater role in stimulating their interests in scientific work than did the high school. Many were more successful in college than in high school and did even better in graduate school.

Doll (1964) summarizes a similar investigation into the backgrounds of one hundred successful men in the arts, business and industry, and the professions:

> 'We were amazed to find that a large minority of these successful people were not only low achievers during their school days, but had registered low IQ's on standardized tests of intelligence. Apparently they had within them that potential which was beyond the range of those limited elements of potential which schools ordinarily identify and develop.'

In far too many instances, parents, teachers, librarians, book publishers, and television producers exploit children by claiming to know what they like to read or what programs they like to watch. One director of children's libraries lectured at length about a particular book for youngsters that she would not give "house room" to, one that she would certainly never purchase—and her audience of librarians were forced to snicker quietly, for the book was the most popular one on their shelves.

Norvell (1958) made an intensive study of children's interests in reading both prose and poetry. In his investigations he found many poems which, although praised by librarians, writers of anthologies, and teachers of English, were rejected by children. Rudman (1954), too, found that so-called experts (including parents) were usually wrong in their designation

Table XIV–1 A Summary of Children's Reading Interests and Parent, Teacher, and Librarian Choices of Reading for Children (Rudman, 1954)

Children's Reading Interests		Parents' Choices for Children		Teachers' Choices for Children		Librarians' Choices for Children	
Category	Per Cent	Category	Per Cent	Category	Per Cent	Category	Per Cent
Literature	34	Literature	31	Literature	20	Famous People	20
Animals	21	Miscellaneous (religion, ethics, school)	17	Other school subjects	19	Literature	18
Sports & Recreation	8	Animals	10	Social Studies	15	Other school subjects	14
Social Studies	8	Sports & Recreation	6	Miscellaneous	13	Social Studies	12
Machines & Applied Science	5	Other school subjects	7	Famous People	6	Miscellaneous	10
Famous People	5	Social Studies	5	Animals	6	Animals	8
Other school subjects	4	Famous People	4	Biological Science	4	Sports & Recreation	6
Miscellaneous	3	Personal Problems	4	Personal Problems	4	Biological Science	6
Physical Science	3	Biological Science	3	Sports & Recreation	3	Personal Problems	3
Biological Science	2	Machines & Applied Science	2	Fine & Applied Arts	3	Fine & Applied Arts	3
Personal Problems	2	Fine & Applied Arts	2	Machines & Applied Science	2	Physical Science	5
Fine & Applied Arts	1	Physical Science	2	Physical Science	2	Machines & Applied Science	5

of subjects children want to read about. Table XIV-1 shows how closely parents, teachers, and librarians agree and how much the three groups disagree with the children regarding reading interests.

Alastair Reid (1963, p. 104) has taken sides with psychologists by writing:

> . . . Children are interested in anything except, possibly, the things they are expected to be interested in; and we might as well lay our world open to them and let them make off with whatever improbable treasure they discover for themselves.

Either adults must adopt this course of action or they must risk turning children against all of those things which adults consider as being of high quality and value.

9. The Child Has a Right to Special Treatment When He Is Handicapped

That robust health, freedom from deformity, high intellectual potential would be assets in achieving personality integration appears to be quite obvious. Indeed, research shows that *generally* the highly intelligent person does deal with his environment effectively (achieves success) and experiences a smaller than average amount of serious mental illness. But those with less intelligence also are found to make admirable adjustments and to achieve internal as well as social integration (Terman, 1954). One's *reaction* to environmental circumstances and hereditary and congenital factors is an essential part of the *Gestalt*.

The presence of congenital defect—visual handicaps, auditory limitations, paralysis, absence of a limb—does limit sharp contact with the environment, and the incidence of personality disintegration is somewhat higher than average for persons (as a group) with such handicaps. However, there are enough successes among those with handicaps that the handicap, by itself, cannot be the explanatory factor. The handicapped are significantly weaker in their potential for self-protection, but their overall adjustment is little different from the nonhandicapped (Wenar, 1954). When parents avoid being oversolicitous, when there is acceptance by key persons (particularly parents), and when appropriate goals and values are learned, then the individual can harmonize his life with his potentialities and live productively. It is not the handicap but the way in which the individual views his handicap as a part of his total self that is the really crucial factor (Carter and Chess, 1951).

The existence of various societies for promoting the study and treatment of cancer, heart disorders, tuberculosis, poliomyelitis, and mental retardation, together with health clinics, supported by either local tax or charity funds, indicates that the child's right to treatment for physical or mental deficiency is functionally recognized. While progress is being made, there is still a largely unfulfilled need for specially trained teachers in all areas of handicap (Mackie and Williams, 1959). In fact, it has been stated that one of the major defects of the American educational system—which purports to pursue vigorously the goal of universal free education—is the dearth of appropriate education for the mentally, emotionally, and physically handicapped.

There are, of course, other kinds of handicaps which could fall logically within this right of children, one being the cultural handicap that is a product of limited educational facilities—as in the rural and slum areas of our nation. Cultural deprivation contributes to delinquency and the underdevelopment of potential. Moreover, the deprivation and discrimination that occurs in the lower social classes is partly responsible for a high incidence of mental illness at that social level (Hollingshead and Redlich, 1958). Because the increased rate of school enrollment over the past thirty years has raised the educational level of the people as a whole, it is essential that society give prime consideration to culturally deprived children—to those whose native environment fails to satisfy or stimulate a desire for exploration, interest in the world, physical growth, language facility, and hence, native intelligence. From birth to the age of four are the crucial years wherein half of all a child's growth in intelligence takes place (Bloom, 1964). If, during the preschool years, underprivileged children are not afforded concentrated programs of cultural enrichment, there is little that can be done later to overcome their consequent physical, mental, social, and moral handicaps.

Excessive and distorted emotional behavior is a handicap not easily dealt with once it gets into the habit stage. In order to recognize disintegrative tendencies beforehand, parents and teachers need a wider and more intensive knowledge of child development, which can be had through observations of many children, through books on the subject, and through developmental studies. Hopefully, too, parents should accept *constructively* the observations and suggestions of teachers who are well-trained to recognize symptoms that may lead to later maladjustments. Oftentimes, parents take a teacher's comments as criticism, and they elect to place the blame rather than correct the situation by whatever means are available. Many emotionally handicapped children today would have been helped during the preschool years if only their maladaptive behavior had been analyzed for causes and rechannelled. And there are some easily recognizable signs, as shown by Baker and Holzworth (1961), who studied the social histories of successful and unsuccessful children. The danger of completely ignoring such symptoms as those shown in Table XIV-2 lies in the fact that as a child grows older he becomes adept at disguising his emotions and inventing devious ways of expressing or hiding them.

Table XIV–2   Incidence of Early Psychosocial Problems (Baker and Holzworth, 1961, p. 138) *

| | Per Cent | |
Type of Problem	Patients	Controls
Enuresis †	44	14
Severe temper tantrums	35	13
Fears or phobias	25	..
Speech difficulties	23	4
Rocking or head banging	16	1
Encopresis [lack of bowel control]	8	..

* Reprinted by permission of the Society for Child Development and the authors.
† Beyond 3 years of age

10. The Child Has a Right to Be Protected from Everything That Might Incite Feelings of Discrimination or Hatred

Prejudice is a social reality full of social and psychological consequences. Many of the effects upon people who experience prejudice in the sense of being discriminated against were discussed in Chapter X; but what of the individual who exhibits prejudice, the one who does the discriminating? We have already stated that the prejudiced person delimits his ability to work with others, but the effects of his intolerance go deeper than a mere aversion to members of certain groups. The intolerant person is one who hates, and hatred stultifies the personality, narrowing an individual's thoughts, feelings, imagination, even experiences. Because he diverts experiences into channels of hate, the hater is less aware of what is going on; he is suspicious, hostile, psychologically destructive, and dangerous to himself and to others. As Levy (1952, p. 305) states: "The phrase 'consumed by hate' may be literally true. For some individuals, as psychiatrists are well aware, pay the price of their hate in physical distress and illness."

On the other hand, Krech (1952, pp. 293–296) reminds us that prejudice is a means for satisfying a particular need for the individual, although that need is not the same one for each prejudiced person. He describes four problems which are often solved for the individual through acquired attitudes of prejudice:

1. Persistent frustration of a need, leading to aggressive acts, which, as a child grows older, demand "targets." Racial propaganda helps supply those targets and gives meaning to otherwise disapproved "blind aggressions."

2. The need to explain an ambiguous crisis (e.g., an economic depres-

sion amid a great wealth of natural resources) leads to scapegoating or sub-scribing to a belief which, though actually false, sounds reasonable.

3. The lure of group acceptances and consequent need for conformity often creates situations in which the individual must accept a group's atti-tudes toward what is or is not good taste, proper behavior, or in accordance with rules. Some of the more common attitudes that an individual meets as he seeks group acceptance are: domestic servants do not eat with the family, a Jew should not marry a Gentile, a Roman Catholic should not attend a Protestant church service, a Mormon does not drink coffee nor a Moham-medan alcohol, the female of the species is inferior to the male.

4. Unhealthy personality patterns create peculiar needs, as when the paranoiac's suspicious nature uses racial prejudice as a justification for his actions. He *creates* incidents wherein his distorted perceptions can become meaningful.

If we are to implement the tenth right of a child, we should give thoughtful consideration to Krech's prescription:

> . . . Always assume that any specific attitude serves some need for the individual who holds it. If we wish to change the attitude, we must first find for the individual some other means to solve his problem or else help him to remove the problem.

SUMMARY

The integrated personality is the goal which most parents have for their children. It refers to the harmonious working together of the individual's desires, abilities, and potentialities so that decisions can be made, acted upon, and lived with. It refers also (and as much) to harmony of self and society—one can adhere to social practices without excessive turmoil. As an adult, an integrated person might work to alter a social injustice while re-specting the views of the perpetrators of the injustice. Integration, in short, refers to a harmonious whole within a social setting and is related to, if not synonymous with, mental health.

There are a number of forces which children may encounter that tend to prevent the achievement of integration. These forces are the ones which cause the child to feel that society does not like him, want him, or have a place for him. They cause him to have a low or negative concept of self.

Factors which promote integrative processes are, of course, need satis-faction and reasonable and consistent demands and expectations. These factors have been defined and combined in various interactive ways in or-der to develop a charter of rights to which each individual child is entitled. Among those rights are acceptance for what the child is, without discrimina-tion; economic and social security; education for self-fulfillment; mental, emotional, and spiritual peace; protection from ill health, disintegrative patterns of behavior, physical defect, and cruelty.

Mothering, parental felicity, kindly but firm and consistent guidance, and recognition of successes based on knowledge of phases of growth are helpful in promoting personality integration. Successful child development is more than a multitude of techniques; it is a condition and outcome of the child's total life and environment.

QUESTIONS AND PROBLEMS

1. What justification is there for considering personality integration as being synonymous with mental health?
2. What are the advantages of using the term "integrative processes" instead of the term "integrated personality"?
3. Do you think of any disintegrative forces which are as serious as, or more serious than, those mentioned in the chapter?
4. Explain how conflicting demands create personality disturbance in a child.
5. If physical strength is an asset to integration, how does it happen that numerous handicapped persons are well integrated—both personally and socially?
6. Is "mothering" an attitude or a set of behaviors?
7. Do you think it is possible for a child to be brought up by domineering parents and still become an integrated personality?
8. Cite a number of examples of how parental felicity—or lack of it—conditions the processes of integration in childhood.
9. What is your evaluation of the substitution of "rights" of children for "needs" of children as used in this chapter?

SELECTED READINGS

A *Survey of Children's Adjustment Over Time*. Minneapolis: Institute of Child Development and Welfare, University of Minnesota, 1959, pamphlet, pp. 42.

BAUGHMAN, E. EARL, and GEORGE S. WELSH, The self-concept and its assessment, in *Personality: A Behavioral Science*. Englewood Cliffs, N.J.: Prentice-Hall, 1962, pp. 339–377.

BERNARD, HAROLD W., *Human Development in Western Culture*, 2nd ed. Boston: Allyn and Bacon, 1966, pp. 359–388.

DINKMEYER, DON C., *Child Development: The Emerging Self*, Englewood Cliffs, N.J.: Prentice-Hall, 1965. Ch. 11.

HURLOCK, ELIZABETH B., *Child Development*, 4th ed. McGraw-Hill, 1964. Ch. 15.

JAHODA, MARIE, *Current Concepts of Positive Mental Health*. Basic Books, 1958.

JERSILD, ARTHUR T., *Child Psychology*, 5th ed. Englewood Cliffs, N.J.: Prentice-Hall, 1960. Ch. 20.

LEVINE, LOUIS S., *Personal and Social Development*. Holt, Rinehart & Winston, 1963. Chs. 6 and 7.

MASLOW, ABRAHAM H., Values, growth, and health, in *Toward a Psychology of Being*. Princeton, N.J.: D. Van Nostrand, 1962, pp. 157–167.

REFERENCES

ARDREY, ROBERT, *African Genesis*. New York: Atheneum, 1961.

BAKER, JOHN W., and ANNETTE HOLZWORTH, Social histories of successful and unsuccessful children, *Child Development*, 1961, 32, 135–149.

BECKER, WESLEY C., The relationship of factors in parental ratings of self and each other to the behavior of kindergarten children as rated by mothers, fathers, and teachers, *Journal of Consulting Psychology*, 1960, 24, 507–527.

BERNARD, HAROLD W., *Human Development in Western Culture*, 2nd ed. Boston: Allyn and Bacon, 1966, p. 417.

BLOOM, BENJAMIN S., *Stability and Change in Human Characteristics*. John Wiley & Sons, 1964.

CARTER, VICTOR E., and STELLA CHESS, Factors influencing the adaptations of organically handicapped children, *American Journal of Orthopsychiatry*, 1951, 21, 827–837.

CATTELL, RAYMOND B., *Personality*. McGraw-Hill, 1950.

COLEMAN, JAMES, *Personality Dynamics and Effective Behavior*. Chicago: Scott, Foresman, 1960.

CONANT, JAMES B., *Slums and Suburbs*. McGraw-Hill, 1961.

DIEKHOFF, JOHN S., The last encyclopedists, *Saturday Review* (September 15, 1962), pp. 62–63.

DOLL, RONALD C., quoted on page 157, "When Children Don't 'Achieve,' " by Lydia Strong, *The New York Times Magazine* (November 15, 1964), pp. 142, 156–157.

ESCALONA, SIBYLLE, Emotional development in the first year of life, in *Transactions of the Conference on Problems of Infancy and Childhood* (M. Senn, ed.). Josiah Macy, Jr. Foundation, 1952, vol. 6, p. 26.

GARRISON, KARL C., ALBERT J. KINGSTON, and ARTHUR S. MCDONALD, *Educational Psychology*, 2nd ed. Appleton-Century-Crofts, 1964, p. 306.

HARDY, MARTHA C., Frequent illness in childhood, physical growth, and final size, *American Journal of Physical Anthropology*, 1938, 23, 241–260.

HECHINGER, FRED M., Mental strains, in *The New York Times* (December 13, 1964), p. E7.

HOLLINGSHEAD, AUGUST B., and FREDERICK C. REDLICH, *Social Class and Mental Illness*. John Wiley & Sons, 1958, p. 199.

INTERNATIONAL FEDERATION OF TEACHERS ASSOCIATIONS. The ten points in the "Charter of Rights" are condensed from the statement adopted at the annual convention at Amsterdam, Holland, August 15, 1950.

KELLEY, EARL C., *In Defense of Youth*. Englewood Cliffs, N.J.: Prentice-Hall, 1962, pp. 7–8.

KRECH, DAVID, Attitudes are acquired, in *Our Children Today* (Sidonie M. Gruenberg, ed.). Viking Press, 1952, pp. 291–303.

LESHAN, EDA J., 'Hard day's night' of today's students, *The New York Times Magazine* (September 27, 1964), pp. 104–106.

LEVY, DAVID M., The toll of intolerance upon the intolerant, in *Our Children Today* (Sidonie M. Gruenberg, ed.). Viking Press, 1952, pp. 304–309.

MACKIE, ROMAINE P., and HAROLD M. WILLIAMS, Teachers of exceptional children, *Review of Educational Research*, 1959, 29, 395–407.

MENNINGER, KARL A., *The Human Mind*. Alfred A. Knopf, 1961, pp. 23, 27.

MILLER, HYMAN, and DOROTHY W. BARUCH, *The Practice of Psychosomatic Medicine as Illustrated in Allergy*. McGraw-Hill, 1956, pp. 27–44.

MONAHAN, THOMAS P., Broken homes by age of delinquent children, *Journal of Social Psychology*, 1960, 51, 387–397.

MOUSTAKAS, CLARK E., *Children in Play Therapy*. McGraw-Hill, 1953.

NORVELL, GEORGE, *What Boys and Girls Like to Read*. Morristown, N.J.: Silver Burdett Co., 1958, pp. 123–134.

O'CONNOR, JOHNSON, Redirecting Americans, *The Atlantic Monthly* (February 1941), *167*, 193–200.

PECK, ROBERT F., ROBERT J. HAVIGHURST, *et al.*, *The Psychology of Character Development*. John Wiley & Sons, 1960.

RADKE, MARIAN J., *The Relation of Parental Authority to Children's Behavior and Attitudes*. University of Minnesota Child Welfare Monographs, No. 22. Minneapolis: University of Minnesota Press, 1946.

RAND, WINIFRED, MARY E. SWEENEY, and E. LEE VINCENT, *Growth and Development of the Young Child*, 5th ed. Philadelphia: Saunders, 1953, p. 384.

REID, ALASTAIR, A poet's view of childhood, *The Atlantic Monthly* (March 1963), *211*, No. 3, 102–104.

RUDMAN, HAROLD, *Interrelationships Among Various Aspects of Children's Interests and Informational Needs and Expectations of Teachers, Parents, and Librarians*. Unpublished doctoral dissertation, College of Education, University of Illinois, 1954.

SEWELL, WILLIAM H., Infant training and the personality of the child, *The American Journal of Sociology*, 1952, *58*, 150–159.

SILBERMAN, CHARLES E., Give slum children a chance, *Harper's* Magazine (May 1964), pp. 37–42.

STRAUSS, SAMUEL, Backgrounds and traits of a group of biological and social scientists, *Dissertation Abstracts*, March–May 1956, *16*, 707–708.

SWIFT, ARTHUR L., JR., Childhood and spiritual values, in *Our Children Today* (Sidonie M. Gruenberg, ed.). Viking Press, 1952, pp. 323–333.

TERMAN, LEWIS M., The discovery and encouragement of exceptional talent, *The American Psychologist*, 1954, *9*, 221–230.

UNITED NATIONS, *First United Nations Congress on the Prevention of Crime and the Treatment of Offenders*. Geneva, August 22—September 3, 1955. A report prepared by the Secretariat for the United Nations, Department of Economic and Social Affairs. New York: The United Nations, 1956, p. 56.

WENAR, CHARLES, The effects of a motor handicap on personality. II. The effects on integrative ability, *Child Development*, 1954, *25*, 287–294.

WHITE HOUSE CONFERENCE ON CHILD HEALTH AND PROTECTION, *Preliminary Committee Reports*. The Century Company, 1930, p. 465.

Appendices

Appendix A

SELECTED, ANNOTATED BIBLIOGRAPHY

ALMY, MILLIE, *Child Development*. Henry Holt, 1955.
Special emphasis is given to adjustments and personality, parent-child relationships, and to the child's relations with his peers. Case studies of six normal children are traced from birth through adolescence.

    AUSUBEL, DAVID P., *Theory and Problems of Child Development*. Grune and Stratton, 1958.
An advanced textbook consisting of four parts: (1) general theoretical and methodological issues in child development; (2) origins, raw materials, and beginning status of behavior and capacity; (3) general theory of personality development; and (4) special aspects of development.

    BALDWIN, ALFRED L., *Behavior and Development in Childhood*. Dryden Press (now Holt, Rinehart & Winston), 1955.
The author sets out to make explicit a theoretical framework to help in predicting how children behave and how they develop. The book is divided into two parts: Part one, how the child behaves; part two, the prediction of personality change.

    BALLER, WARREN R., and DON C. CHARLES, *The Psychology of Human Growth and Development*. Holt, Rinehart & Winston, 1961.
This book was written primarily for students preparing to teach. It is divided into four main parts: I. Orientation to the study of human behavior and development. II. The bio-social foundation of human behavior. III. Development and adjustment. IV. Personality and the school's role in its development.

    BERNARD, HAROLD W., *Human Development in Western Culture*, 2nd ed. Boston: Allyn and Bacon, 1966.
Attention is given by the author to continuity of growth. This book outlines the phases and problems of each successive stage. Part I deals with broad factors in

human development that affect all ages. Part II deals with development in the early years, and Part III with preadolescence, adolescence, and the years of youth. Part IV deals with institutions and concerns which influence development.

DINKMEYER, DON C., *Child Development: The Emerging Self*. Englewood Cliffs, N.J.: Prentice-Hall, 1965.

The early chapters give special attention to theories of child development and to methods of studying children. The chapters on development and learning are followed by chapters dealing with the various areas or directions of development.

ENGLISH, HORACE B., *Dynamics of Child Development*. Holt, Rinehart & Winston, 1961.

The materials are directed to practitioners in the field—parents and teachers. A better understanding of the dynamics of child behavior and development is emphasized as the goal of the text.

GARRISON, KARL C., *Growth and Development*, 2nd ed. Longmans, Green (now McKay), 1959.

In this second edition the author introduced recent data not available when the first edition was published. The chapter outline remains the same, the first chapters dealing with different aspects of growth and the second major part of the book dealing with personality development.

HAWKES, GLENN R., and DAMARIS PEASE, *Behavior and Development from 5 to 12*. Harper and Row, 1962.

The authors have focused their attention on the middle years of childhood. The physical, emotional, social, and intellectual growth of the child are discussed along with material on the family, school, peer group, community, and mass media.

HURLOCK, ELIZABETH B., *Child Development*, 4th ed. McGraw-Hill, 1964.

The high points from many published studies are included in this fourth edition. The author emphasizes the importance of social development as an outgrowth of the child's reaction to his cultural environment.

HUTT, MAX L., and ROBERT G. GIBBY, *The Child: Development and Adjustment*. Boston: Allyn and Bacon, 1959.

The authors' primary consideration involves the way in which the child's personality develops and matures. There is a psychoanalytic orientation in evidence in the treatment of personality structure and development.

JERSILD, ARTHUR T., *Child Psychology*, 5th ed. Englewood Cliffs, N.J.: Prentice-Hall, 1960.

Emphasis is placed upon the family and peer influences on the development of the child. The child's self-concept and personality development are given special consideration throughout the book.

KANNER, LEO, *Child Psychiatry*, 3rd ed. Springfield, Ill.: Charles C. Thomas, 1960.

The psychological consequences of ill health are treated along with different behavior disorders.

MARTIN, WILLIAM E., and CELIA B. STENDLER, *Child Behavior and Development*, rev. ed. Harcourt, Brace, 1959.

The authors emphasize the role of culture in the child's development. The child is regarded as the product of inborn propensities and the cultural forces he encounters.

MUSSEN, PAUL H., ed., *Handbook of Research Methods in Child Development*. John Wiley & Sons, 1960.

A very complete source book prepared by different authors. Considerable attention is given to methods of studying children and to the young child.

MUSSEN, PAUL H., and JOHN J. CONGER, *Child Development and Personality.* 2nd edition, Harper & Bros., 1963.

The authors discuss child growth and development in general at each of five stages: the prenatal, the first two years, the preschool years, middle childhood, and adolescence.

OLSON, WILLARD C., *Child Development,* 2nd ed. Boston: D. C. Heath, 1959. This second edition covers the topics of physical, mental, and emotional development, growth of educational achievement, the child as a whole, human relations in the classroom, the child in the home and community, affective life of the child, and the teacher in individual and group relationships. Emphasis is upon the growth of the child as a whole.

PIKUNAS, JUSTIN, *Fundamental Child Psychology.* Milwaukee: Bruce Publishing Co., 1957.

This text was written primarily for prospective teachers and as a guidebook for parents. The book is divided into four sections: basic approach to child study; phases of development; basic aspects and dimensions of the child's personality; and personality, the self, and child guidance.

STEVENSON, HAROLD W., ed., *Child Psychology.* Chicago: The University of Chicago Press, 1963.

This title is Part I of the sixty-second yearbook of the National Society for the Study of Education. The content focuses on currently active research in the areas of child psychology, notably biological and sociological correlates of behavior; learning, thinking, and perceiving during childhood; and forces relating to aggression, anxiety, and dependency.

STRANG, RUTH, *Introduction to Child Study,* 4th ed. The Macmillan Co., 1959. Special emphasis is given to the dynamics of children's behavior. The importance of the home, school, and community situations in child development is emphasized. Suggestions are given for child study and guidance.

THOMPSON, GEORGE G., *Child Psychology,* 2nd ed. Boston: Houghton, Mifflin, 1962.

Psychological and physiological factors related to child adjustment are systematically presented along with the notion that environmental influences on behavior are continually interrelated to maturation and learning.

THORPE, LOUIS P., *Child Psychology and Development,* 3rd ed. The Ronald Press, 1962.

This book incorporates recent findings on physical, mental, and psychological growth with special emphasis upon the role of the home, school, and community on the child's personal and social development. Consideration is given to the interests, social-sex development, and learning during childhood.

Appendix B

PARTS ONE AND TWO: DEVELOPMENT

Biography of the Unborn (E-B-F, 17 min., B/W, sd.). This film illustrates the development of life from the moment of fertilization to birth.

Children's Emotions (M-H, 22 min., B/W, sd.). A discussion of the characteristics of children's emotions with emphasis on the major emotions.

Developmental Characteristics of Pre-Adolescents (Cor., 18 min., B/W, sd.). An excellent illustration of the successive stages of development toward maturity and the relationship of development to the school curriculum.

Feeling of Hostility (N-F-B, 31 min., B/W, sd.). A case history of a young woman who develops feelings of hostility because she failed to receive affection and understanding from her family.

From Ten to Twelve (N-F-B, 28 min., B/W, sd.). A description of the general characteristics of boys and girls aged ten years to twelve. Also illustrates individual differences.

From Sociable Six to Noisy Nine (M-H, 22 min., B/W, sd.). This film portrays the stages of growth for children of primary grade age: from six to nine years.

Helping the Child to Accept the Do's (E-B-F, 11 min., B/W, sd.). The film illustrates how a child learns to live in a world defined by positive direction and how the personality is influenced by the acceptance of these directions.

Helping the Child to Face the Don'ts (E-B-F, 11 min., B/W, sd.). The film demonstrates how the young child learns to meet and accept restrictions in his life. It portrays the relationship of the restrictions imposed by society to personality development.

438

Importance of Goals (M-H, 19 min., B/W, sd.). The film follows the case of Tommy whose teacher helps him to discover that education is a process of attaining meaningful goals.

Personality and Emotions (E-B-F, 13 min., B/W, sd.). The film provides an overview of the development of emotions from infancy through early childhood.

Principles of Development (M-H, 20 min., B/W, sd.). The film serves as an excellent review of fundamental principles of development.

Testing Intelligence with the Stanford-Binet (P-S-U, 18 min., B/W, sd.). The film demonstrates the methods employed in administering and scoring the Revised Stanford-Binet Scale. The mental age concept is explained and the student is made acquainted with the types of items employed in testing intelligence.

Why Jimmy Can't Read (S-U, 17 min., B/W, sd.). The film illustrates how a reading clinic diagnoses a child with a reading disability.

PART THREE: THE SOCIALIZATION PROCESS

Accent on Learning (O-S-U, 30 min., B/W, sd.). This film explores the meaning of teaching and suggests various creative methods for teaching.

A Counselor's Day (M-H, 12 min., B/W, sd.). The busy day of the counselor is portrayed. The film illustrates the counselor's working relationships with teachers and pupils as well as with his own family.

Angry Boy (I-F-B, 32 min., B/W, sd.). A demonstration of how family tensions engender emotional disturbances in a preadolescent boy. Specialists assist the mother to understand her child and help the boy become better adjusted.

Children Growing Up with Other People (U-W-F, 23 min., B/W, sd.). This film illustrates social adjustment and the problems of cooperating with other people.

Children in Trouble (N-Y-S, 10 min., B/W, sd.). A demonstration of how children get in trouble as a result of a lack of guidance at home, in school, in church, or from community agencies.

Children Learning by Experience (U-W-F, 30 min., B/W, sd.). The relationships between interests, learning, and experiences are demonstrated.

Children's Play (M-H, 27 min., B/W, sd.). Illustrates the role of play in child development and shows how it varies at different grade levels.

Curriculum Based on Child Development (M-H., 12 min., B/W, sd.). The film points out how a good curriculum considers the developmental characteristics of preadolescents and how a good teacher provides learning opportunities for all pupils.

Early Social Behavior (E-B-F, 10 min., B/W, sd.). A portrayal of ten different children aged eight weeks to seven years in various social situations. The behavior shown is analyzed in terms of individual personality differences.

Elementary School Children I: Each Child Is Different (M-H, 15 min., B/W, sd.). This film illustrates how one teacher attempts to discover and meet the needs of individual children.

Elementary School Children II: Discovering Individual Differences (M-H, 25 min., B/W, sd.). A fifth-grade teacher systematically studies the differences in background, abilities, and needs of the various children in the class.

Effective Learning in Elementary School (M-H, 20 min., B/W, sd.). Through a unit approach, a fifth-grade teacher motivates the pupils of the class and integrates the various subject areas in order to make learning effective and meaningful.

Family Circles (N-F-B, 31 min., B/W, sd.). Case studies of children whose families react differently to the needs of their children are portrayed. This film illustrates how parents influence the personal-social development of children.

Feeling of Rejection (N-F-B, 22 min., B/W, sd.). This film illustrates through the use of a case history how early childhood relationships affect emotional adjustment in maturity.

Four Families (M-H, 60 min., B/W, sd.). The film compares family life in India, France, Japan, and Canada. Margaret Mead discusses how the child-rearing practices contribute to a distinctive national character.

He Acts His Age (M-H, 15 min., B/W, sd.). A portrayal of the play activities of children at various age levels. Emphasis is placed upon the importance of understanding the various stages of growth: physical, social, and emotional.

Learning Through Cooperative Planning (Col., 20 min., B/W, sd.). An elementary school cooperates in a community campaign. Each class decides to undertake a special responsibility. The film portrays group learning.

Guidance Problem for School and Home (Col., 17 min., B/W, sd.). The relationship of parental conflicts regarding child-rearing practices is portrayed. How the school and home can cooperate to help a child is illustrated.

Making Learning More Meaningful (M-H, 12 min., B/W, sd.). A third-grade teacher uses the spontaneous interest of her pupils to develop arithmetic skills.

Mike Makes His Mark (N-E-A, 29 min., B/W, sd.). The story of how a mixed-up boy is assisted in making emotional adjustments.

Problem Children (O-D-M-H, 20 min., B/W, sd.). The film demonstrates the methods which a school might employ to help two types of problem cases: one withdrawn and shy and the other hostile and aggressive.

Shyness (M-H, 23 min., B/W, sd.). Through the use of sociometric methods, a teacher discovers three shy children. A psychologist reveals the factors which contribute to the shyness of each child.

Sibling Relations and Personality (M-H, 22 min., B/W, sd.). The relationships a child has with brothers and sisters is demonstrated so as to reveal the importance of sibling relations in personality development.

Social Development (M-H, 16 min., B/W, sd.). Social behavior at different age levels and the reasons underlying changes in behavior as the child develops are examined and analyzed.

The Teacher as Observer and Guide (Col., 20 min., B/W, sd.). Through a series of situations, the film illustrates how the teacher guides and assists various children.

Using Analytical Tools (M-H, 15 min., B/W, sd.). The film demonstrates how a counselor analyses a student's problem. The use of cumulative records, interviews, and tests are illustrated.

Your Children's Play (M-H, 20 min., B/W, sd.). A portrayal of the importance of play activities to learning social skills.

SOURCES OF THE FILMS USED IN APPENDIX B

Col   Columbia University Press
Center for Mass Communication
1125 Amsterdam Avenue
New York, N.Y.

Cor   Coronet Films
Coronet Building
65 East South Water Street
Chicago 1, Illinois

E-B-F   Encyclopedia Britannica Films, Inc.
1150 Wilmette Avenue
Wilmette, Illinois

I-F-B   International Film Bureau, Inc.
57 East Jackson Boulevard
Chicago 4, Illinois

M-H   McGraw-Hill Book Co., Inc.
330 West 42nd Street
New York 36, N.Y.

N-E-A   National Education Association
Publication Sales
Washington, D.C.

N-F-B   National Film Board of Canada
680 Fifth Avenue
New York 19, N.Y.

N-Y-S   New York State Department of Commerce
Film Library
112 State Street
Albany 7, N.Y.

O-D-M-H Ohio Division of Mental Hygiene
Columbus, Ohio

O-S-U   Ohio State University
Department of Photography
Columbus, Ohio

P-S-U   Pennsylvania State University
Psychological Cinema Register
State College, Pa.

S-U   Syracuse University
Audio-Visual Center
Syracuse, N.Y.

U-W-F   United World Films, Inc.
1445 Park Avenue
New York 29, N.Y.

Subject Index

Name Index